Information Processing Approaches to Clinical Psychology

This is a volume in

PERSONALITY, PSYCHOPATHOLOGY, AND PSYCHOTHERAPY
A Series of Monographs, Texts, and Treatises

Under the Editorship of David T. Lykken and Philip C. Kendall

A complete list of titles in this series is available from the publisher upon request.

Information Processing Approaches to Clinical Psychology

Edited by

RICK E. INGRAM

Department of Psychology
San Diego State University
San Diego, California

1986

ACADEMIC PRESS, INC.

Harcourt Brace Jovanovich, Publishers

Orlando San Diego New York Austin
Boston London Sydney Tokyo Toronto

ACADEMIC PRESS, INC.
Orlando, Florida 32887

United Kingdom Edition published by
ACADEMIC PRESS INC. (LONDON) LTD.
24–28 Oval Road, London NW1 7DX

Library of Congress Cataloging in Publication Data

Information processing approaches to clinical
psychology.

(Personality, psychopathology, and psychotherapy series)
Bibliography: p.
Includes index.
1. Clinical psychology—Research. 2. Human information processing—Research. 3. Psychiatry—Research. I. Ingram, Rick E. II. Series: Personality, psychopathology, and psychotherapy. [DNLM: 1. Cognition. 2. Information Theory. 3. Psychology, Clinical. WM 105 I43]
RC467.I54 1986 150 86-3431
ISBN 0–12–371030–8 (hardcover) (alk. paper)
ISBN 0–12–371031–6 (paperback) (alk. paper)

PRINTED IN THE UNITED STATES OF AMERICA

86 87 88 89 9 8 7 6 5 4 3 2 1

Contents

8 An Information Processing Approach to Alcohol Use and Its Consequences
JAY G. HULL AND NORA P. REILLY

9 Information Processing and Autism
ALAN J. LITROWNIK AND ELIZABETH T. MCINNIS

10 An Information Processing Interpretation of Theory and Research in Schizophrenia
DENNIS P. SACCUZZO

III
Implications of an Information Processing Perspective for Assessment and Treatment of Psychopathology

11 Cognitive Assessment of Personality and Psychopathology
WILLIAM NASBY AND JOHN F. KIHLSTROM

12 Information Processing and the Human Change Process
LA PEARL LOGAN WINFREY AND MARVIN R. GOLDFRIED

Preface

It is hardly necessary to document the current interest in cognitive perspectives for understanding and treating behavioral disorders. The growth in recent years in both the quality and quantity of cognitively oriented research attests to the wide appeal of the cognitive approach. Moreover, there are few signs that the enthusiasm for this approach will wane at anytime in the very near future.

Along with this steady growth, the need to begin to articulate the conceptual basis of cognition as it relates to psychological dysfunction has become increasingly clear. Unfortunately, adequate conceptualization has lagged behind the development and implementation of many cognitive clinical interventions. It is only natural, then, that following the lead of cognitive social psychologists, clinical researchers have recently begun to explore the empirical methodologies and theoretical perspectives of cognitive experimental psychology, an area that for at least two decades has been explicitly concerned with understanding the mechanisms of human cognition.

The dominant conceptual perspective in cognitive psychology is currently the information processing paradigm. Accordingly, information processing represents a link to a large body of theory and research in human cognition. As clinical researchers have become cognizant of this link, an increasing amount of information processing based research has been applied to a diversity of clinical areas. Most important, however, this research has not only generated numerous advances in the overall conceptualization of cognitive processes as they relate to psychopathology but it has also engendered conceptual and empirical advances within specific domains of psychological disorders.

The purpose of this volume is to present a broad review of current theory and research that applies the information processing paradigm to clinical psychology and to stimulate continued progress toward understanding, assessing, and treating psychopathology through the application of an information processing perspective. Obviously, not all topics that are relevant to clinical psychology can be covered in a single volume. The contributions included in the present volume, however, were chosen to represent the work of innovative scholars actively applying information processing concepts and/or methods to contemporary clinical issues of concern to a wide range of clinicians and researchers alike. The volume is divided into three broad sections. In Part I, the basic foundations of the information processing paradigm are addressed. In the opening chapter, Rick E. Ingram and Philip C. Kendall present an overview of the contribution that the information processing paradigm can make in advancing clinical science. Attention is devoted to examining the general implications of applying an information processing perspective to the issues of clinical psychopathology. In Chapter 2, Roy Lachman and Janet L. Lachman discuss the origins of the information processing paradigm as well as consider its current theoretical attributes, intellectual commitments, and underlying conceptual and methodological presuppositions. In Chapter 3, James F. Juola gives an overview of a representative sample of the analytical methods employed by experimental cognitive psychologists to evaluate information processing models of human behavior.

Part II focuses broadly on the application of information processing constructs and methods to a variety of contemporary content areas in psychopathology. In Chapter 4, David L. Roth and Don M. Tucker describe how neural control systems exert an influence on information processing and how an examination of these systems can enhance understanding of the information processing, emotional, and interpersonal aspects of psychopathology. Timothy W. Smith in Chapter 5 reviews cognitive research on Type A behavior and cardiovascular disease and then details the implications of these studies for future research employing an information processing paradigm. In Chapter 6, Thomas V. Merluzzi, Thomas E. Rudy, and Mark J. Krejci present an information processing approach to social anxiety and social skills. They address research that focuses on the complexity of social stimuli and how these stimuli are represented or processed. Rick E. Ingram and Michele J. Reed review in Chapter 7 information encoding and retrieval studies in depression with the goal of helping to clarify the major findings and issues in the area. In Chapter 8, Jay G. Hull and Nora P. Reilly broadly integrate the research on alcohol use and information processing. Specifically, they address the effects of alcohol on behavior as mediated by cognitive processes, and the motives to consume alcohol to alter information processing. Alan J. Litrownik and Elizabeth McInnis in Chapter 9 discuss the utility of the information processing perspective for both clarifying our understanding of autism and for focusing research and treatment efforts. Finally, in Chapter 10, Dennis P. Saccuzzo addresses how recent advances in information processing theory can be applied to facilitate clinical understanding of schizophrenia by presenting traditional theories of schizophrenia within the context of information processing concepts, empirical findings, and methods.

Part III addresses the implications of the information processing perspective for the assessment and treatment of psychopathology. In Chapter 11, William Nasby and John F. Kihlstrom examine constructs and methods adapted from the information processing paradigm to elucidate how cognitive mechanisms and processes have implications for the clinical assessment of personality and social psychology. In Chapter 12, La Pearl Logan Winfrey and Marvin R. Goldfried discuss what the information processing perspective suggests for human change processes by reviewing research in schema theory and by noting future research issues. In Chapter 13, Rick E. Ingram and Steven D. Hollon present an information processing perspective on cognitive therapy of depression. Specifically, the processes and procedures of cognitive therapy are conceptualized from an information processing standpoint with the aim of elucidating the mechanisms by which cognitive therapy is effective. Peter A. Magaro, Mark H. Johnson, and Ralph Boring present in Chapter 14 a review of information processing studies addressing the treatment of schizophrenic cognitive and perceptual deficits. Based on this research, they propose a prescriptive information processing treatment approach as well as describe a computer-based treatment battery. In the final chapter of the volume, Dennis C. Turk and Peter Salovey discuss information processing biases in clinicians, a critical but frequently ignored clinical issue. After discussing common sources of clinical judgment bias, they provide suggestions for overcoming these biases in the clinical setting.

I would like to express my gratitude to the contributors for the time, thought, and work that went into each chapter. I would also like to thank those at Academic Press who played such an important role in the preparation and production of this volume. Particular thanks go to Phil Kendall who has been a consistent source of knowledge, encouragement, and inspiration. It is an understatement to say that this volume would not have been completed without Phil's generous assistance. I would also like to thank my family for their continuous support. And finally, I would like to thank Marilyn Bredvold for her constant assistance, interest, support, and encouragement.

I

Foundations of Information Processing Conceptualization and Methodology

1

Cognitive Clinical Psychology: Implications of an Information Processing Perspective

RICK E. INGRAM
Department of Psychology
San Diego State University
San Diego, California 92182

PHILIP C. KENDALL
Department of Psychology
Temple University
Philadelphia, Pennsylvania 19122

The "cognitive revolution" (Mahoney, 1977) in clinical psychology is over. No longer is it rebellious to argue for the existence of cognition, defend its influence or importance in human functioning, or justify it as a legitimate and productive focus of study. Although there are those who are predicting the demise of the cognitive "wave" in favor of other conceptual approaches (see Averill, 1983), cognitive concepts have become firmly entrenched in the vernacular of clinical researchers and clinicians alike. Indeed, cognitive psychology has become mainstream clinical psychology (D. Smith, 1982).

Consistent with the acceptance of cognitive constructs in clinical psychology is the explosive growth in the quantity and quality of empirical research that can be classified as cognitive or cognitive–behavioral. Despite this prodigious clinical interest in cognition, however, one of the most surprising yet salient aspects of this emerging field is its overall lack of guiding conceptual perspectives. Extant theory and research in cognitive clinical psychology spans a wide diversity of cognitive concepts (Arnkoff & Glass, 1982; Kendall & Braswell, 1982), many of which appear to be independent and lacking in cohesiveness. Although some progress has certainly been made in clarifying the theoretical status of cognitively oriented research (e.g., Reiss & Bootzin, 1985), the overall conceptual picture of the field nevertheless remains a challenging and somewhat confusing one.

One reason for such confusion may be traced to the nonparadigmatic nature of current cognitive clinical endeavors. Although clinical research has moved away from strictly behavioral constructs and the stimulus–response paradigm that once dominated psychology, the cognitive shift in clinical psychology has thus far not been accompanied by the emergence of any other dominant conceptual paradigm to take its place. What exists instead is a broad area of interest and inquiry that recognizes and underscores the importance of cognitive variables in human function and dysfunction, but, aside from its continued preference for methodological behaviorism as a research strategy, has no underlying conceptual paradigm to help provide any common thread among the various cognitive theoretical fragments. Similarly, although we currently have a wealth of cognitive clinical data from empirical investigations, it has long been recognized that such data are of very limited utility without any organizing theoretical framework or perspective (see Estes, 1955). Of course, while it is always true that a conceptual paradigm may unproductively constrain one's view of theory and data (e.g., consider the fate of cognitive ideas within the narrow behaviorist paradigm), and appropriate precautions to guard against this should be taken, at the present stage in the development of a cognitive clinical science, the recognition of a conceptual paradigm is essential for continued progress in understanding the cognitive factors involved in personality, psychopathology, and psychotherapy.

Experimental Cognitive Approaches

Clinical psychologists who have drawn heavily on the ideas, concepts, and methods of experimental psychology have benefited greatly. The principals of learning theory initially developed in animal learning laboratories, for example, provided fertile ground for generating an enormous diversity of effective clinical applications (Kanfer & Hagerman, 1985). Given the current clinical interest in cognition, it once again appears that experimental psychology has the potential to offer a good deal to empirically minded clinical psychologists (Arnkoff & Glass, 1982; M. K. Johnson, 1985; Kendall, 1981; Kihlstrom & Nasby, 1981; R. J. Landau & Goldfried, 1981; Safran & Greenberg, 1985). Indeed, for at least the last two decades experimental psychology has been explicitly concerned with explicating the nature of a variety of cognitive processes (Neisser, 1985). Since cognitive clinical psychology has developed relatively independently of the advances made in experimental cognitive psychology (Winfrey & Goldfried, chapter 12, this volume), it is now time to look to this field as a source of guiding information regarding cognitive phenomena. Most importantly, experimental cognitive psychology offers a conceptual paradigm that carries with it an associated body of theoretical concepts, research methodologies, and empirical findings that can facilitate the understanding and examination of cognition as it relates to a variety of clinically relevant concerns.

The Information Processing Approach

The dominant conceptual approach in experimental cognitive psychology is currently the information processing paradigm (J. R. Anderson 1980; R. Lachman, Lachman, & Butterfield, 1979; Neisser, 1976, 1980b). Much has been written about this approach and Lachman and Lachman (chapter 2, this volume) provide a detailed discussion of the assumptions, antecedents, and sociological components of the information processing approach. In the present chapter it will therefore suffice to say a few descriptive words concerning what constitutes the information processing perspective.

We define the information processing paradigm as a conceptual approach which assumes that human functioning can be productively conceptualized and understood in terms of how both environmental and internal information is processed and used. Thus, the paradigm essentially conceptualizes the person as an information processing system and focuses largely upon the structures and operations within the system and how they function in the selection, transformation, encoding, storage, retrieval, and generation of information and behavior. Within the more experimentally based cognitive sciences, the information processing approach generally addresses the analysis of factors such as intelligence, memory, language, and meaning of information. In the arena of clinical interests, information processing constitutes a framework for examining the cognitive mechanisms that underlie and mediate cognition, affect, and behavior, and specifically how these interrelated factors are involved in the conceptualization, assessment, and treatment of psychopathology.

Model or Paradigm?

It is important to note that, in the sense we have invoked the term, *information processing* refers to a broad conceptual paradigm and *not* to a model or theory. As such, information processing provides an umbrella over a confluence of constructs sharing similar assumptions concerning the conceptualization of human cognition (see Lachman & Lachman, chapter 2, this volume). As J. R. Anderson and Bower (1973) have aptly noted, the information processing approach represents "a methodology for theorizing" (p. 136). Within this general information processing paradigm a variety of models and theoretical constructs have been advanced to describe a number of both global and specific cognitive processes. Hence, multistore models (Atkinson & Juola, 1973, 1974; Atkinson & Shiffrin, 1968), levels-of-processing models (Craik & Lockhart, 1972; Craik & Tulving 1975), schema approaches (Neisser 1967), spreading activation constructs (Collins & Loftus, 1975), top-down–bottom-up distinctions (Norman & Bobrow, 1975), global comprehension models (J. R. Anderson, 1976; Norman & Rummelhart, 1975), and numerous other approaches all represent information processing models. While all of these approaches share the common assumption that examining the way information is processed and the mechanisms responsible for this processing is a useful way to understand the functioning of individuals, they generally differ with regard to the specific theoretical constructs employed; their level of analysis; the type, degree, and scope of the problem addressed; and the empirical methods and data considered relevant. The information processing paradigm is thus much more than a single model of cognition: It represents a broad perspective on cognition.

Advantages of the Information Processing Paradigm for Cognitive Clinical Psychology

A growing number of researchers have argued that the information processing paradigm represents a variety of benefits for cognitive clinical psychology (e.g., Bower, 1978; Kanfer & Hagerman, 1985; Mahoney, 1974; Merluzzi, Rudy, & Glass, 1981; among others). In general, an information processing perspective can aid both theoretical and empirical attempts to conceptualize, assess, and treat behavioral dysfunctions. More specific advantages, as we see them, follow.

Building Bridges

Adoption of the information processing approach might best be conceptualized as representing a bridge for cognitive clinical psychology to a diverse and rich body of work in the experimental analysis of cognition. As a conceptual paradigm, information processing offers clinical psychology the potential to help generate and organize data, guide conceptualization and theory, facilitate experimentally based predictions, and ultimately, provide insights into cognitive aspects of psychopathology and psychotherapy. Such an information processing bridge offers several distinct benefits to cognitive clinical researchers.

1. *Theoretical Constructs.* Within information processing psychology, numerous theoretical constructs have been developed to guide conceptualization, prediction, and empirical research on cognition (see Lachman & Lachman, chapter 2, this volume; Juola, chapter 3, this volume). Similar constructs have been

and can continue to be helpful when these same goals are applied to "disordered" cognition. To illustrate the potential these constructs have for increasing our understanding of psychopathology, it is instructive to consider Beck's (1967) cognitive model of depression. In attempting to account for his clinical observations of the symptoms and characteristics of depression, Beck (1967) first invoked the schema construct and notions of "faulty information processing." Since that time the schema construct has generated an enormous amount of theory and research in depression (see Blaney, 1986; Ingram & Reed, chapter 7, this volume) as well as a variety of criticisms (e.g., Coyne & Gotlib, 1983; Seligman, 1980). Hence, information processing constructs have been, and we propose can continue to be, successfully adapted from experimental cognitive psychology to help meaningfully explicate clinically important phenomena.

2. *Methodology.* Taylor and Fiske (1981) have pointed out that little research in the past has been able to examine cognitive processes in any direct fashion. Instead, experimenters examined subject responses to a manipulated variable and then made logical and presumably reasonable inferences as to the underlying cognitive processes responsible for the observed outcome. In cognitive clinical psychology, self-report methods are widely employed to generate such inferences. The potential disadvantages of these methods are widely recognized and will only briefly be mentioned here. Such self-reports, for example, are generally limited to the cognitive products arising from the interaction of various cognitive processes. While the ultimate accessibility of these cognitive products may vary with a number of factors (see Nisbett & Wilson, 1977; Ericsson & Simon, 1980; Hollon & Kriss, 1984; Kendall, 1982), many of the processes that underlie these products may simply be inaccessible to the individual and hence to self-report. It is difficult to imagine, for instance, an individual being accurately aware of and describing the multitude of processes that contribute to the formation of a particular cognition or the processes that bring the cognition to awareness. As Kendall (1981) has noted, temporal factors are also problematic for self-reports. Self-reports intended to tap some cognitions may vary depending upon whether the subject is asked to report the cognition on the spot or after a lapse of time. Social desirability or defensiveness have also been long recognized as a source of contamination for self-report methods. More recently, the notion that self-reports may be adversely affected not only by the desire to deceive others but by a motivation to deceive oneself (Gur & Sackeim, 1979; Sackeim & Gur, 1978) has also been advanced. Finally, particular situations as well as individual differences and the presence of psychopathology may also interact with the above sources of variance to make the accuracy and utility of self-reports further problematic.

Part and parcel of the information processing approach is an empirical methodology developed explicitly to analyze cognition that does not rely exclusively on subject self-reports and is more able to directly assess the parameters of mediating cognitive variables. Additionally, the information processing paradigm relies heavily on rigorous methods for collecting observable and reliable data that serve as the referents of cognitive activity. Adoption of the information processing paradigm therefore allows for adaptation of these associated empirical methods. As a brief example, Saccuzzo and his colleagues (Saccuzzo, Hirt, & Spencer, 1974; Saccuzzo & Miller, 1977; Saccuzzo & Schubert, 1981) have employed a backward masking technology based on information processing that requires subjects to identify certain target stimuli under several varying conditions. By examining the speed and accuracy with which this task is performed, they have been able to generate several inferences concerning the attentional deficits typically found in schizophrenia, without relying on self-reports per se. Although useful data can certainly be gained via self-reports, particularly when it is gathered in as scientifically sound a manner as possible (Kendall, 1981), and information processing methodologies are by no means completely free of the problems that characterize self-reports, we propose that these methods have some distinct advantages over traditional introspective self-report methods.

3. *Findings.* Many of the empirical findings generated within the context of information processing research are potentially useful for clinical researchers. Turning again to the area of depression for an illustration, several experimental findings generated from depth-of-processing experimental methods have been very helpful in disentangling the type of information processed that contributes to depressive symptomatology. In this paradigm it was initially found that information processed according to its semantic attributes was better recalled, and hence presumably more efficiently processed, than information requiring less semantic analysis (Craik & Tulving, 1975). Carrying this finding a step further, T. B. Rogers, Kuiper, and Kirker (1977) found that information relevant to the self was recalled even more efficiently than semantic information. From this result it was only a short step to hypothesizing and demonstrating that depressed individuals recall negatively valenced self-relevant information most efficiently (for a review, see Ingram & Reed, chapter 7, this volume). Thus, findings that are standard in experimental information processing research (i.e., meaningful information is more likely to be recalled) have contributed to both our theoretical and empirical knowledge of depression, and perhaps ultimately to improved methods for treating this disorder. Similar benefits of information processing empirical findings have been and can be obtained in a variety of clinically relevant areas.

Two-Way Bridges

Much of the preceding discussion has focused upon the benefits cognitive clinical psychology can accrue from adopting an information processing perspective. The bridge to experimental cognitive psychology, however, is not unidirectional. We suggest, as do others (Arnkoff, 1980; Arnkoff & Glass, 1982; Merluzzi *et al.*, 1981; Shaw & Dodson, 1981), that there is much that the clinical area can contribute to experimental efforts to understand the nature of basic cognitive mechanisms. Variables that are of particular interest to clinical researchers, for instance, can aid in the generation and evaluation of information processing theories. Examining individual differences as well as systematic differences among various groups of individuals (e.g., social anxiety, and on a more extreme level, psychopathology such as schizophrenia and Alzheimer's disease) are prime examples in this regard. M. K. Johnson (1985), for instance, has reported studies of Korsakoff's syndrome patients which suggest support for a multiple-entry memory model that comprises several separate subsystems. Hence, as data accumulate on the information processing characteristics of psychopathological groups, comparisons to "normal" information processing groups may help to engender insights into the nature of basic and functional cognitive processes.

Traditional targets of cognitive clinical research may also prove valuable to more basic cognitive theory and research. The widespread cognitive clinical investigation of self-statements (Kendall & Hollon, 1981b; Meichenbaum, 1977), attributions (Abramson, Seligman, & Teasdale, 1978; Metalsky & Abramson, 1981), and beliefs (Ellis and Grieger, 1977; Sutton-Simon, 1981), for example, has demonstrated that these cognitions have meaningful effects on emotion and behavior. As yet, there is little research that has addressed the experimental analysis of the information processing mechanisms related to these kinds of cognitions. Inclusion of such variables in basic information processing investigations might help to understand the nature of these processes as well as providing a more unified understanding of the human information processing system. Similarly, other variables of clinical interest such as the effect of situational factors on a variety of phenomena can also be of interest in explicating the functioning of various cognitive mechanisms (Ingram, 1984a; C. R. Snyder, Ingram, & Newburg, 1982).

In addition to potentially increasing our understanding of basic cognitive mechanisms, several more general benefits may also result from an information processing link between clinical and experimental psychology. The inclusion of more clinically relevant variables offers experimental cognitive psychology a measure of ecological validity that some have argued it is currently lacking (Neisser, 1976, 1980a, 1980b). The importance of clinical variables, for example, is frequently rooted in observation of real-world adaptive and maladaptive functioning, and incorporation of such variables therefore provides a link to meaningful human behavior. Most importantly, however, the incorporation of traditionally clinical variables by experimental cognitive psychologists (along with the greater use of the information processing paradigm by clinical researchers) offers a step toward a truly unified and integrated cognitive science that addresses the full spectrum of cognitive behavior (Merluzzi *et al.*, 1981).

Given the complexities, differences, and disagreements within the multitude of topical areas in psychology, this step is not likely to be a simple one, but we nevertheless believe that it is an important one.

One additional example of the contribution that clinical variables can make to understanding basic information processing is in the area of affect. Affect, of course, is a critical concern of clinical researchers and clinicians alike. Within the past several years, a number of researchers have begun to discuss affect and its relationship to cognitive processes (e.g., Bower, 1981; M. S. Clark & Fiske, 1982; Mandler, 1975). As but one example, Bower (1981) has introduced several constructs within an associative network model to account for emotion. He proposes that the cognitive system contains "primitive emotion nodes" that are responsible for the attributes and experience of emotions and that function in the same fashion as memory nodes. These nodes according to Bower are embedded in cognitive networks containing memories and concepts associated with each emotion and, when activated, serve to make the associated memories salient to the individual. Among other things, this model can be invoked to account for a number of experimentally established findings concerning state-dependent learning and recall, thus helping to understand several basic cognitive processes. Although Bower's model may or may not hold up under subsequent empirical and theoretical scrutiny, and some recent work evidences possible shortcomings (e.g., Hasher, Rose, Zacks, Sanft, & Doren, 1985), it clearly attests to the power and utility of incorporating relevant clinical concepts and data into the conceptualization of "normal" cognitive functioning.

Clinical Examples

Having discussed the relevance of information processing perspectives for clinical pursuits, we turn to some illustrations of how an information processing approach might be applied to some diverse areas of clinical interest. The examples of clinically oriented applications that follow are general and are not intended to be comprehensive or exhaustive. Much more specific and detailed proposals are found in the remaining chapters of the present volume.

Conceptualizing Psychopathology

Current cognitive clinical conceptualizations of psychopathology have specified important theoretical links among cognitive variables (e.g., that cognitions such as "dysfunctional" thoughts, beliefs, and attributions are related to affective and behavioral dysfunctions) but have typically not discussed in any complex fashion the various interactions among cognitive, affective, and behavioral variables, or precisely how these particular aspects operate in a given psychopathology. To date, most contemporary cognitive clinical theoretical proposals have been relatively simple linear models which suggest that certain kinds of cognition cause behavioral and affective dysfunctions (Coyne & Gotlib, 1983). Similarly, judging by their present level of interest, previous cognitive approaches (e.g., "ego" or "mentalistic introspection") have not been particularly fruitful in aiding useful conceptual or empirical advances.

A Cognitive Taxonomic System. To provide one illustration of how an information processing perspective may be integrated with clinically relevant theory and research to facilitate theoretical proposals, we describe a cognitive taxonomic system that serves as an organizing framework for the multitude of constructs currently employed in many cognitive theoretical proposals. Building on earlier proposals to differentiate between cognitive structures and processes (e.g., Goldfried & Robbins, 1983; Hollon & Garber, in press; Kihlstrom & Nasby, 1981), Ingram (1983) has proposed that cognition can be viewed as consisting of several interrelated but conceptually distinct components. These components are seen as general classifications of cognitive variables and include structural, propositional, operational, and cognitive product categories (see also Hollon & Kriss, 1984; Ingram & Hollon, chapter 13, this volume; Kendall & Ingram, in press). A representative but not exhaustive list of constructs falling within each category is presented in Table 1.

Cognitive structure can generally be defined as the architecture of the system, that is, the structure(s) in which information is internally organized and represented. It should be noted that the designation of structure does not necessarily imply a "hardware" component, but refers to a functional psychological mecha-

TABLE 1
Representative Constructs within Each Category of Components of the Cognitive Taxonomic System

Schema			
Structure	Propositions	Operations	Products
Short-term memory	Episodic knowledge	Spreading activation Attention	Attributions Decisions
Long-term memory	Semantic knowledge	Cognitive elaboration	Images
Iconic/sensory storage	Internally generated information	Encoding	Thoughts
Cognitive networks/ associative linkages	Beliefs (stored)	Retrieval Speed of information transfer	Beliefs (accessed)
Memory nodes			Recognition/detection of stimuli

nism that serves to store information in some manner. As illustrated in Table 1, examples of structural cognitive components include constructs such as short- and long-term memory. *Cognitive propositions,* on the other hand, can be seen as the information that is actually stored or represented, or the *content* of the cognitive structures such as semantic (general knowledge) and episodic (personal) memory information.[1] Interestingly, although the popular, but rarely explicitly defined (J. R. Anderson, 1980; Kihlstrom & Nasby, 1981) schema concept is frequently referred to as a cognitive structure, most clinical discussion of the concept considers its cognitive propositions or content rather than structural dimensions (e.g., a ''depressive'' or ''anxious'' content schema). Thus, as noted in Table 1, the schema notion encompasses both structural and propositional categories.

Cognitive operations are the various procedures by which the components of the cognitive system interact to function in the processing of information. A number of constructs falling under the heading of cognitive operations are mentioned in Table 1. It should be noted, however, that while some of these may represent distinctly different processes, others may more accurately reflect only differing levels of conceptual analysis. Finally, *cognitive products* can be viewed as the cognitions, or thoughts, that result from the interaction of information, cognitive structures, propositions, and operations. Such cognitive products have generally been the focus of most cognitive clinical research to date (Kendall & Hollon, 1979, 1981a; see Kendall & Korgeski, 1979).

Figure 1 illustrates the potential interrelationship among the various cognitive components in the proposed taxonomic system. As seen in this figure, the different components are viewed as operating in a reciprocal, interactional, and multidirectional fashion. Cognitive propositions are placed inside the cognitive structure category to denote that, within this conceptual system, propositions are stored in an organized manner in some type of structure. Arrows labeled as operations are the cognitive processes that give rise to cognitive products (cognitions), transmit information to, within, between, and from cognitive structures, and otherwise serve to manipulate and alter information. Arrows not labeled as operations are those procedures that may not be *primarily* cognitive in nature, such as the processes by which cognitive, affective, and biochemical variables interact. These latter two factors are included to acknowledge the complex inter-

[1]It should be noted that cognitive *propositions* could have also been labeled *content* since the two terms as used here have virtually identical meaning. The term *propositions,* however, was chosen since content can be used in several ways to describe very different cognitive components, such as in the ''content'' of thoughts or self-statements. Referring to information stored in cognitive structures as propositions is both consistent with experimental cognitive usage and also avoids confusion with current cognitive clinical descriptions of cognition. Similarly, the label *operations* was chosen instead of *processes* since the latter term is widely used in the cognitive clinical literature to denote variables that span across all four taxonomic dimensions.

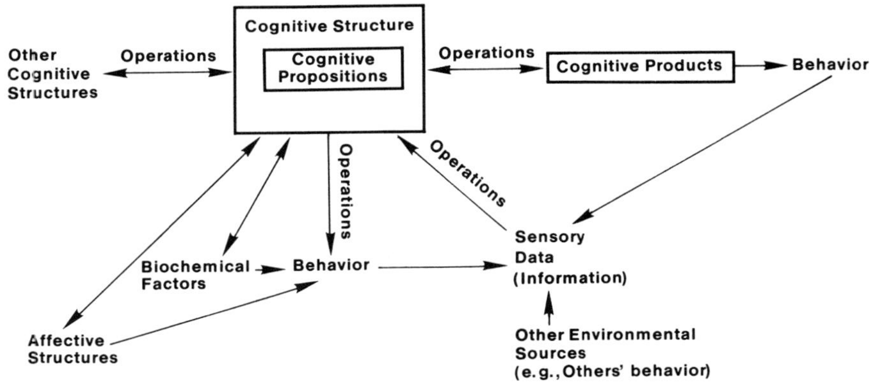

FIG. 1. ***Schematic diagram suggesting the pattern of interrelationships among the various components of the cognitive taxonomic system.***

relationship among the diverse factors that shape human behavior. Behavior is thus affected by a variety of sources including cognitive products (cognitions that lead to behavior), by cognitive structures directly (e.g., "unconscious" cognitive routines such as riding a bike; see Norman, 1981), and by affective and biochemical factors. Behavior also contributes (among other variables) to the sensory/environmental data that the individual processes.

The purpose of this cognitive taxonomic system is not to specify the precise constructs that fall within each category (see Table 1 for examples of divergent cognitive constructs falling into the same cognitive classification). However, while the system itself does not imply what is adaptive or maladaptive cognition, it can be employed to conceptually organize and empirically examine both the unique and shared cognitive features of various forms of psychopathology and psychological dysfunction. To illustrate, a comparison of depression and anxiety might account for not only the similarities between the two disorders, but for their meaningful differences as well. For instance, theory and research suggest that both depression and anxiety are characterized by ruminative, self-focused attentional processes or operations (Ingram, Kendall, Smith, Donnell, & Ronan, 1985; Ingram & Smith, 1984; Sarason, 1975; Wine, 1971). If it can be further assumed that both populations have essentially intact and functional cognitive structures, then a case can be made for suggesting that structures and operations per se are not the key to differentiating these two disorders. Instead, the key may reside in the different propositions contained in the particular cognitive structures that are activated by focused attention, and in the consequent cognitive products. Thus, depressed and anxious individuals may have depressive and anxious cognitive propositions, respectively, that are relatively accessible (Ingram *et al.*, 1985), and thus lead to a different pattern of cognitions. Indeed, in developing assessment devices to measure the self-statements of anxious and depressed subjects, our experience suggests that anxious people *ask* fearful questions (e.g., "What am I doing here?" "What's going to happen?" "Am I going to fail?"), whereas depressed individuals have already *answered* the questions in a negative way (e.g., "I'm a loser," "It always happens to me," "Things never work out") (see also Kendall & Ingram, in press). Thus, while the operations that produce these cognitions are highly similar, the actual content of the productions are quite different.

On the other hand, comparing another psychopathology such as schizophrenia with depression and/or anxiety potentially results in a different pattern of cognitive commonalities and differences. While there may be several peripheral similarities and differences, perhaps the critical difference lies in the structural components. A good deal of evidence demonstrates that schizophrenic individuals show neuropsychological test performances that are remarkably similar to brain-damaged individuals (see Golden, 1978). Could it be, then, that for at least some types of schizophrenia there is a marked structural disorganization that makes this psychopathology unique from other disorders? Similarly, M. K. Johnson (1985) has reported data showing that schizophrenic and manic individuals differ on several cognitive tasks but not on others. Could this suggest that there are deficits in different components of the cognitive systems of these psychotic disorders? Application of an information-processing-based cognitive taxonomy may help to generate research that answers such questions.

The suggested cognitive taxonomic system represents only one perspective of conceptualizing psychopathology that has its roots in an information processing perspective. There are potentially a multitude of others that may be useful. To briefly illustrate another, Norman and Bobrow's (1975) discussion of conceptually driven versus data-driven processes represents a relevant example. According to this distinction, *data-driven processes* refers to the analysis of information guided by the information (i.e., the information actually available in the environment) while *conceptually driven processes* refers to analysis guided by those mechanisms internal to the perceiver. As Neisser (1976) has described, normal functioning is presumably characterized by a balance between both kinds of processes. Conceptual mechanisms may guide where to look for information and fill in the "gaps" when information is not available, but they are also responsive to, and sometimes changed by, the information processed. Could some types of psychopathology be characterized as a deviation from this normal balance where conceptual mechanisms come to dominate at the expense of the impact of incoming information, or vice versa, where information processing is functionally random because conceptual processing mechanisms are underutilized? Or perhaps as M. K. Johnson (1985) has suggested in the case of delusional individuals, could delusion be a fusion of these processes so that they are functionally inseparable? The conceptual data-driven view has similarities with the cognitive taxonomic system mentioned earlier but employs a somewhat different level of analysis and focuses upon different information processing aspects. The point here, of course, is not to compare or contrast these different views but to illustrate how perspectives growing from information processing theory and research provide useful conceptual insights into the cognitive conceptualization of psychopathology.

Clinical Assessment

Clinical assessment derived from the models, methods, and findings of information processing research offers a different perspective on psychological dysfunction than "traditional" assessment. In addition to relying largely on the self-report methods previously discussed, traditional assessment (e.g., projective tests) typically elicits several responses and then examines the accumulation of these responses at the end of the test to generate inferences concerning the cognitive, emotional, and behavioral characteristics of the individual and how the characteristics may be related to psychopathology. Information-processing-based assessment, on the other hand, relies on the theoretical concepts and empirical findings of experimental cognitive psychology. In the realm of intelligence testing, for example, R. J. Sternberg (1981) notes that a knowledge of cognitive psychology can help to relate component test performances to specific mental abilities, and thus recommends supplementing psychometric assessment with theory-based cognitive tasks. Similarly, by adapting and employing cognitive methodologies, the cognitive component presumed to be involved in psychopathology can be examined more directly and independently and then linked to the affective and behavioral characteristics of disordered states. In short, such an approach allows for a greater degree of specificity in regard to the targets of assessment. Although inferential processes are still required, and empirical validity must still be demonstrated, the disadvantages of these processes are accordingly minimized.

One interesting adaptation of information processing research to the problem of assessment employs the concept of a cognitive prototype. A cognitive prototype is an organized constellation of beliefs about what constitutes instances of categories of objects or events (J. R. Anderson, 1980). Horowitz and his colleagues note that a prototype represents a theoretical standard against which individuals can be evaluated; they have employed the prototype concept as a basis for empirically examining the specific cognitions, affect, and behavior characteristics of a number of categories of psychological dysfunction (e.g., L. M. Horowitz, French, Lapid, & Weckler, 1982; L. M. Horowitz, Weckler, & Doren, 1983). They note that by operationally deriving in this manner the critical features of psychopathological or maladaptive prototypes, clinical researchers can not only gain a more precise empirical picture of both the interrelated and distinct components of psychopathologies, but can also improve the clarity and reliability of diagnostic efforts to classify individuals into specific diagnostic categories and subcategories. Moreover, increasingly precise assessment and diagnostic information based on empirically derived psychopathological prototypes is also more able to suggest appropriate treatment modalities as well as help to determine the central features of the disorder that should be targeted by treatment interventions (L. M. Horowitz *et al.*, 1983). An abundant number of other examples of information-processing-based assessment are provided by Kihlstrom and Nasby (1981), R. J. Landau and Goldfried (1981), Nasby and Kihlstrom (chapter 11, this volume), and Merluzzi *et al.* (1981).

Treatment

Kanfer and Hagerman (1985) have noted how empirical data originating in animal learning laboratories greatly contributed to behavior modification, not through the rigid application of the findings of these labs, but by providing clinicians with broad guidelines for examining different sources of variation. In a similar vein, an information-processing-based approach can be highly useful by providing clinicians with a conceptual perspective on the client's cognitive mechanics that helps to explicate a variety of important clinical processes and suggest possible treatment procedures. For instance, what appear to be "reality" distortions by clients may more easily be understood by the therapist with a knowledge of the information processing factors that contribute to the generation of cognitive distortions. Moreover, affect and behavior may be more readily conceptualized in relation to these cognitive processes. Hence, the socially anxious client's dysphoria, behavioral ineptitude in social interactions, and distorted perception of the situation may be treated differently if viewed in relation to cognitive processes. If the clinician is cognizant of how social interactions may trigger a decrease in the processing of environmental information while increasing attention to internally generated information, he or she may better understand the difficulties this kind of processing portends for both personal experience and social interaction.

Although the client's cognitive mechanics are indeed important to understand, they are not the only variables that the information processing paradigm can help to conceptualize. The cognitive processes of the clinician himself or herself are also a critical aspect of any therapeutic interaction and, as such, are potentially biased by a number of cognitive factors. Turk and his colleagues (Turk & Salovey, 1985; chapter 15, this volume; Turk & Speers, 1983) have discussed how the cognitive schemata of clinicians can have a significant impact on their clinical assessment, diagnosis, treatment, and evaluation of treatment responses of the client. On the most basic level, theoretical schemata certainly guide the assessment methods that the clinician employs, the evidence that is subsequently gathered, and ultimately the treatment intervention that is used. More subtly, however, the general cognitive schemata that the clinician possesses of the prototypical "client" may also lead to strong tendencies to process and interpret a wide variety of "normal" cognitions, affect, and behavior in a manner indicative of psychopathology (see also Langer & Abelson, 1974; C. R. Snyder, 1977). Similarly, schemata for specific clients may be developed partially from more "general client" schemata and partially from the client's specific behaviors. Such schemata may constrain how the particular client is subsequently viewed and how his or her behavior is conceptualized and ultimately treated. Therefore, although these types of cognitive processes may generally serve the clinician well by facilitating the categorization and use of a large quantity of information, they also represent some potentially serious problems. While the adoption of an information processing perspective does not guarantee uniform solutions, we propose that it represents a step toward their understanding and eventual resolution. Indeed, based on several information processing concepts, Turk and Salovey (chapter 15, this volume) have proposed several procedures for clinicians to help inoculate themselves against biased information processing.

Another illustration of the relevance of the information processing paradigm pertains to actual treatment interventions. A conceptualization of human information processing in psychopathology can lead to the development and/or refinement of strategies to therapeutically impact these processes. A prime example of such a therapeutic strategy is Beck's (Beck, Rush, Shaw, & Emery, 1979) cognitive therapy of depression. Based generally on information processing constructs such as cognitive schemata, Beck has developed a number of specific cognitive and behavioral strategies to correct "faulty" information processing and the depression that this faulty processing is related to. Although some may disagree with Beck's theoretical tenants (e.g., Coyne & Gotlib, 1983; Seligman, 1981) or with the notion that depressed individuals engage in faulty information processing per se (Alloy & Abramson, 1979, 1982; D. Martin, Abramson & Alloy, 1984), the efficacy of Beck's therapeutic approach has received empirical support (e.g., G. E. Murphy, Simmon, Wetzel, & Lustman, 1984; Rush, Beck, Kovacs, & Hollon, 1977; see also Hollon, 1981). Thus, cognitive therapy of depression is one illustration of how treatment strategies based on information processing concepts and explicitly designed to alter information processing can be effectively developed and employed.

In a related fashion, the information processing approach also offers advantages for measuring the cognitive impact of treatment. Several writers have discussed the importance of examining the precise mechanisms that are affected by treatment and that mediate change (Hollon, 1981; Kendall, 1982; Kendall & Korgeski, 1979; Zeiss, Lewinsohn, & Munoz, 1979). By providing independent evidence for the functioning of various cognitive components, information processing methodologies provide a means for assessing the cognitive mechanisms of change that are related to specific therapeutic outcomes rather than having to infer what intraclient changes might have occurred as a result of therapy. Such an approach thus offers the opportunity to conceptually advance theories of therapeutic change as they relate to cognitive variables, and also, as knowledge accumulates as to cognitive change mediators, to enhance the development of specific and effective therapeutic techniques.

Criticisms, Problems, and Limitations

We have discussed the utility of the information processing perspective and have proposed that it represents a functional bridge to a large body of theory and research in experimental cognitive psychology; yet, information processing approaches are not a panacea for the problems of clinical psychology. There are, to be sure, problems associated with using the information processing paradigm. While fruitful concepts and methods lie on the other side of the bridge, the information processing field should not be construed as unified and characterized by harmony and agreement. As several writers have observed (e.g., Landau & Goldfried, 1981; Neisser, 1976), experimental cognitive psychology has been subject to numerous and occasionally divisive debates over a variety of theoretical and empirical issues. One result of this debate has been the rapid disillusionment with a number of information processing models. Models that conceptualized memory as a series of memory stores (Atkinson & Shiffrin, 1968), for example, were once quite popular in experimental cognitive psychology. Not long after the introduction of such multistore models, however, their popularity waned as it became apparent that the data on which they were based came largely from list-learning experiments (see R. Lachman *et al.*, 1979). Similarly, the levels-of-processing (or depth-of-processing) model (Craik & Lockhart, 1972), once hailed as a viable alternative to multistore models, has also been discarded by many in experimental cognitive psychology, interestingly, for many of the same reasons that multistore models were discarded. This lack of agreement regarding models of human information processing represents a legitimate concern to clinical researchers who might look to this area for cognitive insights. As Landau and Goldfried (1981) note, it is important that cognitive clinical researchers interested in information processing approaches recognize the highly abstract nature of experimental cognitive theory and research. Thus, it would not be wise to simply "transplant" information processing models into a clinical research area, just as it was wise not to transplant animal learning findings directly into human behavior modification efforts (Kanfer & Hagerman, 1985). Rather, researchers will profit the most by borrowing a *perspective* and adapting and modifying information processing constructs and methodologies from that perspective as appropriate to address and explicate clinically relevant problems.

In this way, the current constructs of information processing theory and research can provide frameworks for conceptualizing and empirically examining cognitive variables in psychopathology.

In a similar fashion, even the prospect of adapting "discarded" approaches does not completely preclude clinical utility. Although the conceptual constructs behind many stimulus–response behavioral approaches have been discarded by a number of psychologists, the enormous practical impact that these approaches have had on clinical assessment and intervention can hardly be denied. In a vein closer to information processing, the previously discussed depth-of-processing model, no longer the sole paradigm for experimental cognitive psychology, has proven enlightening for generating empirical data on some of the information processing characteristics that may play an important role in several different psychopathologies (H. Davis, 1979a; Derry & Kuiper, 1981; Ingram, Smith, & Brehm, 1983; T. W. Smith, Ingram, & Brehm, 1983).

It is unlikely that any conceptual approach to the study of human behavior is without criticisms. Unlike other approaches, however, the information processing paradigm may be unique in that one of its earliest proponents is now one of its most articulate critics. In a series of published works, Neisser (1976, 1980a, 1980b, 1985) has challenged information processing research for constructing artificial laboratory experiments requiring inexperienced subjects to perform brief, unusual, and essentially meaningless tasks that are typically measured in reaction times of milliseconds. In short, Neisser has argued that much of what constitutes current information processing research lacks ecological validity and is therefore "unlikely to offer any significant insights into the human condition" (1980b, p. 364).

Such a criticism must be seriously considered by cognitive clinical researchers. It may indeed be that the kinds of experiments Neisser describes make external validity difficult to detect. Moreover, this may be one reason why clinically oriented researchers have been relatively slow to turn to the work of cognitive psychology for help in examining cognitive clinical processes. We know of nothing in the information processing paradigm itself, however, which necessitates that theoretical and empirical work stimulated from it *cannot* be ecologically valid. According to its most basic definition, ecological validity represents the degree to which theoretical models and empirical data can be meaningfully linked to real-world phenomena. Regardless of whether experimental cognitive psychology has presently achieved this goal, the application of an information processing perspective to clinical issues facilitates its movement toward gaining a high degree of such validity. Psychopathology is an issue that has a variety of critical real-world implications. As researchers employing the information processing paradigm continue to make contributions to conceptualizing cognitive aspects of various psychopathological phenomena, to assessing disordered states, and to treating psychopathology, then lack of ecological validity is no longer a relevant shortcoming. The chapters in the present volume are replete with proposals that are promising in this regard.

Criticisms of the information processing approach have also been voiced by some cognitive clinical researchers. Arguing that information processing implies a "passive organism" which merely receives and transfers sensory data through a processing system, Arnkoff (1980), for instance, suggested that "information processing models are inadequate from a clinical perspective because clients are active creators, not passive receivers or automatic transformers of stimuli" (p. 342). Although Arnkoff's criticism may be aimed more at a static and relatively simplistic computer metaphor than at the information processing paradigm, the point is noteworthy; certainly an approach that limits its conceptualization of people to nothing more than passive receivers of information is at best limited and at worst, inaccurate and misleading.

The notion that information processing models imply a passive view of human cognition can probably be traced to a focus in much experimental cognitive empirical work on uncovering the structural characteristics of the mechanisms that transmit sensory information. The concern that examining these "passive" sensory processing structures will not be helpful from a clinical perspective is based upon a narrow definition of what constitutes the appropriate domain of clinical psychology. Thus, while a large part of clinical psychology is indeed concerned with assessing and treating cognitively intact, "neurotic" clients, there are also many areas of clinical psychology that are interested in individuals who are not so cognitively intact. Advances in understanding the cognitive processes involved in autism (Litrownik & McInnes, 1982; chapter 9, this volume), learning-disabled children (D. Goldstein, Hasher, & Stein, 1983), mental retardation (Baumeister, Runcie, & Gardepe, 1984; Spitz, 1973), and schizophrenia (Saccuzzo, chapter 10, this volume; Saccuzzo *et al.,* 1974; Walker & McGuire, 1982) are prime examples of highly relevant clinical concerns that have been facilitated by examining structural deficits in the mechanisms that automatically or "passively" transmit information. Thus, it is appropriate for some areas of clinical psychology to focus solely upon the "passive" transfer of sensory information and how this transfer goes awry.

In addition, while there may be merit in examining such passive information transfer for some clinically relevant disorders, the information processing paradigm itself does not imply that humans are nothing more than passive transformers of stimuli. Even the computer metaphor does not suggest passivity. A computer program inputs symbols; produces numerous transformations, calculations, and reorganizations; combines the input with stored data; puts some results in memory for future use, discards some; and outputs others. Such a process can hardly be seen as a passive flow of information through a system. Similarly, if it can be assumed that individuals do indeed possess some kinds of cognitive structures that are operated via some processes, an information processing perspective that conceptualizes and empirically examines these components can be expedient in elucidating how these structures and operations work to allow for the "active" construction of perception and experience. This has, in fact, been the general concern of much basic information processing research and, as such, is highly relevant to how "disordered" perception is constructed.

By strongly endorsing the advantages of the information processing paradigm, we do not mean to imply that it is the only way to conceptualize psychopathology. A variety of alternative approaches that range across highly diverse conceptual levels of analysis have made numerous and significant contributions to the understanding of normal and abnormal functioning. Despite these contributions, no single approach can account for all facets of human behavior, and the information processing approach is no exception. It is thus important to realize that information processing represents one aspect of a confluence of forces that shape and determine human behavior. Ideally, our understanding of behavior should include not only a knowledge of cognitive contributions to psychopathology, but also of biological, neurological, genetic, environmental, and sociological contributions, and most importantly, of how these various factors interact. Although we have not yet achieved the level of conceptual development or empirical technology sufficient to realize this goal in clinical psychology, it is nevertheless necessary for cognitive clinical researchers to remain open to the contributions of other conceptual approaches and, where possible, to strive for their meaningful integration. It is our belief that the information processing paradigm will facilitate development of the cognitive component of such an eventual integration.

Acknowledgments

We would like to thank David Goldstein and Roy Lachman for their comments on an earlier draft of this chapter.

2

Information Processing Psychology: Origins and Extensions

ROY LACHMAN
Department of Psychology
University of Houston
Houston, Texas 77004

JANET L. LACHMAN
Law Department
Chevron-USA
Houston, Texas 77253

Introduction and Overview

Change seems to be the only thing that is permanent, a fact to which the history of psychology clearly attests. That history is one of shifting coalitions and changing conceptions of the field and its proper objects of study. This volume—which documents and elucidates the blending of information processing psychology and concepts traditionally called clinical psychology—is one of many significant events in that history of change. Most readers of psychology will readily appreciate that such a blending *is* a change; it departs from traditional patterns in that it mixes unlike entities. It is less readily apparent what the entities are, and what conceptual conjunction entails. The present chapter is designed to consider these questions.

The reason that such a book as this is conceived in the first place is that psychologists fall into a broad array of subgroups. The individuals traditionally identified with information processing psychology overlap only slightly with

INFORMATION PROCESSING APPROACHES
TO CLINICAL PSYCHOLOGY

those interested in psychopathology, affective states, and clinical practice. The target audience of such a book is thus a group of scientists and practitioners willing to consider appropriating ideas and methods developed by others for different purposes in different settings. This process of transfer and appropriation is a classical feature of a dynamic science; it is a natural result of the search for solutions to refractory problems. However, until recently, the structure of the groups engaged in such transactions went largely unanalyzed, as did the process itself. There was essentially no coherent account of what was appropriated, or even how to distinguish the recipient from the originating community in the first place. Although our understanding of conceptual and methodological transfer is still largely incomplete, advances have been made in defining the relevant groups or scientific communities that engage in this intriguing process of transfer. We will describe one of these communities, information processing psychology, which offers a potentially rich source of ideas for clinical psychology.

Cognitive psychology refers to the subdiscipline of psychology concerned with the higher mental processes such as thinking, decision making, perception, and memory. Information processing is but one of the orientations that guided the study and systematization of those topics. Because it is the most pervasive orientation, the terms *cognition* and *information processing* are often used interchangeably, although there are several other approaches to cognition having substantial numbers of adherents. The information processing approach has attracted attention far beyond its original domain in the higher mental processes, and it is prospectively of value to areas of psychology traditionally denominated "clinical." It is timely, therefore, to provide a detailed description of the origins of information processing psychology and its current attributes, and to consider its potential contribution to clinical research and practice.

Fortunately for our descriptive objective, the information processing approach emerged contemporaneously with advances in our understanding of scientific fields, coalitions, and communities. Consequently, it is possible to give a contemporary and sophisticated account of the emergence of this particular psychological orientation. As a preliminary, we will determine the contours of any scientific entity such as information processing psychology, and we will consider the relationship of these entities to such terms as *discipline, field,* and *paradigm.* Next we will present an account of information processing psychology itself: its theoretical origins; the various sources of its substantive commitments; and its distinguishing properties, presuppositions, concepts, and methodology. At various points in our deliberations, we will consider the conceptual relationship between information processing and the study of psychopathology and affective states. Specific attention will be given to the opportunities offered, and pitfalls to avoid, in applying information processing concepts to traditionally clinical areas of study.

The Intellectual and Organizational Structure of Scientific Communities

Interacting scientists appear to coalesce into communities whose contours result from both intellectual and organizational factors. Although discussions of scientific approaches often fail to take account of both determinants of structure, both are needed for a clear understanding of the possible referents of concepts such as *disciplinary field, research program, presuppositional system,* and *Kuhnian paradigm.* The interaction between intellectual and organizational factors in determining scientific group boundaries can be illustrated by two contrasting examples. Consider the extraordinary intellectual diversity among members of the American Psychological Association (APA), an organizationally defined group representing the discipline of psychology. Members of the APA can be basic researchers or clinical practitioners; their fields of study range from insects to complex human organizations. Many of them would find each other's work incomprehensible. Then consider the organizational diversity of those individuals intellectually committed to Freudian concepts. Freudians may be found in academic departments from English to psychiatry, holding many different academic degrees, and engaged in a variety of professional activities. Both APA members and Freudians constitute scientific communities, and both reflect some intellectual commonality and some organizational factors. The difference is one of degree; the APA is a group defined primarily by organizational factors and secondarily by intellectual ones, while Freudians are the reverse.

Generically, the problem is one of defining set relationships among scientific communities defined in partly intellectual and partly organizational terms. In psychology, it is rather obvious that intellectually derived definitions yield very different sets and subsets than do organizationally derived ones. This fact is a part of the pattern responsible for certain conspicuous features of our discipline: its seeming chaos, its multifarious subdisciplines, its intradisciplinary rivalries, and its chronic identity crises. The same factor helps motivate certain perennial questions: Is psychology preparadigmatic? multiparadigmatic? aparadigmatic? If it is multiparadigmatic, how many paradigms are there? Is one dominant? These are set inclusion questions, whose answers depend on how the sets are defined. Consequently, it is essential to determine what is meant by *psychology* and *paradigm.* Although answers to the foregoing questions are necessarily conditional, even conditional answers provide guidance in considering nontrivial matters, such as whether the environment is favorable for the emergence of new approaches or the transfer of existing approaches across disciplinary subfields.

The analysis in this chapter will begin by defining *psychology* as an administrative–organizational entity. Membership in the discipline of psychology, while it has intellectual dimensions, is not premised on strictly intellectual considerations. Within the discipline of psychology, there are subgroups of different sizes exerting various amounts of influence. We will consider what it is that distinguishes subgroups within a discipline. Some subgroups have attributes that warrant the designation *paradigm;* we will consider what these attributes are. Finally we will turn our attention to the information processing paradigm and describe its origins and current properties.

Presuppositions and Scientific Communities

A disciplinary field is a political–administrative entity with major organizational dimensions as well as important intellectual ones. The intellectual orientations of scientists interact in complex fashions with organizational politics to shape coalitions of various strengths and sizes. These coalitions range in size and influence from small research teams to monolithic groups whose boundaries are nearly coextensive with those of the discipline. Between these extremes are the orientations such as information processing psychology that can readily be understood in terms of intellectual commitments. An intellectual orientation is vastly more complicated than an administrative entity because its essence is hidden: It inheres in the thought processes of individuals. Accordingly, it is much less stable than an administrative grouping. Furthermore, an intellectual orientation often must be inferred from intellectual products, citation patterns, and scholarly interactions. Nonetheless, coherent scientific communities can be described in terms of the presuppositions determining what their members believe to be the legitimate content of the field, the nature of its underlying reality, and appropriate methods of study. Presuppositions account for strategic decisions of members of the community as to conceptual infrastructure and themata, and their preference for particular types of analogies, formalisms, and research methods. Constellations of such presuppositions underlie major research orientations and have been described as the assumptive core of scientific paradigms (H. I. Brown, 1979).

Cognitive information processing psychology is a scientific community whose members share, to a greater or lesser extent, a common presuppositional system. Individuals with largely common presuppositions can be regarded as members of the same community by virtue of presuppositionally determined activities, even if they engage in relatively autonomous research programs. Researchers studying such strikingly different processes as human problem solving and matching-to-sample procedures with animals may accept the same analogies and conceptual infrastructure and thus belong to the same intellectual orientation.

Membership in an academic department or a scientific and professional society is all or none, and easily identified. But a given individual's participation in a particular presuppositional system falls somewhere on a continuum, from acceptance of a few peripheral elements of the system to near total identification with most of its attributes. Moreover, the size and diversity of intellectual orientations falls on a second continuum, from small research teams to so-called paradigmatic communities consisting of thousands of individual scientists. Not surprisingly, the extent of overlap between the group members depends on the size and diversity of the group. The members of small research teams are nearly identical in orientation; they share common hypotheses, overlapping problems, methods, and theoretical strategies. There also are middle-sized communities; members address a set of problems which are related, but not identical. These individuals are apt to communicate with each other less frequently and more formally than they do with their more direct reference group. Members of large paradigmatic communities share some presuppositions, but they have selected widely different problems to pursue, and their methods reflect the problem domain they have chosen as well as their shared conceptual and thematic presuppositions. Obviously, as the size and diversity of the group increases, the more difficult it will be to characterize the members' shared commitments, and the more individuals there will be who are difficult to classify as members or nonmembers. Even so, sharing part of a conceptual infrastructure may lead to a classification such as *cognitive psychologist* or *behaviorist,* even though members are studying such diverse subjects as humans, animals, children, or business enterprises. Of course, there are some psychologists whose thinking is sufficiently dominated by their problem area that it makes sense to identify them additionally as developmental, organizational, or neuropsychologists. Concepts of scientific community, therefore, tend to be somewhat indeterminate, as are the categories they represent. Nevertheless, a description should be attempted even if it is inevitably imperfect.

Clarification of the Concept of Paradigm

Identification of a scientific subgroup such as information processing psychologists is a feature of the new era in philosophy of science, stimulated largely by the combined work of Kuhn (1962), Polanyi (1964), Toulmin (1963), and some others. The new approach, which we will call for convenience *paradigm theory,* replaced the older doctrine of Vienna Circle Logical Positivism. Known as *logical empiricism* in the United States, logical positivism was the dominant theory of Western science from about 1920 through 1960 (Ayer, 1959). Logical positivists generally subscribed to a unitary notion of canonical validation—namely, that rule-governed procedures based on formal logic are what drives all significant decision-making in science, including which knowledge claims are worth considering and which are to be regarded as proven. The positivists, and some of their close allies (e.g., Popper, 1959), initially believed that the processes of science were neither valid nor interesting unless they could be reduced to the formal logic or Whitehead and Russell's (1910–1913) *Principia mathematica* (H. I. Brown, 1979).

In contrast, paradigm theory takes explicit notice that much scientific decision-making, including decisions as to what is considered a true and correct account of natural phenomena, is made by consortia—decision-making groups consisting of editors, consultants, referees, panels, and the like. While the scientific community strongly values formal representation and logical deduction, many of its decisions are not logical. This is not to say that the decisions are illogical; rather, they are consensual. Consensual decisions shape the community's notions of what problems are worth studying, what interpretations particular kinds of data will support, and what research methods are inadequate to a given problem.

Once it is recognized how important consensual validation is to the advancement of science, it becomes evident that a doctrine of purely canonical validation is seriously incomplete. One of the clearest contrasts between logical positivism and the newer theory of science was the importance of consensual validation in postparadigmatic accounts of the scientific enterprise. This difference, which is perhaps not as widely appreciated as it should be, had far-reaching consequences. As the new philosophy of science focused on consensual as well as canonical validation, there was a concomitant development of interest in the nature and proper characterization of the scientific communities in which the consensus arose. Kuhn (1962) focused on consensus during periods of stability and revolutionary change, using the term *paradigm* to designate scientific communities and their commitments.

Unfortunately, Kuhn gave this word too many different senses. The ambiguity of Kuhn's paradigm concept may reflect his use of physics as a prototypical science. Although he acknowledged a conceptual debt to Piaget (Kuhn, 1962), his concept of paradigm was developed not from psychology, but from episodes almost exclusively in the history of physics and physical chemistry. The generality of the original concept was thus limited by the extent to which these disciplines are representative of science in general. Interestingly, the discipline of physics appears to have had a unique intellectual organization, more through historical accident than the structure of physical reality. For roughly 200 years physics had a single dominant conceptual scheme—Newtonian physics, which included both a comprehensive scientific theory and an encompassing presuppositional system, or complex of related ideas. The theory consisted of the three laws of motion and the inverse-square law of universal gravitation; its major domain was terrestrial and celestial mechanics. The presuppositional system consisted of a family of associated concepts, assumptions, methodological preferences, and behavioral dispositions. Among the most central of these were the conception of physical reality as mass points in motion and an underlying view of space, time, and motion as absolute rather than relative. The paradigm fostered reliance on certain formalisms, such as differential equations, to describe physical systems. It included a commitment to Galilean verification methods, communication, and a willingness to undergo community criticism. What was unique about physics was the extent to which the presuppositional overlap among Newtonians approximated the contours of physics as a discipline. A revolutionary shift to a new presuppositional system, which was associated with relativity theory and quantum mechanics, did not materially change that situation; physics was as unified after the Einsteinian revolution as it had been before. Thus, the presuppositional systems associated with Newton and Einstein were, at separate times, nearly definitive of the discipline of physics—a fact which may account for at least some of the ambiguity of Kuhn's (1962) initial use of the term *paradigm.* Although Kuhn ultimately distinguished between scientific communities and the complex of ideas binding the members of those communities together, not all users of Kuhn's ideas have maintained the distinction. Although it is tempting to seek alternative terminology to avoid confusion, *paradigm* is such a well-known term that we will use it here in a carefully limited sense. In this chapter *paradigm* refers to a research community with a shared presuppositional system. *Presuppositional system,* in turn, refers to the shared intellectual commitments, and common behavioral dispositions, that result in the paradigmatic community being perceived as a group. A presuppositional system includes an interrelated set of concepts, scientific themata and metaphors, methodological formulations, and attitudes. Some attributes of the presuppositional system are primarily intellectual, such as the presuppositions themselves and the complex of beliefs associated with them. Others are behaviors from which the belief system may be inferred; this includes choice of research problems, methodological preferences, and the like. Of course, a presuppositional system does not constitute a monolithic doctrine to which all members of the paradigmatic community universally subscribe. However, it is an internally consistent complex of ideas, accepted by individual scientists in varying degrees and in different configurations at various times. The content of the presuppositional system is largely implicit. It changes over time, both at the individual level and as projected at an abstract level onto the community.

In psychology, a variety of presuppositional systems coexist. These include global assumptions about human nature such as the structure of intelligence, the architecture of cognitive capacities, and the role of environmental contingencies. They suggest the appropriate analogies for mental processes, the propriety of generalization across phylogenies, the efficacy of particular methodologies, and the like. In providing scientific guides such as these, presuppositional systems are a primary force in scientific tradition, decision making, and the advancement of knowledge.

Elements of a Presuppositional System: Themata, Metaphor, and Methodology

The presuppositional system of a scientific community contains elements falling into three categories: thematic, metaphorical, and methodological, with distinct and overlapping attributes. In this section we will first consider *thematic elements,* a concept taken from Holton (1973). Holton identified thematic elements in his examination of the published work, laboratory notes, interview transcripts, and personal correspondence of major scientific figures. Through use of a method he called "thematic analysis," Holton was able to infer in his subjects the presence of of an unshakable commitment to a core set of ideas, which he designated "scientific themata." Themata are the central presuppositions concerning fundamental properties of a discipline's object of study. They give rise to other presuppositional elements—a specific scientific language, interrelated concepts, a unique methodology, and preferences for specific mathematical formalisms.

Holton gives many examples of scientific themata, including Millikan's commitment to an atomistic interpretation of electricity, Weinstein's conviction that a unified theory of elementary physical constituents is possible, and the conviction going as far back as Galileo that observable chaos is to be explained by underlying order and certainty—that every event has a cause. Newton's conception of physical reality as mass points in motion and the related sets of concepts, described earlier, is an interlocking set of thematic elements. To these examples from physics may be added some psychological examples, such as Freud's conviction that all psychopathology results from unconscious conflict, and Skinner's view that observable behavior is due to a prior history of exposure to environmental contingencies. Within the information processing paradigm, examples of scientific themata include Sternberg's belief that mental scanning is decomposable into coherent, isolable, independent subprocesses, and Newell and Simon's idea that intelligent behavior in humans and automata is based upon the operation of a physical symbol system.

Holton showed that themata are retained in the face of shifting theory and practice, contrary evidence, and decades of wilting debate. Although it can be destructive, this commitment is understandable. Scientific discovery is far from an automatic process, and it does not march relentlessly forward. Without thematic guides, scientists could not maintain a direction in the face of unstable experimental outcomes, nor would they have a basis to judge the relative value of conflicting studies. There would be no way to derive a coherent theory from the limitless variety of alternative interpretations of research results. Themata, therefore, provide a source of inspiration and provide sustaining motivation for landmark scientific discovery.

The *methodological elements* of a presuppositional system often follow closely from thematic elements. A firm belief in a particular conception of underlying reality tends to suggest suitable ways to study the phenomenon at hand. For example, it is no accident that Skinner invented the animal box. If all learned behavior can be explained in terms of environmental contingencies, then it follows that animal behavior is representative and any readily available and conveniently sized animal can serve as a research subject. Further, some method must be devised for systematically introducing, deleting, and monitoring environmental contingencies. The so-called Skinner Box follows naturally from the Skinnerian presuppositional system. Similarly, Freud's focus on the study of dreams may well be a consequence of the fact that dreams are not subject to control by the conscious mind and must therefore reflect something else—presumably the unconscious mind which loomed so large in Freud's theories. In the information processing paradigm, Simon's extensive use of computer simulation as his preferred theoretical formalism is predictable from themata emphasizing symbolic operations as central elements in intelligent behavior.

A root *metaphor* may be conceived as a particular type of thema. However, a really compelling metaphor may take on a life of its own and become a central driving force in the development of a problem, a theory, or even an entire field, and hence deserves some discussion of its own. Although analytic distinctions have been made between *metaphor, analogy,* and *model* (Ortony, 1979), these distinctions are unnecessary to the present discussion, and we will use the terms interchangeably.

A good metaphor is part of a thought process that generates a network of similarities between an original context of usage and a new one. Metaphors are used to think about the properties of partially understood phenomena, by analyzing them in terms of familiar systems of relations. Metaphors are part of the reference-fixing process, that is, the process by which scientific terms are attached to nature. The persistence of a given metaphor depends on its ability to accommodate experimental and observational pressure, and only partially on logical considerations. Not only does metaphorical thinking initiate, guide, and support the reference-fixing process in science, it supports the introduction of theoretical concepts and formalisms. The result is the formulation and communication of original conceptions and the construction of new scientific theory.

The ubiquitous use of metaphor goes back to the very beginnings of modern science and is still present in the formulation and development of experimental ideas and formal theory (Boyd, 1979; R. Lachman, 1960). An early example is that of Robert Boyle, who in 1660 analogized the elasticity or "spring" of air with that of lamb's wool. Boyle's analogy helped him demonstrate that air is a compressible material substance having weight (Conant, 1947). There are countless illustrations of metaphors in the growth of scientific knowledge: light conceived as waves, from the already-familiar phenomena of sound waves; heat conduction analogized with the familiar laws of hydrodynamics; the atom viewed as a miniature solar system; and so on. James Clerk Maxwell emphasized the usefulness of analogy in research, describing a physical analogy as "that partial similarity between the laws of one science and those of another which makes each of them illustrate the other" (cited in Nagel, 1961). Maxwell also reported that an analogy with the mathematics of the motions of incompressible fluids was essential to the development of his theory of electricity.

Metaphors have also been influential in the history of psychology, as they are today. The metaphor of association and reflex served well in the early development of learning theory. Freud's theory of unconscious forces, in which a conflict repressed in one area will force its way out somewhere else, reflects an analogy with hydraulics. The past and present of cognitive psychology is also characterized by the use of metaphor; the field actually reflects a successive incorporation of metaphors from communication theory, transformational linguistics, and computer science (R. Lachman *et al.*, 1979; G. A. Miller, 1974). The last of these continues to be pervasively influential; there is no question that the computer metaphor is either implicit or explicit in most cognitive theory and research.

As various chapters in this book illustrate, clinical psychology is in the process of appropriating at least some of the themata, metaphors, and theoretical and experimental methodology of the information processing paradigm. The content of these presuppositional elements, and hence their appropriateness and utility in new contexts, derive in large measure from the presuppositions' intellectual origins. Accordingly, we will now trace the intellectual antecedents of the presuppositional system of contemporary information processing psychology.

Conceptual Origins of Information Processing Psychology

At the most general level, research and theory in information processing psychology are directed at elucidating the properties of the adaptive mechanisms responsible for the apprehension, storage, retrieval, and utilization of information—information that may originate in the external environment or internal somatic and mental states. After two decades of research, cognitive theoretical systems and empirical findings span a formidable array of populations, tasks, and conditions. However, there is far more commonality in the conceptual and intellectual ancestry of information processing than its surface heterogeneity would suggest. The shared commitments underlying the diversity of research in the paradigm can best be understood in terms of the conceptual antecedents from which the presuppositions and practices of the contemporary tradition derive.

Information processing psychology took form in the 1950s and 1960s when external forces began to exert an impact on the experimental psychology of the day. However, the psychological researchers who reflected this impact were not passive recipients of undigested external themata. They incorporated and adapted the external doctrines to produce a subfield that differed dramatically from the parent discipline yet still reflected its most fundamental commitments. The presuppositions and practices of information processing psychology can thus be divided into those originating within experimental psychology and those imported from external sciences. The contributions originating within psychology came from a variety of sources including midcentury neobehaviorism (C. L. Hull, 1943; Spence, 1956), radical behaviorism (Skinner, 1957), classical functionalism (Boring, 1950; Woodworth, 1938), and verbal learning functionalism (Hilgard, 1948; McGeoch, 1942). British experimental psychology (Broadbent, 1958) and studies of human engineering and performance (Howell & Goldstein, 1971) contributed important new concepts and methodologies. Extrapsychological contributors include communication engineering and information theory (Shannon, 1948), transformational linguistics (Chomsky, 1965), computer science (Minsky, 1967; Newell & Simon, 1972), and indirectly, mathematical logic and the formal limits of computation (M. Davis, 1965).

One other development is worth noting at this point. At about the same time that experimental psychology was developing the information processing approach to cognition, an independent approach to cognition was developing from within psychology. This approach, which might be called developmental or structural cognition, was driven by the work of Bruner, Piaget, and others (Kessel & Bevan, 1985). This movement originated in different antecedents and grew in a different direction from information processing. Today it has a well-developed presuppositional system of its own. Although it is not inconsistent with information processing psychology, there is no sign that the two will converge into a unitary approach; it is probably correct to view this tradition as a separate paradigm (see Fig. 1).

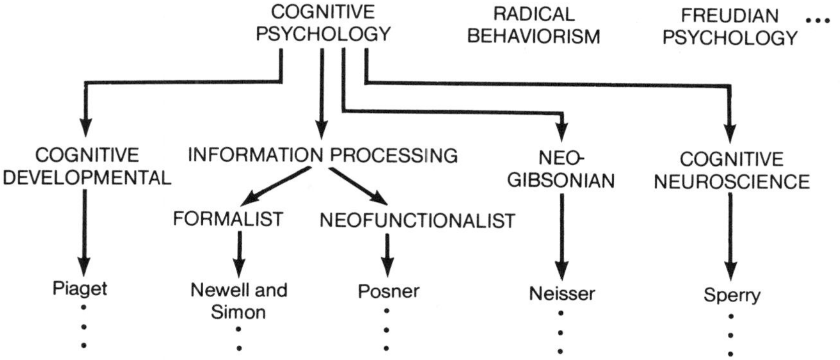

FIG. 1. ***Outline of presuppositional systems in psychology of the 1980s. For techniques being developed to identify critical attributes of the intellectual communities in psychology and initial results, see Krasner and Houts (1984).***

Some of the intellectual antecedents of information processing psychology were affirmatively adopted in whole or in part. Other antecedents, particularly internal ones, shaped the information processing approach in a different way: Certain of their commitments and research programs were explicitly rejected, thus providing points of departure that helped initiate new directions of scientific thinking and experimentation.

Presuppositions from Neobehaviorism

American psychology has always been multiparadigmatic; that is, there has never been universal agreement on a single approach. However, between the 1930s and the 1960s the field was dominated by neobehaviorist presuppositions, and as of about 1950 there was probably more agreement than at any time before or since. Neobehaviorism was basically antimentalistic, concerned with animal behavior, and was committed to extending conditioning principles to all areas of psychology. This commitment contributed to the undoing of neobehaviorist domination of American psychology. The insurmountable difficulties encountered in attempting to extend neobehaviorist theory and method to human symbolic processes (in particular, language capacities) was one of the principal factors leading to the broad acceptance of information processing presuppositions. Particularly oppressive was the disparity between what people can actually do and what was studied in the animal and verbal learning laboratories. People can invent and learn entities ranging from abstract scientific theories and advanced mathematics to modern dance; they can build and operate artifacts from skyscrapers to submarines. Psychological research programs, unfortunately, were heavily concentrated on such limited behaviors as rote learning of nonsense syllables and maze learning by white rats. As disillusionment became widespread, some psychologists turned to external theories to guide their research programs. The result was a massive presuppositional shift away from neobehaviorism—a shift that began in the late 1950s, carried through the 1960s, and was essentially complete by the early 1970s. The coherent and influential research tradition known as information processing was the end product of that shift (R. Lachman *et al.*, 1979). The adoption of cognitive concepts by clinical psychology occurred later and the resulting changes exhibited a unique pattern reflecting the properties and concerns of that field (see Ingram and Kendall, chapter 1 this volume).

As the intellectual reorientation in experimental psychology was taking place, the deficiencies of the neobehaviorist tradition were heavily emphasized by those newly converted to opposing views. The discontinuities were naturally vividly apparent to those involved, who were making a conscious break with their own training and tradition, and many important continuities with the past went unremarked. Today, these can be more clearly appreciated. Some researchers creatively combined the two traditions and produced a very significant scientific product (e.g., Estes, 1982). Perhaps the major source of continuity was an abiding commitment to the Galilean tradition of experimental science. Information processing psychologists shared with their neobehaviorist predecessors a firm belief in empiricism, operationism, and the nomothetic ideal. The central role of experimentation along with related methodological and statistical preferences, therefore, persisted through the intellectual upheavals of the 1960s.

There was also substantive continuity. Although new concepts and methods for the study of memory, language, thinking, and decision making surfaced during the 1960s, interest in particular prior research areas persisted. Many verbal learning psychologists, for example, had studied memory using theories borrowed from neobehaviorist animal research (McGeoch, 1942). Most of them seem to have retained their interest in memory research after accepting information processing presuppositions. They adopted new ways of looking at familiar questions and redesigned their experiments accordingly. For example, the unit of analysis gradually enlarged from nonsense syllables and words (elements seemingly amenable to conditioned association) to larger units of discourse such as sentences, paragraphs, complete stories, and later pictures and other configurational-analogue entities (elements amenable to strategic organization and schemata theory).

Despite these continuities, however, it is undeniable that the information processing movement drew its strength from widespread dissatisfaction with neobehaviorism. Research based on neobehavioristic presuppositions produced a certain number of persistently anomalous outcomes. Some problems that appeared central, such as place versus response learning, steadfastly resisted any experimental resolution at all. The rising cognitive tradition responded by rejecting certain parts of the neobehaviorist presuppositional apparatus: learning as the central problem of psychology, animal data as the source of basic principles, and conditioning as the fundamental form of learning. Perhaps most important, information processing psychologists firmly scuttled the antimentalist emphasis of neobehaviorism, along with its concomitant extreme environmentalism and its exclusive emphasis on the external causes of behavior. Innate capacities were reintroduced, and internal processes such as plans, strategies, images, and decisions were proposed (G. A. Miller, Galanter, & Pribram, 1960). Experiments using human subjects increasingly replaced animal experimentation, and internal mechanisms were coupled with external determinants of behavior to account for the data. Eventually, most researchers concerned with the higher mental processes found internal processes and structural components to be acceptable theoretical elements, and American experimental psychology moved into the information processing age.

As we have indicated, the reorientation was greatly facilitated by a massive influx of themata, metaphors, and methods from external fields, including those that are now called the cognitive sciences (Kintch, Miller, & Polson, 1984), that deal in one way or other with symbols and symbol manipulation: operational mathematics, communications engineering and information theory, linguistics, computer science, and cognitive psychology.

Presuppositions from Information Theory

The stunning development of twentieth-century communication technology occurred because so much was learned about the abstract nature of communication systems. Communication scientists have continuously formulated and tested general laws describing both ideal and real communication systems. In the aftermath of major discoveries, the concepts and laws appropriate to communication systems became metaphors for biological and physical systems that had not previously been viewed as communication channels. Certain psychologists were struck by the potential analogy of the human information processor and the theoretical information channel. Various human abilities were conceived of as part of an information-handling channel with built-in states and limitations. Research was designed to determine the channel's properties and capacities for transmitting different types of information. A number of technical concepts such as *uncertainty, information, bit, source, message, destination, encoding,* and the like, were borrowed from communication theory and incorporated into psychological theory and research (Garner, 1962). A major impetus for this presuppositional, technological, and conceptual transfer to experimental psychology was the work of the mathematician Claude Shannon. Shannon (1948) demonstrated that an explicit relationship existed between certain properties of communication systems and the rate that such a system would process and transmit an ensemble of symbols, and the relationship was independent of the meaning or ultimate utility of those symbols. Shannon's formulation solved a landmark problem in communications technology; however, psychologists were more interested in the general theory of communication in which his solution was embedded. Some concepts derived from Shannon's work continue to influence the thinking of perceptual and engineering psychologists, and probably will for years to come (Garner, 1974). However, outside these areas, the details of information theory have little current influence and will not be presented here. The limited utility of concepts from communication theory probably reflects the fact that they are based on the functions of a physical artifact whose general properties have proved not to be equivalent to those characterizing evolved biological systems (J. L. Lachman & Lachman, 1979).

Presuppositions from Transformational Linguistics

The transfer of theory and method from linguistics to psychology involved no analogy. During the zenith of neobehaviorist domination, many psychologists sought to use concepts from the animal learning laboratory to account for human verbal behavior. Linguists were concerned with precisely the same phenomenon, although they called it language. This terminological difference symbolized fundamentally incompatible themata. Linguists differed sharply from psychologists studying verbal behavior on the importance of various aspects of language. To linguists, novelty and complexity were among the most compelling and central characteristic of language (e.g., Bever, Fodor, & Garrett, 1968). Neobehaviorists, in contrast, focused on repetitive elements of language (Osgood, 1963) and sought simple principles to account for verbal behavior. Most important, linguists repeatedly argued that language had structure. Noam Chomsky (1965), the most prominent linguist of the last two decades, argued that language could never be scientifically explained or understood in radical behaviorist or neobehaviorist terms. These approaches, he insisted, fundamentally misconceived the nature of language by ignoring its most essential properties: structure, ruliness, and grammar. In his view, the use of language must be explained by reference to rules in the user's brain that enable him or her to deal with structure, that is, the systematic relationship between the parts of a sentence such as phrases and clauses. To a linguist, mastering a language involved internalizing the system of rules governing those relationships.

The importance of rules in the head, or "competence," was explicitly formulated by linguists in the *competence/performance* distinction. Performance is actual speech. Linguists and psycholinguists argued for the development of theories of competence and had to postulate innate capacities to do so. They pointed to the compelling fact that children all over the world, learning dramatically different native tongues, begin the acquisition process at about the same age, take about the same length of time to master the essentials of their language, and go through similar steps in the process. What is more, all but the most profoundly retarded accomplish the task, suggesting that at least some aspects of language ability are innate. The child was viewed as a "language acquisition device"—preprogrammed by nature to extract from its environment whatever information is needed to acquire a linguistic system.

Unsurprisingly, when linguistic criticism began to appear in journals (e.g., Chomsky, 1959), the stage was set for a paradigm clash of significant proportions. The criticism in the clash was not unidirectional. The theories and concepts used by linguists, and a growing cadre of psycholinguists who were at home in the information processing tradition, elicited sharp disapproval from neobehaviorists. Such notions as *language acquisition device* and *innate language capacity* seemed hopelessly mentalistic and impossibly retrograde to the radical behaviorists and neobehaviorists, who had come to view their own physicalistic orientation as the benchmark of any behavioral science worthy of the name. Concepts such as *structure* simply would not fit; it is impossible to cast the internalization of structure as the learning of physicalistic stimuli and responses.

Yet Chomsky convincingly argued that people behave as if they have learned rule systems and that grammars are mentally represented; if such neobehaviorist principles as associative contiguity or reinforcement cannot account for this fact, so much the worse for neobehavioristic principles. While linguistics attacked neobehavioristic psychology as anachronistic and witless, the neobehaviorists counterattacked linguistics as antiscientific and muddled. The debate was heated—sometimes downright vitriolic.

Time was the ultimate arbiter of this confrontation. Discouraged by the the poor success of neobehaviorism in constructing theories of language behavior, the nascent proponents of information processing paradigm looked increasingly to transformational linguistics for ideas. Chomsky's theories and presuppositional system were initially borrowed virtually in their entirety. However, the contemporary field is far less dependent on linguistics than it once was, having identified a number of linguistic concepts that are psychologically useless. Psychologists never fully accepted the linguists' rationalist methodology, preferring the experimental approach that was a hallmark of their own discipline. Moreover, events moved on in linguistics; Chomsky's theory, once unrivaled, is no longer so. Considerable work in both cognitive psychology and linguistics now focuses on semantics, conversation, and other social uses of language (H. H. Clark, 1984), easily the weakest parts of Chomsky's theoretical system. Nevertheless, much remains from the early interaction of information processing psychology and linguistics, including the major linguistic arguments against associative theory, the competence–performance distinction, and grammatical rules. Current research seeks to discover the psychological processes or mental operations that underlie linguistic performance in a causal sense, and the kind of knowledge Chomsky called competence will be an important part of these operations. In addition, the productivity and creativity first identified with language is now atttributed to other cognitive activities as well, including perception, memory, thinking, and understanding. Finally, Chomsky's (1980) current work continues to reveal a computational perspective that remains close to a fundamental information processing thema to be described next.

Presuppositions from Computer Science and Artificial Intelligence

The influence of computer science on the development of information processing psychology was at once the most obvious, the most pervasive, and the most subtle. Computer science is a family of loosely related subspecialties, including algorithm theory, numerical methods, programming languages, and artificial intelligence. The latter deals with the programming of processes that exist at only one known locus in nature—human cognition. The appearance of computing machinery, and the conceptual foundations on which it rested, contributed an alternative metaphor for human mental and intellectual capacities

(Haugeland, 1981; G. A. Miller, 1974; G. A. Miller & Gazzaniga, 1984), a theoretical framework with intrinsic themata (Pylyshyn, 1978; Simon, 1981), and a representational and inferential language in which behavioral theories could be expressed (J. R. Anderson, 1983; J. R. Anderson & Bower, 1973; Newell & Simon, 1972). Computer science and artificial intelligence thus became the primary external source of themata, metaphor, and methodology for cognitive psychology, a state of affairs that continues to this day.

Computational themata

The fields of artificial intelligence and information processing psychology actually evolved in tandem. Both are derived, directly or indirectly, from seminal work in mathematical logic; and both are concerned with the properties of cognitive processes such as pattern recognition, language processing, and memory retrieval, all of which are intrinsic components of intelligent behavior. Artificial intelligence is, of course, a subfield of computer science, with which information processing psychology also has close ties. The profoundly significant interplay between computer science and information processing psychology reflects the common origins of the two fields in midcentury work on the logical limitations of computation (Minsky, 1967). Both fields were influenced by the concept of the universal machine, a mathematical formulation culminating from a concerted effort to establish logical foundations for systems of mathematics.

Computer concepts play two different roles within the information processing paradigm. For some, computer processes and mental concepts constitute an analogy of primarily heuristic value. For others, designated in Fig. 1 as formalists, the relationship is a much deeper one. Although human intelligence is biological and the computer is artifactual, both are assumed by the formalists to be instances of the same kind of conceptual entity—a system having quite specific capabilities and empirically verifiable properties. This view is reflected in the "physical symbol hypothesis" (Newell, 1980; Newell & Simon, 1976), which is among the most central computational themata of the formalist branch of the information processing approach.

The physical symbol hypothesis, described in great detail by Newell (1980), stems directly from the same developments in mathematical logic that led to the first computers and that underlie all present-day computer technology. Although mathematical formulations had been based on computational proofs for two millennia, at the close of the nineteenth century the nature of proof remained largely intuitive. There had never been a full formal development of the concept. A major set of unsolved problems in the foundations of mathematics thus concerned the nature of proof and the issues of computability, completeness, and consistency in formal axiomatic systems such as geometry or arithmetic. The landmark work of Whitehead and Russell (1910–1913) indicated that all existing mathematical proof could be given in the logical system that they had invented. Any statement of pure mathematics, it was widely believed, could be proved or disproved in that system. It was assumed that, in a complete and consistent mathematical system, any problem that could be posed could be computed, and equivalent computations would yield the same outcome. Events took a startling turn when Gödel (1931/1965) discovered that it is impossible to formulate a nontrivial system of axioms that could be used to prove its own completeness and consistency. Gödel showed that there were propositions concerning the whole numbers that could neither be proved or disproved in the logical system of Russell and Whitehead. In other words, the matter of computability of particular mathematical problems could not be decided in terms of the axioms of the same system in which the problems are formulated, and such problems were undecidable.

Following the publication of Gödel's incompleteness theorem, as it was called, Alan Turing (1936) published a paper in which he approached the problems of completeness and computability in a more general way. Turing analyzed the properties of an "effective procedure"—a procedure of specific steps or behaviors that lead inevitably to the solution of solvable computational problems. The question can be posed in a number of equivalent forms. How may we be sure that a proposed effective procedure is really complete and leads to a solution rather than continues on forever? How may we know that it is so fully specified that no creative intelligence is required to carry it out? Turing spoke of a simple "calculator" or machine—a mathematical abstraction rather than a physical object. Turing's machine is defined (not built) in terms of how it performs computations. The machine, today called a universal Turing machine, can be described as operating on inputs consisting of symbols located in successive squares on a tape and providing outputs. In his analysis of the process of computation, Turing systematically separated those elements that appear essential from those that are inessential. About five or so remained, such as "move the tape one unit," "erase the symbol on the tape and replace it," and "halt when the computation is complete." He showed that if the machine iteratively applies these five or so elementary steps and the machine stops, the problem is solvable and the procedure is completely specified. Turing proposed that this mathematical machine can carry out any computation that is computable; and if no computational solutions exist, the machine will never stop.

In the nearly 50 years since Turing's publication, no effective procedure for solving a logical or mathematical problem has yet been described that cannot be simulated on a universal Turing machine (Minsky, 1967). Many different subtypes of Turing machines have since been invented. In fact there are an infinite number of these, each of which can be imitated by a universal Turing machine. Turing's paper contained fundamental ideas foreshadowing the invention of the modern digital computer; everything actual computers can do is reducible to the fundamental capabilities of Turing's universal machine.

Turing's discoveries were echoed in two other mathematical papers published the same year (Church, 1936; Post, 1936); these and related work were later shown to be independent formulations of the same class, that is, formally identical (H. Rogers, 1967). Among the various classes of machines that have been demonstrated in the modern theory of recursive functions, four may have psychological relevance. For each of these, there exists a formal grammar that is isomorphic in most important respects with its corresponding machine or automation. Chomsky provided one of the early proofs relating formal grammars to a type of machine (N. A. Chomsky, 1963). But the most central application of the classic work in mathematical logic has been in computer science. For example, it has been shown that high-level programming languages like Pascal or FORTRAN, the compilers associated with them, any other intermediate-level language, and the ultimate hardware machine on which they run are all instantiations of a universal Turing machine (Haugeland, 1981).

For psychology, there are several significant effects of these developments in mathematical logic. The universal Turing machine accomplishes abstract processes in a very concrete way, with a very limited set of operations. It is abstract in the sense that the operations involved are not inextricably tied to any particular physical implementation. However, it is concrete in that it can be realized in a wide range of physical and symbolic devices, including various programming and electronic systems. The concept of a Turing machine thus provides a very concrete basis for characterizing abstract mental operations without appeal to immaterial faculties. Viewed as machines, or as programs which are the logical equivalent of machines, conscious and unconscious mental processes can be conceptually related to behavior and brain processes in logically unproblematic ways—that is, as computer programs relate to hardware. Aspects of human cognitive processes can be conceived of as being governed by internally stored programs relating to neural mechanisms much as computer programs relate to hardware.

The novelty and power of this conception is considerable; it ranks among the more significant advances made in the study of cognitive psychology. The ancient problem of mind interacting with matter vanished with the new conception, and objections to "mental" explanations became irrelevant. What started out in mathematical logic as a precise characterization of mathematical computation that can be effected by nonhuman mechanical means became what could be the central thema of information processing psychology: the human being as an instantiation of a system or a network of systems using stored programs. We call this view the *computational thema* to distinguish it from the notion that computers and humans have some similar properties but are not necessarily instances of the same superordinate category. This latter view is the computer metaphor, which we treat in the next section.

The computer metaphor

Digital computers accept data in the form of symbolic input. They perform a variety of operations on the input, including storage, retrieval, and an array of computational steps. They make decisions in the form of conditional branches, based on the state of the stored data. New expressions are continuously computed by combining symbolic input with symbols already stored in memory; the result is new memory structures, new internal instructions, and some form of symbolic output. It is easy to see that this description of computer information processing includes much of what cognitive psychology is about: sensory input, perceptual recoding, memory storage and retrieval, and motor output.

It is quite likely that the most pervasive contribution of computer science to psychology has been an alternative metaphor for mental and cognitive processes. As we noted earlier, analogies of this sort are enormously important in scientific inquiry, exerting a powerful influence on the selection of research questions, the structure and interpretation of experiments, and the construction of theory. If the fit is reasonable, analogy with a well-understood system may vastly enhance the scientist's grasp of a poorly understood one. And because they are artifacts, many of the properties of physical computing systems and programming languages are reasonably well understood. The analogical fit is more than reasonable; analogies between mind and programs, and computational and cognitive systems are enormously compelling (Haugeland, 1981). Using their knowledge of computer science, therefore, information processing psychologists have theorized about human capacities and behavior using computational concepts in such areas as memory (Shiffrin, 1979), attention (Shiffrin & Schneider, 1977), aging (R. Lachman, Lachman, & Taylor, 1982), language as compilation (Johnson-Laird, 1977), visual information processing (Marr, 1982; Spoehr & Lehmkuhle, 1982), and the programming of motor behavior (Stelmach, 1978). It is important to note that the information processing paradigm reflects a wide range of usages of computational concepts. For those committed to the computational thema, the same explanatory principles apply to human and machine information processing because they are both instantiations of the same superordinate entity—a general-purpose symbol manipulator having the mathematical properties of a Turing machine. Even among those who cannot be identified with the computational thema, commitment to the metaphor varies. Many researchers treat it as a loose comparison between mental processes and the flow of information in a computer program, a comparison that is heuristically useful in generating research and guiding theory. Others are tied more closely to the metaphor and are likely to base their studies and theories on more detailed particulars of computer information processing. They may import such concepts as buffer and compiler, and develop hypothetical mental structures corresponding to them. Many information processing psychologists use the metaphor without articulating their sense of its exactitude; their views must necessarily be inferred from their work.

The computer metaphor and the computational thema have their critics. George Miller, for example, believes their utility to be limited by the fact that the presence of intelligence in biological systems represents an order of complexity far greater than that found in modern computational systems (Machlup & Mansfield, 1983, pp. 57ff.). Stabler (1983) has criticized the computational dimension of Chomsky's theory; he finds no strong evidence for the claim that human mentation is a rule-governed computational device. The cogency of these criticisms depends on whether they are directed at the metaphor or the stronger thematic view. The concept that human intelligence and machine intelligence are essentially the same thing is a claim that will require supporting evidence at some point. However, the computational thema is at an early stage of development; a conclusion one way or the other is presently premature. The computer metaphor, in contrast, needs no evidence beyond its usefulness in guiding research and theory; it is a tool, and if it works, it works. On this issue, the verdict is in. The computer metaphor has been in use for several decades. It has proved to be a thoroughly effective heuristic for cognitive psychology, and its utility shows no sign of diminishing.

Nevertheless, occasional warnings periodically appear against the dangers of a too literal interpretation of any metaphor, including the computer metaphor. In our view, metaphors (however literally interpreted) are seldom to blame for scientific dead ends. Midcentury Hullian psychology, for example, was not undermined by the impoverished telephone switchboard analogy but by a tendency for its research problems to be too parochially generated. Too many studies were derived from lacunae in previous research, and too few from enduring properties of the natural system in question. The result was an inbred and insular science whose later discoveries were heavily dependent on methodology, ungeneralizable, and ultimately uninteresting to anyone but their authors. Similar trends may be present in contemporary information processing psychology, but if they are, it is not because of the computer metaphor. Moreover, attempts to generalize the approach to new areas, such as clinical psychology, will have a wholesome effect on any such tendency to insularity. Contemporary researchers in psychopathology need not fear being misled by the computer metaphor; their real-world concerns will keep them honest.

Methodology: computer simulation

Among the most visible appropriations by psychologists from computer science are inferential and representational languages. Information processing theories are often expressed in ''flow of information'' language and diagrams. This language is reminiscent of computer programs and implicates strong computational themata, loose metaphors, or both. The use of such information-flow language to represent theory also suggests that aspects of the theory can be formalized as computer programs or simulations. It is at this point that information processing psychology overlaps most with artificial intelligence. Computers, of course, can simulate any event, process, or aspect of a system that can be represented in appropriate symbolic form and for which successive states can be specified, at least to a first approximation. The quality of a simulation depends in part on whether the most significant variables have been fully and accurately specified, and whether the instructions given in the program correspond, actually or isomorphically, to the way in which the simulated system actually functions. In this sense even an artificial intelligence program with an information engineering orientation is the programmer's theory of the variables and processes that determine performance.

Simon (1981) has described the relationship between computer simulation and mathematical modeling. Mathematical theory previously was the formalism of choice in both the social and physical sciences. A set of state variables are defined, in the case of models in physics, and a set of simultaneous equations indicate the way these variables change over time. Certain mental processes, particularly those that require controlled attention, are generally viewed as serial processes (Shiffrin & Schneider, 1977). As such, they may be formalized either as difference equations or as an equivalent computer program, or simulation, which traces the paths that the variables specified in the difference equations follow over time. Comparisons with protocols obtained from human subjects test the sufficiency of the mechanisms that have been postulated (e.g., a short-term memory with some specific capacity) to produce the behavior that actually occurs. Many serial cognitive processes such as classic puzzles, algebraic word problems, paired-associate learning, and spelling, to mention a few, have been simulated by computer (Newell & Simon, 1972; Simon, 1979). Additionally, there have been ambitious large-scale cognitive theories postulating various types of internal representations of knowledge and tracing the general flow of information in the organism (J. R. Anderson, 1983; J. R. Anderson & Bower, 1973). These large-scale theories are general in the sense that they should support simulation of a variety of cognitive processes when they are sufficiently developed. Some aspects of such theories have been formalized as conventional stochastic models, while other aspects have been formalized as computer simulations.

From the earliest days of cognitive psychology, simulation as theory produced a number of skeptics. Neisser (1967), for example, found that the computer program analogy had several significant advantages over earlier formulations for cognitive processes; at the same time he dismissed computer simulation as satisfactory cognitive theory (p. 9). More recent criticism has been directed at specific deficiencies in the use of simulation as a way of representing theory. Kintsch, Miller, and Polson (1984) point out that, for any nontrivial simulation, only the author can read and understand the computer code and infer the properties of the underlying theory. Sometimes not even the author can do so. This has led to the publication of simulation theories containing fuzzy descriptions of psychological processes, reflecting concomitantly fuzzy theorizing. Moreover, a procedure called kludging (Lehnert, 1984) is common, where a simulation is made to work by supplementing its theoretical substance with programming tricks. These practices, we think, reflect bad science rather than genuine limitations of computer simulation as a formalism. Bad practices in other contexts need not rule out useful tools. ''Pilot work,'' for example, is sometimes used to select the values of ''extraneous'' variables that give a desired outcome; the result may be a publishable study with no generality. No one would suggest that this practice warrants the elimination of all pilot work, nor that pilot work is a serious limit to the utility of the experimental method. Interestingly, even critics of other information processing themata have recognized that the special contribution of artificial intelligence will be to provide the languages in which cognitive theories can be stated (Miller & Gazzaniga, 1984).

There has been some use of computer simulation in clinical psychology and psychiatry. As an example, Colby (1981) and his associates have been developing a computer simulation of a paranoid personality. Nevertheless, the technique is not yet widely accepted by clinical psychologists. Formalizing a theory by means of simulation is really a brand-new method for stating a scientific theory, a method that capitalizes on the computer's ability to represent and repeat sequences of mind-boggling complexity. Those who are willing to devote a substantial share of their professional effort to pioneering the method for clinical psychology and psychiatry should be encouraged.

Formalist and Neofunctionalist Approaches

After two decades of development, information processing psychology is becoming increasingly diverse, both in its areas of research and its methods of approach. Despite this increasing diversification, two directions are discernable. We will designate them the *formalist* and the *neofunctionalist* approaches. A detailed presentation of these two orientations would require a book-sized monograph; the following presentation is intended simply to define them and capture their highlights.

The *formalist approach* is closely allied with artificial intelligence and places a high value on the detailed development of computer simulations of cognitive processes. Many of the formalists are striving to develop comprehensive formal theories of cognitive processes (e.g., J. R. Anderson, 1983; J. R. Anderson & Bower, 1973; Kintsch, 1982; Newell & Simon, 1972; Simon, 1979). Others are working on theories that span cognitive psychology and artificial intelligence (e..g., Lehnert, 1984; Schank, 1982). Formalist theories are made up of formal components, including one or more simulations that may be in various stages of development. The formalists have been concerned with a variety of cognitive capacities, of which two are particularly noteworthy: long-term memory and problem solving. At the core of formalist theories of long-term memory is the specification of processes that support retrieval from long-term memory (J. R. Anderson, 1983). This focus is not as narrow as it might at first appear; such retrieval is an essential part of virtually all higher mental processes. Theories that include developed procedures for memory retrieval have been concerned with the way knowledge is represented in human memory. Theory and research has been directed at specifying and describing representational format, relationships between stored content and the growth of memory structures, and the general organization of long-term memory. One simulation in the original version and in updates of Anderson's contribution, known as ACT (J. R. Anderson, 1983), takes limited English sentences as input, locates the appropriate information previously stored in memory, and constructs new memory structures that incorporate the content of the input sentence.

Problem-solving theories focus on tracing the thoughts that people have while working on the solution of particular problems. The problems used in this research typically are novel and encountered by the subject for the first time (Simon, 1979). Theories that simulate problem solving start with a detailed account of the mechanisms that are thought to be responsible for effective problem solving. These include characterizations of the problem space and the specification of general strategies of wide applicability, such as means–ends analysis. The simulation itself is an effort to track the symbols that flow through the problem solver's stream of thought, taking account of attentional limits and the processing limits of short-term memory. The simulation includes specified subgoals, and defines both the order and operations that are performed on the transient symbols. Verbal protocols are collected in experiments and compared to the output of the simulation at various points in its sequence of operations. The theory, of which the simulation is one component, is then iteratively modified (Simon, 1981). This type of simulation can capture much of what people actually do when they solve problems. Problem-solving simulations include a wide range of tasks, from solving simple puzzles to the type of problem solving associated with certain forms of scientific discovery.

At the heart of the formalist approach is the computational thema: the presupposition that common principles govern the organization of biological species and intelligent mechanical devices. Both are considered to contain elementary information processing modules, each consisting of a symbol system and a set of computational mechanisms that operate on the symbol system. The strong form of this presupposition takes the brain and the computer as devices that operate on a physical symbol system. Both the brain and computers are considered to contain physical elements that perform such symbolic operations as "read," "compare," and "store," including decision processes that are contingent on the outcomes of comparisons between symbols. The symbol sets represent anything, internal or external, true or imaginary, that is capable of being formulated in symbolic terms. These operations on symbols are, it is presupposed, a sufficient basis for biological intelligence. It is possible that biological intelligence involves a network of information processing modules; such a notion may be needed to deal with the inordinate complexity of mental capacities. However, it is possible to extend the computational thema to a network concept without disturbing the fundamental status of the thema in the formalist approach.

Gains from the formalist approach include both advances in knowledge and new areas of research. For example, problem solving as a process has been substantially clarified, and original research has compared the problem solving of experts with that of novices (e.g., Jefferies, Turner, Polson, & Atwood, 1981). Important conceptual enrichment of the entire paradigm field has also resulted from formalist work, such as the influential distinction between declarative and procedural knowledge, and "protocol analysis" development dealing with the power and limits of introspective methodology (Simon & Ericsson, 1984). These developments, particularly protocol analysis, warrant close scrutiny by clinical psychologists.

The *neofunctionalist approach* is the part of contemporary cognitive psychology that exhibits the greatest continuity with prior psychological traditions. It includes diverse research areas, virtually all of which have precursors in functionalist experimental psychology (Woodworth, 1938). Much neofunctionalist work is characterized by systematic research programs that attempt to formulate the microorganization underlying particular cognitive tasks. Typical experiments are directed toward discovering the major variables influencing cognitive performance and constructing appropriate mathematical representations. Many different methods are used, including mental chronometry (Posner, 1978), quantitative modeling of verbal reports on imagery states (Shepard & Cooper, 1982) or decision processes (Kahneman, Slovic, & Tversky, 1982), and classic procedures of memory measurement (Tulving, 1983), to mention some. Juola's chapter in this volume (chapter 3) affords an excellent overview of cognitive neofunctionalist methodology.

Information processing research in the neofunctionalist tradition is firmly rooted in laboratory studies of human performance. In Posner's (1978) view the approach requires the adaptation of human subjects to particular task environments. Experiments then determine the effects of specific configurations of variables on "the detailed organization of mental processing that obtains in the task environment'' (Posner, 1978, p. 6). However, the relationship among the numerous task environments has not yet been subjected to direct experimental study. A major goal of the neofunctionalist approach is to identify basic, elementary information processes by inference from experimental subjects' behavior and their verbal reports of conscious experience. Most of the experimental literature with this objective attempts to trace the flow of information originating from external stimuli, proceeding through various kinds of inferred internal stages, and ending with an experimental response. Several important areas of neofunctionalist investigation have roots in the early functionalist traditions in psychophysics, perception, and memory. This research is more concerned with basic human capacities than with processing stages. Contemporary memory research, for example, concentrates on factors that facilitate and inhibit memory performance, and subject strategies used to enhance recall, rather than the stages of stimulus fixation in memory. It should be apparent that the computer metaphor plays a different role for the neofunctionalist orientation than for the formalists. Neofunctionalists tend to regard the metaphor as a ''mere'' metaphor and to bind their theories relatively loosely to computational concepts. General rather than specific computational concepts are likeliest to appear in neofunctionalist work.

Posner and McLeod (1982) are among the first to clearly see that a potentially serious cleavage exists in cognitive psychology between the orientations that we have called formalist and neofunctionalist. They also show considerable wisdom in calling for the treatment of the two orientations as complementary rather than competitive. Fortunately, there is no pressing need to take sides. Both approaches provide a rich source of experimental and conceptual technology, of potentially great utility for theory and research in clinical psychology.

Summary and Some Cautions

In this chapter, we have defined *psychology* as an administrative and organizational entity. Within this administrative grouping are diverse and independent intellectual traditions. The communities of like-minded investigators constituting these traditions, we maintained, can be effectively defined in terms of the presuppositional systems that rationalize their research programs. Presuppositional systems contain three types of elements: themata, metaphors, and methodological preferences. The history and contemporary properties of information processing psychology were described by reference to these three elements. We traced the origins and attributes of the computational thema and the computer metaphor, and described the methodology of simulation, stage specification, and basic component analysis. Two major emerging intellectual orientations within the paradigm, the formalist and neofunctionalist, were identified and briefly described.

The commitments of information processing psychology that we have described are neither universal nor final. Like all intellectual traditions, information processing psychology will evolve from within and reflect influences from without. Meanwhile, use of information processing concepts in other fields of psychology can be a valuable two-way street, as these concepts afford valuable ideas to new users, and they in turn supply feedback that will improve and develop the concepts in their original contexts of usage.

Clinically oriented psychologists who use information processing concepts will be most successful if they resist any temptation to redefine their object of study in order to conform it to information processing themata. The human is an evolved organism which probably reflects successive development of systems governed by very different psychological principles (J. L. Lachman & Lachman, 1979). There are countless potential relationships that may obtain among such subsystems. If information processing themata are appropriate only for certain subsystems, they will prove valuable only when that subsystem is implicated in the phenomenon under study. Even then, to the extent subsystems governed by different principles are also involved in the phenomenon, information processing themata may require supplementary principles drawn from different paradigms. The challenge to the clinical researcher will be to distinguish between contexts in which information processing presuppositions are necessary and those in which they may be misleading.

Cognitive psychologists within the information processing paradigm will be among the beneficiaries of those who meet this challenge, for they will develop a much richer view of human psychology as a result. The information processing paradigm has largely ignored the fact that human intellectual capacities evolved in a species whose emotional and appetitive systems were already in place. As a result, the properties of human higher mental processes may be nontrivially determined by predecessor systems, and human intellectual performance may reflect permanent synergy among all subsystems. If this is so, the contemporary information processing paradigm will be a long time in discovering it. As an example, the information processing paradigm concentrates on intellectual performance, while few psychologically interesting phenomena are purely intellectual. Even performance in a cognitive experiment on perception may be influenced by the social context of the experimental setting; the subject's social behavior may reflect the operation of his or her affective system as well as his or her perceptual capacities. The way these systems interact is presently uncharted terrain; those who cannot or will not ignore the noncognitive dimensions of human psychology will be its pioneers. Their work will both extend and establish the limits of information processing themata, to the benefit of us all.

3

Cognitive Psychology and Information Processing: Content and Process Analysis for a Psychology of Mind

James F. Juola
Department of Psychology
University of Kansas
Lawrence, Kansas 66045

Introduction

Cognitive psychology is the study of mental activity related to our perceptions, thoughts, and actions. As such, the objects of study cannot be observed directly; instead the operations and contents of our minds must be inferred from what we can observe. The dominant research methodology in cognitive psychology is based on the information processing paradigm. Humans are viewed as active processors of information in that every behavior, from the recognition of common objects to participation in a conversation, involves the operation of a number of different systems acting in concert. By this view behavior can be modeled as a flow of information through a system in which different processing stages receive inputs from the environment, from memory, or from other stages. Each stage performs operations such as code transformations, memory search and retrieval, or comparisons and other calculations. The output of each stage of processing is passed on to others, culminating in some decision to respond or to sample more data from the environment or to retrieve more information from memory. The goal of most cognitive psychologists is to propose and evaluate

INFORMATION PROCESSING APPROACHES
TO CLINICAL PSYCHOLOGY

information processing models of human behavior that help us to understand some of the more elementary processes involved in such complex behaviors as pattern recognition and reading for comprehension.

Information processing models tend to be task specific in that they attempt to describe a sequence of operations occurring between a stimulus and a response that satisfies the goal defined by the experimenter. Some experimental tasks appear to be narrow, artificial, and lacking in ecological validity, but these concerns miss the point of most cognitive research. That is, it is assumed that fundamental processing stages involved in sensation, perception, memory search, retrieval, decision making, response selection, and response execution are common to strictly controlled laboratory tasks and real-life experiences. In many cases, these assumptions are valid, but in others they are open to question. For example, Haber (1983) has observed that studies of what is visible in tachistoscopic displays are useful mainly for learning about how best to read during lightning storms. Others have argued that even obscure and apparently unnecessary phenomena such as iconic memory have evolved for some reason. Neural activity that persists after a brief visual stimulus might aid perception in normal situations by providing continuity during saccadic eye movements when sensory input is suppressed (e.g., Bridgeman & Mayer, 1983).

There are a number of controversies in cognitive psychology that involve both theoretical and methodological issues. Ecological validity or applicability to natural settings is not as severe a problem for the methodology as are more basic questions of measurement and interpretation. That is, since direct measurements of mental operations are impossible, the entire scientific endeavor rests on indirect measurements and inferential logic. It is precisely for this reason that theoretical analysis is the most powerful practical tool in cognitive psychology. Both in traditional experimental psychology and in computer simulation, the goal is to construct process models that are specific enough about the operations involved in the execution of some task that they are capable of being evaluated against experimental data. In this sense, process models must be potentially falsifiable if they are to be of value. As many cognitive scientists who believe in the value of empiricism have pointed out, it is far better for a theory to be wrong than to be vague, because an incorrect theory that can be shown to be inconsistent with observations can be replaced with a more consistent one, whereas a vague theory might never reveal its inherent inconsistency with the system being modeled (R. Lachman, *et al.*, 1979).

Some perennial theoretical issues in cognitive psychology concern limits and capabilities of the hypothetical information processing system used to model human behavior. It is generally acknowledged that such a system must have a limited-capacity bottleneck somewhere to reflect such phenomena as the immediate memory span (seven plus or minus two items; G. A. Miller, 1956) and our inability to handle more than one attention-demanding task at a time (see Norman, 1976). Limited capacity has traditionally been associated with short-term or working memory, which has been thought of as a storage buffer intervening between two other large-capacity structures, the transient sensory registers and the permanent long-term store (e.g., Atkinson & Shiffrin, 1968). More recently, however, the emphasis has been on process rather than structure (e.g., Craik & Lockhart, 1972), and limits of attentional capacity for processing information have been used to constrain models of behavior (e.g., Schneider & Shiffrin, 1977; Shiffrin & Schneider, 1977). In these process models a distinction is made between automatic processes, which demand no attention or processing capacity for their execution, and controlled processes, which demand the allocation of attentional resources thereby diminishing general system capacity while they are in operation.

Other issues in cognitive psychology include the relative contributions of sensory data and prior knowledge (or bottom-up vs. top-down processes) to task performance. Most tasks are viewed as interactive in that they necessarily require the contributions of sensory-perceptual systems as well as the use of context and prior knowledge for normal execution. It is understood, however, that tasks such as signal detection will emphasize the relatively pure contribution of data-driven, sensory processes whereas tasks such as retrieval from long-term memory emphasize the generative and reconstructive nature of top-down or conceptually driven processes.

This brief introduction to some theoretical and methodological issues in cognitive psychology is intended to illustrate two main points. First, the methods attempt to be analytical in the sense that complex processes which defy understanding can be decomposed, in theory, into simpler ones that can be studied in relative isolation. Thus, the information processing approach holds forth the promise that its models, even when failing to predict a given result, will by their analytic nature be useful in identifying their own faulty components. Second, the methods are relevant for applied problems, particularly in identifying sources of performance differences among subpopulations or individuals. Again, the analysis of complex behaviors into a process model with specific components allows for potential identification, in this case, of individual differences and processing deficits. Of course, it is hardly necessary to remind the reader that wide gulfs remain between the neurophysiological basis of mental processes and our best theoretical representations of such activity. For this reason alone there remains much room for divergent theoretical speculations and alternative methodological approaches to problems in cognitive psychology. We can only hope that continuous progress will be made toward enabling the mind to understand itself in the face of often daunting uncertainties about both cognitive theory and the methods of the information processing paradigm.

In the remainder of this chapter, the information processing approach to cognition will be illustrated with selected examples. These examples demonstrate both the potential theoretical and methodological power of the information processing approach as well as some of the hazards that remain due to our inevitable uncertainty about the exact nature of mental processes. In following sections, research methods employed in the study of perception, attention, memory, and other cognitive processes will be reviewed. Although many of the research paradigms in cognitive psychology have been applied to a variety of subject populations, the use of the methods to localize, understand, and perhaps compensate for processing deficits associated with psychopathology has only begun. It is a fair assumption that attempts by cognitive psychologists to understand mental processes in normal, intelligent adults will of necessity aid our understanding of variations from this norm when they occur for other populations and individuals.

Stage Model Analyses of Response-Time Data

"One of the oldest ideas in experimental psychology is that the time between stimulus and response is occupied by a train of processes or stages—some being mental operations—which are so arranged that one process does not begin until the preceding one has ended" (S. Sternberg, 1969, p. 421). So begins an influential review paper by Sternberg that includes some history of the use of reaction times to analyze mental processes. Donders (1868–1869/1969) pioneered a procedure called the subtractive method in which the difference between average response times in two tasks is used to estimate the duration of the process by which they differ. For example, response times in a simple reaction-time experiment (one stimulus and one response) should be shorter than choice response times (e.g., two possible stimuli with two different response assignments) by the amount of time necessary to make a stimulus discrimination and response selection. There are a number of limitations of the subtractive method of analysis. These include the assumptions that (1) overall response time can be decomposed into a sum of times taken for a sequence of processing stages, and (2) the addition of a new processing requirement to a given task results in the insertion of a corresponding stage without influencing any of the other stages. In many cases these assumptions cannot be validated empirically. This is because many of the standard results in the reaction-time literature can be modeled in alternative ways, such as by serial stage models (e.g., S. Sternberg, 1969, 1975), parallel processing models (e.g., Townsend, 1972, 1974), or so-called cascade models (McClelland, 1979) in which several levels of stimulus analysis are in parallel operation. Since the reaction-time data themselves often are insufficient to discriminate among these various models, converging operations or appeals to parsimony are often used to advocate particular theoretical perspectives.

Perhaps the most compelling use of the subtractive logic of Donders in the modern literature arises from the work of Posner and his colleagues (e.g., Posner & Mitchell, 1967). In a simple letter-matching task, in which subjects are instructed to decide whether or not a given pair of letters have the same name, response times are reliably shorter if the pair are also physically identical (e.g., AA) than if they match only in name (e.g., Aa). For the sake of argument, let us first assume that perceptual and response requirements are the same in both cases. Then the only difference is that, in the physically identical case, a match between two visual codes can trigger a response, whereas in the name identical case, the names for the visual codes must be accessed in long-term memory before a response can be made. Thus, the main difference in response times in the two conditions should be due to the time necessary to access names for stimuli that have been visually encoded. If the additional assumption is made that comparisons of two visual codes are made as rapidly as those for two name codes in memory, then the subtractive procedure would yield an estimate of name retrieval time. Of course, it is just this sort of assumption that has led to questions about the validity of the subtractive method.

Hunt and his colleagues (e.g., Hunt, Lunneborg, & Lewis, 1975) have used the Posner letter-matching task as one means of assessing individual differences in verbal ability. They have shown that people who differ in verbal ability (as measured by performance on college entrance examinations) also differ in the relative advantage shown for physical matches over name matches in the letter-matching task. Hunt (1978) reports that the 60–70 msec advantage that high-verbal college students show for physical matches over names matches increases to about 90 msec for low-verbal students, whereas it doubles for aged adults and young children and triples for mentally retarded children. Relatively low-verbal individuals appear to require extra processing time to access letter names in long-term memory. This conclusion is supported by a variety of converging evidence (Hunt, 1978) that a major source of differences between high- and low-verbal individuals is the accessibility of verbal information in long-term memory.

Short-Term Memory Scanning

An alternative to the subtractive method is the "selective influence" procedure developed by S. Sternberg (1966, 1969, 1975). Rather than changing the task environment by adding or subtracting required processes, the amount of processing required for a given stage is manipulated. For example, stimulus intensity (rather than the presence or absence of a stimulus) or amount of information to be held in memory (as opposed to the presence or absence of a memory load) could be manipulated. Then any observed effects on response times are not due to deletions or additions of processing stages, but rather result from the selective influence of factor levels on the operations of particular stages. It follows directly from the assumptions of a serial stage model that factors which influence separate processing stages should have additive effects, whereas factors which influence at least one stage in common should generally have interactive effects on response times. This additive-factors method of analysis for response-time data has the potential for a wide range of applications, but it has been tested most extensively using the high-speed memory scanning task of S. Sternberg (1966). In Sternberg's task, a small set of items (such as digits or letters) is held in memory in anticipation of a single probe item which might or might not be one of the items in the memory set. Subjects are instructed to indicate rapidly whether or not the probe is a member of the predesignated set. Since the memory set contains only a few familiar items, this task can be performed easily and accurately, and it yields highly reliable results: Response times increase linearly with memory set size in a parallel fashion for positive (probe matches a memory item) and negative (no match) responses.

The model proposed by Sternberg to account for his data has four successive processing stages that intervene between the presentation of the probe and the following positive or negative response. These are (1) encoding, in which the probe is coded into an internal format that is literally comparable with the memory set items; (2) comparison, in which the encoded probe is serially and exhaustively compared with each item of the memory set; (3) decision, in which a positive or negative decision is made; and (4) response, in which the decision is translated into an appropriate response that is then executed. In support of this model S. Sternberg (1969, 1975) has offered the evidence of additive effects of several factors thought to influence these successive stages; that is, respectively, (1) stimulus probe quality (clearly visible or degraded by an overlapping masking pattern), (2) memory set size (one to six items), (3) response type (positive or negative), and (4) response frequency (equal or unequal proportions of positive and negative responses). Since none of these four factors have interactive effects on response times, they are presumed to influence at least four independent stages that occur between stimulus and response.

Perhaps the most counterintuitive aspect of Sternberg's model is that searching for a particular probe through some sort of short-term memory buffer is apparently a serial and exhaustive process; that is, all comparisons are made before a decision is reached regardless of whether or not a match is found during the search. If decisions could be made during the search process itself, then both the number of memory set items and the type of response required should affect a common stage of processing, and they should have interactive effects on the response-time data. Specifically, one would expect the comparison process to take half as long on positive trials as on negative trials, on the average, since if the probe is a member of the memory set, a match could be encountered at any time during the serial search of memory. This interaction is not found in the data, however, as the slope of the response time by set size function is usually similar for both positive and negative responses when the items are simple verbal stimuli such as digits, letters, or words (see H. L. Brown & Kirsner, 1980; Cavanagh,

1972). A consequence of the model, if it is an accurate characterization of the processes being modeled, is that the slope of the response-time function is an estimate of the duration of a single comparison process in memory, as all other processes (viz., encoding, decision, and response) are independent of memory set size. The work of Sternberg has two major contributions for cognitive psychology: (1) Methods have been developed for estimating the durations of mental processes, and (2) the additive-factors logic can be applied to the study of the nature of processing stages in a variety of cognitive tasks.

A number of experiments have used the Sternberg task and additive-factors logic in applied studies of group and individual differences in cognition. For example, MacLeod, Dekaban, and Hunt (cited in Hunt, 1978) report that the drug phenobarbital, when used in relatively high doses for treatment of epilepsy, produces a marked slowing of memory search rate (as indexed by the slope of the obtained response time by memory set size function), whereas epileptic patients who were maintained on a relatively low drug dosage showed no decrease in processing rate. Similarly, overall response times tend to be slower for persons under the influence of marijuana (C. F. Darley, Tinklenberg, Hollister, & Atkinson, 1973) and for hospitalized alcoholics and schizophrenics (Checkosky, cited in S. Sternberg, 1975), but the search rates are not appreciably elevated for these groups. These effects suggest localized processing deficits in stimulus encoding, decision, and response processes rather than in memory search and comparison processes. On the other hand, it has been found that there are slight correlations between the slope of the response-time function obtained in the Sternberg task and verbal intelligence scores within relatively homogeneous populations such as college students (Chiang & Atkinson, 1976; S. Sternberg, 1975), and markedly slower memory search rates are associated with aging and mental retardation (Harris & Fleer, 1974; Hunt, 1978).

Interpretation of Response-Time Data

This discussion of serial stage models has been used to illustrate some of the techniques of the information processing method and to demonstrate how response-time measures can be used to analyze individual and group differences in cognitive processes. Of course, the application of such methods to special populations is useful only if the theoretical analysis is appropriate for identifying, localizing, and understanding population differences when they exist. Although there are a number of viable alternatives to the type of model proposed by S. Sternberg (e.g., Atkinson & Juola, 1973, 1974; Townsend, 1972, 1974), Sternberg's model remains a parsimonious and sufficient account of most of the extant data from short-term memory search studies.

Response times in general are amenable to additive-factors analysis with a few caveats. First, in most cases factors that affect different processing stages should produce additive effects, and factors that affect a common stage should interact, but there are exceptions. Although these relations hold most generally in situations that are adequately described in serial stage models, when operations are occurring in parallel or in cascade, the patterns of obtained results are open to alternative interpretations (McClelland, 1979; Townsend, 1974). Also, even if the serial stage model is an acceptable approximation, it is possible for two factors to affect a common stage in an additive way and for two factors to influence separate stages yet interact with each other. In this latter case, some factor could influence Stage A by changing the quality of its output, and this qualitative change could influence the operation of Stage B. Any other factor found to affect Stage B could then reflect the indirect effects of Stage A processing through an interaction with the first factor (McClelland, 1979; Sternberg, 1969).

Another caveat is that response times are most easily interpretable if they are generated in a nearly error-free environment with the subjects using equivalent response criteria in different experimental conditions. Errors obscure response-time analyses in two ways. First, errors indicate that one or more of the intervening processes between stimulus and response have failed, and in most two-choice response-time situations, failures are as likely to lead to correct responses as they are to produce errors. Thus, a high error rate inevitably points to a contamination of the data for correct trials. A second problem involves various speed–accuracy tradeoff strategies that subjects can employ. A speed emphasis can result in response generation before processing is complete. In this case, the more difficult conditions are more likely to suffer truncations and spurious estimates of their processing time requirements than are the easier conditions in a given experimental context. The use of variable criteria for response decisions in different conditions can also severely limit the usefulness of the additive-factors logic by producing or eliminating interactions among various experimental factors that would not occur if response activation criteria were fixed across conditions (e.g., McClelland, 1979; Pachella, 1974). Thus, optimal conditions for using response times to model cognitive processes are those in which subjects are matching their response criteria across experimental conditions and thereby are responding as quickly as possible while maintaining a uniformly low error rate of about 1 or 2% across conditions. Of course, response times can and have been used as indexes of processing difficulty in a variety of tasks that produce a large number of errors, but the usefulness of response-time data for analyzing a complex task into its hypothetical processing components demands more tightly controlled task environments and performance criteria.

Sensation, Perception, and Attention

Cognitive psychologists commonly distinguish between sensory and perceptual processes, with the former being neurophysiologically determined responses to impinging stimulation and the latter being interpretations of sensory experience based on information activated in memory. Sensation is thus seen as a biological, unconscious, and automatic response to the environment, whereas perception is a conscious, cognitive response to a combination of environmental stimulation and the individual's relevant knowledge, expectations, affective states, and goals. Because the various sensory modalities are constantly providing us with more information than we are capable of responding to, attention is sometimes viewed as a selective process that filters some sensory inputs into a limited-capacity buffer for further processing and, by the same mechanism, filters other sensations away from conscious awareness. Attention is also sometimes equated with the limited-capacity buffer itself, so that stimulus selection and central processing capacity are common but not exactly equivalent realizations of the concept of attention among cognitive psychologists.

Sensory Memory and Selective Attention

The study of sensory processes in cognitive psychology is usually confined to vision and audition, for these are the modalities through which most information that influences cognition enters the system. Sensation begins with the transduction of visible light or audible tones by receptor cells in the retina or cochlea, respectively, that can eventually result in the propagation of nerve impulses to the brain. Cortical areas for the initial registration and analysis of sensory inputs are relatively well identified. Single-cell recording techniques have found that many cortical cells respond only to narrowly defined stimuli such as lines, edges, or angles of particular orientations or to particular frequency modulations in audition (see Hubel & Wiesel, 1979; Kuffler & Nicholls, 1976; Uttal, 1973). Such specificity of responses for individual cells has lent credence to the idea that the sensory system analyzes complex stimuli into sets of component features which are at the basis of subsequent pattern recognition processes (e.g., Neisser, 1967).

The initial registration of sensory information provides us with a continuous wealth of information from which we must choose in order to go about our daily activities. It has long been thought that we can actually "see" or "hear" more than we are consciously aware of or can report, but sensory experiences are apparently subject to rapid decay or are overwritten by new inputs which prevent their continued appreciation in the absence of stimulation. It is further acknowledged that pattern recognition processes take time, and that not every aspect of the stimulus environment can be attended to and processed to a deep enough level to ensure recognition before it is lost from the sensory system.

The first experimental evidence in support of the idea of a large-capacity but rapidly decaying sensory memory was provided by Sperling (1960) and by Averbach and Coriell (1961). Both of these studies demonstrated that people could report only about four or five letters from a brief display containing many letters despite subjects' complaints that more could be seen instantaneously than could be reported. The method used to confirm these subjective reports was to have the observers focus attention on only part of the display and report letters from that part, although the cue for which part to report was not given until after the display had been terminated. In Sperling's study, for example, a brief display containing three rows of letters was followed by a high-, medium-, or low-frequency tone to signal recall of the letters from the top, middle, or bottom row, respectively. Performance in this partial report condition was nearly perfect, indicating that subjects could see most of the letters in a brief display. Whole report, on the other hand, is a task that confounds sensory processes with short-term memory limits and other variables that interfere with performance. That is, although 12–20 letters might be seen clearly enough to be identified under ideal conditions, once the display is turned off, only those letters whose names have been rehearsed are likely to be recalled a few seconds later.

Both Sperling and Averbach and Coriell varied the length of time between the offset of the display and the partial report cue in an attempt to determine how long attention could be directed to part of the sensory image for selective processing of letter names into memory before the sensory information was lost. The results indicated that a partial report advantage over the percentage correctly recalled in the whole report case could be obtained for cue delays of up to about one-half second. The conclusion is that some sensory information, or ''iconic'' image, persists for a fraction of a second after a brief visual display, and this icon can be selectively scanned much as a visual object can be for information specific to some goal. Similar studies of auditory sensory memory have supported the idea that precategorical memories exist for all sensory modalities, and they serve the purpose of holding onto a fairly veridical copy of the stimulus while time-consuming pattern recognition processes are at work in attempts at identification (J. R. Anderson, 1980; Howard, 1984).

Some applications have been made of report procedures to the study of sensory processes and attention in abnormal populations. Spohn, Thetford, and Woodham (1970), for instance, have reported that schizophrenic patients show a lower level of whole report performance than do control subjects when presented with a display containing several items. Because of results such as Spohn *et al.*'s, Saccuzzo, *et al.* (1974) have characterized schizophrenia as being an attention disorder as much as a thought disorder, such that schizophrenic subjects should show deficits in information processing tasks requiring selective attention. Saccuzzo *et al.* presented visual displays containing either a single letter or eight different letters for brief periods of time in a task requiring report of which of two target letters was present in the display. The dependent measure was amount of time the display had to be shown in order to produce an 80% level of correct responses. College students and nonschizophrenic patients required significantly shorter durations for both single-letter and eight-letter displays than did schizophrenic patients at comparable levels of performance. Similar differences were obtained in a condition in which a visual mask followed the display to limit the amount of iconic information available. Saccuzzo and Schubert (1981) replicated these findings in another study showing that a visual information processing deficit was most pronounced for schizophrenics who had been evaluated as having a poor prognosis for recovery. Data from report procedures have thus indicated that schizophrenic patients show a slower rate of abstraction of visual information due, perhaps, to a lesser ability than normal subjects to focus selective attention onto the relevant aspects of the stimulus.

Limits of Attentional Capacity.

The notion of attention as processing capacity is a relatively recent development in cognitive psychology, and it goes hand in hand with the deemphasis on short-term memory as a structural component of the three-store memory system (see Craik & Lockhart, 1972). This is not to deny that we have some limited ability to maintain more than a few different items in immediate memory (G. A. Miller, 1956), but maintenance of memory codes is viewed as only one of a number of different processes than can compete for our limited capacity for processing information. Recently, theorists have felt a need for distinguishing between those processes which tax processing capacity and those that do not (i.e., controlled vs. automatic processes) (LaBerge & Samuels, 1974; Schneider & Shiffrin, 1977; Shiffrin & Schneider, 1977).

Posner (1978, p. 91) has proposed three operational criteria for determining whether or not a process is automatic. These are that automatic processes occur (1) without intention, (2) without conscious awareness, and (3) without interfering with other ongoing mental activities. That is not to say that automatic processes cannot result in interference, as one of the best examples of nonintentional processing occurs in the Stroop effect (Dyer, 1973). It is well-known that the naming time for the color of the ink used to print letters is markedly slowed if the letters spell the name of a different color word. The presumably automatic and nonintentional encoding of a color word results in competition between its name and the name of the ink's color that contributes to the interference effect. Similar interference occurs for naming the color of any word that is primed by the context in which it occurs (e.g., R. E. Warren, 1974; Whitney & Kellas, 1984). That is, it can take longer to name the color of the letters of a word when the word is preceded by a semantically related word or by an appropriate sentence context. Studies of lexical ambiguity have shown that when an ambiguous word is encountered, all of its several meanings are apparently rapidly and automatically activated in long-term memory and remain so for a brief time. Relevant context or expectations then function selectively to maintain a single interpretation for subsequent, conscious processing (e.g., Conrad, 1974; Swinney, 1979).

The context that primes a particular word meaning need not be part of the stimulus environment, but can also be due to the subject's internal state or mood. For example, Gotlib and McCann (1984) have reported that depressed subjects take longer to name the color of depressed-content words than they do for neutral- and manic-content words, whereas nondepressed subjects show no naming-time differences across word types. Apparently, depressed individuals are more likely to have negative-construct concepts activated by related stimulus events than are nondepressed people.

The final notion of automatic processes as those than can occur in parallel with other processes without creating interference has led to a resurgence in the use of dual-task performance as a means of studying attention. That is, unless an automatic process generates a response incompatible with the main task (as in the Stroop phenomenon), automatic processes should generally not interfere with other automatic or controlled processes. In the dual-task case, one task typically is defined as the primary one to which the subject should devote the most attention. Performance in the secondary task can then be used to assess the relative amount of processing capacity engaged by the primary task. For example, Posner and Boies (1971) investigated performance in a secondary simple reaction-time task administered at various times during a primary, letter-matching task. Subjects were instructed to attend to a warning signal followed 500 msec later by a single letter and then after a second by another letter. In the primary task, subjects were to respond as rapidly as possible to the second letter to indicate whether or not it had the same name as the first letter. The secondary task was to respond as rapidly as possible to a white-noise burst whenever it occurred. The results showed that response times to the white-noise burst were flat during presentation of the warning signal and the first letter, but they increased by over 200 msec just before and after presentation of the second letter. These results are consistent with the view that encoding a letter into memory is an automatic process that does not interfere with detection of a white noise signal and the subsequent response to it. However, preparation for and execution of a comparison process involving the names of two letters demands attention that results in poorer performance in the secondary task. Thus, the dual-task method allows for measurement of the relative amounts of attentional capacity allocated to various aspects of a primary task. Ingram (1984a) has recently used this method to assess the amount of attention that individuals pay to therapeutically relevant feedback that is either favorable or unfavorable. Subjects were first exposed to a positive or negative mood manipulation, and then their response times to an auditory signal were measured while they received favorable and unfavorable feedback from a personality inventory. The main result indicated that people who had experienced a negative induced mood paid more attention to negative feedback statements than they did to positive statements. A similar, but non-significant, congruence effect was found for subjects in the positive mood induction condition.

Pattern Recognition

The final topic of this section is pattern recognition, or how we come to recognize each unique stimulus event as matching or exemplifying some earlier experience. Models of pattern recognition have considered both holistic and analytic approaches to the problem (i.e., template matching theories vs. feature analysis theories; Neisser, 1967) and have included as a matter of necessity top-down or conceptually driven processes to enrich the sensory inputs and influence recognition decisions. Pattern recognition has often been thought of as comprising three stages of processing: encoding, comparison, and decision (Juola, 1979; E. E. Smith & Spoehr, 1974). Encoding is primarily a sensory process, in which a holistic iconic image or feature set abstracted from this image is used as the basis for matching or categorization processes. Template matching theories are based on matching holistic sensory images with idealized images or prototypes of categories in memory, whereas the comparison process for feature theories is based on the relative activation levels for all categories in memory after analysis of the sensory input into its component features. Both comparison and decision processes can be influenced by stimulus context and prior knowledge by such strategies as (1) selectively activating certain categories in memory through priming from the environment or through internal processes (e.g., expectations) or states (e.g., moods), (2) limiting comparisons to selected domains of categories in classifying the stimulus (e.g., by comparing something seen flying in the air with known categories of birds), or (3) biasing the decision process such that a particular category is selected to represent the stimulus despite a lack of confirming sensory evidence or even in the face of evidence favoring other categorizations.

Early template and feature theories were criticized because they were too passive, or data driven, to be able to account for some of the phenomena of human pattern recognition behavior. That is, stimulus classification was modeled as a strictly linear process proceeding from sensory input to perceptual coding to semantic representation (see Neisser, 1967). More recent models acknowledge the possibility of interactive processing among levels of coding, such that higher, conceptual levels of analysis could influence the activity of lower levels. The existence of top-down or conceptually driven processing is perhaps best exemplified by several phenomena in speech perception (see Howard, 1984). These include phonemic restoration, context-induced variation, and categorical perception. In phonemic restoration (R. M. Warren, 1970), although a non-speech sound is spliced into a tape of a spoken sentence, listeners fail to hear anything unusual. It is as though the use of the sentence context and knowledge about human speech sounds is sufficient to override contradictory sensory data when they occur. Context-induced variation is the observed tendency for people to use the context in which a particular speech sound is embedded to assist in identification. For example, Ladefoged and Broadbent (1957) demonstrated that an ambiguous syllable could be identified in different ways depending on the particular characteristics of the speaker's voice that preceded the syllable. Apparently, knowledge of articulation effects and compensation for particular vocal characteristics such as accents are part of our normal speech perception processes. Categorical perception is the observation that discrimination between pairs of artificially generated speech sounds is not continuous; discrimination between pairs is much easier if the pair spans a subjective phonemic boundary than if the pair are judged to be members of the same category (e.g., Lisker & Abramson, 1970). This result argues for the rapid and automatic categorization of speech sounds such that some acoustic properties of a spoken syllable are quickly lost or entirely absent from conscious processing to be replaced by the relevant category activated in long-term memory. All of these phenomena underscore the importance of prior knowledge and use of context in pattern recognition processes by which people supplement and expand on sensory data in categorizing stimulus input.

Similar evidence for the use of prior knowledge and context has been found in visual perception. For example, the familiarity of an object and the consistency between it and the scene in which it is embedded both contribute to its recognition speed and accuracy (e.g., Biederman, Glass, & Stacy, 1973; Palmer, 1975). Even simple stimuli such as straight lines or letters of the alphabet are recognized more accurately if they are embedded in relevant meaningful contexts such as drawings of objects (Weisstein & Harris, 1974) or familiar words (Reicher, 1969). Pattern recognition is an interesting and intellectually challenging psychological process because it emphasizes the individual's significant contribution to the interpretation of physical reality. Attempts to duplicate the speed and accuracy with which we classify objects and understand speech using computer technology have met with enormous practical difficulties despite our increased understanding of the involved sensory and perceptual processes. Clearly we need to know more about how knowledge is represented in human memory and how it is used in interpreting sensory data before we can construct viable theories and practical simulations of human pattern recognition processes. These topics are addressed in the final section of this chapter.

Memory and Conceptual Processes

For decades the central distinction in theories of human memory has been between short-term and long-term storage (e.g., Atkinson & Shiffrin, 1968). These stores have been argued to differ in terms of their relative accessibilities (active and conscious vs. inactive and potentially unavailable), capacity (seven plus or minus two items vs. virtually infinite storage), duration (a few seconds without continuous rehearsal vs. practically permanent), coding format (auditory/articulatory vs. semantic), and nature of forgetting (decay or displacement vs. interference with retrieval due to the presence of other memory codes). (See Craik and Lockhart, 1972, and Wickens, 1970, for reviews of these and other arguments for the separation of short- and long-term memories.) Although the distinction between a limited, active (or working) short-term memory and a virtually unlimited, permanent, long-term store remains (e.g., Craik, 1979; Horton & Mills, 1984), recent theory has emphasized other dichotomous issues that sometimes cut across the short- and long-term distinction. These include Paivio's (1971) arguments in favor of separable visual and verbal (or pictorial and linguistic) memory systems and Tulving's (1972) distinction between semantic and episodic memories. Paivio's dual-coding theory argues for the existence of separate but inter-related coding systems in long-term memory for storage and processing of visual-spatial information and of verbal-linguistic information. In Tulving's theory, semantic memory is supposedly based on abstractions from environmental objects and events. It is a general knowledge store that functions as a basis for interpreting sensory inputs as well as for language comprehension. Episodic memory, on the other hand, is a repository for the stored traces of the events themselves, and is thus autobiographical, detailed, and unique to each individual. Each of these issues will be discussed in turn as we move from consideration of short-term memory to long-term memory and the processes of comphrehension and recollection that depend on them.

Evidence for a Separation between Short- and Long-Term Memory Stores

Evidence for a functional distinction, if not a structural one, between short-term and long-term memory stores comes from a variety of sources. Traditionally, these have involved studies of the span of immediate memory and the shapes of serial position curves in free recall data. Ebbinghaus (data presented in Howard, 1984) discovered that there was a discontinuity in his ability to recall a list of items after a single study trial at about a length of seven items. More recent studies have shown that people can recall about five to eight verbal items in serial order after a single presentation. This measure is known as the span of immediate memory, and it shows remarkably small differences across age and educational level. The memory span is unfortunately often used as an estimate of short-term memory capacity, although we know that such a figure must be an overestimate. This is because, in a recall task, we cannot prevent subjects from using whatever information is available to them in memory, and any immediate memory test is likely to show the combined effects of what is currently in short-term or working memory and what can be retrieved from sensory storage and long-term memory. For example, rehearsal can be used to circulate more items through working memory by retrieving them from long-term memory and "refreshing" their codes. Various statistical procedures have been devised in attempts to partial out the unique contributions of working memory to the immediate memory span (e.g., Glanzer, 1982), and these have arrived at estimates in the range of three to five items.

As a list of letters, digits, or words exceeds about seven items, people tend to make errors in both serial and free recall. In serial recall of short lists of items, in which an item is scored as being correctly recalled when it is reported back in the same position that it was presented, a so-called modality effect is found. That is, recall tends to be better for lists of about nine items if they are presented auditorally rather than visually. An analysis of the serial position curves (a plot of the average number of items correctly recalled for each input position of the list) indicates that recall performance is equivalent for auditory and visual presentations for the early part of the list (the primacy region, which generally shows high levels of recall) and the middle portions of the list (where recall levels tend to be lower). The modality effect itself seems to be due entirely to a recency effect for auditory lists—the last item or two tend to be recalled with much higher probabilities for auditory lists than for visual lists, which generally show no recency effect in serial recall (e.g., Crowder & Morton, 1969). Crowder and Morton have argued that this modality effect is due to persisting auditory sensory information (an echoic trace) that remains available long enough to assist with recall of the last item(s) presented. Iconic information for visually presented lists presumably does not last long enough to aid in recall for visual lists. Support for this argument is gained from the finding of a suffix effect; the presentation of a single syllable at the end of an auditory list that does not have to be recalled itself nonetheless eliminates the recency effect and thereby the modality effect as well.

Perhaps the most highly established support for the distinction between short- and long-term memory stores comes from analyses of serial position effects in free recall of long lists of words. In free recall, the words can be recalled in any order, and subjects typically recall the most recently presented items first (and quite accurately) and then more slowly recall items from earlier positions in the list. Besides the finding of a strong recency effect, a primacy effect is also generally found indicating that there is some recall advantage for the first four or five items in a list. These results are consistent with the idea that recently presented items are recalled from a short-term store, and most other items are recalled from long-term memory. The primacy effect would then be due to the fact that the earliest items receive additional attention during study because there are fewer of them to attend to. Later items in a list receive fewer rehearsals and thus are not stored as well in long-term memory (Rundus, 1971). These conclusions are supported by the results of two studies that were designed to introduce factors that should influence short-term or long-term storage separately, and thus should affect only particular portions of the serial position curve. Glanzer and

Cunitz (1966) had their subjects count for 0, 10, or 30 seconds after presentation of the last word in a list and before attemtping recall. The counting task was designed to prevent the maintenance of any words in working memory, and it was successful in eliminating the recency effect in free recall while leaving the primacy and middle portions of the curve intact. Similarly, Murdock (1962) varied presentation rate to affect the amount of time each item could be processed into long-term storage, but the rate was not great enough to prevent word recognition and entry into short-term storage. In agreement with this idea, presentation rate was shown to influence recall levels for early and middle portions of the list, but the recency portion was unchanged.

Similar to these experimental findings, there is a variety of clinical evidence to suggest that certain types of neurological disorders and surgical procedures can lead to selective impairments in short-term or long-term storage. For example, Milner (1966) reports a patient who had surgical lesions bilaterally in the hippocampal region of the brain, and who recovered from surgery with no apparent loss of long-term memory. However, he suffered complete inability to transfer new information from working memory to permanent storage. Shallice and Warrington (1970) report the case of a patient who had a normal long-term memory but abnormal ability to maintain information in working memory (i.e., he had a memory span of only two items). Finally, Oltmanns (1978) reported data in agreement with earlier arguments that the primacy effect in free recall is due to extra attentional processing for earlier items in a list, and that schizophrenia is associated with a deficit in attentional processing. Oltmanns found that the main difference in the serial position curves for schizophrenic patients and normal subjects was that the primacy portion of the curve was lower and flatter for schizophrenic subjects. An information processing analysis of this deficit would be that while maintenance of information in short-term memory is apparently unaffected by schizophrenia, the attentional process that transfers information from short-term to a permanent, long-term representation is deficient in schizophrenic patients.

Forgetting

A second line of argument for the separation of short- and long-term storage stems from differences between the types of forgetting from the two stores. Forgetting in long-term memory is understood to be due to retrieval difficulties mainly because of the enormity of information stored in permanent memory. Any particular code may be difficult to find due to the distracting influence of codes stored earlier (proactive interference) and later (retroactive interference) than the code in question. Forgetting in short-term memory was seen as being different, however, as no forgetting should occur as long as items are free to be maintained by rehearsal. Because of limited capacity, however, items in short-term storage are likely to be replaced and lost if new information is attended to and rehearsed. J. A. Brown (1958) and Peterson and Peterson (1959) independently invented a means for studying forgetting in short-term memory when rehearsal is prevented. In Peterson and Peterson's task, a three-consonant string (CCC) was presented followed by a three-digit number. The subjects' task was to begin counting backwards by threes from the given number until stopped by the experimenter. At that time, the CCC was to be recalled. Forgetting in the Brown–Peterson paradigm was shown to be rapid and profound: Recall accuracy was only about 10% after just 15 sec of counting backward. This rapidity of forgetting was initially seen to be the result of decay of information from short-term storage while rehearsal was prevented. However, Keppel and Underwood (1962) soon presented evidence that forgetting in the Brown–Peterson task is due to interference. They examined performance in the first few trials of the task and found that recall levels for the CCC were almost perfect on the first trial despite the length of time spent counting between presentation of the CCC and its attempted recall. On the second and third trials, however, recall levels were found to drop, especially as the length of the counting interval increased. Keppel and Underwood argued that performance rapidly drops off in the Brown–Peterson task for two reasons. First, there is a build-up of proactive interference over trials such that retrieval of the most recently presented CCC becomes more difficult as there are more of them in memory remaining from previous trials. Second, counting backward interferes with rehearsal such that after about 15 sec of counting, working memory is filled with numbers, and recall depends on what can be retrieved from long-term memory. Thus, the build-up of proactive interference (PI) is a long-term memory phenomenon.

Wickens (1970) made use of this interpretation of the cause of forgetting in the Brown–Peterson paradigm to invent a new method of studying coding of information in long-term memory. He argued that PI would build up over trials as long as the items to be remembered from trial to trial were coded in a similar way in long-term memory, as PI is greatest among similar items. Wickens' method was to select three words to be remembered on each trial followed by 15 sec of counting backward. In order to maximize build-up of PI, Wickens chose all words shown on the first three trials from a single taxonomic category, for example, animal names or articles of clothing. On the fourth trial, an experimental group of subjects was given three words from a new category, whereas the control group received words from the same category as on the first three trials. As expected, the performance for both groups declined steadily across trials, but on the fourth trial, the experimental group was much more likely than the control group to recall all three words correctly. This "release from PI" effect is quite robust and holds the promise to reveal how words are coded in long-term memory. This is because the amount of release from PI shown by the experimental group relative to performance of the control group is a measure of the similarity of coding dimensions for the experimental and control words. Mills and Tyrell (1983) reported an application of this method to sex-stereotypic encoding of occupations. They found that both male and female subjects demonstrated release from PI when occupation words were shifted from female-specific occupations to male-oriented ones. However, only the female subjects showed significant release when masculine occupations preceded feminine ones. Apparently the gender-specific coding of occupation types was more salient for their female subjects than for the males.

Long-Term Memory Encoding and Storage Processes

Studies of long-term memory have shown that successful recall is the end result of a chain of processes including the initial encoding of the stimulus, its storage in memory, and its subsequent retrieval into conscious awareness when needed. A failure in any one of these components can lead to the inability to recall a previous stimulus event, and, therefore, it is usually not obvious which memory process is responsible when a recall failure occurs. Some insight can be gained into the nature of memory processes in general through the study of the individual encoding, storage, and retrieval components of recall.

Since the pioneering work of Ebbinghaus, the dominant means of investigating memory has been to present a list of items for a study period and then test recall after some retention interval. In early studies of memory, encoding processes were often ignored, as most subjects were left to their own devices when given a list to study. It was thought that a given list of nonsense syllables, individual words, or paired-associates would be encoded in roughly equivalent ways across subjects, and that encoding itself would not be a variable of major interest for understanding recall. Yet increasingly, research has shown that manipulations of the types of materials being studied, the structure and context imposed on them, and the instructions given to the subjects during the study period can greatly affect later recall levels. For example, memory is typically better for pictures than for words (e.g., Shepard, 1967), and recall is greater for common, concrete, and imageable nouns than for infrequent and abstract words. In fact, imageability is probably the single most potent variable for predicting recall probability of individual words (Kosslyn & Holyoak, 1982; Paivio, 1971). According to Paivio's dual-coding theory (Paivio, 1969, 1971), highly concrete and imageable nouns can be encoded in two different ways in memory: as verbal (or linguistic) representations and as visual (or spatial) representations that somehow resemble the products of the actual perception of the objects or pictures to which the words refer. Recall probability is then enhanced for concrete words that have been encoded both verbally and visually since a search of memory during a recall attempt is presumably more likely to be successful if two separate versions of an encoded item exist than if only a single code exists in memory.

Further support for dual-coding theory has come from research demonstrating that instructions to form visual images while studying a list of words generally lead to higher recall levels (e.g., Bower, 1972; Paivio, 1971).

The type, or level, of encoding can probably best be manipulated experimentally in an incidental learning situation. In this case, subjects are given some orienting task in which decisions are made about individual words. After a delay, to eliminate any extraneous contributions from short-term memory, subjects are given a surprise memory test. According to levels-of-processing theory (Craik & Lockhart, 1972), deeper levels of encoding engendered by various orienting tasks should produce better long-term memory codes and therefore higher levels of performance in a delayed memory task. For example, Craik and Tulving (1975) presented 60 words, one at a time, to subjects who were given three different types of orienting tasks for 20 words each. The tasks were (1) graphemic, in which subjects indicated whether the given target word was printed in uppercase or lowercase; (2) rhyme, in which they were to decide whether or not the target word rhymed with a given word; and (3) sentence, in which they were to decide whether or not the target word fit congruously into a given sentence context. In a subsequent surprise memory test, subjects remembered about twice as many words in the sentence task as in the rhyme task and about three times as many as in the graphemic task. These results indicate that the memorability of an event is determined by the nature of the encoding operations performed when the event is perceived. When words are encoded to a deep, or semantic, level of analysis, they are remembered much better than when encoding operations focus on their visual or auditory properties.

Long-Term Memory Structures

One result of the levels-of-processing view has been to emphasize that information is stored most effectively when it conforms to the structures and contents already existing in long-term memory. Thus, semantic coding is presumably most effective for long-term retention because information is stored in long-term memory primarily in terms of semantic codes and organized primarily along dimensions of meaning. Tulving (1972) and others have pointed out that people actually are learning nothing new about the words in a list when the list is studied. The task is to develop some means to recall those words that specifically have been studied and to refrain from recalling other words. Models of human memory relevant for recall tasks have typically presumed that long-term memory has both semantic and episodic components. Semantic memory is modeled as a network of interconnected concepts, in which the concept nodes represent core meanings and the links among the nodes define how the concepts are related to one another (e.g., J. R. Anderson, 1983; Collins & Loftus, 1975). This semantic memory is presumed to function as the basis for interpreting sensory experiences as well as speech and print. It is assumed to be based on abstractions of previous experiences and is thus a relatively stable memory system that has many shared structures and processes among individuals of a given cultural–linguistic community (Bahrick & Karis, 1982; Munsat, 1966; Tulving, 1972). In contrast, episodic memory is an autobiographical record of particular experiences tied to specific times and places of occurrence. By its nature, episodic memory is more transient and subject to forgetting. This is because each new input changes the contents of episodic memory and adds to the amount of information than can potentially interfere with search and retrieval processes.

The episodic–semantic memory distinction has generally proved to be a useful metaphor for memory researchers. A list of words learned in a psychology experiment is a particular episode, but the words are interpreted, organized, and stored according to their meanings as defined by the structure and contents of semantic memory. Thus, the importance of semantic coding is underscored by such well-known results that word lists made up of exemplars from taxonomic categories (e.g., vehicles, vegetables, occupations) are learned more easily and retained better if the words are categorized during input, and words presented in a random order tend to be clustered by category during recall (Bousfield, 1953; M. D. Murphy & Puff, 1982). Recall also can be enhanced by providing cues, such as superordinate category labels, that are semantically related to studied words during the recall interval (e.g., Bahrick, 1969). The conclusion is that, if models of long-term memory acknowledge a distinction between semantic and episodic memories, there must remain sufficient interconnections between them so that semantic properties of what is learned influences both storage and retrieval of information in episodic memory.

Retrieval from Long-Term Memory

The final link in successful memory of a previous event is the ability to retrieve the necessary information from memory so that the relevant experience can be recollected or reconstructed. The typical methods used for studying memory include free (or serial) recall, cued recall, and recognition. Free recall is often a relatively insensitive measure of what has been stored, particularly after lengthy retention intervals. Information that has been accurately encoded and stored (and hence is available in memory) might not be accessible during a retrieval attempt due to the enormity of information stored in memory and interference among competing memory traces. Thus, cued recall, in which some specific contextual or associative hint is provided, or recognition, in which a token stimulus is presented and the subject has to determine whether or not it had been studied earlier, is more likely to produce successful retrieval than is uncued recall. Although the probabilities of correct responding are typically higher in cued recall and recognition than in free recall, the data must be interpreted with caution. This is because in most cases the probability of a correct response obtained by chance guessing is negligible in free recall, but can be substantial in cued recall and can be 50% in a yes–no recognition test for a given item. Procedures for correcting performance levels for guessing exist for both cued recall and recognition and should be used before the data are analyzed (e.g., Murdock, 1982; Watkins & Gardiner, 1982).

Studies of cued recall have revealed that the best cues are those that tend to remind the subject of the context and interpretation of the original stimulus event, a fact incorporated into the principle of encoding specificity (e.g., Thomson & Tulving, 1970; Tulving & Thomson, 1973). Although strong associates of previously studied words are generally better retrieval cues than are weak associates, this finding can be reversed if weak associates are presented along with the studied words both during the study interval and as recall cues. According to Tulving and Thomson (1973, p. 369), "Specific encoding operations performed on what is perceived determine what is stored, and what is stored determines what retrieval cues are effective in providing access to what is stored." The principle of encoding specificity generalizes to other situations in which better recall is obtained when the study and test environments are matched as well as when internal states such as drug dosage and mood are equivalent during study and test intervals (see Watkins & Gardiner, 1982). Bower (1981) has reported a series of studies in which subjects' moods were elevated or depressed through hypnotic suggestions. Strong mood congruency effects were found for subjects' recollections of recent pleasant or unpleasant experiences as well as for childhood memories. Bower suggests that the subject's "current mood activates and primes mood-congruent categories into readiness, and these are used in expectation-driven or top-down processing to classify and assimilate indeterminate experiences" (p. 140). Such effects of depressed mood on the relative accessibility of unpleasant thoughts and memories have been claimed to be part of a vicious cycle between depression and cognition that serves to perpetuate certain affective disorders (D. M. Clark & Teasdale, 1982; Teasdale & Fogarty, 1979).

Schema Theory and Comprehension Processes

Perhaps the most important recent development in cognitive psychology anticipated by Tulving's (1972) paper on the episodic–semantic memory distinction is the emphasis on the roles of previously existing knowledge structures in memory and comprehension processes. The beneficial effects of semantic coding and organization on memory processes have been studied extensively in list-learning experiments (e.g., Mandler, 1967; Tulving, 1962; Watkins & Gardiner, 1982). It is also recognized that knowledge structures in long-term memory function generally in interpreting environmental events, in comprehending speech and written text, and in reconstructive recall. Thus, just as individual words or objects are recognized and encoded with respect to particular conceptual representations in semantic memory, environmental events, conversations, and stories presumably are interpreted and remembered in terms of larger scale memory structures generally called schemata.

Schema theory can be traced back at least to the work of Bartlett (1932), who developed it as a means of explanation for the systematic distortions that he observed in his subjects' recollections of stories rendered days and weeks after their original readings. In general, peoples' memories of what they have witnessed or read demonstrate that recall is not a literal or verbatim representation of experience. Rather, some aspects of what has been experienced are forgotten, whereas other details are recalled, and elaborations and distortions consistent with the subjects' knowledge and biases further remove the content of recall from that which originally occurred. Under laboratory conditions, it is possible to demonstrate that stimuli consistent with subjects' interpretations, inferences, and conclusions will be "recognized" as being part of the original experience even if they had not, in fact, been presented (for reviews, see Thorndyke, 1984; Voss, Tyler, & Bisanz, 1982).

Schemata are viewed as more specific theoretical structures than concepts and the relations among them stored in semantic memory. A schema can be thought of as a cluster of knowledge representing a generic procedure (e.g., making bread), an object or percept (e.g., a person's office), an event or event sequence (e.g., driving to work), or a social situation (e.g., dining out with a friend). These clusters provide skeleton structures that can be instantiated with details of the particular object or event being represented (Thorndyke, 1984). In this way, schemata can be seen to benefit encoding and storage processes as well as subsequent reconstructive retrieval processes. However, distortions and other inaccuracies in both perception and recall can result from an inexact fit between experience and the most relevant schema in memory. In encoding sensory information or comprehending spoken or written language, schemata can function to guide processing by indicating which aspects of the input merit attention and what their critical values are. Relevant schemata also generate expectations about part–whole relations and sequences of events likely to occur, thus assisting the observer to find structure in the environment. Similarly, schemata can function during recall to produce likely inferences and elaborations consistent with a schema despite their absence in the original incident (e.g., Bower, Black, & Turner, 1979).

Conclusions

The present chapter has reviewed some of the theoretical content of cognitive psychology along with some of the information processing methods used to develop and extend cognitive theory. Some examples have also been given of applications of contemporary research techniques to specific abnormal populations and the study of individual differences in cognition. The review has necessarily been selective, and many interesting findings in areas such as reasoning, problem solving, and psycholinguistic behavior have been omitted entirely. However, those topics in perception and memory that have been discussed were chosen specifically because they have the firmer foundation in cognitive theory and research methodology. The information processing approach has proved its usefulness as a metaphor for understanding complex human behaviors (e.g., Lachman & Lachman, this volume) as well as for providing a means of studying and understanding individual differences in cognition. It is mainly the analytical theory behind the approach that enables us to localize and understand particular deficits in cognitive abilities. Work with abnormal groups and individuals should not only help psychologists to identify the nature of processing deficits associated with various forms of psychopathology, but should also be of aid for compensatory training and treatment as well.

Acknowledgments

I thank Thomas Cocklin, F. Richard Ferraro, Rick Ingram, and especially Sonia Ann Juola for helpful comments and encouragement during the preparation of this chapter.

II

Contributions of the Information Processing Perspective to Experimental Psychopathology Theory and Research

4

Neural Systems in the Emotional Control of Information Processing

DAVID L. ROTH*
Department of Psychology
University of Kansas
Lawrence, Kansas 66045

DON M. TUCKER
Department of Psychology
University of Oregon
Eugene, Oregon 97403

Most theorists of human information processing readily acknowledge that cognitive processes are dependent on neural events. Yet information processing theories in psychology have progressed, for the most part, in isolation from an explosion of findings in the neurosciences. As these findings continue to accumulate, it is becoming increasingly possible to develop information processing models that incorporate the operational characteristics of brain systems. The brain is inherently involved in both emotion and cognition, and the relations between emotion and thought might be more fully understood by considering the adaptive functions of neural systems. Because alterations in both cognition and brain function are often observed in disorders such as schizophrenia and depression, a biologically based information processing approach might provide an especially useful framework for the conceptualization of psychopathology.

In this chapter we discuss the influences on information processing provided by certain neural control systems (Tucker & Williamson, 1984). Different neural

*Present address: Department of Psychology, University of Alabama at Birmingham, University Station, AL, 35294.

systems provide opposing biases on attention and working memory, and the functional interaction of these neural systems results in a dynamic control on cognition in the natural environment. We describe how neural systems adjust processing activities to serve emotional needs, and we suggest that the study of brain systems can contribute to the understanding of cognitive, emotional, and interpersonal aspects of psychopathology.

Neural Control Systems and Attention

In order to survive, organisms must receive and organize incoming perceptual data. Neural systems governing perceptual processing must open information channels so that the organism can receive and process information originating in the external environment. Equally essential for survival is the organism's ability to perform motor acts. The neural systems that regulate motor behavior place a different set of demands on the information processing of the organism. Voluntary actions are controlled from within. Processing activities are directed by internal information to control the execution of motor sequences. Thus, while perceptual systems produce a bias to process novel, external information, motor systems require a bias to process stable, internal information.

Biologically, certain areas of the central nervous system have been identified as serving primarily afferent or efferent functions. Specific areas in the posterior cerebral cortex analyze incoming sensory data, and the motor strip of the frontal cortex contains neurons that initiate voluntary motor actions. Yet most structures of the central nervous system do not completely serve either ''input'' or ''output'' functions. The primary function of the central nervous system is to integrate information processing so that incoming perceptual information can result in adaptive action. Because perceptual and motor neural systems place very different demands on immediate information processing, some type of functional interaction between these systems must take place. A cybernetic model of perceptual and motor control may help explain how information processing systems are dynamically adjusted to handle changing survival demands.

Information Processing in Neural Systems

Habituation is an example of the dynamic association between stimulus and response in the biological organism. During habituation, an organism's response to a repetitive stimulus adaptively decreases. Groves and Thompson (1970) described processes in the spinal cord that occur during the habituation of simple reflexes. One neural pathway quickly decreases its activity in the presence of a repetitive stimulus, and another neural pathway slowly increments and maintains its activity with continued stimulation. These neural pathways exist separately from direct afferent and efferent pathways. Instead, these systems provide a detection of novelty or repetitiveness in external stimulation, and they exert a primitive control on the processing of information from stimulus to response.

In the hierarchical structure of central nervous system organization, more recently evolved neural systems modulate the functioning of more primitive systems. Yet there appears to be a strong continuity in the regulatory principles of neural structures. Higher systems appear to have elaborated on the control principles of the more primitive systems. Pribram and McGuinness (1975) suggested that the most complex systems of attentional control in the human brain have maintained a continuity with the simple control principles of spinal pathways. Although information processing in the brain is substantially more complex, the controls on the brain's processing activities may resemble more primitive control mechanisms.

Pribram and McGuinness (1975) distinguished two systems in the brain that control attention. An *arousal system* governs the phasic responding to external information, and an *activation system* maintains a tonic internal readiness for action. The amygdala is the central structure in the arousal system, with important pathways extending to the hypothalamus and the frontal cortex. The activation system is centered at the basal ganglia of the extrapyramidal motor system. McGuinness and Pribram (1980) suggested that these two systems could also be differentiated in terms of their neurochemical substrate. Reciprocal norepinephrine and serotonin pathways are important for arousal. These pathways innervate widespread brain areas to support wakefulness and responsivity to perceptual input. The tonic readiness of activation is provided by dopamine pathways extending from the substantia nigra in combination with acetylcholine influences on the basal ganglia.

Tucker and Williamson (1984) elaborated on this model by considering the regulatory characteristics of activation and arousal. The norepinephrine-mediated neurons that support arousal do not simply lead to increased neural activity when stimulated. Norepinephrine inhibits spontaneous neural activity, and this primes neural pathways to be responsive to perceptual input (Aston-Jones & Bloom, 1981; Bloom, Schulman, & Koob, in press). Because it habituates in the presence of repetitive input, the arousal system provides a mechanism such that novel events are especially likely to alter the brain's information processing activities.

A different type of regulatory bias is found in the control of motor behavior. The dopaminergic pathway supporting motor processes does not simply lead to increased motor activity; this system produces a bias in information processing to maintain constancy in motor operations. At excessive levels of dopaminergic activity, behavior becomes routinized and stereotyped (Iversen, 1977). Activation thus provides a bias toward redundancy in the information content of processing channels (Tucker & Williamson, 1984).

These control systems may be essential not only in regulating elementary perceptual and motor operations, but in controlling attention in complex cognitive activities. Tucker and Williamson (1984) propose that the cybernetics of activation and arousal may be fundamental to the specialized cognitive capacities of the left and right cerebral hemispheres. The redundancy bias of activation allows the left hemisphere its focal attentional mode, which in turn is integral to its analytic cognition. Arousal, on the other hand, applies a bias to habituate to constancy. This bias may underlie the right hemisphere's holistic perceptual skills.

Grossberg (1982) also suggested that attention is controlled by two complementary neural systems. After examining the mathematics of neural networks and theories of conditioning, Grossberg proposed that one system controls short-term memory during expected events and maintains internal representations, whereas another system is responsible for resetting short-term memory and orienting processing activities to unexpected events.

Separate neural systems thus seem to regulate the phasic orienting to novel external events and the tonic maintenance of internal operations. The two systems function simultaneously, and through their differential constraints on attention and short-term memory, they maintain a dynamic equilibrium in the organism's information processing.

Psychological Theories of Attention

A central issue for information processing theories is how large amounts of sensory input can be organized to allow meaningful behavior. At some point, processing activities are focused. Some information is selected for further processing at the expense of other information.

Early information processing theories in psychology were concerned with identifying "bottlenecks," stages where information was filtered and reduced on its journey from sensation to response (e.g., Broadbent, 1958; Deutsch & Deutsch, 1963; Triesmann, 1964). These theories pioneered the information processing model of attention, although each theory required modifications to explain many experimental findings (see Kahneman, 1973; R. Lachman, Lachman, & Butterfield, 1979). One problem shared by many early theories was that they were unidirectional; they described only the processing of information emanating from the external environment. The task of the processor was seen as perceiving and organizing externally produced input.

An important realization was that information in memory greatly influences how external stimulation is processed. Neisser (1967) emphasized the active role of stored information in the construction of perception. In Neisser's model, "preattentive" processes provide a crude organization of sensory input, and "focal attention" allows inputs to be more fully constructed and processed.

Focusing is active, not the result of a passive filter. Perception not only precedes memory; memory influences the process of perception. In this model, the convergence of external sensation and internal representation (analysis by synthesis) determines the contents of current conscious processing.

Other recent information processing models also maintain that both perceptual and memory systems influence the allocation of attention (e.g., Carver & Scheier, 1981; Kahneman, 1973). Novel stimulation generally increases the extent to which attention is controlled by perceptual input (Berlyne, 1960, 1974; Carver & Scheier, 1981; Kahneman, 1973). Memory systems allow attention to be focused on information that is pertinent to internal concerns. When external stimulation becomes repetitive or redundant, perceptual systems habituate. Memory systems, on the other hand, function to preserve repetitiveness. To store information is to maintain information constancy in anticipation of future needs.

Internal and External Controls on Attention

The refinements that have been made in the psychological theories of attention are in many ways consistent with the commonalities that have emerged in the neural models. The differing biases on information processing produced by the brain's activation and arousal systems may be important in understanding how attention is controlled by both existing internal representations and novel external stimulations. The regulatory effects of arousal orient the brain to control by external input (Pribram & McGuinness, 1975; Tucker & Williamson, 1984). The habituation bias leads the brain to be responsive to new data, rather than to information that matches current working memory. With this responsiveness to novel input, processing capacities can be directed to unique environmental information. Many aspects of data-limited processes (Norman & Bobrow, 1975) and preattentive processes (Neisser, 1967) seem to rely on the regulatory influences of arousal.

The regulatory influence that emerges from the motor system tends to maintain the constancy of information in current stores (Tucker & Williamson, 1984). Activation allows the performance of a specific motor sequence in spite of the continual distraction of sensory stimulation. Through this regulatory influence, activation allows the internal control of attention. The redundancy bias causes the organism's cognition and behavior to be directed by the limited contents of working memory. Thus, attention can be focused on matters that are pertinent to internal motivations.

The question posed by early attention theorists—how meaningful information is selected from the overload of data encountering the senses—must be answered in large part in terms of the semantic processes that determine what is meaningful and what is not. Yet the controls on the brain's state of functioning may be integral to how semantic constraints regulate information flow. In one way that the brain is turned on, arousal, novel perception dominates, and the current channel contents reflect a broad but transient representation of the sensory array. In another way that the brain's level of functioning is augmented, activation, attention becomes more focused, more closely directed by the information in current memory stores.

Controls on Processing Allocation

Another area of interest to information processing theorists is the nature of the limits on attentional capacity. Posner (1978, 1982) reviewed evidence that some processes, such as access to word meanings, may occur automatically, without placing demands on a limited attentional resource. This led to the notion of parallel pathway activation (where *activation* in Posner's usage refers to engagement of relevant domains of semantic memory rather than to motor readiness). In contrast to this more automatic form of attention, tasks that call for coordination of conscious cognitive processes seem to draw on a limited capacity system that proceeds in a serial rather than parallel fashion.

The limited capacity system described by Posner seems to have similarities to the control of the motor readiness system. With the constricted representational scope produced by a redundancy bias, processing can be focused on a single task. This same influence allows information to be manipulated through the execution of serial operations. As more processing resources are applied to a resource-limited task, performance on the task may improve (Norman & Bobrow, 1975). Yet, this allocation of processing capacity may reduce the opportunities to successfully execute a simultaneous cognitive operation. The focusing of limited processing resources must be carefully controlled internally, in accordance with current motivational needs.

A more automatic form of control occurs for many perceptual operations. Novel input seems to prime certain pathways in memory without the organism having to exert effortful attention. Although the activation system and its associated redundancy bias seem important for effortful, limited capacity attentional processes, it is possible that the neural control provided by the arousal system may be relevant for explaining the parallel pathway engagement that places minimal demands on attentional capacity. Certainly there are aspects of parallel pathway engagement that are not explained by a simple arousal mechanism. These pathways exist in semantic memory and they subserve a routinized activity. Yet, it appears that well-established semantic networks can be engaged very easily, perhaps automatically, with little attentional focusing from the motor readiness system.

Controls on Information Flow

Information processing theorists have convincingly illustrated that attention can be directed by semantic processes. An important direction of control is thus top-down. A person holds the concept that a task is important to complete, and activation is augmented so that sufficient redundancy is maintained in processing channels to keep attention focused on the task until it is completed. Alternatively, the expectation that something interesting is about to happen may enhance arousal, and this enhances perceptual responsivity to novel external events.

Another important direction of control is bottom-up, where elementary regulatory processes alter the nature of current cognitive representation. This direction of control may be especially useful for understanding the cognitive dysfunctions that occur in psychopathology. The psychotic, in addition to having irrational ideas, has fragmented attentional processes. This may result from a dysfunction at a more elementary level of attentional control.

The elementary neural control systems derived above do not change brain function diffusely. Both activation and arousal systems impose an inherent negative feedback on their target processes (Tucker & Williamson, 1984). Activation increases the functioning of motor systems, but it also augments the redundancy of that functioning. Arousal increases perceptual responsivity, yet it applies a habituation bias to limit that responsivity. These effects alter the nature of the information in working memory. They also alter the nature of the interface between working memory and long-term storage.

Under the redundancy bias of activation, a few pieces of information are thoroughly represented in working memory. This restriction in scope limits the range of engaged domains in long-term memory. Only a few domains are engaged, but each of these has a high probability of successful retrieval. The thorough analysis of this limited information allows it to be easily manipulated. Arithmetic and the syntactic ordering of language require a tight attentional control and a limited engagement of long-term memory.

The negative feedback inherent to perceptual arousal influences memory in many ways that are opposite to those of motoric activation. Constant input leads to a decrement in brain responsivity such that the effects of novel input are facilitated. Under this influence, perception is directed toward filling working memory with a broad array of new information, as opposed to maintaining a narrow range of existing contents. If we again assume that access to long-term memory is dependent on the engagement provided by the information in working memory, the broad scope of information in working memory facilitated by arousal leads to a very different mode of memory access. An expansive interface is produced. This broad scope is not achieved free of cost, however. Given limits to representational capacity, this allocation over such broad areas causes the contents of working memory to be ephemeral. For many kinds of cognition, arousal does not provide appropriate attentional control. The focusing of activation is necessary to maintain the contents of working memory to allow extended analysis to occur.

Asymmetric Control of Cognition

The question of limited attentional capacity has also been raised in neuropsychological research on hemispheric specialization. Because disordered hemispheric function has been linked with symptoms of psychopathology (Flor-Henry, 1976; Tucker, 1981; Walker & McGuire, 1982), a consideration of how hemispheric processing capacities are related to attentional controls may be important for understanding information processing dysfunctions.

Tucker and Williamson (1984) pointed to several lines of evidence linking the functional specialization of the cerebral hemispheres to the regulatory characteristics of activation and arousal. For example, although both hemispheres contain sensory reception and motor control areas, the higher level control of complex perceptual and motor operations appears to be more lateralized. Early in this century, Hughlings Jackson (J. Taylor, 1958) concluded that the left hemisphere handles expressive functions, whereas the right hemisphere is better equipped for higher level receptive operations. More recently, Semmes (1968) suggested that the left hemisphere's specialization for motor control and the right hemisphere's proficiency for perceptual integration are fundamental to the cognitive differences between the two hemispheres.

The left hemisphere processes information in a single-channel, serial fashion (Bradshaw & Nettleton, 1981; S. Cohen, 1973). Consistent with the notion that the left hemisphere is specialized for the higher order utilization of the redundancy bias of activation, the left hemisphere's analytic cognition requires the ability to focus attention, and its sequential processing resembles the type of control necessary to execute voluntary actions. Tasks that engage the left hemisphere, therefore, may be more likely to show effects that suggest a limited-capacity, serial processing system.

Kinsbourne (1974) reviewed observations on the task performance of commissurotomy patients (persons whose cerebral hemispheres have been surgically disconnected in order to control severe epileptic seizures) in an attempt to determine the roles of the two hemispheres for controlling attention. On simple perceptual tasks, such as the ability to recognize geometric shapes, the two hemispheres appeared to be similar in their ability to maintain attention. However, when the task demands increased, requiring more control over cognitive execution, the left hemisphere was usually found to be superior. Kinsbourne (1974) concluded that the left hemisphere controls focal attention. Similarly, Dimond and Beaumont (1973) suggested that the left hemisphere is important for maintaining an active, vigilant form of attention. Activation, through its tonic neural readiness and redundancy bias, seems to provide a capability to keep attention focused over an extended period of time.

The sequential, focused control on processing provided by activation can be easily disrupted if attention is attracted by a novel stimulus. The right hemisphere's more parallel mode of operation (Bradshaw & Nettleton, 1981; S. Cohen, 1973) can tolerate a looser, multitasking mode of processing. A more holistic allocation of working memory seems essential to receptive, but not active, attention. The habituation bias of arousal serves to maintain a global representation of the changes occurring in external space. Heilman and Van Den Abell (1979) found that warning stimuli were more effective in reducing reaction time if presented to the right rather than left hemisphere. A number of clinical studies have shown that attentional neglect of external space is more often observed following brain damage to the right rather than left hemisphere (Heilman, Watson, & Valenstein, 1985).

Methods from research on visual information processing have recently been applied to the study of attentional neglect in brain-damaged persons (Posner, Walker, Friedrich, & Rafal, in press). The results confirm that the ability to direct attention to areas of the visual field is impaired after parietal lesions, particularly those of the right hemisphere. Using chronometric methods, Posner *et al.* were able to determine that the right hemisphere's importance is not just in maintaining spatial orientation within the visual array, but in the actual disengagement of attention from one part of the field so that it can be directed elsewhere. This finding seems consistent with the right hemisphere's facility for orienting processing to novel environmental information (E. Goldberg & Costa, 1981; Tucker & Williamson, 1984).

The higher order of control of attention has been described as a specialty of both the left (e.g., Kinsbourne, 1974) and right hemisphere (e.g., Heilman & Van Den Abell, 1980). We suggest that each hemisphere contributes uniquely to attentional control and that these contributions are different qualitatively. Hemispheric specialization may have evolved as an elaboration of the fundamental differences between anterior and posterior brain systems. Pribram (1981) described the posterior brain as *participatory* because it provides an automatic processing of events in the external environment. The forebrain was depicted as *episodic* because it provides the control necessary for planned interactions with the environment. The attentional skills of the right hemisphere seem to draw on the operational characteristics of arousal to provide a receptive awareness of the changes occurring in the external environment. The attentional characteristics and cognitive skills of the left hemisphere, on the other hand, seem essential for the higher order control of voluntary action and expression.

Information processing analyses promise to be most useful when framed in a context of human functioning in a social world. Systems of attentional control must be described not only in terms of structure, but in terms of purpose as well. The neural systems that augment brain function do so in response to survival demands. As much as they are attentional control systems, activation and arousal are motivational and emotional systems.

Adaptive Neural Control

Like information processing research, the study of emotion has often been concerned with definition and description. A great deal of inquiry has been directed toward determining how many basic emotions there are, where they originate, and how they are expressed. What seems needed is a framework for considering the *functions* of emotions—how they regulate information processing and interpersonal relations.

An advantage of examining both information processing and emotional functioning in a neuropsychological framework is that neural systems are inherently adaptive. Neural systems adjust processing activities according to the demands of survival. Through a biological framework, it may be possible to consider how emotion is inherently involved in the control of information processing.

Emotional Response to Stress

The importance of novel environmental information in the arousal of acute emotional reactions is obvious. To turn a placid animal into an angry or fearful one requires the appearance of a new threat in the environment. In order to meet the demands of a threatening situation, changes in information processing and physiological functioning must occur.

Increased norepinephrine turnover in the brain occurs in response to a stressful event (Anisman, 1978; Maynert & Levi, 1964; Tanaka *et al.*, 1982). In addition to influencing information processing, the emotional arousal of the brain leads to endocrinological changes through the hypothalamic control of pituitary–adrenal cortex and sympathetic–adrenal medulla systems (Dunn & Kramarcy, 1984; Mason, 1975). The emotional response to stress involves not only resetting the brain's information processing activities but also adjusting the body's metabolic functions.

After the organism has been aroused, the question becomes how the organism deals with the situation. Aversive stimulation often leads to action. At a primitive level this may involve a decision to fight or flee. Anxiety, which may be accentuated by heightened physiological arousal, serves to augment the motivation to initiate a coping strategy. Attentional focusing is necessary to implement and maintain an attempt to deal with the stressor.

Under ideal situations, stressors are perceived, information processing and metabolic functioning are adjusted, and motor operations are activated to control the aversive aspects of the experience. Unfortunately, not all stressors are controllable. Under these circumstances, a different type of adaptation may be desirable. If the world consists of uncontrollable forces that cause pain, then a decreased responsivity to external stimulation might be the only way to reduce that pain.

Weiss, Stone, and Harrell (1970) found that norepinephrine systems adapt to prolonged aversive stimulation. Animals who could control aversive stimulation showed enhanced norepinephrine stores, whereas yoked controls who could not control the occurrence of the stressor showed norepinephrine depletions. Thus, if it is advantageous to process external information, norepinephrine systems appear to adapt to provide even greater capacity to do so. If the organism has been exposed to uncontrollable stressors, norepinephrine systems may adapt in an attempt to reduce sensitivity to perceptual input. This reduced responsivity to external information may interfere with the ability to learn new environmental contingencies. Learned helplessness (Seligman & Maier, 1967) may result from norepinephrine depletions (Weiss *et al.*, 1970). The progression from anxiety to helplessness in response to uncontrollable aversive events (Seligman, 1975) may reflect not only cognitive events, but the inherent functional characteristics of neural systems.

Motivation and Emotion as Control Processes

Because different neural systems subserve perceptual and motor operations, it is reasonable to suggest that different adaptive control processes are involved in the regulation of those operations. We suggest that activation controls voluntary action in accordance with motivational processes, and the emotional aspects of arousal exert control over ongoing perception.

The arousal system that modulates perceptual responsiveness does so as a function of mood level. Although aversive arousal usually leads to action, pleasurable arousal can lead to augmented perception. With a high mood level, such as that sometimes observed in mania, emotional sensitivity is enhanced. During a depressed mood, the sensitivity to, and hedonic value of, external stimulation is reduced.

Certain basic emotions, such as anger, fear, sadness, joy, and surprise, are innate; they are similarly perceived and spontaneously expressed across all cultures and some animal species (Chevalier-Skolnikoff, 1973; Darwin, 1872; Ekman, 1971). In humans, the holistic processing skills of the right hemisphere appear to be important for the nonverbal perception and expression of these emotions (Heilman, Bowers, & Valenstein, 1985; Tucker, 1981). These emotional reactions further lead to the direction of attention to salient external stimuli. Conversely, one's level of mood, or emotional responsiveness, can directly determine the extent to which information processing can be oriented to arousing external events.

Motor functions are regulated by a different type of control process. Voluntary motor sequences are initiated in accordance with internal motivations. Actions are initiated to attempt to gain some internal control over a situation in the environment. The strength of this desire to gain internal control can be enhanced by anxiety. The augmented activation that results leads to a restriction in the range of information processing in order to support the selection and execution of an appropriate motor sequence. Chronically high anxiety appears to involve an overactivated left hemisphere (Tucker, Antes, Stenslie, & Barnhardt, 1978; Tyler and Tucker, 1982). In our model, the subjective experience of anxiety reflects an attempt to focus cognition and control behavior internally. Thus, any perceived loss of control may exacerbate this subjective feeling of anxiety.

Internal and External Emotional Experience

By considering the functioning of distinct neural systems, it may be possible to integrate both external and internal aspects of emotional experience into a more comprehensive model. A threat in the environment results in the filling of processing channels with salient environmental information. A certain spontaneous facial expression (Ekman, 1971) and endocrinological adjustment (Mason, 1975) may also occur. Simultaneously, activation provides an internal focus that supports the execution of a coping attempt. When the external information is analyzed with respect to internal representations, the emotional state may be consciously labeled (Schacter & Singer, 1962). It is emotional arousal that orients the organism to the stressor and internal motivation that governs strategic interactions with the situation. If the specific coping attempt is successful in handling the situation, it is likely that an internal representation will be developed for use in similar situations in the future. If the coping attempt is unsuccessful, a state of anxiety may persist as long as a desire to gain control over the situation is maintained.

In addition to reacting to external situations, internal processing systems may contribute to the way such situations are received and interpreted. By developing expectancies and restricting the breadth of information input, certain aspects of emotional arousal can be controlled. Leventhal, Brown, Shacham, and Engquist (1979) found that distress reactions to painful stimuli can be reduced by providing concrete, but nonthreatening, information about the sensation prior to its experience. Such information may reduce the ''novelty'' of the aversive stimulation and therefore limit the extent to which it controls processing. Leventhal (1980) proposed that emotion involves an interaction between a relatively automatic, preattentive arousal process and a conscious analysis of the arousal with respect to an internal schema. Strategic development of this internal schema seems to be effective for helping persons tolerate aversive experiences.

There are certainly many other ways that externally sensitive and internally controlled processes converge to influence emotional experience. What seems clear is that feelings of all types are dependent on the activity and interaction of neural systems. The activation and arousal systems described here are distinct in their adaptive functions. Because these neural systems have evolved in accordance with the demands of survival, the biases they provide on information processing activities are intricately linked with current emotional and motivational states. The ultimate challenge for the biological organism is to successfully coordinate these complementary neural systems so that its behavior in the social environment can be satisfactorily regulated.

Social Adjustment and Psychopathology

In addition to disturbances in cognition and affect, psychopathology involves disordered interpersonal functioning. A formidable task for both information processing theories and neurophysiological models is to extend their concepts to explain human behavior in social contexts. Information processing research has helped clarify the ways in which people construct knowledge about themselves and handle information about others. An integration of these formulations with observations on neural systems may help explain how cognition and emotion are intricately involved in social interaction.

Processing Social Information

By necessity, human beings must process information about themselves differently from the way they process information about others. This is because it is impossible for people to observe themselves the way they observe others. One's actions, while serving as novel stimulations to another observer, are the enactments of redundant internal representations to oneself.

Duval and Wicklund (1972) suggested that attentional processes can be directed either outward toward the environment or inward toward the self. They defined the latter as a state of *objective self-awareness*. More generally, Carver and Scheier (1981) suggested that attentional processes can be focused on external or internal sources of information. *Self-focused attention* is one type of focus on internal information. Although one can process information about the self from a source that is external to the self, Carver and Scheier (1981) maintain that this type of information is processed with respect to the internal representations of oneself, or one's self-schemata. They propose that even when the source of self-referent information is external, attention is primarily focused on the internal self-schemata and not on environmental change.

Knowledge about the self is organized in extensively developed, verbally mediated, cognitive schemata (Markus, 1977; T. B. Rogers *et al.*, 1977). Findings from studies using manipulations to control encoding indicate that verbal structures for organizing information about the self are more extensively developed than verbal structures for processing information about both familiar and unfamiliar others (Kuiper & Rogers, 1979; Lord, 1980). One's knowledge about oneself is an abstraction, an object of one's own thoughts. The self-schemata involved provide a very useful function. They allow a person to build a system of knowledge about oneself in spite of the inherent difficulties in observing oneself as just another object in the environment.

The research supporting the importance of verbal self-schemata may have detected differences in the processing of information about self and others that are more qualitative than quantitative in nature. The suggestion that information about oneself is processed differently from information about other people is supported by some research findings in this area. Using verbal encoding controls, Lord (1980) replicated the finding that words associated with the self were better remembered than words associated with both familiar and unfamiliar others. However, when a similar procedure using imagery was examined, an interesting change in the results was obtained. Specifically, the objects that were associated with others using an imagery procedure were better remembered that those objects that were imagined in association with the self. Lord (1980) concluded that there is a tendency to process information about the self verbally, whereas information about other people is processed more imaginally.

These two complementary systems for processing social information are strikingly similar to the cognitive specializations frequently attributed to the cerebral hemispheres. Because other people do provide novel stimulation that attracts attention, it is possible that information about others is more extensively handled by the externally oriented arousal system. Knowledge about oneself, however, is a relatively stable, internal representation, and the activation system is probably necessary to focus attention on that internal information. The tonic maintenance of this stable internal representation is probably best achieved through the use of verbal labels. Because the systems that allow self-awareness are distinct from those that govern social sensitivity, there are likely to be differences in the processing of information about the self and others not only in terms of cognitive structure but in terms of adaptive purpose as well.

Social Arousal and Self-Evaluation

Dahl (1979) used psychoanalytic concepts to theorize on the social and self-evaluative aspects of emotional experience. Certain emotions, such as anger, sadness, and fear, are social appetites; they are aroused by external objects, and they demand behavioral action to attain satisfaction. Additionally, internal cognitive appraisals on the extent to which the social appetites have been satisfied define a different set of emotions, a set in which the self is the object of the emotion. When the social appetites have not been satisfied, different internal states may result from qualitatively different self-evaluations. In Dahl's model, anxiety is the appraisal that appetites exist and satisfaction will be difficult to attain, whereas depression is the appraisal that satisfaction is impossible and that the arousal of more appetites is undesirable.

This conceptualization of anxiety is consistent with the notion of anxiety as a motivational influence on the activation system. The self-evaluation that satisfaction will be difficult to achieve can lead to greater attentional focusing and effort. In the case of depression, it is important to differentiate between depressed mood, which involves a decreased responsivity to the social environment, and depressive cognition, which involves negative self-evaluation. Both anxiety (Sarason, 1975) and depression (Ingram & Smith, 1984) may be associated with exaggerated self-focused attention. The nature of this attentional effect, however, can be quite different. In anxiety, social appetites have not been abandoned, and self-focused attention may reflect an increased motivation to gain internal control and activate coping attempts. During depression, social influences on attention are reduced, and self-focused attention may result from the failure of perceptual systems to orient processing to novel external events.

The internal analysis of one's social arousals and one's ability to satisfactorily deal with those arousals results in self-evaluations, and ultimately, in the development of a self-concept. Because the processing systems responsible for social emotionality and self-awareness are different, a functional interaction between these systems must take place to allow the development of interpersonal relationships. Through this model, it may become apparent how disordered information processing is associated with disordered interpersonal functioning.

Psychopathology

Ideally, the brain's processing controls operate in some sort of functional harmony and balance. Alterations in the activity and coordination of brain systems are the neuropsychological substrates of variations in personality and symptoms of psychopathology. Neural control systems must be dynamic so that if it serves one's needs to attend to the environment, processes that are sensitive to environmental novelty will dominate cerebral activity, whereas if one feels a need to focus on one's internal concerns, systems that restrict attention to relevant internal information can direct cognitive processing. Furthermore, a functional interaction of the processing systems is needed. If one's self-concept is going to be related to one's social life, then the self-concept must develop in accordance with events in the external environment.

A severe disruption in this functional harmony and interaction of neural systems may be observed as a psychosis. The psychotic person is one whose internal thoughts are not functionally related to the reality of the external environment. The thoughts of psychotic individuals are often restricted to redundant, internal delusions, and these internal thoughts are often not easily changed by external information. In general, a psychosis appears to involve some type of dissociation between internal and external information processing.

The anterior cortex is intricately involved in motor control and, through its interconnections with limbic structures, emotional arousal. Thus, the anterior cortex is an important area of interface between activation and arousal, and it might be expected that certain symptoms of psychosis involve disordered frontal and anterior temporal lobe function. Evidence from a variety of studies suggest that the "negative" symptoms of chronic schizophrenia, such as social withdrawal and affective blunting, are often accompanied by neurodiagnostic indications of diffuse frontal lobe pathology (Seidman, 1983). Temporal lobe dysfunction has also been implicated in some types of psychoses (Flor-Henry, 1976).

Several investigators have suggested that schizophrenia is characterized by an overactivated left hemisphere (e.g., Flor-Henry, 1976; Gur, 1978; see Walker & McGuire, 1982). Gjerde (1983) suggested that many of the information processing alterations observed during schizophrenia could result from an attentional capacity deficit due to information overload. Through excessive activation, the left hemisphere might appear overly excited, and information processing might then be overly restricted to internal information. Because dopamine is an important biochemical substrate of activation (McGuinness & Pribram, 1980; Tucker & Williamson, 1984), it seems reasonable to suggest that the dopamine overactivity hypothesized to underlie schizophrenia (Kety, 1980; Meltzer, 1979) might be linked to internal cognitive processing that is excessively stereotyped and isolated. The deficits in transfering input information from iconic storage to short-term memory (Braff & Saccuzzo, 1981; Saccuzzo & Braff, 1981) and the typical slowed reaction times of schizophrenics may also reflect a decreased capability to allocate attention to external information under excessive internal activation. Additionally, the affective blunting and social withdrawal characteristic of schizophrenia could result from information processing that is excessively restricted to internal information.

Unlike psychotic thought disturbance, the affective disorders do not usually involve unrealistically isolated internal processing. Instead, the person's emotional sensitivity to the social environment seems to be poorly balanced in affective disorders. Depression is characterized by a lack of social emotionality, and mania involves exaggerated emotional responsivity.

A popular model of affective dysfunction is that depression is caused by a lack, and mania by an excess, of norepinephrine activity in the brain (Schildkraut, 1965). Along with attentional control characteristics, the arousal system subserves important hedonic functions. The anhedonia of the depressive may reflect a fundamental inability to be aroused by external stimulation. Uncontrollable environmental stress, which depletes norepinephrine (Weiss *et al.*, 1970), probably contributes to the onset of depression (Paykel *et al.*, 1969). Lewinsohn, Hoberman, Teri, and Hautzinger (1985) hypothesize that stressful life events trigger dysphoric emotion and self-focused attention. These effects are then believed to combine to produce a number of other symptoms, such as negative self-perceptions.

Reduced social emotionality may actually be desirable during prolonged, uncontrollable stress. However, once the stressors become more manageable, this lack of sensitivity to the external environment is no longer adaptive. Indeed, adequate sensitivity to external events is necessary to learn new environmental contingencies. Negative self-evaluations may also contribute to lowered social emotionality. Because of negative expectations, the depressed person tends to avoid social situations and therefore fails to experience novel external stimulation in the social environment.

The fact that depression may involve both decreased social emotionality and exaggerated self-focused attention has direct implications for psychotherapy. Insight-oriented therapy is probably not desirable for someone who already excessively focuses information processing on the self. Cognitive–behavioral therapies (e.g., Hollon & Beck, 1979) include treatment approaches that target both depressed mood level and dysfunctional cognition. Self-defeating thoughts are explicitly analyzed in a logical way in cognitive therapies; this strategy utilizes the focusing attributes of activation to inspect the self-evaluations that are also inherently associated with the same internally focused activation system. At the same time, many cognitive–behavioral therapies include "experiments" in which the person is put into a relatively safe, emotionally arousing situation. Because the "experiments" often initially involve rather simple behavioral demands, some emotional satisfaction is likely to occur after successful experiences, and this may break the low mood and rejuvenate the arousal system.

Imbalances in internal control may contribute to other types of psychopathological symptoms. A lack of self-control is inherent in impulsive and sociopathic tendencies. Exaggerated emotional display and insufficient internal control also characterize the hysterical personality (Shapiro, 1965). Conversely, chronic anxiety and obsessive–compulsive personality traits may reflect exaggerated strivings for internal control. In general, we suggest that many symptoms of psychopathology can be seen as consistent with the functioning and interaction of neural control systems. Conceptualizations that extend across biological, cognitive, and social levels of analysis can be developed by considering the functioning of neural systems of emotional control on information processing.

Although there are controversies over how to interpret many findings in the neurosciences, theoretical advances in neuropsychology can be used to develop an understanding of the relations between neurophysiological systems and observable behavior. It is becoming possible to determine the links between neurochemical alterations and disordered thought processes. Similarly, it should be possible to provide assessments on a person's disordered attentional and affective functioning and address the specific neural regulatory systems that may be involved.

Throughout this discussion, we have suggested that information processing theorists should consider biological constraints and emotional controls on cognition in the natural environment in addition to describing the parameters of processing activities in controlled laboratory experiments. We have described a model whereby attention and cognition are adjusted by elementary neural control systems. The qualitative differences in information handling between motoric activation and perceptual arousal seem integral to the qualitative changes that occur in cognition and affect during psychopathology. Through the study of these regulatory systems, it seems possible that the importance of both external and internal influences on human functioning in the social world can be more fully appreciated.

5

Type A Behavior and Cardiovascular Disease: An Information Processing Approach

TIMOTHY W. SMITH
Department of Psychology
University of Utah
Salt Lake City, Utah 84112

Overview of Coronary Heart Disease

The mortality associated with coronary heart disease (CHD) has declined somewhat over the past 15 years. Nonetheless, this illness remains the leading cause of death in the United States. About 650,000 people die from CHD each year in this country, and approximately 4,000,000 cases of the disease exist at any given time (Castelli, 1980). When such figures are multiplied by the financial and personal costs associated with an individual case of CHD, the scope of this health problem becomes uncomfortably clear.

Coronary heart disease has three clinical manifestations. Myocardial infarction (MI), or heart attack, involves the death of portions of the heart muscle due to prolonged lack of blood supply. Angina pectoris (AP) is sharp pain caused by temporarily reduced blood flow to the heart muscle. Sudden death is caused by a severe disruption in heart rhythm that prevents the heart from functioning effectively. Coronary artery disease (CAD), a narrowing of the blood vessels supplying the heart muscle, is the condition underlying each of these manifestations. This narrowing of the blood vessels, or atherosclerosis, is a progressive condition, beginning in early adulthood or adolescence. Blood platelets, fatty substances, and smooth muscle cells combine to form a slowly growing deposit, or

INFORMATION PROCESSING APPROACHES TO CLINICAL PSYCHOLOGY

plaque, on the interior lining of the coronary artery. Eventually, these deposits impede blood flow enough to produce the clinical manifestations of CHD (Daniel, 1980).

Epidemiological research has identified a now familiar sounding list of factors that place individuals at risk for developing CHD. These include high serum cholesterol, elevated blood pressure, smoking, sex, age, and family history of the disease (Kannel, 1979). Identification of these risk factors has been invaluable in guiding basic research efforts designed to clarify the etiology of CHD and CAD, as well as interventions intended to reduce the incidence of the disease.

Though undeniably important, the traditional list of risk factors has proved incomplete. These risk factors can account for only about half of the CHD cases developing each year. The inability of standard risk factors to predict accurately a majority of CHD cases has led to increased attention to psychological and social risk factors (Jenkins, 1976). The suggestion that psychological factors such as anger and stress are causally related to heart disease has a long history (Osler, 1892; Trousseau, 1882) and has been supported by recent empirical research.

Type A Behavior and Risk of Coronary Heart Disease

Perhaps the most notable among the psychological risk factors identified by this renewed interest is the Type A behavior pattern (TABP). Cardiologists Meyer Friedman and Ray Rosenman (1959) observed a specific set of behavioral characteristics that seemed typical of CHD patients. These included exaggerated achievement striving, competitiveness, hostility, time urgency, impatience, and loud, explosive speech. Friedman and Rosenman labeled such persons Type A; individuals characterized by the relative absence of these behaviors were called Type B. It should be noted that these differences between Type A and Type B persons are not always present, rather they emerge in response to challenging and demanding situations. Friedman and Rosenman (1959) developed a structured interview (SI) to assess the TABP and found these characteristics to be more common among CHD patients than other patient groups.

The most compelling evidence establishing the TABP as a risk factor, however, came from two large-scale, prospective studies. Using the SI and the Jenkins Activity Survey (JAS), a self-report questionnaire method of assessing the TABP, the Western Collaborative Group Study found that previously healthy Type A individuals were about twice as likely to develop CHD as were their Type B counterparts. This risk was independent of and equivalent to the risk associated with standard risk factors (Jenkins, Rosenman, & Zyzanski, 1974; Rosenman *et al.,* 1975). Subsequently, another self-report measure of the

TABP, the Framingham Type A Scale (FTAS), was found in an independent sample to predict the development of CHD in previously healthy persons, again independently of standard risk factors (Haynes, Feinleib, & Kannel, 1980). This and similar evidence has led to the widespread acceptance of the TABP as an independent risk factor of the same magnitude as those traditionally associated with CHD (Review Panel on Coronary-Prone Behavior and Coronary Heart Disease, 1981).

Physiological Reactivity: The Link between Behavior and Disease

The mechanism by which Type A behavior contributes to CHD has received much attention. The hypothesis guiding the related research maintains that the TABP leads to CHD through excessive physiological reactivity (R. B. Williams, 1975, 1978). In brief, it is suggested that Type A's, relative to Type B's, respond to challenging and demanding situations with enhanced, sympathetically mediated physiological responses. Type A's and B's do not appear to differ in static, basal levels of autonomic activity. Rather, Type A's demonstrate greater *changes* in sympathetic activity in response to challenging and demanding stimuli. These responses include elevated blood pressure and heart rate; increases in circulating epinephine, norepinephrine, and cortisol; mobilization of plasma lipids; and increased blood platelet aggregation. Such responses are believed to injure the lining of the coronary arteries, providing the site for the subsequent development of atherosclerotic plaques. Further, this set of physiological responses promotes the mobilization and accumulation of atherosclerotic material at the site of the injury. Finally, physiological reactivity, in the presence of established CAD, may precipitate acute clinical manifestations of CHD such as MI, AP, or sudden death.

Evidence from a variety of sources is consistent with this model. Though many questions remain, a large body of animal research indicates that the physiological responses described above are related to the development of CAD, as well as subsequent MI and sudden death (see Schneiderman, 1983, for a review). Further, many studies have demonstrated that Type A's respond to challenging and demanding stimuli with greater cardiovascular and neuroendocrine activity than do Type B's (for reviews, see Houston, 1983; D. S. Krantz, Glass, Schaeffer, & Davia, 1982; Matthews, 1982). While this evidence is far from conclusive, physiological reactivity does represent the most likely process underlying the association between the TABP and CHD observed in epidemiological studies.

The Nature of Type A Behavior and Reactivity

Clarification of factors that maintain Type A behavior and the associated physiological responses would be of great utility in understanding, preventing, and treating CHD. Not surprisingly, then, psychological factors responsible for the differences between Type A and Type B persons in their behavioral and physiological responses to stressful situations have been the subject of much attention. D. C. Glass (1977) has provided a motivational analysis. Briefly, he asserts that the TABP represents an attempt to assert and maintain control over one's environment. Type A's are hypothesized to be more likely to perceive threats to their control and more motivated to maintain control. The Type A's physiological reactivity, in turn, is viewed as a result of effortful attempts to assert and maintain control. This model is supported by the results of studies examining the behavioral responses of Type A's to threats to their control (Brunson & Matthews, 1981; D. C. Glass, 1977; Strube & Werner, 1985). Further, efforts to assert control over stressful stimuli have been found to produce enhanced physiological reactivity, both in general (Houston, 1972; T. W. Smith, Houston, & Stucky, 1985; Solomon, Holmes, & McCaul, 1980) and for Type A's in particular (Pittner, Houston, & Spiridigliozzi, 1983).

Matthews and Siegel (1982, 1983) have provided a cognitive social learning theory approach. These authors have suggested that overt Type A behavior is the result of a strong value in productivity and achievement, combined with ambiguous standards for evaluating performance. Thus, situations that represent opportunities for achievement, but lack explicit standards for evaluating success, are likely to elicit the aggressive striving typical of Type A's. Further, there is evidence to suggest that this pattern may be influenced by the nature of parents' responses to the achievement-related behavior of their children (D. C. Glass, 1977; Matthews, 1977).

Biological models have also been proposed. For example, Krantz and his colleagues (D. S. Krantz & Durel, 1983; D. S. Krantz, Arabian, Davia, & Parker, 1982; D. S. Krantz, Durel *et al.*, 1982) have suggested that many of the overt behaviors comprising the TABP reflect an underlying constitutional factor. In short, Type A behavior and the associated physiological responsiveness to stressors are viewed as caused by the same factor—a constitutionally based tendency toward sympathetic reactivity.

Cognitive Factors in Type A Behavior

Motivational, social learning, and biological factors may indeed account for many of the overt behavioral and physiological responses demonstrated by Type A persons. Recent cognitive approaches to personality (e.g., Cantor & Kihlstrom, 1981, 1982), however, seem likely to provide additional, important insights into the TABP. Examination of the ways in which Type A's perceive situations, attend to task demands, and process information regarding their activities may identify psychological processes responsible for the behavioral and physiological differences between Type A and Type B persons. Indeed, recent research points to several potentially important cognitive processes associated with the TABP. To date, this research has not borrowed extensively from the conceptual and methodological armamentarium of the information processing paradigm (e.g., Ingram & Kendall; Lachman & Lachman; Juola; chapters 1, 2, 3, this volume). As a result, many of these studies do not reflect the precision associated with those studies typical of experimental cognitive psychology. Instead, somewhat older concepts from the cognitive traditions in personality and social psychology (e.g., attributions, appraisal, cognitive coping, self-evaluation) have been employed. In what follows, the existing cognitive research on the TABP will be reviewed. This research will be reviewed from the perspective of what it reveals about the basis of Type A behavior, and about the source of the physiological responses believed to link the pattern to disease. Subsequently, implications of this research for future studies using information processing paradigms and for the clinical task of modifying Type A behavior will be discussed.

Appraisal of Task and Interpersonal Situations

Several studies indicate that Type A's processing of situational information (i.e., cognitive appraisal) may be an important influence on their overt and physiological responses. A recent study by T. W. Smith and Brehm (1981b) of person perception demonstrated that Type A's differ from Type B's in their appraisal of potential competitors. Type A and B subjects listened to two individuals engaged in a competitive game (i.e., the Prisoner's Dilemma Game). After the game was concluded, one half of the subjects were informed that they would engage in the game with one of the players they had just observed (i.e., expectant observer condition); the other half of the subjects expected simply to observe the two original players participate in another game (i.e., passive observer condition). Subjects then evaluated the observed players on a number of trait adjectives. The results indicated that Type A subjects in the expectant observer condition rated their future opponent as more competitive and hard driving than did Type A's rating the same individual when they did not expect to compete with him or her (i.e., passive observer condition). Further, Type B's demonstrated the opposite of this pattern; subjects expecting to compete rated the target as less competitive than did those not expecting to compete. Thus, Type A's expecting to interact with the target appraised him or her as more competitive than did Type A's who simply expected to observe the target a second time, even though these appraisals were based on identical information. Type B's expecting to interact, on the other hand, generated more benign appraisals than did Type B's in the observer role. These results indicate that Type A's tend to appraise their interpersonal interactions as involving more challenge and demand than do Type B's.

Similar differences between Type A and Type B persons have been found in their appraisal of the degree of challenge inherent in other stimuli. For example, Type A's have also been found to set higher performance goals prior to task performance (Snow, 1978) and classroom examinations (Grimm & Yarnold, 1984) than do Type B's, suggesting differential appraisal of the degree of demand.

This research suggests that Type A's are characterized by the tendency to process or appraise a variety of stimuli as more challenging and demanding compared to Type B's. What effects are such cognitive processes likely to have on overt Type A behavior and physiological reactivity? It is likely that such appraisals will prompt aggressive, competitive, and achievement-striving behavior commensurate with the perceived demands of the situation. Further, a study by Gastorf (1981) suggests that such differences in cognitive appraisal influence cardiovascular responses. Type A and B subjects were exposed to either an objectively easy or difficult anagram task. Half of the subjects were led to expect an easy task; the other half expected a difficult one. Type B's evidenced elevated task-related cardiovascular responses only when they encountered a difficult task they had accurately expected to be difficult. In contrast, Type A's evidenced elevated cardiovascular responses to both the easy and difficult tasks if they *expected* the task to be difficult. They demonstrated lower levels of cardiovascular response, equivalent to Type B's, only when they expected and performed an objectively easy task. Type A's prior cognitive appraisal of task demand, therefore, influenced their physiological response.

As noted above, D. C. Glass (1977) has suggested that the TABP represents a style of responding to perceived threats to one's control over environmental events. The results of several studies are consistent with this view (Brunson & Matthews, 1981; Dembroski, MacDougall, & Musante, 1984; D. C. Glass, 1977; Strube & Werner, 1985). Other research has indicated that cognitive processes may mediate this hyperresponsivity to control threats. Specifically, Type A's appear to be more likely to *appraise* a situation as representing a threat to their control. For example, Carver (1980) found that Type A's appraised a persuasive communication as more coercive than did Type B's, particularly when the objective level of coercion was low. Not only are Type A's more likely to view stimuli as potential control threats, their attempts to reassert control appear to be mediated by a greater tendency to view events as under their control (Rhodewalt & Davison, 1983). That is, Type A's enhanced sensitivity to control threats may be due to their greater tendency to appraise events as potentially controllable.

The tendency to view events as controllable and the sensitivity for perceiving events as threats to control are likely to contribute to Type A's physiological responsivity. Such appraisal processes would lead Type A's to attempt to assert control over events more frequently and more aggressively than would their Type B counterparts. As mentioned above, attempts to assert control are associated with increased physiological arousal (Houston, 1972; Smith, Houston, & Stucky, 1985), especially when control is difficult to achieve (Manuck, Harvey, Lechleiter, & Neal, 1978; Solomon *et al.*, 1980). Further, Type A's respond to control threats with greater reactivity than do Type B's (Pitner, *et al.*, 1983). Thus, Type A's greater tendency to appraise situations as representing challenge, demand, and threats to control is likely to elicit aggressive striving with corresponding levels of physiological arousal.

Cognitive Activity during Task Performance

The results of two recent studies indicate that during task performance Type A's focus their attention on the task to a greater degree than do Type B's. Both studies employed a standard information processing paradigm that required subjects to work on a task designated as primary, along with a secondary, concurrent task. Performance on the secondary task is used as an index of attention allocation, since the capacity for cognitive processing is assumed to be limited. Thus, increased attention to the primary task would disrupt performance on the secondary task (R. Lachman *et al.*, 1979). Matthews and Brunson (1979, experiment 1) asked subjects to perform concurrently a task presented to the subjects as primary (i.e., Stroop Color-Word Interference Test) and a task described as of secondary importance (i.e., reaction time). Relative to Type B's, Type A's performed better on the primary task but worse on the secondary task. This pattern presumably reflects more processing capacity allocated to the primary task, and hence, more rigidly focused attention to the primary task.

Similar results were reported in the second study. Stern, Harris, and Elverum (1981) assigned Type A and Type B subjects to separate conditions. In one condition, an arithmetic task was designated as primary, and a recall task embedded within the arithmetic task was designated as secondary. In another condition, the recall task was designated as primary, and the arithmetic task was embedded and secondary. In both conditions, Type A's demonstrated better performance than Type B's on the primary task, but they simultaneously performed less well on the secondary task. Again, this pattern of results suggests that Type A's allocate their attentional resources to primary tasks, at the cost of poorer performance on secondary tasks.

The focused attention of Type A's has also been demonstrated in a recent study of concept formation processes. Humphries, Carver, and Newman (1983) asked subjects to view a series of complex stimuli (i.e., strings of letters in a concept formation task) and then indicate their degree of confidence of having seen the stimuli previously. The pattern of confidence ratings during the subsequent recognition task indicated that Type A's had attended to frequently occurring, central attributes of the stimuli to a greater degree than did Type B's. Further, this pattern of increased attention to central features of the stimulus series occurred only under conditions of high challenge, that is, when the task was presented as a test of intelligence. These results suggest that the focused attention of Type A's occurs even when primary aspects of a task are not explicitly defined as such, and further that this cognitive characteristic is elicited by challenging conditions.

The focused attention of Type A's may be related to the physiological reactivity believed to link the behavior pattern and CHD. As Humphries *et al.* (1983) note, Type A's respond to challenge by focusing their attention more exclusively than do Type B's on central stimuli. As a result, these stimuli are likely to be subjectively more salient to the Type A. Previous research suggests that greater subjective salience can produce enhanced responsivity to the salient stimulus (e.g., Scheier, 1976). Thus, Type A's behavioral and physiological reactivity may be, in part, a result of the increased salience of threatening or demanding stimuli engendered by their focused attention. Though perhaps facilitating task performance, the Type A's attentional processes may magnify the degree of challenge and demand they see in their surroundings and elicit corresponding physiological changes.

A second, potential connection between attentional style and physiological reactivity is somewhat more direct. As noted by J. R. Jennings (1983), the results of a variety of studies indicate that the proportion of attentional capacity allocated to task demands is positively related to the degree of heart rate, blood pressure, and neuroendocrine response (e.g., J. R. Jennings, 1983; Surwitt, Williams, & Shapiro, 1982). Thus, if Type A's typically allocate a greater proportion of their attentional capacity during task performance, this would result in more frequent and exaggerated episodes of physiological responsivity.

Exaggerated attention to task demands is not the only difference between Type A and Type B persons during task performance. A second, important aspect of the Type A cognitive style concerns coping strategies. Type A's, in contrast to Type B's, report using the cognitive coping strategies of denial and suppression of aversive physical and emotional states during task performance (Pittner & Houston, 1980; Pittner *et al.*, 1983). That is, Type A's report that while in stressful situations, they actively avoid attention to negative affect (e.g., anxiety, tension) and physical symptoms (e.g., pain, fatigue). Such cognitive coping strategies are consistent with another recent study on symptom reporting during task performance. Weidner and Matthews (1978) asked Type A and B subjects to report on their level of fatigue either during or after completing a demanding aversive task. Type A's expecting to continue in the task reported fewer physical symptoms and less fatigue than did Type A's who were finished with the task. Reports of the latter group of Type A's were equivalent to the reports of Type B's. Further, expectations concerning continuation of the task did not influence the symptom and fatigue reports of Type B's. This suppression of aversive physical and emotional states, perhaps in combination with the attentional style described above, may account for the fact that Type A's work closer to their capacity on physical tasks than do Type B's while simultaneously reporting lower levels of fatigue (Carver, Coleman, & Glass, 1976). It is interesting to note that this underreporting of fatigue by Type A's has been demonstrated in 11-year-old children (Matthews & Volkin, 1981). Clearly, this pattern of cognitive coping may be physiologically taxing, especially if it persists over many years. The same sensations or symptoms which Type A's suppress often prompt individual's to avoid or withdraw from stressful situations.

Evaluation of Performances

The research reviewed above suggests that Type A's and B's differ in their initial cognitive appraisals of situations and in their cognitive activity during task performance. Other research indicates that Type A's demonstrate a distinct cognitive pattern *after* task performances as well.

Type A's tend to view a given level of performance as less satisfactory than do Type B's. Manuck and Garland (1979), for example, found Type A's to be less satisfied with their performances on a challenging task than were Type B's, even when they did not differ in their objective level of performance. Similarly, Suls, Becker, and Mullen (1981) found that relative to Type B's, Type A's described themselves as likely to be more upset over a hypothetical failure.

While Type A's are harsh judges of their performances, they also tend to attribute these same outcomes to internal factors. Brunson and Matthews (1981) found that Type A's attributed their failure on an experimental task to internal factors to a greater extent than did Type B's. Consistent with this finding, Rhodewalt (in press) found that Type A's were more likely to attribute hypothetical negative events to internal factors than were Type B's.

It is not immediately apparent how the self-evaluative and attributional style of Type A's would lead directly to increased physiological reactivity. It is apparent, however, these processes might prompt an increased display of overt Type A behaviors. Recall that Type A's set higher self-standards for performance (Grimm & Yarnold, 1984; Snow, 1978). The combination of higher standards on the one hand and lower evaluations of performance on the other is likely to leave Type A's with a larger discrepancy between desired and perceived levels of accomplishment than that found in Type B's. When combined with Type A's more negative response to failure (Gastorf & Teevan, 1980), belief in the necessity of achievement (T. W. Smith & Brehm, 1981a), and tendency to attribute negative outcomes to internal factors (Brunson & Matthews, 1981; Rhodewalt,

1984), this discrepancy is likely to prompt the aggressive achievement striving typical of Type A's. This type of cycle is, of course, the basis of several cognitive models of motivation and self-regulatory behavior (Bandura, 1977a; Carver & Scheier, 1982; Kanfer, 1980).

Recently, Type A versus B differences in self-evaluative or self-regulatory behaviors have been observed in children. Matthews and Siegel (1983) found that Type A fourth-grade students, compared to their Type B classmates, evaluated their task performances against harsher standards. Thus, the Type A's tendency to be self-critical may appear early.

The Context of Type A Cognitive Processes

The cognitive processes outlined here seem to be important components of the Type A pattern. Consideration of cognitive factors in isolation, however, presents a problem. It is a problem detailed in Coyne's (1982) critique of the role of cognition in depression. Briefly, Coyne argues that by abstracting cognitive processes from the set of interacting personal and environmental concomitants of depression, one risks generating an artificially limited model of depressive cognition and a woefully incomplete understanding of depression itself:

> Without an understanding of the depressed person's ecological niche and its characteristic responsiveness and of the informational consequences of the depressed person's behavior, we are unlikely to achieve an adequate model of the cognitive processes associated with depression. (p. 9)

The same contextual issues are critical in understanding the Type A cognitive style. Typical information processing paradigms, along with other cognitive–behavioral traditions, are often employed without attention to this potential limitation. Cognitive social learning theory (Bandura, 1977b; Mischel, 1973), and the emerging cognitive-social approach to personality (Cantor & Kihlstrom, 1981, 1982), however, provide a rich framework for exploring reciprocal relationships between cognitive processes, overt behavior, and situational factors associated with Type A behavior. The explicit rejection of unidirectional causal models and the adherence to the principle of reciprocal determinism (Bandura, 1977) is a central theme in these perspectives. Thus as Mischel (1973) indicates, important cognitive factors are placed within their equally important behavioral and situational context:

> The person continuously influences the "situations" of his life as well as being affected by them in a mutual, organic two-way interaction. These interactions reflect not only the person's reactions to conditions but also his active selection and modification of conditions through his cognitions and actions. (p. 278)

One such interactional factor useful in understanding Type A behavior is the kind of situations individuals choose to enter. M. Snyder (1981a) has argued convincingly that choice of situations is an often overlooked determinant of behavior. Three studies have demonstrated that Type A's, relative to Type B's, prefer participation in more demanding, challenging tasks (Holmes, McGilley, & Houston, 1984; Lutz & Holmes, 1984; Ortega & Pipal, 1984). Such preferences place Type A's in the kind of situations where they demonstrate the most physiological reactivity compared to Type B's (Holmes *et al.*, 1984). Other research suggests that such choices may place Type A's in environments which, in turn, elicit more Type A behavior. D. C. Glass (1977) found that Type A's report greater involvement in academic and extracurricular activities in school. Waldron *et al.* (1980), on the other hand, found that academic pressure or demand produces increases in Type A behavior over time.

A second interactional issue important in understanding Type A behavior concerns the effect of overt Type A behavior on the social environment. The tendency for Type A's to exhibit interpersonal aggression and competition is well documented (Carver & Glass, 1978; Holmes & Will, 1985; Strube *et al.*, 1984; Van Egeren, 1979a, 1979b; Van Egeren, Abelson, & Sniderman, 1983). Such interpersonal responses are likely to elicit aggressive, competitive behaviors from others, thereby changing the "ecological niche" of the Type A. Such changes in the social environment are likely to elicit additional Type A behavior and associated physiological consequences. The results of several studies support this notion. The competitive behavior of Type A's in game situations, for example, has been found to prompt like responses from others and to be associated with greater cardiovascular arousal (Van Egeren, 1979a, 1979b; Van Egeren *et al.*, 1983). Further, competition has been found to elicit elevated levels of circulating catecholamines in Type A's, especially when the competitive partner is hostile (Friedman, Byers, Diamant, & Rosenman, 1975; D. C. Glass *et al.*, 1980). Thus, the competitive, aggressive behavior of Type A's is likely to propel stressful interpersonal cycles with negative physiological results.

Even this brief consideration of the situation choices and interpersonal behaviors of Type A's underscores the importance of contextual factors and reciprocal processes in understanding the Type A cognitive style and its potential role in hastening disease. When this set of interacting processes is considered, it is apparent that the Type A pattern represents a challenge and demand-engendering style (T. W. Smith & Anderson, 1986). In contrast to Type B persons, Type A's construct a subjectively and objectively challenging and demanding environment. They do this by choosing to enter demanding situations, appraising a given situation as involving more challenge, focusing their attention and suppressing negative sensations during task performance, eliciting challenging and demanding behavior from others via their own overt behaviors, and retrospectively evaluating their performance harshly. These processes may occur separately, but probably often occur in combinations. Further, they are likely to occur both in brief, isolated episodes and in habitual interaction patterns.

Two important results emerge from this interactional pattern. First, Type A's continuously construct, cognitively and objectively, an environment that elicits and perhaps even rewards additional Type A behavior. Second, Type A's continuously increase the frequency and duration of their contact with precisely those stimuli previously found to elicit exaggerated physiological responses in Type A's—challenges and demands. The cumulative, pathogenic effect of this cycle is an increase in the physiological reactivity believed to link Type A behavior and CHD. It is important to note that the cognitive behavior of the Type A is a key component in this interactional process.

From an even broader perspective, it is important to note that the cognitive interactional aspects of the TABP are embedded within other levels of organization. Other authors have suggested that the intrapersonal and interpersonal aspects of the TABP are best understood within the context of institutional and cultural factors (Margolis, McLeroy, Runyan, & Kaplan, 1983; Price, 1983). For example, characteristics of an individual's place of employment (e.g., employee expectations, stressfulness, number of subordinates) are associated with the prevalence of the TABP and the degree of negative health outcomes associated with this pattern (Matteson & Ivancevich, 1982; Mettlin, 1976). Further, cultural influences on the ways in which competitiveness and achievement are expressed may also influence the prevalence and characteristics of the TABP, as well as its relationship to health (J. B. Cohen *et al.*, 1979). By articulating the relationships among the physiological, cognitive, interpersonal, institutional and cultural aspects of the TABP, this area of research would move closer to the "biopsychosocial" perspective currently advocated in many areas of medicine and related disciplines (Engel, 1977; G. E. Schwartz, 1982).

Present Limitations and Future Directions

The present discussion must be qualified in two important respects. First, it is clear that the Type A pattern is not a unitary phenomenon. It is by definition a set of characteristics. The individual characteristics (e.g., hostility, time urgency) may not be equivalently related to physiological reactivity (Dembroski *et al.*, 1978) or CHD (Matthews, Glass, Rosenman, & Bortner, 1977). Further, the various methods of assessing TABP are only modestly intercorrelated (Chesney, Black, Chadwick, & Rosenman, 1981; Mathews, Krantz, Dembroski, & MacDougall, 1982) and demonstrate different degrees of association with other factors linked to CHD (e.g., anxiety, Chesney *et al.*, 1981; T. W. Smith, Houston, & Zurawski, 1983). Thus, any attempts to examine information processing aspects of the TABP must be careful to recognize potentially important differences among the components of the pattern and among its usual operational definitions.

Second, the present discussion focused solely on physiological reactivity as the mechanism linking behavior and disease. Other links are plausible, some of which may involve cognitive processes. For example, J. R. Jennings (1983) has argued that Type A's tendency toward focused attention may lead to the deterioration of other health-related resources. Multiplied over weeks and years, the Type A's task-focused style may produce insufficient attention to social cues, resulting in the deterioration of social networks among co-workers, friends, and family. These social networks might otherwise be useful in coping with stress (Cobb, 1976).

Recent research by Matthews and her colleagues (Matthews, Siegel, Kuller, Thompson, & Varat, 1983) describes another potential cognitive link between Type A behavior and CHD events. In a study of MI survivors, Matthews *et al.* found that Type A behavior was associated with a longer delay between the onset of symptoms and the appraisal of the symptoms as interfering with daily activities. Thus, part of the risk associated with Type A behavior may involve the individual's response to health cues. Interestingly, this response to MI symptoms is quite consistent with the suppression and denial of negative affect and fatigue characteristic of Type A's during task performance (Carver *et al.*, 1976; Pittner & Houston, 1980). Finally, the tendency for Type A's to perceive and react against threats to their control may influence the ways they respond to the prescriptions and proscriptions inherent in medical treatment. Such aspects of medical care are likely to represent threats to control for Type A's. As a result, they may be less compliant (Rhodewalt & Strube, 1985). Poor adherence to health care regimens could be a source of risk for Type A's, particularly those with developing CAD or established CHD. Thus, several potential additional links exist between the TABP and disease. These links also, however, suggest the importance of the Type A cognitive style.

These qualifications aside, the present perspective has potentially important implications for the modification of Type A behavior. Given the evidence establishing the pattern as a CHD risk factor, several clinical interventions for Type A behavior have been evaluated (see Suinn, 1982, for a review). Such interventions are complicated by several difficult issues. For example, it is unclear exactly which of the several components of the multifaceted Type A pattern are linked to CHD. Further, many of the Type A characteristics (e.g., achievement striving) are highly valued and often adaptive. Indeed, in a sample of academic psychologists, Matthews, Helmreich, Beane, and Lucker (1980) found Type A behavior to be positively associated with the quality of scholarly production, as measured by the number of annual citations of subjects' publications in the Social Science Citation Index. Thus, attempts to modify Type A behavior run the risk of reducing instrumental characteristics that may not actually represent a threat to health (Roskies, 1980). This situation is a likely source of difficult decisions for therapists. It is also likely to be a source of firm resistance from clients who do not feel sick. Indeed, the Type A may report deep enjoyment in creating challenges and meeting demands.

The value of modifying Type A behavior in post-MI patients, however, has recently been demonstrated. While Type A behavior is a significant risk factor in populations of healthy persons, it is a still better predictor of recurrent CHD events in persons already manifesting CHD symptoms (Jenkins, Zyzanski, & Rosenman, 1976). Modification of the TABP in this group seems important and appears to be feasible. Friedman *et al.* (1984) randomly assigned post-MI patients to either a condition including a Type A intervention along with usual cardiac care counseling (i.e., information on diet, exercise, and medication) or usual care alone. At the end of a 3-year follow-up, the intervention group evidenced significantly less Type A behavior. Further, the intervention group demonstrated approximately half the rate of recurrent cardiac events as that demonstrated by the control group ($p < .005$). These findings provide important evidence regarding the feasibility and value of such interventions, at least in high-risk populations.

Unfortunately, most of the interventions for Type A behavior lack an empirically based conceptual foundation. Rather they attempt simply to dampen physiological reactivity and/or educate clients concerning Type A behavior and possible alternative ways of behaving. The cognitive and interactional processes outlined here may provide the beginning of a list of empirically defined targets to be included in such interventions. If these cognitive and interactional processes are indeed as central to the Type A pattern as they appear, they could make fruitful starting points for therapeutic efforts. It is clear that additional research is needed, however. The cognitive and interactional processes already identified need further refinement. Also, it is unlikely that this list is exhaustive. Perhaps the greatest use of existing information processing paradigms would be the further mapping of the Type A cognitive style. For example, the efficiency with which Type A's perceive, encode, and recall information regarding environmental challenges and demands, or regarding self-relevant performances, could be assessed. A rich repertoire of cognitive tasks exists for such an assessment (e.g., Kihlstrom & Nasby, 1981). At the very least, such efforts would add consideration of an interesting individual difference variable to current paradigms in cognitive psychology. But greater benefits are obviously possible. Clarification of the cognitive psychology of Type A behavior could assist efforts to reduce the costs of our foremost health problem.

6

Social Skill and Anxiety: Information Processing Perspectives

THOMAS V. MERLUZZI
Department of Psychology
University of Notre Dame
Notre Dame, Indiana 46556

THOMAS E. RUDY
School of Medicine
University of Pittsburgh
Pittsburgh, Pennsylvania 15260

MARK J. KREJCI
Department of Psychology
University of Notre Dame
Notre Dame, Indiana 46556

Introduction

Although our social world is inherently complex, the research methods employed to understand how social stimuli are perceived, processed, represented, and acted upon have not kept pace with theoretical recognitions of this complexity (e.g., Festinger, 1954; Kelly, 1955; Triandis, 1972). Dissatisfaction with traditional research methods has led clinical and social psychologists to adopt more information-processing-type research methods in order to understand cognitive processes that may mediate various types of social experience and behavior. In fact, Simon (1976) has argued that the more traditional research methods and data analytic tools are incompatible with social psychologists' emerging interest in cognitive processes.

> The variance analysis paradigm, designed to test whether particular stimulus variables do or do not have an effect upon response variables, is largely useless for discovering and testing process models to explain what goes on between the appearance of a stimulus and performance of responses. These traditional methods are particularly inappropriate when both stimulus and responses are complex. (p. 261)

While most clinical psychologists would not disagree with Simon's emphasis on the importance of understanding the mediating processes that underlie social behavior, his dismissal of the analysis of variance model may not be as widely accepted. This reaction is perhaps in part due to the fact that, although methodology serves as the foundation for all clinical research endeavors, surprisingly little has been written about clinical research methods. Notable exceptions have been the *Handbook of Research Methods in Clinical Psychology* (Kendall & Butcher, 1982) and *Research Design in Clinical Psychology* (Kazdin, 1980); however, these texts did not address recent information processing methodological advances, especially as applied to social skills research.

The chapters in this volume aptly present the value of espousing the information processing paradigm (IPP) as an approach to understanding clinical phenomena. Therefore, little space will be devoted in this chapter to that subject. In the terminology of George Kelly's personal construct theory, the integration of the IPP with the study of psychopathology allows us to elaborate our constructs concerning the conduct of research in social anxiety. That is, we may be open to new perspectives that would not be possible without the IPP. Hopefully, this synthesis will not result in our mimicking the methods of experimental cognitive psychology, but rather, by operating within the major tenets of the IPP, result in our developing relevant methods of studying clinical phenomena.

In this chapter we present information processing approaches to social anxiety and social skill. Our approach to presenting this information will be to highlight research in three areas that have attempted to take into account the complexity of social stimuli while focusing on how the information in these complex stimuli are represented or processed. First, we will present a study conducted in 1984 that illustrates how social skill affects the social–cognitive schemata people use to represent social information. Consistent with Kelly (1955) and more recently Mischel (1981), who have advocated for the importance of knowing how people categorize and construe information, we have used multidimensional scaling (MDS) (see Rudy & Merluzzi, 1984a) to recover social cognitive schemata that people use to represent social information. Next we will present a study (Pryor & Merluzzi, 1984) that represents the use of scripted (see Schank & Abelson, 1977) social information. In that study we assessed the degree to which the availability of social scripts or sequential behavior patterns (i.e., first date) differs as a function of dating expertise or skill. Finally, we will present a study (Rudy & Merluzzi, 1984c) that assessed the manner in which complex social information is processed in order to make decisions leading to social responses. It should be noted that the studies presented here focus on how individuals process information contained in social situations and not on how social anxiety affects information processing about the self (see T. W. Smith, Ingram, & Brehm, 1983).

General Theoretical Perspective

From a theoretical perspective our research is based upon the notion that personality is the result of a dynamic interaction of the individual with the social environment. Early theorists such as Harry Stack Sullivan (1953) and George Kelly (1955) and more current theorists such as Mischel (1973) and Bandura (1977b) have endorsed the social constructive nature of personality. For Bandura, in particular, "psychological functioning is explained in terms of a continuous reciprocal interaction of personal and environmental determinants" (pp. 11–12). Also, Kelly's (1955) concept of *constructive alternativism* presents the individual as one who attempts to construe one's self and environment in a way that maximizes prediction of events. As we change and events change we must modify our constructions of events to maximize prediction. Thus, the manner in which we construe social events has an impact on our behavior, which affects the social context, which in turn affects our behavior, and so on. The result of this social cognitive process is the construction of schemata and interaction episodes that are used to predict and regulate future interaction.

While our program of research does not tap the dynamic interactive aspects of the social construction of personality, we have attempted to assess how people construe social situations, how scripted information is used, and how people integrate information in social decision making.

Methodological Perspectives

The methods chosen for each of the three topics (schemata, scripts, and decision making) have a rich history in psychological research. In the study dealing with recovering social cognitive schemata, we used methods of data collection and analyses (MDS) that have a strong psychometric tradition (Kruskal & Wish, 1978) and have been used in psychophysical and social research for years. The use of three-way MDS allows us to study how people represent social information while retaining individual differences such as social skill or anxiety level. Thus, we are able to determine how all subjects represent social information and, in particular, how individuals varying in social skill or anxiety differ in their relative emphasis of certain kinds of social information. A 1983 issue of *Applied Psychological Measurement* (Vol. 7) and, in particular, an article by L. E. Jones (1983) in that issue illustrate the usefulness of MDS methods of data collection and analysis.

Similarly, the script has been a well-researched and useful concept in representing abstract knowledge structures (Abelson, 1981). For example, Bower *et al.* (1979), Nottenburg and Shoben (1980) and Graesser, Woll, Kowalski, and Smith (1980) have studied the properties, structure, and content of scripted information. Additionally, its utility for studying clinical phenomena has been suggested by Landau and Goldfried (1981). An attempt was made to follow, to a great extent, the methods of examining the general content and organization of scripted information found in Bower *et al.* (1979). Finally, a speed-sorting task was conducted to test some of the assumptions of Abelson's strong versus weak scripts.

In the decision-making study, social decision models were derived from methods suggested by N. T. Anderson (1974a, 1974b). These methods of recovering decision models take into account the simultaneous processing of components of social situations and emphasize how subjects integrate information contained in social situations.

Role of Emotion

There are many treatises on the roles of cognition and emotion (see Winfrey & Goldfried, chapter 12, this volume, for an overview). Therefore, we will gracefully sidestep the controversy and indicate that we side with Fiske (1981), who proposed a process she referred to as "schema triggered affect." While Fiske and her colleagues have studied affect concerning persons, we might extrapolate from her findings and apply these to total social situations. That is, complex social situations may consist of a person with certain attributes, an interaction with that person based on some situation-specific social behavior, and a setting or context. Thus, in our research on assertion as a social skill, an unreasonable request made by a high-status person may trigger a different emotional reaction than that same request delivered by a low-status person. However, our decision-modeling research suggests that it is not just the target *person* that would determine the affective response but also the type of behavior the target person is displaying. *Thus, a simple additive or component model would not explain the data as well as a complex schemata or interactive model.* Also, as the reader will discover in the schema section, low-skilled subjects will at times neglect or not emphasize emotion or arousal in planning a response to social situations. Thus, while arousal may be triggered by difficult social situations, it may be eschewed in favor of other information in the selection of social responses.

In the script research we might speculate that, while socially skilled and socially anxious individuals might share the same script or knowledge structure, they would differ in the predictability of events. Moreover, the skilled person would have more subroutines in the script to handle aberrations that may occur in the scripted sequence. Thus, there may be some matching of the behavior sequence with the script contained in memory. Affect may be triggered by a poor match; further, the uncertainty as a function of having weak scripts or not having subroutines to handle aberrations may also trigger affective responses.

In sum, an extrapolation of the schema-triggered approach offered by Fiske (1981) here suggests that certain information in social situations may fit a schema which provokes affect. This information may be used, which may in turn lead to some action, plan, or goal.

Models of Social Anxiety and Skill

Prior to embarking on a presentation of the research we will present an overview of existing models of social anxiety. This overview is intended to frame the information processing approaches in the context of existing models of social anxiety.

Prevalent models of social anxiety may be divided into four categories: conditioning, skills deficit, social learning, and cognitive. The conditioning model has as its basis the classical conditioning of fear responses. Avoidance and fear of social interaction is learned through the association of early fear-provoking situations with social interaction. Theoretically, mere exposure to social interaction should decrease the fear response. While many people may reduce social inhibition by mere exposure to social interaction, avoidance also may contribute to the persistence of the fears by reducing exposure to social interactions. This avoidance may be evident in the person's life-style, choice of occupation, recreation and leisure, and the like. If one needs therapy for social anxiety, the treatment consistent with the conditioning model is systematic desensitization or flooding.

The skills-deficit model has used as its basis the operant paradigm. Social anxiety is viewed as a deficiency in learnable skills. The socially anxious person's learning environment may be construed as one that did not reinforce (or punished) socially skilled behaviors. The persistence of the problem may be a result of the socially anxious person's inability to execute socially skilled behaviors that will be reinforced.

The social learning models are an extension and liberalization of the operant model. Essentially, the etiology of social anxiety may be viewed in terms of poor role models whereby the observational learning sequence as outlined by Bandura (1977b) results in the acquisition of withdrawn or phobic-like behaviors in children. The consequences and reinforcing value of our social behavior may, as adults, maintain social phobias for certain types of social situations. From a social learning perspective, disinhibition of social anxiety can occur by seeing others engage in the threatening behavior without adverse consequences. Treatments based on modeling attempt to change the behavior expectancy and/or outcome expectancy. In fact, there is some evidence to indicate that behavioral differences between socially anxious and nonsocially anxious people may be less prominent than differences in self-evaluation and outcome expectancies (see C. R. Glass & Merluzzi, 1981).

The cognitive approach to social anxiety is to a great extent an extension of the social learning approach in that it relies on principles that are consistent with social learning theory such as the acquisition and cognitive representation of information. However, the cognitive approach may extend farther to include methods and concepts from experimental cognitive psychology. The obvious advantage to this extension is, as the chapters in this book illustrate, the ability to draw on the paradigm that guides these efforts (i.e., the IPP) and the adaptation of models and methods for the study of clinical phenomena. One of the hazards is that the information processing approach is not well equipped to account for the etiology of social anxiety. However, if one considers the logical connection between cognitive psychology and social learning theory, then the problem of etiology is solved. In fact, D. Hamilton (1979) has proposed an information processing model of social anxiety that takes into account the parent–child interaction as an explanation for information processing deficits.

What may be intriguing about the cognitive or information processing extension of social learning theory is that there may arise out of this research new implications for treatment that are not obvious from the research that takes an exclusive classical conditioning or operant model perspective. Further, the methods used in experimental cognitive psychology may help elaborate some principles contained in social learning theory (see Bower, 1978). For example, in this chapter we will be presenting data in three areas—schemata, scripts, and decision making—that have direct relevance for social learning theory and self-regulation and have counterparts in experimental cognitive psychology.

Finally, in the concluding section at the end of this chapter we will speculate on how information about the self may influence the course of information processing. In particular, we will focus on control theory as an approach that may integrate information processing and social learning theory.

Research in Schema Recovery, Scripts, and Decision Making

In the next sections we will briefly review three research strategies that appear to hold promise in advancing social skills research methods from an information processing perspective: (a) recovery of schemata via MDS, (b) scripted information, and (c) decision-making approaches. Additionally, we will summarize three empirical investigations from our laboratory that illustrate the potential utility of these methods.

Multidimensional Scaling and Its Application to Social Skills Research

The first discussions of MDS were presented by Richardson (1938) and Young and Householder (1938). However, it was not until the work of Shepard (1962) and Kruskal (1964) that MDS was seen as an applicable research method in psychology. During the past 20 years, MDS research methods have been effectively applied in numerous areas of psychological research, including consumer, social, cognitive, clinical, and vocational psychology.

Multidimensional scaling has been defined as "a body of knowledge involving (1) a set of statistical techniques for estimating the parameters in and assessing the fit of various spatial distance models for proximity or preference data and (2) the coordinate representations of stimulus structure that result from such statistical techniques" (M. L. Davison, 1983, p. 373). Thus, like factor analysis, MDS refers to a wide collection of mathematical techniques that enable the investigator to uncover "hidden structure" in a data base. The purpose of this section is not to provide a description of MDS statistical techniques, but rather to provide an overview of how MDS may provide unique information regarding social processes, that is, information that cannot be obtained from other more traditional research approaches. Several good, nontechnical descriptions of MDS statistical approaches are already available (e.g., Carroll & Arabie, 1980; Kruskal & Wish, 1978: Schiffman, Reynolds, & Young, 1981), and we (Rudy & Merluzzi, 1984b) have published a comprehensive discussion of designing and analyzing MDS experiments, with a special focus on the application of MDS to social skills research.

In general, applications of MDS research methods to social phenomena have attempted to investigate the structure of individuals' perceptions and conceptions about themselves and others, interpersonal relationships, social episodes, social situations, and attributions. A leading pioneer in this research has been Lawrence Jones (e.g., M. L. Davison & Jones, 1976; L. E. Jones, 1982; L. E. Jones & Young, 1972), who has effectively linked the methodology of MDS with several theories of interpersonal perception and social cognition. Based on the assumption that people organize and summarize their knowledge about relevant social domains (e.g., persons, social environments, interpersonal behaviors, and social roles) into cognitive structures, and that these cognitive structures in turn shape the perception, encoding, and interpretation of future inputs from those domains, L. E. Jones (1983) asserts that the desired representation of an individual's social structure can be, in part, achieved by MDS. More specifically, by simply asking an individual to make general similarity judgments (the most frequent unit of analysis in MDS) about social stimuli, the application of MDS statistical analyses to those similarity judgments can yield a wealth of information about the individual's social constructs. Research by Jones and his colleagues (e.g., M. L.

Davison & Jones, 1976; L. E. Jones & Young, 1972) and other investigators (e.g., Forgas, 1978; Kaman, Shiklar, & Hautaluoma, 1979; Wish, 1976) has demonstrated that MDS methods can contribute directly to our understanding of the cognitive states and processes that may mediate interpersonal behavior.

Although MDS methodology has had a rich 12-year history in social-psychological research, its applicability to clinical research has generally not been recognized. There are, however, some exceptions. Sprouse and Brush (1980) and Stiles, Tupler, and Carpenter (1982) have demonstrated that MDS methods can be effectively utilized to understand the nature and development of interpersonal perceptions for members of psychotherapy groups. Several more assessment-oriented studies also suggest that MDS methods may be useful from the standpoint of an information processing approach to psychopathology. For example, R. Landau (1980) found that MDS effectively uncovered cognitive schemata that discriminated between subjects with dog phobia and those without, and Rudy *et al.* (1982) found significant differences between low- and high-assertive subjects' perceptions of both positive and negative types of assertion situations.

Using multidimensional scaling to assess social–cognitive schemata

We will now briefly review one in a series of studies that we (Rudy & Merluzzi, 1984a) have conducted to assess the utility of MDS methods to measure cognitive schemata that may be important in assertiveness. The current emphasis on cognitive interventions to remediate social anxiety and nonassertive behavior has established the need for methodological studies regarding cognitive assessment methods and measures of change (C. R. Glass & Merluzzi, 1981).

The Conflict Resolution Inventory (CRI), developed by McFall and Lillesand (1971), was used to test 60 undergraduate males for level of assertiveness. Following a procedure outlined by R. M. Schwartz and Gottman (1976), 6 low-assertive, 6 moderate-assertive, and 6 high-assertive subjects were selected to complete the rest of the experiment.

The primary stimuli used in this experiment were 18 assertion vignettes that were developed from a previous study (Rudy *et al.,* 1982). The stimuli were factorially arranged utilizing three Types of Assertion (someone asking to borrow $25, someone asking you to change tables, and someone cutting in front of you while you are waiting in line) by three Target Persons (intimates, friends and acquaintances, and status/authority people) by two Environmental Contexts (formal and informal). Thus, a three (Type of Assertion) by three (Target Person) by two (Environment) full factorial design was employed. In addition to the 18 assertion vignettes, 12 bipolar scales were also used to aid in the interpretation of the MDS stimulus space.

The 18 assertion vignettes were used to create three separate response booklets. The first booklet consisted of a single page that contained all 18 assertion vignettes. In this booklet subjects were instructed to create a single, absolute rank-ordering of the situations from the perspective of the difficulty of responding to each situation. More specifically, subjects were asked to assign the number 1 to the situation they felt would be the easiest one for them to respond to through 18, the situation they felt would be the most difficult for them to respond to (ties were not allowed). The second booklet also consisted of a single page that contained all 18 of the assertion vignettes. In this booklet, subjects were again requested to create a single rank-ordering of the situations; however, this time rankings were from 1 to 18 in terms of their likelihood of refusing to comply in each situation. The third booklet contained the 18 vignettes and 12 bipolar rating scales. Next, six 18 by 18 symmetric proximity matrices were created and then processed by the ALSCAL computer program (Takane, Young, & deLeeuw, 1977), and a nonmetric INDSCAL analysis (Carroll & Chang, 1970) was conducted. A two-dimensional solution appeared to be adequate for these data and accounted for 55.2% of the total variance in the eight matrices (a three-dimensional solution added only 1.4% more variance accounted for).

The mean ratings on 12 bipolar scales were used to aid in the interpretation of the INDSCAL group stimulus space. The approach most commonly used to help interpret MDS stimulus spaces is based on a multiple regression or vector model (Kruskal & Wish, 1978). Both multiple regression and canonical correlation procedures were used to interpret the group space that resulted from the INDS-

TABLE 1
Multiple Regression of Bipolar Ratings on INDSCAL Dimensions

	Regression weights (direction cosines)		
Bipolar scales	Dim. 1	Dim. 2	*R*
Socially appropriate vs. socially inappropriate	−.995	−.099	.810***
Informal vs. formal	.263	.965	.588*
Irritating vs. nonirritating	.085	.996	.826***
Threatening vs. nonthreatening	.228	.974	.586*
Tense vs. relaxed	.124	.992	.751**
Exactly equal power vs. very unequal power	−.809	.588	.716**
Cooperative vs. competitive	.023	−1.000	.835***
Fair vs. unfair	−.148	−.989	.733**
Easy vs. difficult	−.074	−.997	.562
Similar roles and behavior vs. different roles and behavior	−.138	−.990	.565
Unfamiliar vs. familiar	.384	−.923	.561
Friendly vs. hostile	.301	−.953	.797***

*$p < .05$.
**$p < .01$.
***$p < .001$.

CAL analysis of the six proximity matrices. Table 1 contains the results of these analyses. The results of the multiple regression analyses indicated that (a) there were a number of significant multiple correlations and (b) a number of scales had high regression weights on one dimension matched with low regression weights on the other. Thus, the INDSCAL dimensions appeared to be psychologically meaningful, unique, and could be interpreted in an objective manner.

Inspection of the high regression weights contained in Table 1 for Dimension 1 indicates that this dimension was recovered well by the social appropriateness bipolar. The ANOVA main effects for Dimension 1 indicated that the stimulus coordinates were primarily discriminating the levels of the Person factor, $F(2,12) = 10.62$, $p < .002$. The relatively high regression weight for the exactly equal power versus very unequal power bipolar also confirmed that this dimension was apparently addressing the status level of the target person. Thus, it appeared that this dimension could be interpreted as a social appropriateness/status dimension.

As displayed in Table 1, five bipolar scales have high loadings on Dimension 2. These results indicated that the stimuli at one end of this dimension were rated as competitive, irritating, tense, unfair, and hostile; and at the other end, as cooperative, nonirritating, relaxed, fair, and friendly. In sum, these results suggested that this dimension reflected the degree of unreasonableness, hostility, and emotional arousal that subjects perceived in the 18 assertion vignettes. Taken together, this dimension could perhaps best be labeled as an arousal/antagonism dimension.

In addition to providing a group stimulus space for these 18 assertion vignettes for each of the three experimental groups and the two rank-ordering tasks, the INDSCAL analysis also provided a set of dimension weights that indicated how important the two dimensions were in subjects' judgments of the assertion situations. The raw and normalized dimension weights that resulted from this INDSCAL analysis are presented in Table 2. Inspection of Table 2 indicates that all three experimental groups for both ranking tasks used both dimensions to some degree.

A closer examination of the normalized dimension weights for the difficulty-of-responding task indicated that the low and high experimental groups were not significantly different from each other in their use of these two dimensions. These two groups slightly weighted Dimension 1 as more important, yet both the social appropriateness/status and the arousal/antagonism dimensions were important to them as they made their difficulty-of-responding judgments. On the other hand, in the moderate assertives' difficulty-of-responding judgments, their use of Dimension 1 was significantly less, and their use of Dimension 2 was significantly greater than predicted by chance (a Monte-Carlo-type procedure was conducted to test for significantly different dimension weights; see Rudy and Merluzzi, 1984b, for more details). Apparently, then, the social appropriateness/status dimension was not used as much by this group. Rather, they felt

TABLE 2
INDSCAL Dimension Weights for the Two Ranking Task and the Four Experimental Groups

Group	Task	Dimension 1	Dimension 2	Weight ratios (Dim. 1/Dim. 2)	RSQ
Low	Difficulty of responding	.451 (.793)	.347 (.610)	1.30	.324
	Likelihood of refusing	.775 (.940)*	.280 (.399)**	2.77	.678
Moderate	Difficulty of responding	.478 (.579)***	.666 (.815)***	0.71	.667
	Likelihood of refusing	.558 (.700)	.569 (.714)	0.98	.635
High	Difficulty of responding	.548 (.713)	.539 (.701)	1.02	.592
	Likelihood of refusing	.492 (.763)	.417 (.646)	1.18	.416

Note. Numbers in parentheses are normalized dimension weights so that their sum of squares equals 1.
*$p < .05$.
**$p < .010$.
***$p < .001$.

that the level of arousal/antagonism in the situations was a more important concept as they made their difficulty-of-responding judgments.

When the weight ratios for the likelihood-of-refusing task were examined (Table 2) several major shifts occurred. First of all, the importance of the social appropriateness/status dimension increased for all three experimental groups. Further, inspection of Table 2 revealed that this dimension was no longer significantly less important for any of the experimental groups. And lastly, the arousal/antagonism dimension (Dimension 2) was no longer significantly more important for the moderate group. Thus, it can be concluded that the moderate- and high-assertive groups were not significantly different from each other in their use of these two dimensions. Furthermore, inspection of their weight ratios indicated that the subjects in these two groups weighted both dimensions as approximately equal in importance in making their likelihood-of-refusing judgments.

More important, however, was the finding that the low assertives weighted the social appropriateness/status dimension as significantly more important and the arousal/antagonism dimension as significantly less important. Examination of their normalized dimension weights suggested that they almost exclusively used the social appropriateness/status dimension in making their likelihood-of-refusing judgments. Additionally, inspection of the weight ratios for the low group contained in Table 2 indicated a large increase in the importance of Dimension 1 for the likelihood-of-refusing task when compared to the difficulty-of-responding task.

In sum, the above results suggested that what had occurred in this INDSCAL analysis was analogous to a task by group interaction. The low-assertive group appeared to have been more affected by the likelihood-of-refusing task than were the moderate- and high-assertive groups. This became clearer when the weight ratios are examined. As displayed in Table 2, the weight ratios were calculated by dividing the weight for Dimension 1 by the weight for Dimension 2. Thus, as the size of this ratio increased, so too did the importance placed on Dimension 1 relative to Dimension 2. The low experimental group had a large increase in their weight ratio for the likelihood-of-refusing task; however, only a slight increase occurred for the moderate and high experimental groups. In other words, the utilization of the common dimensions between the two ranking tasks did not change much for the moderate and high groups but did change for the low assertive group.

In general, the results of this study offered empirical support to the hypothesized value of using MDS methods to assess the cognitive constructs that may facilitate or inhibit assertive behavior. Additionally, the similarity between high- and low-assertive subjects' dimension weights on the difficulty ranking task suggests that lower assertive individuals have ''access'' to the information that may be important in processing social information but may eschew the arousal/antagonism dimension in favor of the status-of-the-target dimension when contemplating the likelihood of behaving assertively. These findings do suggest that low assertives are not cognitively deficient but do narrow their schema to a single dimension when assessing their intention to behave assertively. Future research might focus on the link between assessing the likelihood of asserting and actual assertive behavior.

Social Scripts

Schank and Abelson (1977) described a script as a stereotyped sequence of behaviors for a particular event. Scripts for many activities are stored in memory (e.g., getting ready for work, going to a restaurant) and may represent cohesive sequences of events that are highly predictable. The utility of scripts is obvious: We use them to plan our behavior in variety of situations; thus, they help us understand behaviors in situations and serve as guideposts for our own behavior. Also, while several scripts may be brought to bear on one situation, we may tend to choose the most ''available'' script. Further, Abelson (1981) has described strong and weak scripts: Strong scripts occur in an orderly temporal sequence where the events are causally linked. For example, a restaurant script would be a strong script where "looking at the menu" would precede "ordering food", which would precede "receiving food." In that script the order is rather fixed and the events are to a great extent causally linked.

Our (Pryor & Merluzzi, 1984) research has focused on scripts that are of particular relevance to the college population: "getting a date" and "going on a first date." The importance of these scripts is well documented in surveys of the concerns of college students. For example, Arkowitz, Hinton, Perl, and Himandi (1978) reported that one-third of college men and women sampled said that they were somewhat or very anxious concerning dating. Martinson and Zerface (1970) reported that dating problems ranked higher than career choice among the students they sampled.

Scripts may be construed as a consensual set of behaviors and expectancies that allow individuals to interact smoothly. We chose *dating expertise* as an individual difference variable that may be related to the use of dating scripts. If one has had more experience in dating, then this expertise may lead to having a stronger script and in general that script may be associated with more cohesive cognitive organization than novices' knowledge (Fiske, Kinder, & Larter, 1983). This conclusion was based on the notion that the temporal and causal connections may be enhanced or strengthened by dating experience. On the other hand, we did not anticipate any content differences as a function of dating expertise because we anticipated that knowledge of dating can be acquired vicariously.

In the first two studies conducted we examined the general content and organization of scripts concerning "getting a date" and "first date." Subjects generated about 20 actions that occur on a first date and when a male asks a female out. Protocols were tabulated and scripts formed by putting similar actions together. There was a good deal of general agreement concerning the actions and events listed. In fact, correlations indicated that both high and low dating frequency subjects and both males and females mentioned the same actions. In further analyses a different set of subjects were instructed to place slash marks in the script where they perceived boundaries between parts of the story. Regardless of their dating frequency, subjects tended to see similar components in the scripts. This was evidenced by a consistency in how subjects divided the script into logical units.

The findings noted above are consistent with those of Bower *et al.* (1979) with respect to the consensual nature of the content and structure of the script. We then sought to test whether these consensually shared scripts would be used differently by expert daters (those who have had many dates with different people) and novice daters. Based on Fiske *et al.* (1983) we proposed that expert daters might have a more cohesive cognitive representation of the scripts and would be able to use them in tasks involving processing script-relevant information.

We defined experts as those who reported having dated six or more different people in the last year. Novices were those who dated three or fewer different people in the past year. Our pilot study (Pryor & Merluzzi, 1984) included 8 expert and 11 novice males.

Subjects were first given ‘‘attending a lecture’’ and ‘‘getting up in the morning’’ scripts to familiarize them with the task. Subjects were given a speed sorting task in which they were given the components of each of four scripts on index cards and sorted the scripts into what they thought was the correct order. Each of the four sorts was timed.

All subjects' sorts corresponded highly with the original script order. We found little or no differences in processing time between novices and experts on the scripts unrelated to dating and no differences in sequence were noted between experts and novices. In terms of processing time for the dating scripts, we found that experts sorted scripts into the appropriate orders on the average of 22.5 seconds faster than novices, a difference that was statistically significant. We also obtained a main effect of scripts, which simply reflected the fact that the ‘‘first date’’ scripts contained more items than the ‘‘getting a date’’ script.

These pilot study data confirm that the content and organization of scripts did not vary as a function of dating expertise. On the other hand, it appears that experts as opposed to novices find it easier to use their cognitive representation of scripts when required to impose order on a random sequence of events related to dating. We can infer that experts have more cohesive scripts based on more experience with the scripted behavior sequence. Further, we can speculate that experts compared to novices are more likely to ‘‘chunk’’ the scripted behaviors (i.e., use larger units to represent behavior sequences in the script), thus being able to have more information in working memory to make comparisons between the correct order and the random sequence. Similarly, expertise may enhance script availability (Kahneman, Slovic, & Tversky, 1982). In sum, the expert dater may not differ from the novices in terms of the content of scripts concerning dating but may differ in availability and ease of use. Further research in this area will focus on abberations and interruptions in dating scripts.

Decision-Making Approaches

Decision making is usually conceptualized as a multistage process. First, the problem is represented, that is, goals, alternative actions, possible events, and potential outcomes are defined. Second, the probabilities and/or utilities of events and consequences are judged. Third, the actions are evaluated in terms of the probabilities and utilities of their potential consequences. Finally, an action is chosen according to the decision criterion used by the decision maker.

Dissatisfaction with traditional models of social skills, which view social skills deficits as the result of either maladaptive anxiety (e.g., Wolpe & Lazarus,

1966) or the lack of necessary skills for effective social behavior (e.g., A. A. Lazarus, 1971), has led several researchers to propose that social skills are, at least in part, determined by the types of decision-making strategies that people employ in social situations. For example, Fiedler and Beach (1978) have examined the feasibility of casting assertive behavior into an expectancy/decision-making model. Specifically, they proposed that people may weigh the consequences that might follow assertive or nonassertive behavior and then choose the most favorable course. Indeed, Fielder and Beach found that, when faced with unreasonable requests, significant differences between subjects choosing refusal or compliance were found as a function of their estimates of the probability that specific consequences might occur. No differences, however, were found in the value or importance attributed to these consequences. These findings, as well as those of Kuperminc and Heimberg (1983), suggest that decision making, an information processing type of task, may be an important cognitive mediator between experiencing social situations and the expression of assertive behavior. Further, the "skills deficit" observed in nonassertiveness may be related to an information processing deficit, that is, the inability to accurately estimate the consequences of assertion.

Information Integration Research in Social Decision Making

Working within the framework of "information integration theory (IIT)," Anderson and his colleagues have shown that simple algebraic models describe information use quite well in an impressive variety of judgmental, decision making, attitudinal, and perceptual tasks (e.g., N. T. Anderson, 1974a, 1974b). Basically, information integration approaches to decision making are concerned with establishing structural models, that is, describing the relationship between stimulus and response, or between input and output.

Information integration theory differs markedly from many expectancy value models of decision making which draw upon a compositional or "build-up" approach. The subjective expectancy approaches to decision making assume that the total utility for some multiattribute stimulus can be found as a weighted sum of the stimulus' perceived attribute levels and associated value ratings, as separately judged by the respondent (Wilkie & Pessemier, 1973). In contrast, IIT, using a more realistic format, is based on a decompositional approach in which respondents react to a set of total profile descriptions. It is the job of the researcher to find some type of composition rule (e.g., an additive one) that is most consistent with the respondent's overall preferences. This approach provides a more satisfactory formulation of decision making under uncertainty. It does not postulate that people's behavior is determined by the following process: (a) assigning utilities and subjective probabilities to outcomes and events, respectively, (b) multiplying the utility of each outcome by its subjective probability of occurrence, and (c) choosing the alternative for which the sum of these products is maximal (D. H. Krantz & Tversky, 1971). For this reason, the application of subjective expected utility models does not seem appropriate in the decision modeling of such a complex phenomenon as assertion. In fact, regression approaches to modeling human judgment have in general been criticized (Hoffman, 1968; Ytema & Torgerson, 1961). Two of the most frequently highlighted shortcomings of these models have been (a) their difficulty to detect configuralities and (b) the use of the correlation between the proposed model and data as an index by which to measure the correctness of a theoretical model. M. H. Birnbaum (1973), for example, has shown that under some conditions the wrong model can yield higher correlations than the appropriate model.

To our knowledge, IIT has not been applied to the study of decision making in complex social situations. To test the applicability of integration theory as an information processing method of assessing social skill, we (Rudy & Merluzzi, 1984c) conducted a pilot study that involved 20 undergraduate males. Our basic experimental procedure and findings are outlined below.

The stimuli judged in this experiment consisted of 32 of the 84 assertion vignettes created from the results obtained by Rudy *et al.* (1982). Four types of assertion situations were chosen: paying a compliment, defending someone being verbally abused, someone cutting in front of you while you are waiting in line, and someone asking to borrow $25. These four types of assertion were selected because subjects in a pilot study noted them as increasingly more difficult. These assertion situations were combined with four different types of target persons (intimates, friends and acquaintances, service workers, and status/authority persons) and two types of environmental situations (formal and informal). This process resulted in a four (Type of Assertion) by four (Target Persons) by two (Environments) full factorial design.

Each of the 32 vignettes was printed on the top of separate pages. If the vignette portrayed a negative assertion situation, the question "How easy or difficult would it be for you to refuse to comply in this situation?" followed. If it was a positive assertion situation, the question "How easy or difficult would it be for you to speak out in this situation?" followed. Below each question a 100-point rating scale ranging from very easy (0) to very difficult (100) was printed. Multiple random orders were created, and subjects rated the 32 assertion vignettes three times over a 3-week period.

A major consideration and prerequisite to meaningful decision modeling and other statistical analyses is the response consistency of subjects. Pearson product moment correlations computed for difficulty ratings over the three replications indicated that a majority of subjects (65%) displayed a high degree of consistency in their difficulty ratings. For these subjects, all r values were greater than .7 ($p < .0001$). A smaller group of subjects (20%) can be described as marginally consistent. Their average r values ranged from .5 to .7, which were significant

TABLE 3
Group ANOVA for Difficulty Ratings

Variable	*SS*	*df*	E
Replications (R)	150.20	2	0.16
Type (T)	27485.03	3	33.43**
Person (P)	162007.81	3	35.39**
Environment (E)	19924.08	1	12.72*
R × T	1976.41	6	0.93
R × P	1936.84	6	1.39
R × E	997.44	2	2.51
T × P	321136.44	9	33.08**
T × E	5907.58	3	2.45
P × E	1848.32	3	1.28
R × T × P	4502.65	18	0.87
R × T × E	1073.99	6	0.69
R × P × E	1424.66	6	0.96
T × P × E	41473.38	9	5.91**
R × T × P × E	3974.28	18	1.22

*$p < .01$.
**$p < .001$.

at the .001 level. Although three subjects were classified as inconsistent (their average r values were less than .5), even these subjects displayed rather high consistency between two replications. Results for two of these three subjects suggested practice helped them develop more consistency. In sum, these correlations indicated that subjects understood the difficulty rating task required of them, the stimuli rated were apparently unambiguous, and thus respectable internal reliability was achieved. Additionally, correlations of this magnitude suggested that many of the subjects utilized a well-developed decision rule or strategy in their assessment of the degree of difficulty in assertion situations.

Subjects' rating responses were submitted to an overall repeated measures analysis of variance, with Types of Assertion (T), Target Persons (P), Environmental Contexts (E), and Replications (R) considered as fixed factors. The results of this analysis are displayed in Table 3. Because we were most concerned with being able to conduct individual ANOVAs, the fact that the Replications factor was not nonsignificant and did not significantly interact with any of the other factors provided support for an additive repeated measures model. Given these findings, each subject's difficulty ratings were submitted to a repeated measures ANOVA, with the three replications treated as the within subjects factor. These analyses allowed us to determine how each subject employed the T, P, and E components of the assertion vignettes in deciding whether to respond to a specific situation in an assertive manner.

TABLE 4
Omega Squared Estimates for Each Subject

Subject	T	P	E	T × P	T × E	P × E	T × P × E	Total
1	.228	.130	.047	.329	.017	.017	.069	.837
2	.133	.055	.052	.359	.002	.010	.178	.789
3	.083	.145	.000	.370	.003	.000	.072	.673
4	.207	.099	.051	.027	.010	.013	.050	.457
5	.455	.014	.000	.267	.010	.002	.062	.810
6	.091	.169	.075	.253	.036	.021	.109	.754
7	.046	.218	.000	.288	.084	.000	.222	.858
8	.342	.107	.005	.369	.002	.015	.053	.893
9	.626	.103	.000	.227	.000	.003	.004	.963
10	.170	.337	.110	.044	.015	.009	.119	.804
11	.061	.152	.000	.431	.001	.012	.095	.752
12	.000	.006	.058	.285	.043	.096	.042	.530
13	.434	.071	.052	.240	.000	.024	.075	.896
14	.174	.068	.008	.283	.033	.002	.050	.618
15	.415	.000	.000	.495	.000	.001	.019	.930
16	.213	.126	.000	.186	.000	.002	.120	.647
17	.342	.035	.000	.396	.000	.003	.007	.783
18	.037	.050	.000	.198	.035	.001	.051	.372
19	.140	.331	.027	.090	.036	.000	.122	.746
20	.163	.204	.009	.225	.000	.000	.043	.644

Because effects that are significant in the analysis of variance may be quite insignificant in terms of the amount of variance they account for, it is often more useful to look at the proportion of variance estimates (omega squared) for each subject (Hays, 1973). Computational procedures for computing omega squared for components in a repeated measures ANOVA are given by Dodd and Schultz (1973). The proportion of variance estimates for each subject are presented in Table 4. Immediately apparent were the large differences between subjects. For example, the omega squared values for the Type component range from .626 for Subject 9 to .000 for Subject 12.

Similar to the results displayed in Table 3, the omega squared results contained in Table 4 demonstrated the strength of the T × P interaction effects. For 85% of the subjects, their T × P omega squared scores accounted for more than 10% of the total variance. Thus, many of these were apparently processing the assertion information in a configural or multiplicative manner. Table 4 also demonstrated the importance of the Type and Person components. For 70% of the subjects, component T accounted for more than 10% of the total variance. Of somewhat lesser importance was the P component. This component accounted for more than 10% of the variance for 55% of the subjects.

The E, T × E, P × E, and T × P × E effects were far less important. Only

25% of the subjects had omega squared scores above .10 for T × P × E. Only one subject had an omega score above .1 for the E factor, and none of the subjects had omega scores above .1 for the T × E and P × E effects. As expected, subjects classified as inconsistant (4, 12, 18) have the lowest omega squared totals.

The results of this study appear to substantiate the hypothesis that, in social situations requiring an assertive expression, an individuals' behavior (at least decision behavior) is functionally related to the social context of the interpersonal interaction. Also, the results suggest a stimulus-specificity theory of assertiviness. That is, an individual who decides to be assertive in one interpersonal context may not choose to be assertive in a different interpersonal environment. Further, the social environment seems to be determined by a multiplicative relationship between the type of assertion and the target person. That is, the difficulty in responding assertively was jointly determined by the target person in the situation and the type of assertive behavior called for in the situation.

Conclusion: Control Processes in Social Skill–Dynamic Information Processing

In this chapter we have related three studies that have attempted to study social skill from an information processing perspective. The studies reported can be construed as tapping various aspects of social interaction. In the case of the MDS study we assessed the general dimensions used to construe social situations and determine response probability; in the information integration study we assessed how complex information is processed in social decision making; in the script research we assessed the strength of certain behavior sequences as a function of expertise. In each instance we have taken a glimpse at a portion of what might be described as the complexity of human social interaction. However, our research does not account for the dynamic, interactive nature of social interaction and does not account for "on-line" assessment of social information.

A more innovative approach to the study of social skill and anxiety would integrate the research we have conducted into a broader theoretical framework that would include the dynamic interactive processes and, at the same time, include the information processing perspective. A control theory model developed by Powers (1973) and elaborated upon by Carver and Scheier (1983) may provide the framework that can guide these research efforts. Essentially, the central theory proposed by Carver and Scheier (1983) has as its basis the self-regulation of behavior based on several components, and framed within a negative feedback loop the components are as follows: (a) an assessment or perception of a situation; (b) a comparison of the perception with some reference point, standard, or expectation; (c) an action to reduce the discrepancy between the perception and the reference point; (d) an assessment of the impact of the action; and (e) an assessment or perception of the situation. This last step closes the feedback loop and, in essence, starts the cycle again.

The major thrust of control theory, in the research of Carver and Scheier, has focused on the comparison processes and the impact of self-focused attention on discrepancy reduction. In terms of social anxiety these processes would be occurring "on-line" in the sense that our social performance would be checked against our expectancies or goals in a situation, and our behavior would be adjusted to reduce the discrepancy between our perception of how the social interaction is proceeding and our goals or expectations. These control processes occur at various levels; thus, there is a hierarchy of feedback systems. At lower levels the control processes might involve regulation of physical or motoric responses. For example, gesturing friendship by touching would involve control of muscles and movement of the hand at one level and have more abstract control functions at a more superordinate level. At the superordinate level the individual may be trying to control the display of being a sensitive caring person. If our perception of the impact of our actions is discrepant from our goal, we might engage in other actions to reduce the discrepancy or we might withdraw (as in the learned helplessness model) mentally or physically. For example, if the person who was the recipient of a "friendly" touch were to show discomfort or subtle cues that touching was inappropriate, we could try another means of gesturing friendship. However, after repeated efforts failed we could withdraw from discrepancy reduction efforts.

From this brief discussion of control theory as it relates to social skill, it is evident that expectancies with respect to social interaction can vary as a function of social skill. Thus, low expectancies in the case of socially anxious persons, can lead to extreme efforts for discrepancy reduction and in many instances to withdrawal. However, the control processes involved are similar to highly skilled individuals in that discrepancy reduction is the goal. The critical difference is that discrepancy reduction efforts by skilled persons, in most instances, would be less effortful and more successful than low-skilled people. For a more elaborate description of Carver and Scheier's control theory, the reader is encouraged to consult Carver and Scheier (1983).

In terms of the research we have presented, control processes may be involved in the ongoing behaviors of a script. Because each sequence in the script involves behaving in a "script-consistent" fashion, deviations from that sequence can be monitored and used to modify one's behavior to return to the script. Person's with stronger scripts would be expected to invoke corrective discrepancy-reducing behaviors more successfully than those with weak scripts.

With respect to the MDS and information integrative research, both fit neatly into the control model by providing schematic organization of social information. Thus, as new events or situations are encountered, existing knowledge structures are used to interpret the new information. These matches of schemata with new information provide some behavior-specifying information. For example, when a situation calls for assertion, the individual will scan the status of the target person and the behavior of the target before constructing the initial actions. For example, the higher the status of the target person the more likely the goal or expectation would be to not assert gracefully, particularly if the high-status or authority person is verbally abusing someone or cutting in front of you in line. This tendency, according to our research, would be more prevalent in low-assertive people; whereas, with friends asserting is easier than with high-status persons regardless of the behavior. Thus, the knowledge base or schemata accessed by MDS or our decision-making research may provide the necessary information to develop the goal or expectancy in the social situation thereby providing the basis for the assessment of the discrepancy between the goal of the social interaction and the actual progression of events. One would expect, as Kelly (1955) has noted, that the knowledge base could change based on successive interactions where the discrepancy reduction attempts did not succeed based on a faulty knowledge base.

While the conceptualization of control theory as a dynamic information processing approach to social skill is speculative, we also hope that it is provocative. There is a need for an integrating framework that may take into account the dynamic aspects of social interaction that is also grounded in information processing. From this perspective perhaps the treatment of social skills deficiencies may be based more on accurate knowledge of the deficits rather than the success of existing treatments.

7

Information Encoding and Retrieval Processes in Depression: Findings, Issues, and Future Directions

RICK E. INGRAM
Department of Psychology
San Diego State University
San Diego, California 92182

MICHELE R. REED
Department of Psychology
University of Houston
Houston, Texas 77004

A number of theoretical approaches to depression have begun to emphasize information processing concepts as being at the core of depressive symptomatology. Beck's well-known model (1967), for instance, proposes that negative cognitive schemata distort the processing of information and serve to maintain depression. Although Beck's theory is the most widely known, compatible cognitive models by Kuiper (Kuiper, Derry, & MacDonald, 1982), Teasdale (1983, 1986), and Ingram (1984b) have also assigned a central role to information processing in depression. Moreover, even the "behavioral" models proposed by Lewinsohn (Lewinsohn, Hoberman, Teri & Hautzinger, 1985) and Rehm (1977) incorporate significant elements of information processing. Rehm (1977), for example, maintains that selective monitoring of negative information is an important component of depression while Lewinsohn's (Lewinsohn *et al.*, 1985) revised model views attentional processes as being at the root of a number of the cognitive and behavioral features associated with the disorder.

Paralleling this theoretical interest, empirical research on the information processing mechanisms of depression has also begun to accumulate. Although *information processing* may be operationally defined in a variety of ways (see Lachman & Lachman, chapter 3, this volume), a number of depression processing studies have begun to specifically examine the encoding and retrieval of information. *Encoding* studies, for instance, are those that make information available to be processed by individuals with varying levels of depression, and then use some index (typically information recall) to generate inferences as to how it was encoded. In contrast, *retrieval* studies examine information that has been encoded and stored at some previous preexperimental time to determine what factors affect its retrieval from long-term memory. Although only a subset of the cognitive factors addressed by extant depression research, encoding and retrieval processes are critical components of most information processing conceptualizations of depression and, as such, have important implications for understanding the processes that potentially mediate the multitude of cognitive deficits observed in depression. As these processes become better understood, it becomes increasingly possible to disentangle the ultimate contributions of cognitive mechanisms to depression and, hopefully, to develop accurate guidelines for generating optimally effective psychotherapeutic techniques. More broadly, an enhanced conceptualization of the information processing mechanisms operating in depression also portends implications for understanding the relationship between affect and cognition in general. Thus, the present chapter will briefly review and highlight the relevant outcomes of studies examining encoding and retrieval processes. Although this review will not be exhaustive, it will focus on research efforts that are representative of the empirical literature in depression. We will then discuss the salient methodological issues engendered by these studies and, although we will sidestep the issue of cognitive causes of depression, we will conclude with a discussion of some theoretical issues generated by encoding and retrieval empirical research (see also Blaney, 1986).

Encoding Studies

Following Tulving (1972), extant encoding studies can be conceptualized as focusing primarily on the processing or either semantic or episodic information.[1] *Semantic information* refers generally to knowledge and meaning and thus distinguishes studies that examine the processing of information relevant to individuals' knowledge or conception of themselves. *Episodic information,* on the

[1]It should be noted that the authors of these studies have not necessarily categorized the research in this manner. Nevertheless, such a distinction seems an accurate and reasonable way to organize the existing literature.

other hand, is autobiographical in nature and is therefore concerned with memory for personal and behavioral events in the individual's experience (e.g., memory for task performance).

Processing Semantic Information

Perhaps the first study to examine semantic information encoding in depression was reported by H. Davis (1979a), who employed a methodology from experimental cognitive psychology known as the depth-of-processing paradigm. Derived originally from memory research (Craik & Lockhart, 1972; Craik & Tulving, 1975) for use in determining the encoding of self-referent information (T. B. Rogers, Kuiper, & Kirker, 1977), the depth-of-processing paradigm presents individuals with stimulus adjectives and asks them to rate each adjective on a specified dimension. Theoretically, each dimension forces the individual to process the stimulus at a different cognitive level or depth in order to accurately perform the rating task. The deepest processing stage is thought to be the self-referent level since it is here that the individual has the greatest store of information available (i.e., information about one's self, or the self-schema). In order to assess the depth to which information is processed, an incidental recall task for the stimulus words is given immediately following the encoding phase of the paradigm. Craik and his colleagues have argued that information which is the most extensively (deeply) processed will leave a relatively stronger memory trace and is the most likely to be recalled in a free recall task.

According to current depressive information processing models, depressed people should have a greater store of negative information accessible at the self-referent level, and thus, stimulus information that is depressive in nature should be efficiently processed by these individuals. H. Davis (1979a) thus presented depressed patients with a depth-of-processing task and then examined recall rates for information encoded at various processing levels. For nondepressed control subjects, the expected recall superiority of self-referent processed information was found, indicating the presence of an organized schema to facilitate the encoding and subsequent recall of the information. For depressed subjects, this self-referent enhancement was not found; recall rates for self-referent information and information processed at a more general semantic level were roughly equivalent, a finding that caused H. Davis (1979a) to suggest the possibility that "the negative self-schema is depression does not exist" (p. 107). Unfortunately, as has been pointed out several times, since H. Davis (1979a) examined only recall rates across the various processing tasks (i.e., how many stimulus adjectives were recalled) and not whether depressed subjects recalled more negative or depressive *content* adjectives, this particular use of the depth-of-processing paradigm was unable to test the conceptually appropriate question of negative information processing in depression (Derry & Kuiper, 1981, Ingram *et al.*,

1983; Kihlstrom & Nasby, 1981). Two similar depressive information-processing studies (H. Davis, 1979b; H. Davis & Unruh, 1981) suffered from the same problem.

Building on Davis' examination of information processing in depression, Derry and Kuiper (1981) addressed the same issue with a more appropriate use of the depth-of-processing methodology. Employing the same paradigm, Derry and Kuiper (1981) developed an adjective list that contained both depressive (e.g., loser, inferior, hopeless) and nondepressive (e.g., amiable, sociable, capable) content. Consistent with the negative information processing hypothesis, Derry and Kuiper (1981) found that by using these stimuli, clinically depressed subjects recalled significantly more self-referent encoded depressive content than nondepressive content while both normal and nondepressed psychiatric control subjects showed the reverse of this pattern; they recalled more nondepressive than depressive self-referent information.

The same depth-of-processing paradigm was also utilized in two experiments reported by Kuiper and Derry (1982) with mildly depressed college students. In the first experiment, nondepressed subjects recalled more nondepressive than depressive self-referent information, while depressed subjects showed superior recall for *both* depressive and nondepressive self-referent content. In the second experiment, this pattern was again repeated although there was a nonsignificant trend for depressed subjects to recall more depressive than nondepressive self-referent adjectives. Based on a comparison of these results with their earlier research using clinically depressed subjects, Kuiper and Derry (1982) noted that "whereas mild depressives process both nondepressed and depressed content in terms of their self-schemas, more severe clinical depressives are only capable of effectively self-referencing pathologically oriented material" (p. 79). A closer inspection of the means reported in these studies, however, indicates that this conclusion may be somewhat premature. While it is true that mildly depressed subjects processed positive and negative content with relatively equal facility, it is not the case that clinically depressed subjects were completely devoid of any positive self-referent processing. In the Derry and Kuiper (1981) study, for example, clinically depressed subjects showed a self-referent positive information recall rate of 16%, precisely the same as Kuiper and Derry's (1982) mildly depressed subjects in Experiment 2 and not substantially under the rate for mildly depressed subjects in Experiment 1. Thus, these studies suggest some equivalence between clinical from subclinical depression with regard to processing self-referent information.

Several other studies have examined incidental recall in depression. McDowall (1984), for instance, found that in a free-recall situation depressed patients recalled more previously presented unpleasant words (e.g., ridicule, misery) than pleasant words (e.g., beauty, kind). Employing a depth-of-processing paradigm, Hammen, Miklowitz, and Dyck (in press) found evidence that the strength of processing depressive information (i.e., stimulus adjectives with depressive content) is related to not only the severity of the depression but to the duration of the depressive episode as well. Furthermore, Hammen *et al.* (in press) showed that when individuals were no longer depressed, they no longer evidenced enhanced processing of depressive information. Similarly, in a two-part study, Slife, Miura, Thompson, Shapiro, and Gallagher (1984) demonstrated that elderly depressed patients recalled more trigrams that they had previously rated as disliking than trigrams they had rated as liking. Two control groups showed the opposite pattern. In the second part of the study, depressed patients who underwent psychotherapy reversed this trend over the course of therapy and showed enhanced recall of liked trigrams, a result consistent with Hammen *et al.*'s. (in press) finding that depressive information processing occurs only when the individual is actually depressed.

One study has examined the encoding of personal information in depression within the context of a social interaction. Gotlib (1983) had depressed and nondepressed inpatients and nondepressed controls interact with opposite-sex strangers. Following this interaction, subjects were given a rating sheet that had purportedly been completed by a concealed observer of the interaction. Each sheet contained prearranged ratings on 13 bipolar adjectives that represented a number of evaluative dimensions (e.g., inadequate–adequate, unlikable–likable). After disclosing their reactions to these ratings, subjects were asked to reproduce from memory the ratings on a blank sheet. Results indicated that depressed subjects recalled these ratings to be significantly more negative than actually was the case, while on the other hand, neither of the nondepressed groups were inaccurate in their recall. Gotlib (1983) suggested that these results clearly reflected a negative distortion by depressed individuals in the recall of social feedback.

Several studies have also examined the impact of situational manipulations on information encoding in depression. Ingram *et al.* (1983), for instance, provided both depressed and nondepressed college students with either a success or failure experience immediately preceding a depth-of-processing task. Unlike Derry and Kuiper (1981) and Kuiper and Derry (1982), however, the stimulus adjectives in the processing task were not predetermined to be of either depressive or non-depressive content. Instead, the stimulus words used by T. B. Rogers *et al.* (1977), which contain a range of content, were employed. Following the depth-of-processing task, all subjects were asked to rate each word that had appeared on the task for favorability and self-descriptiveness. Based on these ratings, the mean personal favorability of the words recalled on the incidental recall portion of the task were examined. For nondepressed subjects, the self-referent favorability of recalled words encoded under the self-referent task was significantly higher in the success condition than in the failure condition. These subjects also evidenced significantly more favorable self-references recalled in the success condition than did depressed subjects in the success condition. For depressed subjects, there were no differences in personal favorability recall between the success and failure conditions, a finding that led the authors to suggest that depressed subjects failed to make use of the success experience to activate the processing of positive self-referent information as did the nondepressed subjects. Although the lack of a baseline comparison group not receiving either a success or failure experience makes these interpretations tentative, Ingram *et al.* (1983) suggested that depression might be characterized by a deficit in the ability to process positive information rather than by an oversensitivity to negative information.

In another study addressing the impact of situational manipulations, Dyck (1983) found results that appeared to conflict with Ingram *et al.*'s (1983). In this study, depressed and nondepressed college students were instructed to recall either a happy or sad personal experience. After completing a manipulation check item that asked subjects to rate on a 7-point scale whether they felt happy or sad, they participated in a depth-of-processing task where depressive and nondepressive adjectives were rated on a self-referent scale and an incidental recall task was then performed. Collapsed across the mood induction variable, results indicated that nondepressed subjects recalled significantly fewer negative words than did depressed subjects while there was no difference between depressed and nondepressed subjects in the recall of positive words. When the mood induction variable was considered, findings showed that depressed subjects recalled significantly more theoretically defined schema-congruent words (i.e., negative words that were rated as descriptive and positive words that were rated as nondescriptive) in the sad condition than in the happy condition (29 vs. 16%). Alternatively, nondepressed subjects did not show any differential recall as a function of the happy/sad mood manipulation (23% happy vs. 22% sad). Although Dyck (1983) concluded from these findings that information processing in depression might be more dependent on mood activation than for nondepressed individuals, interpretation of these results is problematic; the manipulation check employed appears to be highly susceptible to demand characteristics (e.g., subjects being asked to rate whether they felt happy or sad immediately after being told to think of something happy or sad). Thus, while significant effects might certainly be engendered by this kind of manipulation, particularly for already depressed subjects told to think of something sad in their own memory, it may have been much less effective for subjects not currently experiencing any depression.

From a somewhat different vantage point than the studies previously described, several studies have examined whether the ongoing information processing in depression might interfere with encoding of other information. Using a standard information processing methodology, for example, Krames and MacDonald (1985) presented both depressed and nondepressed outpatients with a dual cognitive task where they were required to learn a list of words (primary task) while at the same time being shown numbers of varying length and being asked to write them down (secondary task). This methodology assumes that individuals' cognitive processing capacity is limited, and as two tasks vie for this capacity, performance on the primary task will deteriorate as the secondary task becomes more demanding. Under conditions of moderate and high secondary task interference (longer numbers), both depressed and nondepressed subjects showed equivalent interference effects on primary task performance. Interestingly, however, under low secondary task interference, depressed subjects continued to show poor performance relative to nondepressed subjects. These results were subsequently replicated in a study by Vredenberg and Krames (1983) using a conceptually similar experimental paradigm. Results of both studies thus suggested the possibility that in conditions of low experimenter controlled cognitive interference, depressed subjects' current cognitive activity is capable of interfering with external information processing to a significant degree.

This conclusion receives additional support from a study by Gotlib and McCann (1984), who addressed the issue of cognitive interference in depression through the use of a modified Stroop task. Depressed and nondepressed college students viewed rapidly presented words with depressed, neutral, and manic content, and the subjects were asked to name the colors that the words were printed in. Gotlib and McCann (1984) reasoned that the presence of ongoing negative cognitive activity might interfere with the color-naming response latencies for depressive content words. Consistent with this hypothesis, they found slower response times to these words for depressed subjects but not for the nondepressed group, who showed no differences across any of the word conditions. In a second experiment to test whether these results might be due to transient mood effects, Gotlib and McCann (1984) repeated their procedure by using a Velten mood induction with nondepressed college students. While results indicated significant group differences on a manipulation adjective checklist, no differences were found on the Stroop task between subjects given either a depression, elation, or neutral mood induction. Although this was interpreted to indicate that mood itself is not a sufficient determinant of depressive interference effects, the possibility of demand characteristics on the manipulation item checklist must make this interpretation somewhat tentative.

Finally, Zuroff, Colussy, and Wielgus (1983) have noted that information processing research in depression may inadvertently be measuring response biases in depressed subject recall independent of information encoding, storage, and retrieval processes. In an attempt to test this proposition, Zuroff *et al.* (1983) employed a paradigm similar to one developed by D. Roth and Rehm (1980) where depressed and nondepressed college student subjects first examined 20 positive and 20 negative adjectives, rated them for self-descriptiveness, and then selected the 10 positive and 10 negative adjectives they felt were most descriptive. Subjects were then given 1-hour, 2-day, and 7-day delayed recall tests for the 10 positive and 10 negative most self-descriptive adjectives as well as a 7-day recognition test. In addition to examining recall and recognition rates for these adjectives, Zuroff *et al.* (1983) also performed a signal detection analysis on the recognition test, the results of which suggested that depressed subjects employed a more liberal criterion in making recognition judgments for negative information rather than more efficiently remembering this kind of information. Unfortunately, several serious flaws in Zuroff *et al.*'s (1983) methodology preclude drawing this conclusion. As M. Martin and Clark (in press) have pointed out, the D. Roth and Rehm (1980) paradigm employed may be insensitive to selective memory effects thus rendering it a questionable methodology for this kind of study. More importantly, they also note that the particular statistical comparisons employed by Zuroff *et al.* (1983) were not appropriate to address the conceptual issue of response biases. Additionally, with regard to the recall findings reported by Zuroff *et al.* (1983), conclusions can not be drawn since they were collapsed over all three recall periods.

Episodic Processing Studies

In one of the first studies to investigate the processing of behavioral information in depression, Wener and Rehm (1975) presented a pseudotest of social intelligence to both depressed and nondepressed subjects. Subjects ostensibly were reinforced for task performance accuracy, but actually were told they were correct at a predetermined high (80%) or low (20%) rate and were later asked to recall the percentage of correct responses they received. In both the high- and low-reinforcement conditions, depressed subjects underestimated the percentage of correct feedback, a finding interpreted by the authors as indicating that depressed individuals were more sensitive to negative than positive reinforcement.

Adding a punishment condition to this recall-of-reinforcement paradigm, Nelson and Craighead (1977) reinforced or punished college students for performance on an ambiguous task at either a high (70%) or low (30%) rate. Depressed subjects recalled being reinforced significantly less accurately than did controls in the high-reinforcement condition, while in the low-reinforcement condition estimates of reinforcement did not differ between the depressed and nondepressed groups. In the punishment conditions this pattern was largely reversed. There were no differences in recall of punishment at the high rate; both the depressed and nondepressed groups were fairly accurate. However, at the low-punishment rate, depressed subjects recalled receiving more punishment than did the nondepressed subjects, who significantly underestimated the negative feedback they had received. In other words, the depressed subjects were somewhat more accurate than the controls in the recall of punishment while the nondepressed subjects were generally more accurate in the recall of reinforcement.

Gotlib (1981) also addressed the recall of reinforcement in depression. Employing depressed inpatients, nondepressed inpatients, and nondepressed nonpatients, the recall of self-reinforcements and punishments administered on a verbal recognition task was examined. Gotlib (1981) found that depressed subjects recalled significantly more self-punishments than was actually the case and significantly more than either of the control groups. The biggest significant differences, however, were found for self-reinforcements. Here, depressed subjects recalled substantially fewer reinforcements than they actually made and fewer than either of the control groups recalled making.

In another study, DeMonbreun and Craighead (1977) employed the same recall of reinforcement paradigm with clinically depressed and nondepressed control subjects. In addition to examining the recall of punishment and reinforcement, they also sought to investigate whether potential distortions in this recall occurred at the point where individuals first perceived the reinforcing or punishing stimuli, or at some later information processing stage. In order to accomplish this, an ambiguous task was employed, and performance feedback on each trial was conveyed to subjects by presentation of one of several slides, varying in shades of light gray to black. Subjects were instructed that the darkest slide indicated a 100% acceptable answer, the next darkest slide indicated a 75% acceptable answer, and the lightest and next lightest slides represented 100% and 75% unacceptable answers, respectively. A midrange gray or ambiguous slide that was not mentioned to subjects was also included. After performance feedback, subjects were to indicate which of the feedback slides they received. Additionally, the experiment was divided into two parts; during the first 40 trials subjects received an equal number of all performance feedback slides, while during the second 40 trials, half of the subjects received a high rate of "acceptable" responses while the other half received a low rate of acceptable responses.

Results indicated that all subjects responded to the undefined midrange slide as positive approximately half the time and as negative approximately half the time, thus providing no support for hypotheses concerning distortions in the initial perception of these kinds of stimuli. After the first half of the study, depressed subjects tended to recall receiving less positive feedback than they actually did, but the difference was not significant. After the second 40 trials, depressed subjects in the *high*-reinforcement condition significantly underestimated the amount of positive feedback received as well as recalling significantly less of such feedback than the control groups. In the low-feedback condition no group differences were obtained. DeMonbreun and Craighead (1977) thus concluded that recall distortion in their depressed subjects occurred only when the rate of positive reinforcement is high.

Using a task similar to that employed by DeMonbreun and Craighead (1977), Craighead, Hickey, and DeMonbreun (1979) investigated recall as well as stimulus perception again using ambiguous performance feedback (i.e., feedback from unidentified slides) in students who were selected to be depressed and anxious, nondepressed and anxious, or nondepressed and nonanxious, respectively. Inconsistent with previous depression theory and research, no significant differences were found between any group on any measure. As noted by Sacco (1981), however, these negative findings were most likely the result of a lack of significant differences in depression or anxiety among any of the experimental groups. That is, inspection of depression and anxiety means on measures taken immediately before the experiment was conducted indicated that the previously selected depressed and anxious subjects were no longer depressed or anxious. Hence, this experiment does not appear to have employed groups with any meaningful psychopathological differences.

Employing a similar experimental paradigm, Dykman and Volpicelli (1983) presented depressed and nondepressed college students with 40 trials of a dot-estimation task. Subjects then received good, average, poor, or ambiguous (i.e., undefined) feedback that was conveyed by brightness of a red light bulb. Additionally, in order to examine whether the subjective importance of the experimental task affected information processing, half of the subjects were told that the task reflected the possession of "special mental abilities," while for the remaining half, the evaluative significance of the task was downplayed.

Initial analyses indicated no significant differences in recall, classification of initial stimuli (as good, average, or poor), or on a measure of latency to classify the stimuli. However, after inspection of the data, subsequent analyses indicated significant differences between groups in ambiguous stimulus classification during the last 20 experimental trials. Although Dykman and Volpicelli (1983) interpreted this as depressed individuals "negatively biasing" their stimulus perception of ambiguous feedback, inspection of the means shows only that depressed and nondepressed subjects significantly differed and suggests that nondepressed individuals may have been more likely to overinterpret this feedback as positive (rather than depressed subjects showing a negative bias). Dykman and Volpicelli (1983) also found significant differences in response latencies such that depressed subjects showed progressively longer times to classify the feedback as it became more positive while nondepressed subjects showed the opposite trend. In contrast, no differences were found in the recall of feedback nor were any differences on any measure found for the personal importance manipulation.

J. E. Johnson, Petzel, Hartney, and Morgan (1983) examined the effects of successful completion of tasks versus failure to complete tasks within a recall-of-reinforcement paradigm. The tasks involved were 20 paper-and-pencil tests of analytic abilities, half of which the subjects were allowed to complete, and half of which were interrupted prior to completion. Depressed college students recalled significantly more of the uncompleted tasks than the completed tasks, while nondepressed college students demonstrated the opposite trend by recalling significantly more of the completed tasks than the uncompleted tasks. Based on these recall differences, J. E. Johnson *et al.* (1983) argued that these findings were "consistent with Beck's (1967) assumption that the depressive minimizes those things he/she does well and maximizes those things he/she does poorly'' (p. 55).

Employing a different approach to examining the encoding of behavioral information, Finkel, Glass, and Merluzzi (1982) provided depressed and nondepressed college students with either a high proportion of positive self-referent statements, a low proportion of positive self-referent statements, or neutral, non-self-referent statements and then asked them to rate each statement on a 7-point scale as to how positively or negatively they perceived the statement. Following these ratings, subjects were asked to recall how many of the statements that they had ''judged to be any degree positive.'' Recall results indicated that depressed subjects recalled judging significantly fewer statements positive than nondepressed subjects when the proportion of such statements was high, but not when the predetermined proportion was low or when the statements were neutral. It is not clear from the data presented, however, whether this decreased recall of positive statements for the depression group was a cognitive underestimate of the amount of statements they rated positively, or an accurate reflection of the fact that they rated fewer statements as positive than did nondepressed subjects (which other data in the study suggest that they did).

In a study employing depressed and nondepressed psychiatric patients, D. Roth and Rehm (1980) examined the processing of both semantic and episodic information. After rating a group of positive and negative adjectives on a personal accuracy scale, subjects were asked to choose the 10 positive and 10 negative words that were most self-descriptive. After a 10-minute filler task they were then given a recall and recognition task for these words, neither of which later yielded significant group differences. Subjects also participated in a social interaction task where they were videotaped in a role-playing procedure and then later asked to rate their number of positive social responses (e.g., head nods) and negative social responses (e.g., hand rubbing). Comparison to objective videotape raters indicated that depressed subjects perceived an accurate number of negative responses and significantly less positive responses than was actually the case. Nondepressed subjects perceived significantly fewer of both positive and negative responses than did the objective raters. Roth and Rehm appropriately pointed out that these results might either be due to differences in selective information processing or to differences in the stringency of decision criteria employed. Either way it seems clear that depressed individuals in this study ''underperceived'' their socially appropriate responses.

Studies of Retrieval of Personal memory

As previously described, retrieval studies refer to those which examine the factors affecting the retrieval of pre-experimentally stored information. Although there are several different methodological tacts that retrieval studies can take, in the present section we will limit our review to those studies in which depressed subjects retrieved previously stored personal memories.

Lloyd and Lishman (1975) reported probably the first study of this type. In this study, depressed patients were presented with a series of neutral stimulus words and then asked to recall either a pleasant or unpleasant personal experience that was somehow associated with each word. Employing the latency to retrieve each of these kinds of experiences as the dependent measure, they found that the more severe the depression, the less time it took to retrieve unpleasant memories and the greater the time to report pleasant experiences.

Noting the strictly correlational basis of the Lloyd and Lishman (1975) findings, Teasdale and Fogarty (1979) followed up this study by manipulating mood in normal college students and examining the retrieval time of pleasant and unpleasant memories. Using the same strategy as Lloyd and Lishman (1975), college students were induced into either an elated or depressed state with the Velten mood induction procedure (Velten, 1968) and were then asked to recall either a pleasant or unpleasant experience in response to a neutral stimulus word. Results indicated that, when elated, pleasant memories were recalled significantly more quickly than when subjects were in a depressed condition. No significant differences in responses latencies were found between the elated and depressed states for unpleasant memories. Thus, only pleasant and not unpleasant material appeared to be affected by the experimenter-induced mood.

In two similar experiments, Teasdale, Taylor, and Fogarty (1980) and Teasdale and Taylor (1981) examined the probability of memory retrieval in depression. Subjects were again induced into an elated or depressed mood and were then asked to recall a memory but were not given any instructions concerning what kind of memory to recall. On a different day and not under the effects of the mood manipulation, subjects were asked to rate the pleasantness of the previously recalled memories. Using these ratings to determine which memories were pleasant, results of both studies indicated that in the depressed mood, subjects recalled significantly fewer pleasant memories than while in the elated condition. The opposite was true for unpleasant memories: Fewer were recalled in the elated mood than in the depressed mood. Similar results were obtained by Teasdale and Russell (1983) and by D. M. Clark and Teasdale (1985), although the latter findings were limited to females, suggesting the possibility of potential sex differences in depressive information processing.

Turning to clinical depression, D. M. Clark and Teasdale (1982) subsequently replicated the earlier results by examining diurnal variations in the mood of depressed inpatients. Using the same paradigm but with natural mood variations rather than mood inductions, it was again found that high levels of depression were related to significantly more unpleasant than pleasant memories recalled. For time periods of relatively low depression levels in these same patients, more pleasant than unpleasant memories were retrieved.

At least two other studies have examined personal memory retrieval processes in individuals with depressed mood. In one, Natale and Hantas (1982) found that college students who had been induced into an elated mood using the Velten procedure recalled a significantly greater number of happy memories than subjects induced into a depressed mood. Elated subjects also recalled significantly more happy than sad memories while depression-induced subjects recalled a fairly equal number of happy and sad memories. When compared to a baseline group not receiving any mood induction, the elation induction significantly increased the number of happy memories recalled while the depression induction significantly decreased the number of happy memories retrieved. For sad content, only in the elation condition was there a decrease in memory. For the depressed condition, no increase was seen in sad memories relative to the baseline group; both depressed- and normal-mood subjects recalled roughly the same number of these memories. These results are generally consistent with an experiment reported by M. Snyder and White (1982) that is relevant to the actual retrieval of information. In the first of three experiments, college students were induced into either an elated or depressed mood and asked to recall events that happened to them the past week, good events that happened to them during the past week, and finally, bad events that happened to them the past week. Results indicated that when asked to recall these events, elated subjects recalled more happy events while depressed subjects recalled more unhappy events. The number of neutral events did not differ as a function of the mood manipulation. When subjects were specifically asked to recall either good or bad events, once again elated subjects recalled more positive events and depressed mood subjects recalled more negative.

General Findings

As always, diverse methodologies, different conceptual perspectives, and a variety of specific research questions make it difficult to draw conclusions about an area as a whole. Given the methodological and theoretical issues remaining to be addressed, more than tentative conclusions concerning encoding and retrieval in depression are not possible. Nevertheless, based on the research available to date, we will attempt to delineate some general, and hopefully promising, trends in the data.

With regard to the encoding of semantic information, the bulk of available evidence suggests that depressed individuals relative to nondepressives do indeed experience an enhanced processing of negative or depressively oriented information. The efficient processing of positive or nondepressive information, on the other hand, seems to be more variable with some studies indicating decrements in positive processing (e.g., Ingram *et al.*, 1983) and others suggesting no such decrements (e.g., Kuiper & Derry, 1982). Such findings may point to positive information encoding as simply a variable process in depression, or alternatively, that extant research has been variable in its ability to accurately assess this process. The most consistent picture emerging from the data so far, however, is that enhanced *negative* encoding may be the key factor in semantic information processing.

This provides somewhat of a contrast to episodic information encoding studies. Here the picture seems to be one of depressed individuals being impacted at the *positive* rather than the negative information level. That is, the less accurate encoding (underestimation) of positive information seems to be the critical process for depressed individuals rather than the distorted overestimation of negative information. It may thus be that, as depressed individuals are primed by extant and salient negative semantic structures, congruent episodic information is processed efficiently while incongruent (positive) is distorted.

Although there are some exceptions, when retrieval studies are considered, the processing of positive and negative information in depression appears to be more symmetrical than for either semantic or episodic encoding processes. That is, while again the retrieval of negative information seems to be consistently enhanced, the retrieval of positive information appears to be more consistently diminished as well. There may be several reasons for this, one of which might be primarily methodological. Whereas encoding studies typically employ already depressed students or patients, retrieval studies usually rely on the manipulation of mood in normal student subjects. While differences may be due to different subject populations per se, an intriguing possibility has to do with the mood assessed, particularly when subjects in retrieval studies are given elation manipulations. In encoding studies, control subjects, while not depressed, are probably not all that elated either (consider the attitude of many introductory psychology students sitting in a psychology experiment) and thus probably have a more "neutral" mood. More symmetrical retrieval findings, particularly with regard to positive processing may therefore be partially due to the added mood dimension that an elated condition brings to previously neutral mood subjects.

An additional possibility for different encoding and retrieval patterns may reflect the operation of somewhat different processes. Encoding, for example, is more restrained by factors external to the person such as the kind of information available in the environment. Variable positive or nondepressive processing may hence be a function of the information available to be processed. Even if the depressed individual's cognitive system more efficiently encodes negative information, positive information may be accurately encoded if, for example, a large amount of positive information "overwhelms" the system. Retrieval of information, on the other hand, would seem less constrained by these external factors and more dependent on solely internal factors. Without these constraints, affect may be more likely to be the prime determinant of what information is retrieved, facilitating consistent information and inhibiting inconsistent. Therefore, retrieval processes may be more "pure" mood related than encoding.

Issues

The previous discussion has summarized a number of findings that are relevant to encoding and retrieval processes in depression. In this section, we will suggest several issues that might profitably be considered by future theory and research (see also Blaney (1986) for a discussion of related issues). Since information processing and depression are related in complexly numerous ways, the issues raised here are intended to be illustrative rather than exhaustive of the factors to be considered potentially important for understanding the role of information processing in depression. Although by no means exclusive, these issues can be divided into two conceptually broad categories: *methodological issues* that bear upon our ability to adequately and accurately assess information processing in depression, and *theoretical issues* pertaining to questions needing to be addressed to further our understanding of this relationship.

Methodological Issues

One methodological issue that is germane to all research but particularly critical to information processing research in depression is the appropriate use of experimental stimuli. The issue is perhaps best illustrated in H. Davis' (e.g., 1979a, 1979b) initial information processing studies that did not examine the content of the stimulus information processed by depressed subjects. The simplest remedy to this problem is to develop stimuli that contain negative/depressive content. Using precisely this strategy, Derry and Kuiper (1981) found that such stimuli led to impressive selective processing effects with clinically depressed subjects. Even this remedy, however, may not completely solve the problem. Although this particular depressive content stimuli does indeed appear appropriate for clinical levels of depression, it may be less so when applied to subclinical forms of the disorder. Much of the content of this stimuli is strongly depressive, for instance, leading to the possibility that it may not effectively tap the current cognitive content of mildly depressed individuals. Finding "null" results, or at least a different pattern of results, with this stimuli for mildly depressed subjects may thus mean that these individuals have an inefficient self-schema, or alternatively, that this depressive content stimuli did not fit their particular depressive self-schema. An intriguing possibility in this regard, may be a state/trait-like distinction between mildly and severely depressive self-schemata. For example, if mildly, and presumably transiently, depressed individuals were presented with "state" depressive-content descriptors (e.g., blue, criticized, troubled), would they deeply and efficiently process and recall this information, and would clinically depressed individuals be more likely to respond to ''trait'' descriptors (e.g., loser, weak, inadequate)? Whatever the ultimate answer to this or similar questions, it is important to note that researchers must take care to construct stimuli that are appropriate to tap the cognitive dimensions of theoretical interest.

An additional methodological issue concerns the type of measure employed to assess encoding and retrieval processes. The majority of studies reviewed in the present chapter have employed recall measures in this vein while, on the other hand, some studies have adopted recognition memory measures. In general, these latter studies have not been as successful in finding selective processing effects in depression (e.g., Roth & Rehm, 1980; Zuroff *et al.*, 1983). Although recall and recognition measures may tap somewhat different cognitive processes, on a more fundamental methodological level, recognition is generally acknowledged to be a less difficult memory task than recall (Tulving, 1985). Hence, the relative ease of recognition may render it too insensitive to be a useful measure in this arena. Moreover, it may also be particularly susceptible to response bias effects: While depressed subjects may be more willing to endorse negative items that they do not remember seeing previously, nondepressed subjects may be correspondingly more willing to censor the reporting of negative items that they do in fact remember. Thus, as with the previously mentioned issue of stimuli appropriateness, researchers must also ensure that their dependent measures are sensitive enough to tap the particular information processing intricacies of interest. Additionally, more care should be taken to ensure that what is being tapped is what is being perceived by subjects rather than what they are perceiving and then *deciding* to report to the experimenter. Although no method is entirely free of this problem, methods that require subjects to recall or reconstruct the actual information presented (e.g., recall which words were presented) are probably less susceptible than those presenting information and then asking subjects to make estimates about it. The creative use of experimental cognitive-based methods employed by Gotlib and McCann (1984) and Krames and McDonald (1985) are excellent examples of sophisticated measures that may help to solve some of these potential problems.

A final methodological issue concerns the impact of mood manipulations on depressed subjects. Both Gotlib and McCann (1984) and Dyck (1983) have suggested that different kinds of mood manipulations may affect different kinds of cognitive processes. Apart from these potentially differential effects, however, it may also be the case that mood manipulations impact no cognitive processes. In the Ingram *et al.* (1983) study, for instance, it was found that depressed individuals did not respond positively to a success manipulation. In retrospect, this is hardly surprising; why should success on a brief test in a psychology experiment offset the depression a student is experiencing as the result of, say for example, the death of a friend or the loss of a meaningful relationship? It is therefore crucial for researchers not only to develop effective manipulations, but also to adequately and thoroughly assess their impact. Different situations and moods may indeed affect cognitive processes differently. The implementation of appropriate and effective manipulations (even if only transiently effective) will help facilitate the answer to this question.

Theoretical Issues

In addition to the methodological issues that invariably become salient as research in an area begins to accumulate, there are also a number interesting theoretical questions that arise. One particularly relevant issue that has yet to be explicitly addressed concerns the parameters of the information to be processed and how it interacts with depressive characteristics. Information can vary on a number of dimensions. Gotlib (1983) and Dykman and Volpicelli (1983) have noted, for instance, that a number of studies of information processing in depression have employed information that is highly impersonal (e.g., performance feedback on a letter recognition task). On a somewhat more abstract level, in the present review we have also distinguished between semantic and episodic information. As evidenced by the data currently available, it seems that these different kinds of information may indeed be processed differently as a function of depression level and, more importantly, may also contribute to the maintenance and/or features of depression in different manners. Although by no means complete or mutually exclusive, several other potentially interesting categories of information can also be distinguished. Some examples include the *target* of the information (whether it is specifically about the individual as opposed to social information concerning others), the general *favorability* of the information (e.g., positive/favorable, negative/unfavorable), the *content* of the information (e.g., neutral, depressive, anxious, manic, assertive, aggressive), information *congruence* (does it fit with the individual's own self-concept?), and finally, as previously suggested by Gotlib (1983), the *personal relevance* of the information. All of these categories would seem to be important and interactive dimensions that merit theoretical and empirical scrutiny. At the very least, however, future studies would be wise to refrain from drawing conclusions about how depressives process information without reference to the specific type of information under study.

Related to the issue of information categories in depressive processing is the issue of depressive categories. Although we have used the generic term *depression* to refer to a multifaceted symptom constellation with depressed mood as the defining characteristic, it is widely recognized that depression is not a unitary, homogeneous disorder. It is also widely recognized that there is very little consensus concerning the classification, symptoms, and conceptual boundaries of various depressive disorders (Andreason, 1982; Depue & Monroe, 1978). While acknowledging the disagreement over depression classification, however, there are several broad categories that in the most general sense do seem to be agreed upon. We have already touched upon the severity distinction in studies that have employed subjects ranging from normal subjects with induced depression, to mildly depressed college students, to clinically depressed inpatients. Although the extant research has shown some evidence generally supportive of the notion that information processing in these disorders is similar in at least a qualitative sense, research has yet to explicitly examine the specifics of potential information processing differences in different severity levels.

One classification that also merits study is the unipolar–bipolar distinction. Previous research has either limited itself exclusively to unipolar depression or has not made a distinction between the two. Finding information processing differences in unipolar and bipolar depression would not only be of great theoretical interest, but because much psychosocial–cognitive therapy is based on the premise that "correcting faulty information processing" is the basis for effective treatment (see Ingram & Hollon, this volume), such research may also have direct practical importance as well. An examination of other categories such as reactive–endogenous and neurotic–psychotic might prove interesting as well. More broadly, how information processing is affected by, and in turn affects, a variety of different moods (e.g., depression, mania) is of tremendous theoretical interest for understanding the relationship between affect and cognition (Hammen, 1983a). Finally, addressing information processing in individuals theoretically vulnerable to depression but not presently depressed, and in children experiencing depressive affect, as Kuiper (Kuiper, Olinger, MacDonald, & Shaw, 1985) and Hammen (Hamman, 1985; Hamman, Marks, Mayol, & deMayo, 1985; Hamman, Marks, de Mayo & Mayol, 1985; Hammen & Zupan, 1984), respectively, have taken the lead in doing, may also provide important data on how information processing may ultimately contribute to depression.

Depression is not the only psychopathology that has received information processing attention. Albeit from a markedly different conceptual framework, other disorders such as schizophrenia have a long history of information processing interest (see Saccuzzo, this volume). It therefore may be important that researchers not only examine the characteristics of information processing in depression, but in other psychopathologies as well. Although the use of nondepressed–psychopathological control groups is a legitimate and useful research strategy, the amount of information we can gain from this procedure is limited. A more comprehensive understanding of information processing in depression requires not only that we employ control groups but that we specifically examine the information processing commonalities and differences between depression and other psychopathologies. Such comparisons would help to pinpoint both the unique and shared cognitive features of depression and would suggest important theoretical and important implications for depression in particular and for psychopathological functioning in general.

One current controversy in the depression literature pertains to the relative accuracy or distortion of cognition in depression. A. T. Beck's (1967) traditional position that depressed people distort the processing of information in systematically negative ways has been challenged by several sources (e.g., Alloy & Abramson, 1979, 1982; Lewinsohn, Mischel, Chaplin, & Barton, 1980; Sackeim, 1983). The bottom line of this challenge is that "a rapidly growing body of empirical work suggests that depressed peoples' perceptions and inferences are actually more realistic and accurate than those of nondepressed people" (Alloy, 1982, p. 2). Although the research discussed in the present chapter was not designed specifically to address this issue, several studies do bear upon it. Generally, these studies have shown mixed results, suggesting that sometimes depressed individuals "distort" information (e.g., Gotlib, 1983; Nelson & Craighead, 1977-reinforcement condition) and sometimes they do not (Nelson & Craighead, 1977-punishment condition). These mixed results therefore strongly suggest that the accuracy of information processing in depression is determined by a number of complex factors and that general conclusions as to distortion or accuracy are probably premature. More fundamentally, although accuracy can easily be operationalized in laboratory situations, the notion of accuracy/distortion has not been adequately conceptually defined (D. L. Roth & Ingram, 1985). A. T. Beck's (1967) contention, for example, implies a *distortion by commission* definition where depressed individuals somehow "change" positive or neutral information into negative information to fit their depressive schema. An equally likely but very different definition of distortion is a *distortion by omission* notion. In such a case, depressed individuals may process negative information very accurately while cognitively ignoring positive information (the converse may be just as likely for nondepressed individuals). The overall effect of this processing style would thus be distortion because of the imbalance of information attended to relative to what was available. Whether this or other conceptualizations of distortion are useful, it is important for future research to reach some degree of consensus as to what constitutes distortion or accuracy before the phenomenon can be examined and conclusions drawn.

One final issue we will raise concerns the nature of information processing in depression as it is typically assessed. Schneider and Shiffrin (1977; Shiffrin & Schneider, 1977) have proposed an important distinction between automatic and controlled information processing. The principal behind this distinction is that automatic processing, as the name implies, occurs in an automatic almost mechanistic manner without any significant control by the individual. Controlled processing, on the other hand, involves a process where the individual exerts some control over how the information is processed. Information processing studies in depression to date have almost exclusively examined the productions (e.g., word recall) of subjects and found these productions to be different for depressed subjects than for nondepressed subjects. Theoretically, these studies assume that some combination of automatic processes are behind this content. Studies that attribute recall to factors such as schema functioning, for instance, implicitly assume that the processes involved in this recall automatically "happen" without much control by the individual. Similarly, episodic information processing studies examine perception of information through recall estimates with the assumption that this perception automatically occurs to subjects and is then reported. Without denying the validity and importance of automatic information processing in depression, we propose that it is also useful to examine information control processes in depression. While the study reported by Zuroff *et al.* (1983) suffers from serious methodological flaws, the point that some apparent selective memory effects in depression may be mediated by what subjects are *willing* to report is one that warrants consideration. There may in fact be differences in how depressed and nondepressed individuals attempt to control aspects of how they process information. When nondepressed people encounter a depressing thought, for instance, do they search their memory for positive thoughts to counter it while depression-prone individuals instead focus on the depressing thought? This is, of course, only one very simple example of a large number of hypothetical questions concerning control process differences. It illustrates, however, not only the importance of distinguishing between automatic and controlled processing but also of specifically examining potential differences among groups in the operation of these processes. Certain kinds of automatic processing are undoubtedly a critical component of depression. Certain kinds of control processes may also be an important key to understanding the disorder.

Obviously the preceding discussion has not been able to cover all of the methodological or theoretical issues that are relevant to information processing in depression, but has instead attempted to focus upon some of the more salient ones to be considered. Elucidating the role of cognitive variables in depression is an extremely complicated and demanding challenge. If, however, it is reasonable to assume that cognition contributes to depression in some nontrivial manner, then understanding the information processing basis of this disorder can ultimately help researchers to successfully meet this challenge. Depressive information processing research has shown signs of steady growth in recent years. Through continued growth, both in uncovering the information processing mechanisms of depression, and in integrating knowledge of these mechanisms with other cognitive and noncognitive perspectives, it is our hope that this research can bring us closer to an understanding of the essential elements that underlie depression.

Acknowledgments

We would like to thank the Cognitive Clinical Research Group at San Diego State and Constance Hammen for their helpful comments on an earlier draft of this chapter.

8

An Information Processing Approach to Alcohol Use and Its Consequences

JAY G. HULL
NORA P. REILLY
Department of Psychology
Dartmouth College
Hanover, New Hampshire 03755

The present chapter will attempt a broad integration of research on alcohol use and information processing. The principal aims of the chapter will be to show interconnections between a variety of alcohol effects that are all too often considered in isolation, while at the same time disentangling effects that are sometimes mistakenly treated as equivalent. While several theories and research traditions will be reviewed, we will try to avoid emphasizing any one approach to the exclusion of others.

The chapter is organized into three sections. These sections examine (a) the effects of alcohol on cognitive processes, (b) the effects of alcohol on behavior by virtue of its effects on cognitive processes, and (c) the motive to consume alcohol in order to achieve its effects on cognitive processes.

The Effects of Alcohol Use on Information Processing

Research on the effects of alcohol on information processing can be divided into those studies interested in the acute effects of intoxication and those interested in the long-term effects of chronic alcohol abuse. Within each of these

INFORMATION PROCESSING APPROACHES TO CLINICAL PSYCHOLOGY

areas, studies have been conducted that attempt to determine not only the nature of alcohol effects on learning and memory, but also the processes responsible for those effects.

Acute Effects of Alcohol Intoxication on Information Processing

In general, memory for information processed in the intoxicated state is impaired relative to memory for information processed in the sober state.[1] A consensus has formed among researchers that the locus of these effects resides in the effects of alcohol on the storage of information. Thus, several researchers have proposed that alcohol-induced cognitive impairment is located in central information processes as opposed to more peripheral sensory or motor mechanisms (e.g., Moskowitz, 1973). Among these central processes, the acquisition of new information would appear to be particularly vulnerable to alcohol effects (see Ryback, 1971).

In attempting to delineate the central processes most susceptible to alcohol impairment, researchers have contrasted the effects of being intoxicated while learning new information and while trying to recall old information. Differences in the effects of alcohol in these two cases are attributed to the impact of intoxication on either information storage or retrieval. In order to investigate storage processes, retrieval tasks must be selected that involve minimal competing processing (Parker, Birnbaum, & Noble, 1976). Evidence pertaining only to retrieval processes must ensure that all storage processes are equivalent and then attempt to manipulate factors such as differential retrieval cues. With some exceptions (e.g., H. L. Williams & Rundell, 1984), this literature has demonstrated that information storage processes are more impaired by intoxication than retrieval processes. Thus, I. M. Birnbaum and Parker (1977) report a number of well-designed studies that demonstrate that storage of both verbal and visual

[1]Under certain specific conditions, alcohol intoxication can actually result in improved memory. Two recently documented effects involve retrograde facilitation and state-dependent learning. In retrograde facilitation, memory for information processed in the sober state is improved by immediately *subsequent* intoxication (e.g., Mueller, Lisman, & Spear, 1983; Parker *et al.*, 1981). The exact reason for retrograde facilitation remains unclear. Some researchers argue that alcohol primes the consolidation of memory traces, while other researchers argue that information processed just prior to intoxication is facilitated because alcohol interferes with the processing of subsequent, potentially competing information.

A different kind of memory facilitation occurs in state-dependent learning. In this case, memory for information previously learned in an intoxicated state is better when one is subsequently intoxicated than when one is sober. In a review of 57 studies, Eich (1980) found that with few exceptions successes in demonstrating state dependency were restricted to studies in which retrieval was performed in the absence of any observable prompts; failures occurred when memory was tested in the presence of discretely identifiable retrieval cues. In effect, a salient external cue overrides the cue of pharmacological state. The result is ordinary cued retrieval. When identifiable cues are unavailable, the default operation appears to be to use nonsalient cues such as drug state.

information is impaired by acute alcohol ingestion, while information learned under sober conditions can be retrieved equally well under both sober and intoxicated conditions.

Given that alcohol impairs information processing through its effect on storage, which storage processes are most impaired? One way to approach this question is to examine the types of tasks and the contexts in which alcohol has its greatest effects on memory. Some tasks are more susceptible to alcohol impairment than others. Free recall tasks have regularly displayed alcohol effects (e.g., I. M. Birnbaum, Parker, Hartley, & Noble, 1978; Rosen & Lee, 1976; Rundell & Williams, 1977) as have tasks of word recognition (e.g., Parker *et al.*, 1976; H. L. Williams & Rundell, 1984). Alcohol intoxication has also shown repeated effects in simple tasks involving associative linkages such as clustering or paired-associate lists (e.g., Parker *et al.*, 1976; Rosen & Lee, 1976; Rundell & Williams, 1977). It is particularly important to note that the organizational cues in these studies were neither obvious nor strong. Furthermore, when such cues are strengthened, alcohol has less of an effect on cued retrieval tasks such as category cuing and recognition testing (cf., I. M. Birnbaum & Parker, 1977; Rosen & Lee, 1976). By implication, then, alcohol may impair storage by decreasing the use of organizational strategies during the acquisition of information. When such strategies are provided by the experimenter, alcohol appears to have less of an effect.

The hypothesis that alcohol impairs information processing by inhibiting the use of organizational strategies was explicitly tested in an experiment by I. M. Birnbaum *et al.* (1978). In this study, intoxicated subjects performed significantly worse than sober subjects on three trials of free recall. Furthermore, sober subjects showed a significantly faster rate of acquisition of words over trials, as well as significantly better organization of words into categories. Of greater interest is the fact that cueing by the experimenter produced more improvement in recall for intoxicated than sober subjects. By implication, alcohol has its effects by disrupting the subject's spontaneous tendency to use associative cues.

A second experiment by these authors controlled for storage processes in order to examine the effects of alcohol on retrieval. At the same level of intoxication as in the first experiment, retrieval was unimpaired. Free recall and paired-associate lists were learned while sober and retrieved 1 week later in either a sober or intoxicated state. As in previous research no effect of alcohol was obtained for speed, accuracy, or use of cues in recall. Taken together, these experiments suggest that alcohol impairs the storage of information and that this impairment is related to the use of associative cues.

Building on these findings, I. M. Birnbaum, Johnson, Hartley, and Taylor (1980) proposed that alcohol debilitates information storage by inhibiting the use of elaboration strategies or schemata. Thus, it has been shown that elaboration (i.e., the classification and integration of new information with previously acquired information) facilitates storage and retention of information (e.g., Bransford & Johnson, 1973; Hasher, Griffin, & Johnson, 1977). It is possible that alcohol debilitates storage by reducing the likelihood that elaborative information will be either generated or efficiently used by intoxicated subjects in processing new information. I. M. Birnbaum *et al.* (1980) conducted three experiments to determine whether the provision of elaborative schemata would reduce alcohol-induced memory impairment. Sober and intoxicated subjects learned a series of words and then performed a recognition task. Some subjects were provided context words along with the target word, while other subjects were only presented with the target. The provision of context words did not affect the performance of sober subjects. However, intoxicated subjects made significantly fewer ''false alarm'' errors when the context words were presented in conjunction with the target. I. M. Birnbaum *et al.* (1980) concluded that the alcohol-induced deficit involved the production of elaborative schemata: Intoxicated subjects benefited from elaboration when it was provided for them by the experimenter (the context condition), but apparently they did not generate the necessary elaboration on their own.

The research and conclusions drawn by Birnbaum and her colleagues remain somewhat controversial. A more recent experiment by Hashtroudi, Parker, DeLisi, and Wyatt (1983) found that provision of a highly effective elaborator enhanced recall for sober subjects and not intoxicated subjects. In this experiment, subjects either generated their own elaborators or were provided elaborators by the experimenter. The elaborators were either simple (related to the target in a nonspecific way) or precise (two explicit cues integrated into a single prompt). It was found that precise elaborators (both provided and self-generated) significantly improved the performance of sober but not intoxicated subjects. If anything, then, use of a highly effective encoding strategy exacerbated rather than diminished the effect of alcohol on cognitive performance. Hashtroudi *et al.* (1983) offer a nonspecific, methodological account for the discrepancy of their findings with those of I. M. Birnbaum *et al.* (1980). Other more recent studies have failed to find that alcohol-induced deficits are related to the spontaneous tendency of subjects to produce elaborative traces (H. L. Williams & Rundell, 1984) or the depth of processing required by the task (Fleming, Miller, & Adesso, 1983). These results bring into question Birnbaum's claim that alcohol has its effects by virtue of inhibiting the propensity of subjects to use complex organizational strategies.

On the basis of this brief review, it can be concluded that alcohol impairs information processing by creating a deficit in information storage. Somewhat more tentatively, it is suggested that such impairment is greatest when the situational context lacks strong organizational cues. By implication, alcohol may have its effects by disrupting organizational processes. The obvious task of future research is to determine the exact nature of the affected processes and the strategies necessary to overcome these deficits.

Chronic Effects of Alcohol Use on Information Processing

Up to this point, we have examined the effects of alcohol on information processing by comparing memory in intoxicated versus sober social drinkers. It is also possible that alcohol has long-term effects on cognitive performance. We will begin by examining the effects of long-term social drinking and then conclude this section with an examination of the effects of long-term alcohol abuse and Korsakoff's syndrome, a severe memory disorder involving amnesia.

Chronic effects of moderate to heavy alcohol consumption

Parker and Noble (1977) examined cognitive impairment in male social drinkers. Neither frequency of drinking nor the amount of alcohol consumed over a lifetime was significantly related to sober performance on a battery of neuropsychological tests. On the other hand, the average amount of drinking the subjects reported on one occasion proved to be positively and significantly associated with impaired performance. MacVane, Butters, Montgomery, and Farber (1982) replicated this result, as did Parker, Birnbaum, Boyd, and Noble (1980), using younger subjects (male college students). This effect appears to be strongest in the heavy drinkers, although it is also present in the nonheavy drinkers (Parker & Noble, 1980). Finally, older subjects seem to be more affected than younger subjects (Parker & Noble, 1980).

Cognitive impairment is not limited to males. M. K. Jones and Jones (1980) conducted a study of female social drinkers and reported that sober memory performance in moderate drinkers was significantly worse than that in light drinkers. Hannon, Day, Butler, Larson, and Casey (1983) tested both men and women while sober and found decreased cognitive performance to be associated with both quantity of alcohol consumed per occasion *and* total lifetime consumption. Their data also suggest that drinking has a differential effect on the two sexes. For men only, frequency of alcohol consumption was actually associated with improved performance on some tasks. The authors suggest that women may be more neuropsychologically impaired than men by exposure to alcohol.

While cognitive loss is related to chronic alcohol use, it may also be true that cognitive improvement would result from changes in drinking patterns. The possible reversibility of alcohol-related impairment in social drinkers has not yet been examined. Nevertheless, a study by Poulos, Wolff, Zilm, Kaplan, and Cappell (1981) suggests that the impairment of recall may be *reduced* by repeated daily exposure to alcohol in nonalcoholics. These authors suggest that this is evidence of tolerance to alcohol-induced impairment, although we would not rule out the alternative that their results reflect increased familiarity with the requirements of the particular memory task.

The chronic effects of alcohol abuse on information processing

Given that chronic social drinking is associated with some forms of cognitive impairment, it is not surprising that long-term alcohol abuse leads to more severe deterioration in cognitive function. Indeed, Ryback (1971) has proposed a continuum of alcohol-related memory deficits ranging from memory loss in the social drinker to blackouts among alcoholics to amnesia among patients with Korsakoff's syndrome. In support of such a continuum, we have seen that some degree of cognitive impairment is associated with increased alcohol consumption in social drinkers. In turn, alcoholics show greater impairment than social drinkers.

It is typically agreed that detoxified male alcoholics tend to display performance deficits on perceptual–spatial, nonverbal abstract reasoning, and problem-solving tasks, although general verbal intelligence remains relatively unaffected (e.g., Parsons, 1977; Tartar, 1975). Parsons (1977) and Wilkinson and Carlen (1980) suggest that deficits such as these imply that brain dysfunction occurs in many male alcoholics. Fabian, Parsons, and Silberstein (1981) found highly similar performance patterns between male and female alcoholics. Similarly, Silberstein and Parsons (1981) found that male and female alcoholics are equivalently impaired on some tests, although women displayed deficits on fewer measures than men. General neuropsychological decrements in alcoholics have also been validated cross-culturally, as demonstrated by Loberg's (1980) study in Norway and Wilkinson and Carlen's (1980) report on Canadian alcoholics.

There is evidence to suggest that deficits accrued from chronic alcoholism are not necessarily permanent. Schau, O'Leary, and Chaney (1980) report results consistent with the notion that reversibility is related to the cessation of drinking and that improvements may be detectable even if some relapse occurs. This improvement, however, does not reach the level of performance attained by nonalcoholic controls. Studies by O'Leary, Radford, Chaney, and Schau (1977) and Hester, Smith, and Jackson (1980) further support this latter observation.

Much of the current research on neuropsychological deficits in alcoholics concerns general memory impairment. At the same time, such memory loss would appear to be more characteristic of some alcoholics than others. Thus, Ryan and Butters (1980) found that alcoholics without memory complaints performed on par with nonalcoholic controls on both clinical and experimental memory tasks. On the other hand, alcoholics who complained of memory deficits performed worse than either alcoholics without complaints or nonalcoholics on these same tasks. In fact, these "complaining" alcoholics overlapped with the performance of alcoholics diagnosed as having Korsakoff's syndrome.

As with more general neuropsychological deficits, there is some evidence that memory disorders in alcoholics can improve with abstinence from alcohol. Cermak and Ryback (1976) found that older alcoholic patients tested on a short-term memory task upon hospital admission perform on par with patients with Korsakoff's. After a 1-month abstinence, however, these older alcoholics performed more comparably with alcoholics without Korsakoff's, perhaps indicating a continuum of "improvement" as well as one of impairment.

Korsakoff's syndrome

Korsakoff's syndrome is classically described as a pure disorder of memory, sudden in onset, that affects a small proportion of chronic alcoholics (see Ryan, 1980). Individuals with this condition display severe anterograde and retrograde amnesia. In contrast to the amnesia associated with an alcoholic blackout, the amnesia experienced by a Korsakoff's patient need not be associated with a drinking bout: There is a deterioration in the ability to process information under conditions of complete sobriety.

Butters and Cermak (1974) and Cutting (1979) provide some evidence that, within individuals with Korsakoff's, memory impairment can be divided into two distinct categories of neuropsychological deficits: those of visual–spatial functions (e.g., nonverbal visual memory) and those of complex verbal (semantic) memory. The former deficit may be a characteristic of all chronic alcoholics, whereas the latter is specific to patients with Korsakoff's. Cutting (1979) gave Korsakoff's, non-Korsakoff's alcoholic, and nonalcoholic subjects picture recognition and verbal learning tasks. On a test of pattern memory, alcoholics and subjects with Korsakoff's were comparable to each other, but both were inferior to nonalcoholics. On tests of verbal learning and object picture memory, individuals with Korsakoff's were impaired relative to both alcoholic and nonalcoholic subjects. Consistent with these results, Butters and Cermak (1976) found that alcoholics with Korsakoff's were impaired relative to alcoholics without Korsakoff's on a test of meaning*ful* nonverbal memory (object recognition), but not on a test of meaning*less* nonverbal memory (pattern recognition). By implication, the cognitive deficit associated with Korsakoff's syndrome would appear to be specific to the processing of information according to its meaning.

What is responsible for the Korsakoff's deficit? As with acute intoxication, much of the literature suggests that persons with Korsakoff's have trouble with information acquisition and storage. Cermak, Reale, and DeLuca (1977) found that subjects with Korsakoff's were capable of obtaining a small amount of verbal information through constant rehearsal, although this material was rapidly forgotten when rehearsal was prevented (Cermak & Butters, 1973). G. G. Brown, Rosenbaum, Lewis, and Rourke (1980) also found that persons with Korsakoff's rehearse information at a lower rate than either alcoholics without Korsakoff's or normal subjects. Furthermore, statistically controlling for this rate eliminated differences on recall performance among the groups. Cermak and Butters (1973) also report that subjects with Korsakoff's use inefficient rehearsal strategies and in addition may inadequately analyze the categories of target words to be remembered (see also Cermak & Butters, 1972). Finally, Cermak, Naus, and Reale (1976) reported that when forced to learn a word list, subjects with Korsakoff's are much more likely to use rote rehearsal than more effective associative techniques such as elaboration. All of these studies suggest that impairment of information storage is associated with Korsakoff's syndrome. To some extent, this impairment is due to a rehearsal deficit. However, some research suggests that persons with Korsakoff's are also impaired in their use of more sophisticated encoding strategies. As in the literature on acute intoxication, researchers have begun to focus on elaboration processes as a key element in storage deficits for alcoholics and persons with Korsakoff's.

That alcoholics have difficulty with sophisticated encoding strategies is suggested in a study by Ryan (1980). In this experiment, subjects learned a word list to mastery and then recalled the information both immediately and 5 hours later with the aid of either a simple or complex cue. When told to learn the noun-pair lists in the simple orienting task, alcoholics were unable to spontaneously generate their own sophisticated mnemonics and learned the list significantly slower than controls. This difference disappeared when more complex elaborative learning cues were provided. Alcoholics also forgot more words than controls over the 5-hour period when simple retrieval cues were used, but this difference again disappeared when the words had been learned in sentences and then cued with these sentences at recall. Ryan (1980) concluded that alcoholics can generate mnemonics spontaneously, but do so using simplistic and inefficient encoding strategies.[2] Similarly, Cermak and his colleagues (Cermak, Butters, & Gerrein, 1973; Cermak & Reale, 1978) report that Korsakoff's alcoholics are more likely to focus on structural or phonemic characteristics of words rather than their semantic characteristics. Use of such lower level encoding strategies could itself account for memory deficits (cf. Craik, 1979b).

This levels-of-processing approach led Cermak and Reale (1978) to suggest that the anterograde amnesia suffered by persons with Korsakoff's results from their tendency not to perform deep (semantic) analyses of target material and that their retention of material can be improved with instruction to do so. Thus, it is

[2]It should be noted that these alcoholics were also less able to later recall words that had been learned to mastery. In contrast to work on the acute effects of intoxication, this effect suggests a retrieval as well as an encoding deficit among alcoholics.

known that although persons with Korsakoff's display impairment in semantic organization, they still have an ability to use associative information (D. C. Rubin & Butters, 1981). Furthermore, subjects with Korsakoff's do show improved performance when strongly associated semantic cues are used at both input and retrieval (Cermak, Uhly, & Reale, 1980). The suggestion is that persons with Korsakoff's do not spontaneously employ higher order encoding strategies but can benefit from their use when they are provided by the experimenter.

Although there are findings that do not fit an encoding account (see Glosser, Butters, & Samuels, 1976; McDowall, 1981), we feel justified in making the general conclusion that persons with Korsakoff's display deficits in the acquisition and storage of information; and further that these deficits appear to involve impairment of rehearsal and organizational strategies. It should be noted that there is a clear similarity between such a conclusion regarding the chronic effects of alcohol and earlier claims regarding the acute effects of alcohol. With these effects in mind, we will now examine the hypothesis that alcohol affects subsequent social behavior by virtue of its effects on cognition.

Social and Behavioral Consequences of Alcohol-Induced Cognitive Impairment

The Question of Behavioral Disinhibition

It is part of the common lore that alcohol intoxication results in behavioral disinhibition. At the same time, researchers and theorists in the area disagree on whether behavioral disinhibition occurs (see MacAndrew & Edgerton, 1969) and, if so, which processes are responsible. Much of the empirical research on alcohol-related behavioral disinhibition has investigated aggressive responses.

Alcohol and aggression

Experimental studies on alcohol and aggression have generally found that alcohol increases aggression in response to provocation. Many of these studies have employed a competition paradigm. In this type of experiment, subjects believe that they are competing with another subject on a task with multiple trials. Before each competitive trial, the subject selects a shock intensity setting for the opponent to receive in the event that the opponent loses on that trial. Trial winners do not receive shocks but are informed of the shock intensity (set by their opponent) that they would have received had they lost. In actuality, the opponent is simulated. The subject's shock intensity settings constitute the measure of aggression. Using this paradigm, researchers have found that intoxicated subjects behave more aggressively than either placebo or no-beverage control subjects and that high doses of alcohol lead to more aggression than low doses of alcohol (see S. P. Taylor and Leonard, 1983, for a review).

It would appear that the inherently threatening nature of the experimental setting in these studies is crucial to the finding that alcohol increases aggression. Studies that have employed the nonthreatening teacher–learner paradigm developed by Buss (1961) have failed to find that alcohol intoxication increases aggression (e.g., Bennett, Buss, & Carpenter, 1969). Furthermore, S. P. Taylor, Gammon, and Capasso (1976) manipulated the degree of threat involved in the competition paradigm and found a threat by intoxication interaction: Alcohol increased aggression, but only under conditions of threat. Similar results were found in other studies (see S. P. Taylor & Leonard, 1983). We will briefly consider three different models that have been offered to account for the effects of alcohol on aggression.

Two theoretical traditions do not appear to provide acceptable accounts of the above results. According to a pharmacological disinhibition model, alcohol impairs cortical functions responsible for the inhibitory control of behavior. As a consequence, behavior comes under control of more primitive subcortical centers in the brain. The result is the release of innate aggressive tendencies. Since such a model assumes that alcohol invariably increases aggressive tendencies, it would appear to be contradicted by evidence associating the effect of alcohol with the provocative character of the stimulus.

As an alternative to the pharmacological disinhibition model, some theorists have proposed a cognitive expectation model. According to this analysis, the knowledge that one has consumed alcohol rather than the pharmacological effect of the drug is responsible for aggressive behavior. In fact, research has demonstrated that cognitions about one's level of intoxication have effects on social behaviors that are independent of the pharmacological effects of the drug (see Marlatt & Rohsenow, 1980). At the same time, this model has difficulty accounting for the findings on aggression reviewed above. Thus, increasing the actual alcohol content of a beverage has been shown to increase aggression in response to provocation even when expectancies have been controlled such that all subjects think they have consumed alcohol. Such a finding suggests that alcohol intoxication has effects independent of subjects' cognitive expectations.

Recent evidence appears to favor a third model of alcohol and aggression. According to the cognitive impairment model, alcohol intoxication leads to behavioral disinhibition by disrupting the processing of information that is necessary for effective self-regulation. Applied to aggression, the logic of such a model is as follows: Alcohol intoxication impairs information processing; as a consequence, the actions of another person are interpreted in a relatively random fashion; the perceived arbitrary nature of the other's actions are more likely to evoke aggressive behavior. Pernanen (1976) argued that the cognitive effect of alcohol that is responsible for this pattern of behavior involves a narrowing of the perceptual field that effectively reduces the number of cues available to the intoxicated person. In a model that will be considered in the following section, J. G. Hull (1981) argued that the effect responsible for this pattern of behavior involves a deficit in higher order encoding strategies used in information storage. In a similar fashion, S. P. Taylor and Leonard (1983) have argued that the cognitive effect is related to the fact that "intoxicated individuals produce relatively superficial associations and impoverished conceptualizations" (p. 96). Each of these models have in common the assumption that alcohol has its effects on social behaviors by virtue of its effects on cognition. We will now review two studies that offer evidence in support of this hypothesis.

In an experiment by Zeichner and Pihl (1979), alcohol intoxication apparently increased aggression by virtue of inhibiting the individual's ability to process information pertinent to the consequences of his or her behavior. In brief, subjects participated in what was described as a reaction-time/pain-perception experiment. Each subject was told that they would receive a tone of varying loudness from their partner. After a 5-sec exposure to the relatively unpleasant tone, subjects were to press a button that would both terminate the tone and send a shock to their partner. Shocks could be delivered for various durations and at various intensities. The subject was led to believe that after receiving the shock the partner would communicate to the subject the degree of pain he or she felt by means of the level of the subsequent tone choice.

For half the subjects in this experiment, the degree of tone loudness was fully correlated with the shock intensities chosen by the subjects. For the remaining subjects, the tone loudness varied randomly. Given that the tones are correlated with previous shock intensity, one might reasonably expect that subjects would moderate their delivery of shocks in order to avoid loud tones. Given that the tones are random, one might reasonably expect that subjects would deliver more intense shocks in an effort to punish the irresponsible behavior of the other. In fact, this pattern was characteristic of subjects who had not consumed a beverage or had consumed a placebo they thought contained alcohol. On the other hand, subjects who consumed a beverage that actually contained alcohol were unaffected by the tone contingencies. Instead, these subjects apparently based their responses on the strength of the preceding tone regardless of whether it occurred in a random or correlated pattern. According to the authors, these findings "suggest that the occurrence of aggressive behavior following the ingestion of alcohol may in part be due to the individual's inability to process information pertinent to the consequences of his behavior" (p. 159).

A subsequent experiment by Zeichner and Pihl (1980) suggests that one of the crucial cognitive variables in the regulation of sober but not intoxicated behavior involves the attribution of intent. Using a reaction-time/pain-perception design, these authors varied what subjects were told about their partner's use of the tones. One-half of the subjects were told that the partner had no control over the tones. Such tones were therefore delivered with neutral intent. The remaining subjects were told that the partner had full control of the tones. High decibel levels were therefore indicative of malicious intent. For measures of both shock intensity and duration there was an intent by drinking interaction such that the intoxicated group was less affected by the manipulation of intent than either a placebo or nondrinking control. Once again, the behavior of the intoxicated group was mainly a function of the decibel level of the preceding tone regardless of intent. Most strikingly, under neutral intent conditions, the correlation of tone level and shock intensity was highly significant in alcohol groups and nonsignificant in both placebo and nondrinking groups.

Taken together, these two studies indicate that alcohol intoxication decreases the extent to which aggressive behavior is based on objective situational contingencies and perceived intent of the other. It is suggested that such behavioral disinhibition follows from the effect of alcohol on information processing related to self-regulation. At the same time, as Zeichner and Pihl (1980) point out, it is unclear whether intoxicated individuals differ from sober individuals in their degree of self-control because they do not efficiently process self-relevant information or because they simply choose to disregard it. One recent model of alcohol-related behaviors is based on the hypothesis that alcohol has its effects by virtue of inhibiting the processing of self-relevant information.

The self-awareness model of the behavioral consequences of alcohol use

J. G. Hull (1981) has proposed that alcohol functions to reduce an individual's level of self-awareness by inhibiting the processing of information about self. As a consequence, alcohol is proposed to disrupt self-evaluation and self-regulation (see J. G. Hull & Levy, 1979). This analysis builds on two lines of research on cognitive processes. According to the literature reviewed in the first part of the present chapter, alcohol interferes with higher order encoding processes. According to the recent literature on cognitive prototypes, self acts as a schema for encoding information (e.g., Markus, 1977; T. B. Rogers *et al.*, 1977). J. G. Hull (1981) integrated these two literatures and proposed that alcohol affects processing of information about self by decreasing use of self-relevant encoding schemes.

If alcohol interferes with processing information about self by inhibiting use of self-relevant encoding schemes, it should have the opposite behavioral effects of variables that increase use of such schemes. In a study by J. G. Hull and Levy (1979), highly self-aware individuals were especially likely to remember information that had been encoded according to its self-relevance. J. G. Hull (1981) therefore proposed that alcohol has the ultimate effect of decreasing self-awareness by inhibiting the encoding of information according to its self-relevance. This proposition has two corollaries: (a) Alcohol decreases self-awareness, and (b) it does so by inhibiting higher order cognitive processes related to the encoding of information in terms of its self-relevance. Subsequent research has examined each of these corollaries.

That alcohol can have the effect of reducing self-awareness was demonstrated in two studies reported by J. G. Hull, Levenson, Young, and Sher (1983). As measures of self-awareness, previous studies have assessed both relative frequency of first-person pronouns in speech (e.g., D. A. Davis & Brock, 1975) and frequency of self-focused responses on the Exner (1973) sentence completion questionnaire (e.g., Carver & Scheier, 1978). J. G. Hull *et al.* combined these methods in an open-ended speech format: Subjects gave short speeches about themselves that were then coded for relative frequency of self-focused statements according to the Exner scheme and first-person pronouns. The speeches took place after subjects had consumed either an alcoholic or a placebo beverage. In accord with predictions, alcohol significantly reduced the relative frequency of self-focused statements. In addition, it resulted in a marginally significant reduction in the relative frequency of first-person pronouns. A second experiment demonstrated that this effect did not depend on subjects' expectancies regarding the alcoholic content of their beverage.

Although these experiments support the corollary that alcohol reduces self-awareness, they do not provide evidence of how this occurs. J. G. Hull *et al.* (1983) report a third study that attempted to test the corollary that alcohol reduces self-awareness by inhibiting the encoding of information according to its self-relevance. The experiment involved an incidental memory paradigm developed by T. B. Rogers *et al.* (1977) to investigate self-relevant encoding processes. Using this paradigm, J. G. Hull and Levy (1979) demonstrated that individuals high in private self-consciousness (the dispositional counterpart to situational manipulations of self-awareness) were especially likely to recall information encoded according to its self-relevance in comparison to low self-conscious individuals.

Experiment 3 by J. G. Hull *et al.* (1983) replicated the procedures of T. B. Rogers *et al.* (1977) and J. G. Hull and Levy (1979) under sober and intoxicated conditions with high and low private self-conscious groups. In accord with predictions, there was an interaction of self-consciousness and alcohol consumption. High self-conscious individuals recalled more words encoded according to their self-relevance than low self-conscious individuals under placebo conditions and alcohol consumption eliminated this difference. In other words, alcohol eliminated the self-consciousness contribution to the processing of self-relevant information. These findings support the proposition that alcohol consumption reduces self-awareness by inhibiting the process of encoding information in terms of its self-relevance.

J. G. Hull (1981) proposed that alcohol intoxication has certain behavioral consequences as a function of its self-awareness reduction properties. Specifically, alcohol was proposed to affect behavior by inhibiting processes related to self-regulation. A 1985 experiment tested hypotheses related to this aspect of the model (J. G. Hull & Young, 1985). The experiment involved the Prisoner's Dilemma Game (a mixed-motive game that allows for either cooperative or competitive play). Prior to consuming an alcohol or placebo beverage, subjects read instructions on how to play the game. The instructions included a strategy section. For half of the subjects, this section emphasized a competitive game-playing strategy, for the remaining subjects this section emphasized a cooperative strategy. Following beverage consumption and absorption, subjects reread the instruction-strategy sheet and played the game. Although subjects thought that they were playing against each other, they actually played against a preprogrammed strategy. For purposes of analysis, subjects were divided according to their dispositional public self-consciousness.

Most interesting for the present discussion, analyses suggested that alcohol had effects on the self-regulation of game-playing behavior by interfering with self-regulation vis-à-vis the situational standard. Thus, to the extent that subjects self-regulate their behavior with respect to the standard presented on the instruction-strategy sheet, game-playing behavior should be a direct function of attention to the sheet: More attention to the cooperative sheet should increase cooperativeness and more attention to the competitive sheet should increase competitiveness. To test such an hypothesis, amount of time subjects spent reading the instruction sheet just prior to playing the game was correlated with amount of competitive play. Consistent with expectations, the two strongest correlations occurred for sober high public self-conscious subjects: the longer such subjects attended to competitive instructions, the more competitively they played; the longer they attended to cooperative instructions, the less competitively they played, and these two correlations were significantly different from each other. However, among *intoxicated* high public self-conscious subjects, these correlations were in the opposite direction and did not differ from each other. By implication, sober high public self-conscious individuals regulate their game-playing vis-à-vis situational standards of appropriate behavior. Intoxication appears to disrupt such self-regulation: Although subjects spent time attending to the material, they were doing so in such a way that it did not affect their subsequent behavior. Interestingly enough, the correlations among intoxicated high public self-conscious subjects were virtually identical to those of sober low self-conscious subjects. Furthermore, none of the correlations for sober or intoxicated low public self-conscious individuals were significant, and none were significantly different from each other. Once again, it would appear that alcohol is having effects by virtue of eliminating the self-consciousness contribution to behavior.

Cognitive Deficits and the Motive to Consume Alcohol: The Self-Awareness Model of Alcohol Use

While alcohol would appear to have social and behavioral consequences as a function of its effects on cognition, it is also possible that individuals consume alcohol in part in order to achieve a cognitive deficit. Past research has shown that increased self-awareness is associated with increased negative self-evaluation following failure and increased positive self-evaluation following success (see J. G. Hull & Levy, 1979). Furthermore, it has been found that individuals try to avoid self-awareness following failure and increase self-awareness following success. Given that alcohol consumption decreases self-awareness, it follows that self-aware individuals should show increased alcohol consumption following failure and decreased consumption following success.

J. G. Hull and Young (1983) conducted an experiment to test this analysis. Subjects completed a questionnaire booklet that included the self-consciousness inventory (Fenigstein, Scheier, & Buss, 1975). They then worked on intelligence-type tasks and were randomly assigned success or failure feedback. Immediate overt signs of pleasure–displeasure in response to this feedback were recorded as an indication of reactivity to the manipulation. Subjects were then released to participate in a second, ostensibly unrelated experiment during which they completed a mood measure and then tasted and rated a series of wines. This wine-tasting procedure has been used in several previous experiments to assess alcohol consumption under ad-lib conditions (e.g., R. L. Higgins & Marlatt, 1975).

For purposes of analysis, individuals were divided into high and low private self-consciousness groups. In accord with predictions, high self-conscious individuals showed significantly more overt pleasure–displeasure in response to the success–failure feedback than did low self-conscious individuals. In addition, analyses of the mood measures revealed the predicted interaction of self-consciousness and success–failure such that high self-conscious subjects who received failure feedback reported significantly more negative moods than high self-conscious subjects receiving success feedback. Low self-conscious individuals fell between these extremes and did not vary according to success–failure feedback. Finally, as predicted, there was a significant interaction of self-consciousness and success–failure on the measure of wine consumption. High self-conscious subjects given failure feedback drank significantly more wine than high self-conscious subjects given success feedback. Again, low self-conscious individuals fell between these extremes and did not vary according to success–failure feedback.

While these results support the self-awareness model of alcohol consumption, it is also necessary to determine if they can generalize to conditions outside of the laboratory. J. G. Hull, Young, and Jouriles (in press) report two studies that apply predictions from the model to alcohol consumption in the real world. In both studies, the basic prediction was that life events indicative of success and failure should be more strongly related to alcohol consumption among individuals high as opposed to low in dispositional private self-consciousness. In the first study, this analysis was successfully used to predict relapse rates among detoxified alcoholics. Following release from the detoxification center, high self-conscious alcoholics who had experienced predominantly negative life events were particularly likely to relapse to pretreatment levels of drinking. High self-conscious alcoholics who had experienced predominantly positive life events were particularly likely not to relapse. The quality of life events had no effect on relapse rate of low self-conscious alcoholics. In the second study, the model was successfully used to predict alcohol consumption rates among high school adolescents. Again, high self-conscious individuals who were experiencing negative self-relevant events (poor grades in school) were especially likely to consume alcohol. High self-conscious individuals who were experiencing positive self-relevant events consumed significantly less alcohol. The quality of self-relevant events had a significantly smaller effect on the drinking of low self-conscious individuals. In addition, this interaction of self-consciousness and the quality of self-relevant events remained a significant predictor of consumption even after several other known predictors of alcohol use were statistically taken into account.

Together with the experimental study by J. G. Hull and Young (1983), these experiments indicate the generality of the self-awareness model. Alcohol use has been shown to be a joint function of an individual's level of private self-consciousness and personal success–failure. This interaction has been demonstrated across different populations (adolescents, college students, and middle-aged adults), different patterns of alcohol use (social drinkers and alcoholics), different indicators of self-relevant life experiences (experimentally manipulated success–failure, reported academic performance, and reported performance of a significant role), and different measures of alcohol use (situationally measured wine consumption, self-reported alcohol consumption, and measures of alcoholic relapse). Furthermore, the results of the second study by J. G. Hull *et al.* (in press) suggest that this relationship is relatively independent of environmental and behavioral factors previously shown to be directly related to alcohol use.

Summary and Conclusions

In conclusion, it would appear that alcohol has pharmacological effects on information processing. In particular, intoxication appears to debilitate the acquisition and storage of information. At the same time, it appears to have minimal effects on retrieval of information. While some research suggests that these storage deficits are due to the effects of alcohol on the production and use of encoding-elaboration strategies, there is enough research that is inconsistent with this hypothesis to warrant caution at this time.

In addition to effects related to acute intoxication, chronic use of alcohol also appears to have a detrimental effect on information processing. While long-term moderate use is associated with some memory impairment, the most severe effects are related to memory in alcoholic and patients with Korsakoff's syndrome. Once again, this chronic impairment appears to be due to deficits in the storage of information. As in the literature on acute intoxication, researchers have begun to focus on encoding-elaboration strategies as key elements in this storage deficit.

Several recent models propose that, by virtue of its effects on cognition, alcohol has the ultimate effect of disinhibiting social behavior. In one form or another, these models presume that alcohol disrupts processes related to self-regulation. Recent research suggests the utility of this analysis. At the same time, future research needs to more precisely identify the cognitive mechanisms responsible for these effects and to provide more direct evidence of these mediational processes.

According to one recent model, individuals sometimes consume alcohol in order to achieve cognitive impairment. Thus, the self-awareness model presumes that individuals occasionally feel uncomfortable as a consequence of cognitive processes related to self-evaluation. Under these conditions, alcohol consumption may be motivated by a desire to inhibit the utilization of self-referent encoding schemes. Recent research has provided support for this analysis.

It is hoped that this summary of the current state of research on alcohol and information processing has demonstrated the interconnections between a variety of alcohol effects. In addition, it is hoped that we have made clear the areas in which the evidence is weakest in support of a particular point of view. It is our conviction that the cognitive approach to alcohol use has resulted in real progress in understanding some of the causes and effects of alcohol consumption. At the same time, more convincing evidence is necessary in areas where the role of information processing is implicit or where the research has presented conflicting results. Hopefully future research will clarify that which present research only suggests.

9

Information Processing and Autism

ALAN J. LITROWNIK
Department of Psychology
San Diego State University
San Diego, California 92182

ELIZABETH T. MCINNIS
Los Niños Education Center
San Diego, California 92120

Introduction

It was a little over 40 years ago that Kanner (1943) first described 11 cases that he claimed represented a new syndrome, early infantile autism. In this relatively brief period a considerable body of research has been generated in an effort to understand and treat this puzzling disorder. While many etiological theories have been proposed, none has been unequivocally supported nor have we been successful in developing effective treatments.

Why is this the state of our understanding? In an earlier review of cognitive and perceptual deficits in autism (Litrownik & McInnis, 1982), we pointed out that not only have diagnostic issues limited interpretation of research findings, but also the lack of a unifying conceptual framework. Without this conceptual framework, research efforts are fragmented and contribute little to an overall understanding of this disorder. To remedy this situation, we presented an information processing framework that we believed would help integrate diverse areas of research, direct future research efforts, and thus contribute to our general understanding of autism and its treatment. In the present chapter we continue to rely on this conceptual foundation, that is, information processing, while recognizing the need to expand our framework in order to accommodate the flood of information emerging from the biological perspective.

Our goals in this chapter are to (1) provide a brief description of diagnostic issues in autism, (2) present a general framework for understanding the search for etiology and pathogenesis, (3) present the information processing model used in our earlier review along with a summary of the conclusions drawn from that review, (4) summarize recent work in the most promising areas identified in this first review (i.e., neurophysiological/psychophysiological indexes of processing, hemispheric functioning, and attentional deficits) and (5) illustrate the utility of the information processing perspective for not only clarifying our understanding of autism, but also for focusing our treatment and research efforts.

Infantile Autism: Diagnosis and Current Focus

In order to understand the diagnostic issues related to autism, one must keep in mind that autism is a syndrome, that is, a group of symptoms that together characterize a specific condition. While some consensus has developed regarding the list of symptoms associated with the diagnostic label "autism," problems arise from the fact that not all those individuals identified as autistic exhibit all of these symptoms, nor do they exhibit the same degree of symptom severity. None of these symptoms is exclusively associated with autism, and there is no consensus as to which or how many symptoms must be exhibited.

Two sets of diagnostic criteria have received some endorsement from the *Journal of Autism and Developmental Disorders* (Schopler, 1978). One was formulated by Rutter (1978) based on a review of literature, and the second was formulated by a committee of the National Society for Autistic Children (1978). To further complicate matters, the latest revision of the *Diagnostic and Statistical Manual of Mental Disorders* (1980) includes autism for the first time. In comparing these three sets of criteria, the lists have three items in common (although worded somewhat differently): (1) age of onset prior to 30 months, (2) pervasive lack of responsiveness to other people, and (3) delayed and deviant language development. Other criteria mentioned on at least one of these lists include peculiar interest in or attachment to animate and inanimate objects; disturbances in the rate of appearance of physical, social, and language skills; abnormal responses to sensory input; absence of delusions, hallucinations, loosening of associations, and incoherence.

In the past 10 years most, if not all, professionals who work with autistic children have come to the conclusion that there is some organic involvement in the disorder. Some (e.g., D. J. Cohen & Shaywitz, 1982) point to the early onset of the disorder and to its pervasiveness, which they see as suggesting a critical central nervous system (CNS) dysfunction. Others acknowledge the likelihood of organic involvement but dismiss its relevance for treatment (Lovaas, 1979).

In any case, the promise of discovering the underlying organic deficit has led to an almost frenzied search for biological markers and localization of the CNS dysfunction. New and better techniques for assessing biochemical/metabolic functioning (e.g., chemical assays and positron emission tomography [PET] scans that measure glucose utilization in the brain), neuroanatomy (e.g., computed tomography [CT] scans and magnetic resonant imaging [MRI]), and neurophysiology (e.g., event-related potentials [ERPs]) have also been responsible for this flurry of recent activity and optimism. Unfortunately, much of this work has been in response to the new technological developments rather than being based on theoretical formulations or prior empirical studies. While we can remain optimistic about what these new methods will allow us to learn about biochemical functioning, neuroanatomy, and neurophysiology, there is less reason to expect that an explanation for autism will be forthcoming. Silver and Segal (1984) caution that, while biological factors may be necessary to fully understand the functioning organism, these factors are not sufficient to explain all the complexities of human behavior. Thus, an integration of biological and psychological perspectives is required if we hope to understand normal as well as abnormal development.

Levels of Focus

In our previous review of the psychological literature dealing with autism (see Litrownik & McInnis, 1982), we introduced a working model of information processing that allowed us to (1) organize empirical reports, (2) summarize our current understanding of this disorder, and (3) identify promising areas for future work as well as strategies for conducting this work. Given the recent focus on biological functioning, it is apparent that an information processing approach will further our understanding of autism only if it is viewed from a broader interdisciplinary framework. The following conceptual framework is presented in an attempt to integrate approaches while also demonstrating the continued utility of viewing autism from an information processing perspective.

Gross Etiology and Pathogenesis

The first step in this integration requires that we identify various levels of focus or analysis. Identification of these levels in the causal chain does not argue for a reductionist explanation of autism but rather sets the stage for considering the role that each level plays in the development, maintenance, and treatment of

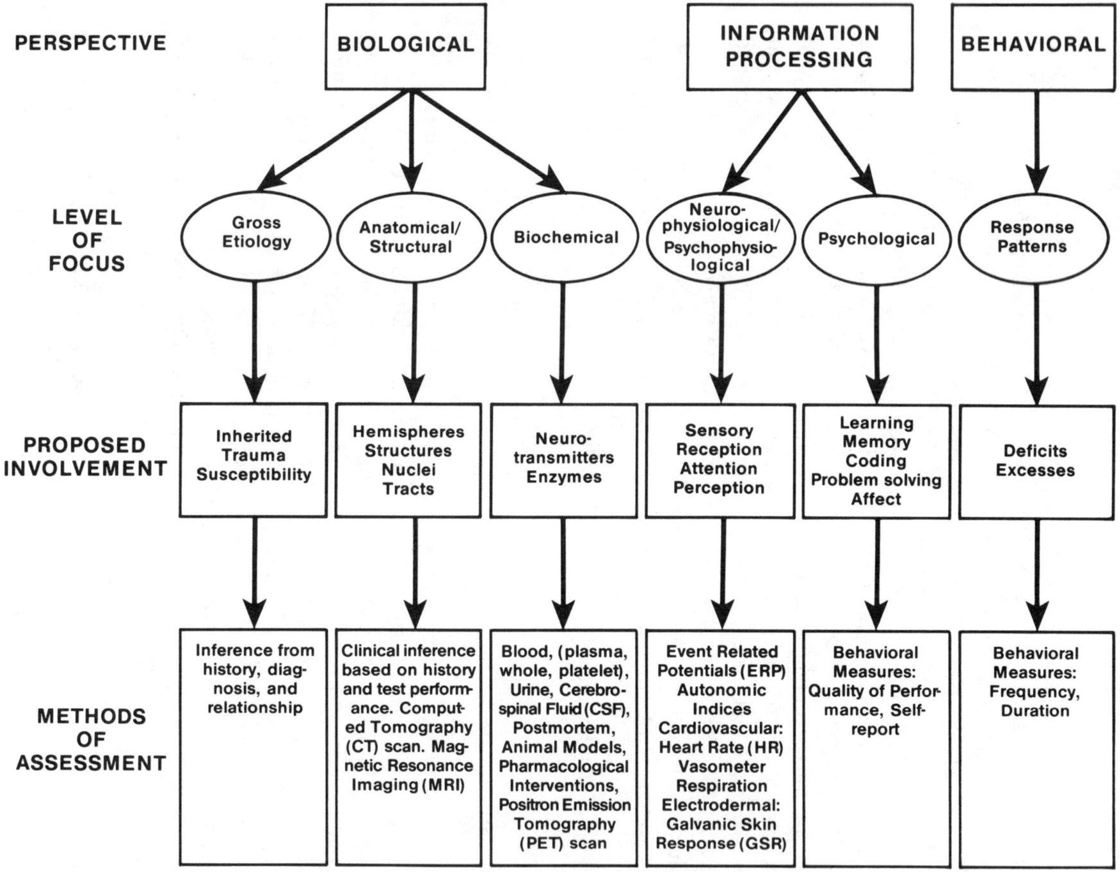

FIG. 1. *A conceptual framework for integrating perspectives: autism and levels of focus, proposed involvement, and methods of assessment.*

the disorder. These levels, methods of assessment, and perspectives that serve to direct our understanding are presented in Fig. 1.

At the first level we recognize that a single gene or traumatic event (i.e., physical or viral) could be responsible for the direct expression of autism, though most professionals now agree that autism is the result of multiple etiologies that are expressed in some common pattern (e.g., Coleman, 1979). This common expression could be observed as a CNS or biochemical lesion, neural defect, sensory dysfunction, attentional deficit, or inappropriate overt response that occurs either singly or in combination.

An important distinction is made between etiology and pathogenesis or common expression. That is, specific etiological factors can directly or indirectly determine the primary dysfunction or pathogenesis. For example, an etiological agent could be directly responsible for a specific biochemical lesion or pathogenesis (e.g., lack of an enzyme) or the biological system could be more susceptible to environmental insult (e.g., Ciaranello, VandenBerg, & Anders, 1982).

Structural Focus

Not only have structures such as the hippocampus (Boucher, 1978), thalamus (Coleman, 1979), and mesolimbic cortex (Prior, 1984) been identified as possible lesion sites, but also the more general left side of the cortex (see Fein, Humes, Kaplan, Lucci, & Waterhouse, 1984). Indirect methods have been utilized almost exclusively to produce this list of possible brain damage sites. As Maurer and Damasio (1982) explain, ''standard methods of clinical inference'' are used to develop plausable hypotheses about hemispheres, lobes, and structures that might be damaged. This method first requires that we agree that autism is an organic disorder of the CNS. We must also accept the propositions that (1) autism can be identified and differentiated from other disorders and common behavioral problems described, and (2) various functions (e.g., motor, communication, attention) in the intact CNS can be identified as occurring in specified parts of the brain (i.e., there is a specific anatomical structure responsible for that function). Clinical inference can then be applied in an effort to explain observed behavioral dysfunctions in autism by pointing to parts of the CNS believed to be responsible for normal behavioral functions.

There are some serious problems with this method. Though most agree there is an organic base for autism, the reliability and validity of attempts to identify common deficits (e.g., cognitive, linguistic, attentional) in autism have been questioned (see Fein *et al.,* 1984). The second proposition regarding the relationship between CNS structure and function, and the resulting inferences about structures responsible for observed common deficits, are tenuous at best. Phillips (1982) points out that it is possible to get the same end (i.e., functioning) via quite different approaches (i.e., pathways, neural structures). Thus, there is not a simple one-to-one relationship between structure and function in the CNS. Direct methods for assessing brain anatomy do exist. The invasive pneumoencephalogram has been replaced by the CT scan. This radiologic technique has been applied to autistic populations with mixed results (Fein *et al.*, 1984). While CT scanning procedures can be standardized, significant methodological problems exist in their interpretation (Reider, Mann, Weinberger, van Kammen, & Post, 1983).

Newer and more powerful techniques, for example, MRI, continue to be developed. As previously suggested, these slices of the brain will have little meaning if we do not consider how they are related to the processing of information and ultimate response patterns. Specifically, we need to know more about CNS functioning and the various strategies that are utilized to accomplish a specific objective. With additional knowledge about processing strategies available for a given task, we may be able to move closer to localizing involved neurological structures (Phillips, 1982).

Biochemical Focus

Biochemical involvement in autism has been related to toxic effects due to abnormal enzyme levels (e.g., of monoamine oxidase) as well as dysfunction in neurotransmitter systems (e.g., catecholamine, indolamine). These systems and the specific chemical neurotransmitters allow for transmission of information from one neuron to another.

While different neurotransmitters may be active in the same lobe (temporal, frontal, etc.) or structure (hippocampus, thalamus, etc.), discrete collections of nerve cells (i.e., nuclei) and axon bundles that are made of nuclei (i.e., tracts) generally involve a single neurotransmitter. Three transmitters have been implicated in the pathogenesis of autism: serotonin, norepinephrine, and dopamine (e.g., Campbell, Anderson, Deutsch, & Green, 1984; Ritvo, Freeman, Geller, & Yuwiler, 1983). It is easy to understand why these three have generated such interest when we identify the nuclei and tracts that contain these transmitters (i.e., where they originate, terminate, and the functions they mediate or determine). Specifically, serotonergic activity modulates emotionality, sleep, learning and memory, appetite, sensory perception, and neuroendocrine secretions located in the brainstem, hypothalamus, and limbic systems. Neurons utilizing norepinephrine arise in the medulla and project to limbic, hypothalamus, and cortical structures. Thus, they are involved in activity level, arousal, attention, memory, learning, and emotionality. Dopamine has been associated with neurons that originate in the midbrain and hypothalamus with projections to limbic and cortical structures as well as the pituitary gland. These structures and regions are involved in emotionality, affect, cognition, and attention (see Ciaranello *et al.*, 1982).

As D. J. Cohen and Young (1977) point out, our understanding of neurotransmitter systems in general, and in autism specifically, is limited by the indirect methods available for obtaining information about brain metabolism (e.g., sampling metabolized neurotransmitters in the blood, urine, and cerebrospinal fluid [CSF]; using animal models and pharmacological interventions). There is no guarantee that these methods represent brain metabolism. Even with more direct methods (e.g., postmortem examination, PET scan) it is difficult to interpret how levels of neurotransmitters and their metabolites are related to autism. That is, it is not likely that one neurotransmitter would be responsible for the observed syndrome of autism. There is much activity and organizing that occurs between the action of a neurotransmitter and actual functioning of the nervous system. Biological and physiological processes in the brain interact to determine nervous system functioning, and numerous secondary factors (e.g., diet, high activity level) could be responsible for observed differences in neurotransmitter metabolism (D. J. Cohen & Young, 1977; Gillberg, Trygstad, & Foss, 1982).

Physiological, Psychological, and Behavioral Focuses

The next two levels, neurophysiological/psychophysiological and psychological, are incorporated in an information processing perspective. At the present time researchers interested in autism seem to be approaching the problem from two diverse points of view. On the one hand are the behavioral clinicians who have been focusing upon the behavioral manifestations of autism and their modification through environmental manipulations, the last level. At the other extreme are the neurobiologists who have been concerned with the identification of specific CNS dysfunctions in autism. As D. J. Cohen and Shaywitz (1982) have pointed out, there is a need to bridge the gap which exists between the clinical and basic researchers. It is our contention that an information processing perspective which incorporates the neurophysiological/psychophysiological and psychological levels can function as such a bridge, providing a means of organizing and interpreting research which approaches autism from both the clinical/behavioral and biological perspectives. In addition to providing an organizational framework which can aid in the understanding of current research results, it can also provide direction to future research efforts.

Information Processing

The remainder of the chapter is devoted to the application of an information processing perspective to understanding autism. We begin by presenting an overview of a previously proposed model of information processing and a summary of our empirical review based on this model (see Litrownik & McInnis,

1982, for a complete presentation of the model and review of the empirical literature).

Working Conceptual Model

The model described in our earlier review was not proposed as an explanatory theory but rather as a framework from which we could better understand the functioning of individuals who display autistic symptomology. It was our hope that increased understanding would suggest new areas of research and ultimately lead to improved methods of treatment. Our objective remains the same, as we briefly describe the previously presented model which includes four levels of processing.

Two component mechanisms are proposed at the *sensory-receptor level*. The first is the individual's sensory systems (e.g., visual, auditory) and their structural parts (e.g., cornea, lens, retina; eardrum, middle ear, cochlea) which respond to specific forms of physical energy (e.g., light and sound waves). The second component is the sensory register which temporarily stores large amounts of information for a short time after the external stimulus has been withdrawn. Each receptor system is seen as having its own register which briefly stores minimally processed information from which information is selected for further processing.

At the *initial processing level,* information from the sensory registers is selected for subsequent presentation at the higher cortical levels. Since information in the sensory registers decays rapidly, an important parameter at this level is the speed with which information is selected and organized for further processing. Another important parameter at this level is the processing capacity or breadth of attention. Breadth of attention appears to be a structural feature of this level as opposed to other types of attentional process which seem to be under control of the individual and influenced by past experience, instructional sets, and expectations.

Information selected at the initial level is prepared for retrieval at the *higher processing level.* This preparation includes initial temporary storage of selected information, which is then made available for coding or constructive transformations. In the coding or transformation process the information is related to prior cognitive structures or stores of information. It is assumed that at this level information from separate sensory registers enters a single coding system.

The last level, the *executive level,* includes retrieving information, generating response alternatives, and selecting an alternative for performance. Information that has been stored is retrieved in response to the demands of the situation the individual is experiencing. Retrieval of information will necessarily be determined by prior processing, as well as by task demands and learner variables.

Summary of Earlier Literature Review

In our earlier chapter we reviewed studies as they related to the first three levels of processing. While the levels can be conceptually separated, most research has involved processing on all levels. Behavioral measures necessarily involve all four processing levels, while physiological correlates of processing at the earliest level can be obtained without the influence of higher processing levels. However, inferences about processing at a given level can be made if the influence of the higher levels is minimized and adequate processing at the lower levels can be ensured. Recognizing these limitations we reviewed relevant empirical reports that were available through the middle of 1981 and as a result reached the following conclusions about the functioning of autistic children at the sensory-receptor, initial, and higher processing levels.

Sensory-receptor level

The question of whether there is a dysfunction in the activation of the peripheral sense organs had received little systematic attention from researchers. We concluded, based on available work, that at least some autistic children exhibit signs of dysfunction at the sensory-receptor level. Support for this conclusion came from reports that autistic children (1) either failed to show any brainstem response to an auditory stimulus or evidenced delayed brainstem transmission times for both auditory and visual stimulation, (2) tend to prefer and work harder for higher levels of auditory and vestibular input than comparison groups, (3) differ from other populations in terms of how they respond to and utilize input from different sense modalities, and (4) are not as responsive to vestibular input as comparison groups. Since the reviewed research indicated that autistic individuals may have abnormalities at the sensory-receptor level, it is possible that deficits observed at higher levels may also be the result of problems which begin at this first level.

Initial processing level

Attentional mechanisms responsible for initial processing (scanning, selection, and transfer of information to the higher levels) had generated a great deal of research. The general conclusions derived from this body of research were that autistic children (1) spend less time visually scanning their environment and do not shift their visual fixation from one display to another as often as normal and retarded children; (2) are able to attend to as many simultaneously presented cues as normal children of the same mental age; (3) tend to be too selective in responding to multiple cues, though this may be more related to mental age than autism; and (4) are not able to learn incidentially as are normal children.

Higher processing level

Our review at this level focused upon the physiological correlates of CNS functioning, evidence of specialization of hemispheric functioning, and research related to basic cognitive operations (memory, coding, cross-modal transfer of information). Major conclusions based on this body of research included (1) autistic children evidence abnormal cortical responses and may have diminished cortical responsiveness and a longer processing time than normal children; (2) the left hemisphere may be abnormal in autistic individuals; (3) memory storage in autistic children seems to be a rote echo box store, which is adequate if the input does not exceed the immediate memory span or require coding; (4) autistic children have difficulty coding information (abstracting rules and recognizing redundancy) regardless of the input modality; (5) spatial information is easier for autistic children to code than information requiring temporal coding strategies; and (6) autistic children have more difficulty than normal children with tasks requiring cross-modal transfer of information, for example, the translation of visual input such as reading into an auditory code so that a verbal response can be made.

Promising Research

After completing our initial review we noted that most of the work had focused on specific functions while failing to consider the effects of other processing levels on observed performance. Problems with the heterogeneity of the autistic populations studied and inappropriate or nonexistent comparison groups also limited conclusions based on these empirical reports. Nevertheless, there appeared to be several areas which seemed to deserve further attention, for example, ERPs, autonomic indexes, hemispheric functioning, and attentional deficits. In the following sections we review and update developments that have taken place in these areas since our last review.

Event-related potentials

A relatively recent development in the search for specific neurological dysfunctions in autism has been the use of ERP measures with autistic populations. Electrical patterns which represent brain-wave activity in response to repeated presentations of sensory stimuli are averaged, which cancels out background electrical activity and allows for the identification of the small magnitude changes which occur in response to a stimulus. These potentials are generally identified by the sense modality involved and by the typical latency associated with the response. Those waves associated with latencies of 0 to 80 msec can be viewed as reflecting transmission and storage of sensory information and are usually obtained while the subject is passively experiencing the presentation of sensory stimulation. Waves associated with latencies of 100 to 1000 msec are identified with cognitive processing and are generally obtained while the subject is performing a cognitive task (Polich & Starr, 1984). In reviewing the evoked potential work done with autistic children we will group studies according to the waves measured.

AUDITORY BRAINSTEM POTENTIAL (ABP). Seven waves (Waves I–VII) have been identified in the transmission of auditory stimuli through the brainstem. These seven waves occur within 10 msec of the presentation of the auditory stimulus. Wave I is thought to reflect activity of the 8th cranial nerve and its latency to represent peripheral transmission time; Wave II, activity of the cochlear nuclei; Wave III, the olivary complex of the pons; and Waves IV and V, the rostral pons and midbrain. The difference between Waves I and V is assumed to measure brainstem transmission time (Polich & Starr, 1984).

Table 1 provides a summary of eight studies conducted between 1978 and 1983 which have investigated auditory brainstem responses of autistic children. Methodologically these studies are quite similar: All presented an auditory stimulus (clicks) at intensities which generally ranged from 60 to 90 dB and measured the evoked potentials at the vertex location (Cz) of the scalp. Two studies presented the stimuli binaurally, the rest used a monaural presentation. Normal control groups were used in all these studies and two studies included clinical groups other than autistic (minimum brain damage, psychotic).

While abnormalities in evoked potentials were reported for the autistic group in all these studies, not all autistic children exhibited abnormalities. These studies provided individual data indicating that anywhere from 44 to 80% of the autistic sample showed completely normal responses (Gillberg, Rosenhall, & Johansson, 1983; Novick *et al.*, 1980; Skoff *et al.*, 1980). Evidence of delays in peripheral transmission time for autistic children (Wave I latency) was reported in two studies (Student & Sohmer, 1978; Tanguay, 1981), but this finding was not replicated by the other investigators. No consistent results were seen in relation to which ear received stimulation. Skoff *et al.* (1980) found more abnormal responses for left-ear stimulation, while Tanguay (1981) found more abnormalities for the right. The most common finding across studies was evidence of delays in central transmission time for some autistic children in each sample (increased Wave I–IV latencies). At least some evidence of this type of abnormality was reported in every study reviewed.

In addition to focusing on the presence or absence of abnormal ABPs, two studies also looked for behavioral correlates associated with the presence of abnormal ABPs. Gillberg *et al.* (1983) assessed a subset of their autistic group for postrotary nystagmus. They report that three of four children with no nystagmus had abnormal ABPs, whereas only one of four with nystagmus did. They also assessed the entire autistic group for muscle hypotonia and found that 7 of

TABLE 1
Brainstem-Evoked Potentials

Author	Subjects	Controls	Method	Results[a]
Student & Sohmer (1978)	15 Autistic, 4–12 yr, sedated	12 Normals, similar ages, 2 coma	Monaural clicks, 75 dB, 10 per sec	No AEP in 5 autistics (cochlear hearing loss) Autistics with AEPs had significantly longer Wave I latency and I–IV interpeak intervals
Sohmer & Student (1978)	13 Autistics, 4–12 yr, sedated 16 MBD, 3–11 yr 10 retarded, 2–8 yr	18 Normals, 4–12 yr, 4 sedated, 1 coma	Monaural clicks, 10 per sec, 75 dB above threshold	No AEP in 4 autistics (cochlear hearing loss) No Wave IV & V in 2 mentally retarded subjects No difference in Wave I latency between normals & autistics All experimental groups, I–IV interval significantly longer No difference between sedated and not sedated
Rosenblum, Arick Krug, Stubbs, Young, & Pelson (1980)	6 Autistics (4 males), 5–15 yr, sedated	6 Normals matched for age & sex	Binaural clicks, 10 per sec, 60 dB above adult threshold	Autistic group: Wave I–IV interval significantly longer Autistic group: Waves III & IV latencies significantly longer Autistic group: AEPs significantly more variable
Novick, Vaughn, Kurtzburg, & Simon (1980)	5 Autistic adolescents	5 Normals, age matched	Binaural clicks, 10 per sec, 90 dB SPL	Normal latency found for 4 autistics Significantly longer I–IV latencies for 1 autistic
Skoff, Mirsky, & Turner (1980)	16 Autistic (9 males), 5–13 yr	20 Normals (10 males, 10 females), 5–16 yr	Monaural clicks, 10 per sec, 60 dB above adult threshold	Autistic group: significantly longer I–IV & III–V latencies Autistic group: 9 had abnormal AEPs, significantly more abnormal AEPs in left ear

				No difference in Wave I latency between groups
Fein, Skoff, & Mirsky (1981)	15 Autistics, 1 schizophrenic, 5–13 yr	20 Normals, 5–16 yr	Monaural clicks, 10 per sec, 60 dB above adult threshold	Autistic group: significantly longer I–IV & III–V latencies No difference in Wave I latency between groups Autistic group: 7 had normal AEPs, 9 had abnormal AEPs Abnormal AEPs more frequent in left ear Behavioral differences (autistics with normal AEPs vs. autistics with abnormal AEPs); no difference in language, perception, or motor behavior; more pathology in attention & social behavior; all with seizures & all not right-handed had abnormal AEPs
Gillberg, Rosenhall, & Johansson (1983)	24 Autistics (19 males), 2–21 yr 7 Psychotics, 8–13 yr	31 Normals (16 males), 5–21 yr, IQs > 85	Monaural clicks, 10 per sec, 20–80 dB Postrotary nystagmus measurements in 8 autistics	AEPs abnormal in 8 autistics Autistics with abnormal AEPs: 6 had longer Wave V & I–IV latencies Autistic group: no overlap in I–IV latencies with normal group No postrotary nystagmus in 4 autistics (3 had abnormal AEPs vs. abnormal AEPs in 1 of 4 with nystagmus)
Tanguay (1981)	16 Autistics, 2–13 yr	16 Normals	Monaural clicks, 20, 50, & 100 per sec; 42, 57, 72 dB above adult threshold	Autistic group: Wave I latency longer for right ear Autistic group: longer latencies for I–III, III–V, & I–V Autistic group: 50% had at least one interval latency which was 3 *SD*s above the mean for normals

[a]AEP, auditory-evoked potentials.

TABLE 2
Cognitive-Evoked Potentials

Author	Subjects	Controls	Method	Results
Novick, Kurtzburg, & Vaughn (1979)	3 Autistic (3 males), adolescents	3 Normals (3 males), adolescents	Monaural 50 dB tone, 1 per sec; 10 msec light, 1 per sec. 1st condition: 10% of stimuli randomly omitted, response to omissions 2nd condition: No response to omissions	Autistic group: both auditory P3–P400 & visual P4–P500 small or absent Autistic group: N1–P2 smaller (not significant) Autistic group: 1st condition smaller ratio (missing stimulus/stimulus present) with auditory stimulus Autistic group: 2nd condition smaller ratio with both auditory & visual stimuli
Novick, Vaughn, Kurtzberg, & Simon (1980)	5 Autistic adolescents	5 Normals, adolescents	Middle latency Binaural clicks, 1 & 3 per sec, 90 dB Auditory discrimination task Binaural tone, 1 per sec, 90 dB; response required to low pitch tones; 10% of stimuli low pitch (signals) Missing stimulus 10% of binaural tones omitted 1st Condition: Respond to omission 2nd Condition: No response required	Middle latencies Autistic group: P2 amplitudes significantly smaller No difference between groups in P60 & N100 shape or latency Auditory discrimination task Autistic group: abnormal AEPs to signals & P3 amplitudes significantly smaller No Reaction Time (RT) difference between groups in response to signals Autistic group: less accurate in response to signals than normals Missing stimulus Autistic were able to detect a missing stimulus, their P3 amplitudes significantly smaller with & without a response
Martineau, Garreau, Barthelemy, Callaway, & Lelord (1981)	12 Autistics (6 males), average age = 7	11 Normal (6 males), average age = 7	Conditioning paradigm CS was 4-msec tone 25 dB above threshold; UCS was .1-msec 200 lux light; measured middle latencies; vitamin B6 given to all subjects	Autistic group: Before B6, P2 latency significantly longer to CS–UCS pair N1–P1 amplitudes significantly smaller to UCS Autistic group: With B6, N1 & P2 latencies significantly longer to UCS & CS–

				UCS pair, P2 significantly longer latency to CS Autistic group: AEP changes with B6 were in normal direction
Niwa, Ohta, & Yamazaki (1983)	4 Autistics (4 males), 12–17 yr 4 Downs (3 males), 11–17 yr	5 Normals (4 males), 11–22 yr	Stimulus was 200-msec 1-kHz tone, 50 dB SL; target stimulus was 900-kHz tone (P = .15); three-task condition: listening, counting, key-pressing	Listening: Autistic group had lower (nonsignificant) P3 Counting: 2 Autistics had P3s similar to normal; 2 autistics & 4 Down's could not do the counting Key press: All autistics and 2 Down's could not key press
Courchesne, Kilman, Galambos, & Lincoln (1983)	7 Autistics, nonretarded, 13–21 yr	7 Normals, age matched	Positive stimulus (words me, *you*) & novel sounds 200-msec, 65 dB above threshold Listening condition: 90% *me*, 10% *you* Task condition: Respond to *you* (10% *you*) Respond to *you* (10% *you*, 10% novel)	Autistic group: accurate in response to target; RT a little slower Listening condition: no significant difference between groups Autistic group: smaller P3 & N800 amplitudes to novel sounds, N800 latencies longer to target stimulus Listen vs. task conditions: normals P3 amplitudes to target stimuli higher in task than listen; Autistic P3 was not higher in task condition; Both groups N800 amplitudes higher in task condition than listening condition No significant difference between groups in N1 & P2
Martineau, Garreau, Barthelemy, & Lelord (1984)	15 Autistics (8 males), average age = 8, IQs 20–70	18 Normals (9 males), average age = 8	Conditioning paradigm CS was 4-msec tone 25 dB above threshold; UCS was 1200 lux flash 800 msec after CS; measured middle latencies	Autistic group: CS alone, P3 amplitude larger & all latencies shorter (had fewer P3 response than normals) Autistic group: UCS-CS paired, P1, P2, P3 amplitude decreased (same ampls increased in normals), were fewer responses and were more variable in autistic group

Note. The following abbreviations are used in this table: CS, conditioned stimulus; UCS, unconditioned stimulus.

the 8 autistics with abnormal ABPs also had hypontonia, whereas only 1 of 16 autistics with normal ABPs displayed hypotonia. Fein, Skoff, and Mirsky (1981) compared the behavioral profiles of a group of autistic children who had abnormal ABPs with a group which did not. They did not find any difference between these two groups in terms of language, perceptual, or motor behaviors, but they did find that the three children in the sample who had seizures and the four who were not fully right-handed had abnormal ABPs. Perhaps their most significant finding was that the group with abnormal ABPs showed a higher degree of pathology in terms of attention and social accessibility.

MIDDLE TO LONG LATENCY POTENTIALS. Table 2 presents a summary of six studies which investigated ERPs which occur 10–1000 msec after the stimulus presentation. Middle latency potentials occur between 10 and 50 msec after the stimulus and are generally labeled based on whether they are in the positive (P) or negative (N) direction with the order being indicated by lowercase letters a, b, or c (e.g., Na, Pa). Late latency potentials occur between 50 and 250 msec after the stimulus and are labeled P1, N1, P2, and N2. Long latency potentials occur 250–400+ msec after stimulus presentation and are labeled P3 or P300. The neuroanatomical origins of the middle, late, and long latency potentials are largely unknown. The middle latency potentials are largely unaffected by endogenous variables such as attention. The late and long latency potentials, on the other hand, are strongly influenced by subject variables such as attention, detection, decision, and anticipation, and therefore reflect information processing at the higher levels. The studies investigating late and long latency waves have either used a conditioning paradigm or more commonly one which requires the subject to detect a stimulus change. These studies usually present a sequence of stimuli and then on a random basis either change or omit one of the stimuli. There are usually two conditions: one where the subject passively experiences the change and another where they must make some kind of a response (e.g., key press) to the stimulus change. All of the studies used auditory stimuli, and three studies also included a visual stimulus.

Middle latency abnormalities were found in autistic subjects, but the findings were not consistent across studies. Novick, Kurtzberg, and Vaughn (1979) and Courchesne, Kilman, Galambos, and Lincoln (1983) found no significant differences in N1, P2 responses between autistic and normals, whereas Novick *et al.* (1980) reported a significantly smaller P2 amplitude in the autistic group. Martineau, Garreau, Barthelemy, Callaway, and Lelord (1981) found a significantly longer P2 latency in the autistic group and a significantly smaller peak to peak amplitude of N1–P1 in the autistic group, while Martineau, Garreau, Barthelemy, and Lelord (1984) reported shorter P1, N1, P2, and N2 latencies for autistic subjects.

More consistent findings have been reported for the long latency waves, specifically P3. Evidence of significantly smaller P3 amplitudes in response to stimulus changes was reported by Novick *et al.* (1979, 1980). These results were found in both a passive listening condition and a condition which required a response. Courchesne *et al.* (1983) and Niwa, Ohta, and Yamazaki (1983) also found smaller P3 amplitudes in their autistic groups. Martineau *et al.* (1984), on the other hand, reported large P3 amplitudes (although their autistic group had fewer P3 responses than normal).

In general, the ERP research supports the hypothesis of neurological dysfunction in autism. It appears that the brainstem transmission time of auditory input is delayed in many autistic children, and abnormalities are also found in the cortical potentials in response to both visual and auditory stimuli. While this area of research appears very promising, the studies reported to date have been done with very small samples, and thus the results should be regarded as preliminary. Since abnormalities have been found at both the initial and higher levels of processing, it would seem important to begin investigating both brainstem and cortical potentials in the same subjects. Novick *et al.* (1980) did look at both the early and late potentials in five subjects, but they did not report whether the one subject who exhibited an abnormal brainstem transmission time in their study also evidenced abnormalities in cortical potentials.

Autonomic indexes

In our previous review we suggested that initial processing and sensory-receptor levels deserved more attention. Specifically, reviews of prior research efforts point to possible perceptual and attentional abnormalities. Most of the research we reviewed that focused on sensory, perceptual, and attentional processes relied on verbal and motor responses of the autistic individuals studied. Such reports not only lack reliability but also are confounded by other deficits that characterize autism, for example, developmental delays (Prior, 1984) and lack of cooperation (D. J. Cohen & Johnson, 1977).

After reviewing psychophysiological studies of autism, A. L. James and Barry (1980b) indicated their surprise at the limited use of such nonverbal, noninvasive measures (e.g., autonomic indexes) of attentional and perceptual processing. These indexes include measures of cardiovascular and electrodermal activity. The cardiovascular measures that can be used are (1) heart rate (HR) in response to changing stimuli (i.e., phasic) as well as prolonged stimulus exposure (i.e., tonic); (2) vasometer responses such as blood pressure (BP), peripheral blood flow (PBF), and peripheral vascular resistance (PVR); and (3) respiration rate, which is highly correlated with HR. These measures appear to provide an index of general arousal and anxiety, with more specific information about attentional processes coming from measures of autonomic responsiveness to specific inputs. For example, HR changes in response to specific stimuli may include deceleration or acceleration, which reflects orienting (attention) or startle (defensive response), respectively (see Palkovitz & Wiesenfeld, 1980). Vasometer responses vary with the focus of attention or readiness to respond to external stimulation. That is, an external focus results in decreased PBF and increased PVR. Internal attention, such as that required when solving math problems, is related to increased PBF and decreased PVR (D. J. Cohen & Johnson, 1977). These measures have been used to infer whether an individual is ready to receive external information (i.e., sensory readiness) or is attempting to screen out such external stimulation (i.g., sensory rejection). Though electrodermal activity, for example, galvinic skin response (GSR), is a popular measure of arousal and attention, it has been infrequently used with autistic populations. Respiratory activity in autistics has been, for the most part, ignored.

After reviewing the few research studies that applied these autonomic measures in an attempt to further understand the functioning of autistic children, A. L. James and Barry (1980b) concluded that (1) HR levels and GSR measures of autistic children fell within the general range though there appeared to be more variability within these individuals; (2) HR changes in response to specific stimulus presentations appeared to be less orderly, and tended to be more intense and of shorter latency and duration in autistic children; and (3) there was some suggestion that vasometer responses may be related to autistic deficits.

These conclusions were based on a few preliminary studies. Most importantly, A. L. James and Barry (1980b) call for further investigations to clarify suggestive deficits based on the few preliminary studies reviewed. Since this review, others have similarly called for additional investigations of autonomic responses in autistic children (D. J. Cohen & Shaywitz, 1982). In spite of these urgings and the suggestive preliminary reports, very few researchers have responded.

Cohen and his colleagues (Kootz & Cohen, 1981; Kootz, Marinelli, & Cohen, 1982) did examine cardiovascular correlates (HR, PBF, PVR) of attention while their autistic subjects either rested, interacted with an adult, or performed on a reaction-time task. In the first study, the autistic children's HR changed as a function of the task presented, but not to the same degree as normal children, and overall HR appeared to be elevated in these children. These equivocal results were interpreted by Kootz and Cohen (1981) as suggesting that autistic children are in a state of heightened autonomic nervous system arousal and thus tend to reject sensory information. Since autonomic indexes of such an approach to incoming environmental stimulation were not supportive of this claim, Kootz *et al.* (1982) reexamined some of the same autistic children after classifying them as either high or low functioning based on whether or not they reached a criterion for training on the reaction-time task. Not only did the lower functioning group perform worse on the reaction-time task (as expected) but also evidenced significantly greater PBF and lower PVR. The results of this study suggest that there is a great deal of heterogeneity in those identified as autistic, and heightened states of autonomic arousal and resultant sensory rejection may be characteristic of lower functioning autistic children.

Palkovitz and Wiesenfeld (1980) presented the results of HR and GSR measures of 10 autistic and 10 CA-matched normals to (1) a pure tone, (2) nonsense verbalization (''Sponzelnirem shern''), and (3) a meaningful verbal statement (''Listen to me, (name)''). Resting GSR was higher in the autistic group overall with neither group responding differentially to the auditory inputs. Examination of HR change yielded significant deceleration trends in the normal group that suggested orienting to all three inputs. Changes in HR in the autistic group were not as easy to interpret as they were of lower magnitude (i.e., 3–4 beats/min as compared to 8–9 beats/min in the normal group) and were not consistent (i.e., evidence of both deceleration and acceleration). Nevertheless, Palkovitz and Wiesenfeld (1980) claimed that these results provide additional evidence supporting the notion that autistic children ''tend to respond autonomically with defensive patterns to stimuli'' (p. 357).

A. L. James and Barry (1980a) measured respiration rate and pulse amplitude changes of 20 autistic, 20 retarded, and 20 normal children in response to repeated presentations of an auditory input. Both the retarded and normal groups evidenced habituation while the autistic children did not. In addition, the autistic children differed from the other two groups in that the magnitude of their vascular system responses was enhanced. The finding that these responses are related to chronological age led A. L. James and Barry (1980a) to conclude that autistic children ''may display a general developmental lag in phasic vascular response measures'' (p. 541) as opposed to a general heightened level of autonomic activity and resulting defensive autonomic pattern of responsiveness.

These studies all attempted to relate autonomic measures to the theoretical proposition that autistic children are overaroused and thus react to external stimulation defensively. While some (e.g., Zentall & Zentall, 1983) are willing to accept these reported results as highly supportive of this explanation, it appears that a more cautious interpretation is warranted. Specifically, autonomic responses of autistic children are extremely variable, both between and within individuals, and there is some suggestion that higher magnitude responses are related to age such that responses of autistic children are indicative of an immature autonomic system and not a relatively stable pattern of hyperarousal.

Our current research efforts have attempted to utilize autonomic indexes of attention to assess early levels of information processing rather than gathering confirmatory support for the overarousal hypothesis. We have just finished assessing six autistic children's autonomic responsiveness to auditory inputs that varied in terms of duration (40, 250, and 500 msec) and location (right or left ear). Analyses of HR changes in response to onset and offset of these inputs yielded some interesting results. Specifically, deceleration or evidence of orienting was found in response to changes presented to the left ear (right hemisphere) for all durations, and for all but the 40-msec duration presented to the right ear (left hemisphere). Thus, there was some indication that these autistic children were not as responsive autonomically to changes in brief duration inputs presented to the right ear. This preliminary finding is extremely intriguing given (1) the many proposed language deficits in autism, (2) proposed left-hemisphere involvement, (3) the importance of brief duration inputs in making discriminations between consonant phonemes, and (4) the suggestion that the auditory system includes two component neural pathways, one that responds to brief duration inputs and another that responds to longer duration inputs (see Gersuni, 1965).

In addition to these most promising preliminary reports, autonomic indexes have been used to provide information about attentional processing as it relates to performance. Specifically, Zouzounis (1981) observed HR changes in three groups of normals (five subjects in each age group 4–6, 10–12, and 18–21) and two 15-year-old autistics. The subjects were observed as they learned to press a button in the presence of a multiple cue (auditory and visual) and not press during intertrial intervals; they were then presented with single cue (auditory, visual) test trials. This serial discrimination paradigm with test or probe trials has been used to assess stimulus overselectivity in autistic individuals (see the subsection on attentional deficits later in this chapter).

One of the autistic adolescents and one of the 4- to 6-year-olds responded overselectively, that is, they pressed the button in the presence of one cue but not the other. Different patterns of autonomic responsiveness were observed in the four groups. The 18- to 21-year-olds showed cardiac acceleration to all inputs throughout, the 4- to 6-year-olds evidenced acceleration in response to the multiple cue at the end of training and responded to single cue test trials with HR deceleration, and the 10- to 12-year-olds evidenced acceleration to the multiple cues at the beginning of training only and showed deceleration to the single cue probe trials only at the beginning of the test session. In general, the magnitude of HR changes for these three groups decreased over training and testing sessions. The two autistic adolescents responded autonomically to all inputs but (1) it took longer for them to reach peak cardiac change than the normal groups, (2) the magnitude of their change increased over training and testing sessions, (3) they took longer to return to prestimulus HR levels, (4) they evidenced cardiac acceleration to the multiple cue training stimulus as did the 18- to 21-year-olds, and (5) they responded to the single cue probe trials with cardiac deceleration as did the 4- to 6-year-olds. Not only do these results help to clarify the relationship between attentional processing and behavioral output, but they also suggest that autonomic responsiveness of autistic children to specific inputs is qualitatively different from nonhandicapped populations.

Frankel, Simmons, Fichter, and Freeman (1984) observed pulse rate changes in autistic, normal, and retarded children who were similarly exposed to a multiple cue (auditory and visual) serial discrimination task with subsequent single cue (auditory, visual) probe trials. While five of seven autistic subjects pressed a bar in the presence of one cue but not the other, pulse rate changes indicated that the autistic children were equally responsive autonomically to each cue presented singly. The authors were puzzled by this finding. In our review of attentional deficits later in this chapter, we apply an information processing approach that helps to put the pieces of this puzzle together into a meaningful picture.

Hemispheric functioning

In our earlier review several lines of research were presented which seemed to support the hypothesis that left-hemispheric dysfunction was associated with autism. These research findings included reported enlargement in the left temporal horn in 15 of 17 autistic children, reports of increased preference for activities (music) associated with the right hemisphere and increased incidence of left-handedness in autistic children, and evidence from CT scans which found a higher than normal incidence of larger right hemispheres (relative to the left) in an autistic sample. We concluded that, before any definite conclusions could be made, these studies need to be replicated and that more appropriate control groups which would control for mental age and level of language functioning needed to be used.

Fein *et al.* (1984) have recently presented a comprehensive review of research related to the hypothesis of left-hemisphere dysfunction in autism. Language impairment in autism is frequently cited as supporting a hypothesis of left-hemisphere dysfunction. After reviewing this literature, Fein *et al.* reject this hypothesis, citing evidence that autistic children exhibit a wide range of language deficits, that the phonological and syntactic aspects of their language may be more delayed than deviant, that frequently observed abnormalities in prosodic and pragmatic aspects of language are more suggestive of right- rather than left-hemisphere involvement, that only some autistic children show verbal deficits relative to perceptual performance, and that formal tests of verbal and visual-spatial functions may be confounded by task demands and information processing differences. In reviewing the research on handedness they found that the reported incidence of left-handedness varied from study to study depending upon how handedness was defined. It was their conclusion after summarizing the results across studies that the percentage of left-handedness is similar to that in other clinical groups and is consistent with Satz's model of equal incidence of right- and left-brain insult. More recent anatomical studies (e.g., Tasi & Stewart, 1982) failed to replicate the reversed asymmetry reported previously and, further, failed to identify consistent evidence of specific morphological abnormalities in autistic subjects. After reviewing the electrophysiological studies, they conclude as we do that there is no consistent pattern of laterality associated with observed abnormalities, but in those individual cases where unilateral dysfunctions were observed they tended to occur more frequently on the left. Their general conclusion regarding the nature of the evidence for left-hemisphere dysfunction in autism is that it is very weak and probably occurs only in a subgroup of the autistic population.

The concept of hemispheric specialization is not as simplistic as was initially presented and thus may not be as useful in contributing to the understanding of autistic dysfunction as was once hoped. Allen (1983) in a recent review of models of hemispheric function points out that there is no general model of hemispheric functioning which allows for the integration of research in this area, but rather a number of limited models associated with specific topic domains such as handedness, language, and visual-spatial performance. He identifies five classes of models based on their conception of underlying mechanisms: (1) unilateral models, which assume only one hemisphere performs a given psychological process; (2) positive interactive models, which assume that both hemispheres perform the function simultaneously and interact in a positive fashion; (3) negative interactive models, where the assumption is that both hemispheres can perform a given function, but that one inhibits or suppresses the activities of the other; (4) parallel models, where the assumption is that the hemispheres operate simultaneously and independently; and (5) allocation models, which assume that both hemispheres have the capacity to perform but that in a given situation only one does. Given the lack of a cohesive theoretical framework and limited understanding of underlying neurological functioning, it would appear that this once promising area currently contributes very little to our understanding of dysfunction in autism.

Attentional deficits

Not only does an information processing perspective serve to direct research activities, but it also provides a framework in which proposed dysfunctions can be formulated. Probably the best example of this former function comes when we examine the proposed attentional deficit, stimulus overselectivity, in autistic children. Stimulus overselectivity or overselective attention was first introduced in an effort to describe the observed performances of autistic children (Lovaas, Schreibman, Koegel, & Rehm, 1971). In this study and subsequent studies (see Litrownik & McInnis, 1982, for a review), the children were initially trained to respond to one stimulus complex (S+) and not to another (S−). Once the serial or simultaneous discrimination was acquired, components of the complex were presented individually. It was assumed that performance on these probe trials would assess the degree to which each stimulus component controlled responding. In each instance it was observed that the autistic children were highly selective in their response to the multiple cue complexes. Specifically, they tended to respond to one component of the stimulus complex and not to others.

Though the term *stimulus overselectivity* was first introduced by Lovaas *et al.* (1971) to describe this apparent restricted responding, it has since acquired much surplus meaning. That is, stimulus overselectivity has been called upon to explain the autistic child's failure to develop speech, respond to social stimuli, acquire appropriate emotional responses, learn observationally, and generalize acquired responses to other similar situations (see Lovaas, Koegel, & Schreibman, 1979). This descriptive term has become an explanatory concept that is now the focus of intervention efforts.

While some (e.g., A. D. Ross & Pelham, 1981) see this as a "model of clinical research," we (Litrownik, 1984; Litrownik & McInnis, 1982; Litrownik, McInnis, Wetzel-Pritchard, & Filipelli, 1978) and others (Edwards, Shigley, & Edwards, 1976; A. L. James & Barry, 1980b; Prior, 1984; Prior & McGillivray, 1980) have not only questioned the applied relevance of the reported interventions but also the significance of the described deficit.

Though stimulus overselectivity initially emerged from a conditioning (stimulus–response, or S–R) perspective as a summary descriptive term for performance in the two discrimination paradigms, unwarranted generalizations continue to be made. For example, Gersten (1983) argued that there are a host of empirical studies demonstrating overselectivity in autism and that "stimulus overselectivity refers to a learner's failure to attend to more than one component of a complex stimulus" (p. 62).

There are some S–R theorists that recognize the limits of this claimed deficit (e.g., Bickel, Stella, & Etzel, 1984; Cook, Anderson, & Rincover, 1982). Bickel *et al.* (1984) assume that all responses are controlled and therefore observed "chance" responding to experimenter-manipulated cues is due to control by some other source. They conclude that apparent overselectivity does not preclude learning, is a type of responding in specific environmental contexts, can be understood if conditions of control are determined, and can be treated if we can identify the hierarchy of control (i.e., eliminate higher priority competing stimuli, and utilize transfer of stimulus control procedures such as within stimulus prompts). Cook *et al.* (1982) similarly point out that task parameters are most important in determining autistic responsiveness. As a result they argue that stimulus overselectivity is not a generalized way in which autistic individuals view the world. While on the one hand they recognize the limited meaning of one construct (i.e., overselectivity) they introduce another, tunnel vision, to explain observed responding of autistic children.

Attempts to understand attentional processing in autistic individuals as well as develop more promising interventions are necessarily limited by the conditioning or S–R perspective. While some (e.g., Prior, 1984) simply dismiss overselectivity as diagnostically irrelevant due to its modifiability and relationship to age and stimulus variables, we believe that a focus on understanding how information is differentially processed will not only give us a clearer picture of autism but also provide suggestions for treatment.

It is clear that restricted responding in autistic children has been observed when single-cue probe trials have followed the acquisition of a multiple-cue serial or simultaneous discrimination (e.g., Frankel *et al.,* 1984; Gersten, 1983; Lovaas *et al.,* 1979). On the other hand, autistic children have not evidenced restricted responding to multiple cues when assessed in match-to-sample (Litrownik *et al.,* 1978) and conditional learning (Koegel & Schreibman, 1977; Prior & McGillivray, 1980) paradigms, nor when bidimensional (rather than unidimensional) probe trials were used to assess stimulus control after a multiple cue simultaneous discrimination had been acquired (Edwards *et al.,* 1976).

In an effort to understand these apparent disparate findings, we presented a conceptual model, borrowing from experimental cognitive psychology, that identified at least three different attentional processes (Litrownik & McInnis, 1982). Prior models, as well as subsequent discussions of attention from an information processing perspective (e.g., Mulder, 1983), provide a consensus: Attention includes components of (1) selection, (2) alertness or scanning of the environment, and (3) a limiting parameter that defines capacity for the allocation of attention.

Analysis of the procedures used to assess restricted responding, the results of these assessments, and the differentiated attentional components suggest (1) selection strategies of autistic children do show a developmental lag when assessed via single-cue probe trials only, (2) this lag is modifiable as selection is a function of higher processes (e.g., cognitive structures, learning sets), and (3) autistic children have the capacity to attend to multiple inputs.

Butler and Rabinowitz (1981) offer a logical explanation for this observed developmental lag. First, they point out that solutions to multiple component discrimination tasks can be based on each of the components individually or on a combination of the components (i.e., compound). Not only is there evidence indicating that the preferred solution (component or compound) is related to developmental level (i.e., younger children are more likely to utilize compound solutions), but also within the same multiple cue discrimination some of the cues are utilized as individual components and some as part of a compound in order to solve the discrimination (Butler & Rabinowitz, 1981; Campione, McGrath, & Rabinowitz, 1971). If assessment of stimulus control following acquisition of a multiple-cue discrimination problem includes presentations of single cues, the compounds used in the solution are destroyed. When this occurs the child will repond to individual cues that were solved on a component basis but not to those cues that were solved on a compound basis. The observed result is "stimulus overselectivity."

Reports by Frankel *et al.* (1984) and Zouzounis (1981) indicate that autistic individuals show cardiac deceleration in response to each single cue probe even though they may be responding overtly to only one. This suggests that autistic individuals do not restrict their attention to a limited number of multiple cues but may restrict overt responses. The implications of this understanding for treatment are extremely encouraging. Specifically, the cognitive strategies used to solve multiple-cue discriminations have been modified in younger, normally developing children (House, 1979). Schreibman, Koegel, and Craig (1977) did report that restricted responding of an autistic child diminished with repeated presentations of multiple-cue discrimination and single-probe test trials. The acquisition of the learning set by this autistic child provides some support for the claim that a more appropriate cognitive strategy can be developed in autistic children.

Summary, Conclusions, and Suggestions for the Future

We initially presented an interdisciplinary framework that identified general perspectives and more specific levels of analysis that have been applied in an effort to better understand and treat infantile autism. While the current focus of most researchers is on discovering biological factors responsible for autism, interventions have relied primarily on methods derived from the behavioral perspective. A possible point where these two interests, that is, search for underlying etiology and/or pathogenesis and treatment, can meet is at the information processing perspective. Specifically, we argued that identification of processing deficits in autistic individuals should provide opportunities to hypothesize about specific biological involvement (i.e., structural, biochemical). Newer and more powerful techniques (e.g., MRI, CT scan, PET scan, chemical assays) can then be focused on examining specific structures and neurotransmitter systems rather than being applied in general because they are available. A better understanding of how information is processed by autistic persons should also lead to more effective behavioral interventions.

In an effort to begin this task we briefly described a working model of information processing that we had previously proposed, presented a summary of a review based on this model (through 1980), and identified areas of research that appeared to be most promising. We focused our present review on updating developments in these areas. Suggested deficits at the sensory-receptor and initial processing levels were supported by recent neurophysiological (ERP) and psychophysiological (autonomic indexes) measures of autistic populations. Results of the few studies reviewed indicate that, as a population, autistic individuals evidence abnormalities at the earliest levels of processing: sensory-receptor and initial. Specifically, peripheral and central transmission time as measured by ABPs were delayed, orienting to brief-duration auditory inputs presented to the left hemisphere was not observed, and changes in HR as a function of specific inputs were of a greater magnitude and lasted for a longer period of time than in normal comparison groups. While these abnormalities were observed in the autistic populations studied, researchers noted that not all autistic individuals evidenced them. Factors such as general level of functioning, hypotonia, postrotary nystagmus, attention, and social accessibility were related to this variability in responding.

An update of research examining proposed left-hemisphere dysfunction in autism revealed that support for this hypothesis, once thought to be promising, was equivocal at best. In addition, attempts to understand autism are grossly oversimplified when explained by left-hemisphere damage. More specific deficits, for example, left-hemisphere insensitivity to brief duration auditory inputs, are more likely to result in furthering our understanding of autism as well as focusing efforts to identify biological involvement.

Recent work examining attentional functioning, for example, overselectivity, supports our proposed distinction between active selection, noting, and capacity. Restricted responding continues to be observed in most, but not all, autistic individuals when they are assessed in a specific paradigm (i.e., simultaneous or serial discrimination with multiple cues followed by single-cue probe trials). Autonomic responses indicate that even those autistic individuals who fail to respond behaviorally to all cues presented singly do respond to them autonomically. It is our contention that attentional functioning of autistic persons can be better understood when viewed from an information processing perspective and that effective, relevant treatment procedures can be identified.

We end this chapter with the all-too-familiar call for additional research and study. But, as we did following our previous review, we offer some specific suggestions for how this work should be conducted. First of all, it is apparent that many autistic individuals evidence deficits at early levels of processing. It is also evident that there is a great deal of variability in the performance (and thus processing) of those identified as autistic, due to diagnostic and methodological problems as well as the possibility of multiple involvement (i.e., same symptoms resulting from different dysfunctions). In order to identify common deficits, develop more effective intervention strategies, and formulate hypotheses about biological involvement that will direct the application of advancing technology, we need to systematically assess processing in autistic and comparison populations. These assessments must allow for establishing relationships between various measures, for example, behavioral, neurophysiological, and psychophysiological, as well as provide an opportunity to identify clusters of individuals who present common problems.

10

An Information Processing Interpretation of Theory and Research in Schizophrenia

DENNIS P. SACCUZZO
Department of Psychology
San Diego State University
San Diego, California 92182

Recently there has been a surge of interest in information processing methodology (J. R. Anderson, 1980; Freides, 1974; D. H. Krantz, 1969; Lachman & Lachman chapter 2 this volume; Teichner & Krebs, 1974). This work has culminated in the advancement of psychological theory through the application of information processing models to issues of theoretical importance (J. R. Anderson, 1973; Erdelyi, 1974; Rumelhart & Siple, 1974; Ulehla & Adams, 1973). Information processing theories and models and signal detection methodology have also been applied to the study of abnormal behavior, most notably schizophrenia (Callaway & Naghdi, 1982). A number of excellent review articles (Cromwell, 1978b; Gjerde, 1983; Kietzman, Spring, & Zubin, 1980; Knight, 1984; Nuechterlein & Dawson, 1984) and an entire book (Magaro, 1980), which provide comprehensive overviews of the information processing literature in schizophrenia, are available.

The present discussion will consider how recent advances in information processing theory can be applied to enhance our understanding of schizophrenia. Traditional theories will be recast in terms of more modern information processing concepts. Empirical and methodological issues will then be considered in the context of a focused discussion of one attempt to analyze information processing in schizophrenia and related schizophrenia spectrum disorders.

One way theorists have attempted to deal with the overwhelming number of books and articles on schizophrenia has been their attempt to find an underlying explanation or cause of the syndrome. Such an explanation would help clarify conflicting results and, hopefully, lead to the early detection and perhaps prevention of this mysterious human problem. Bleuler (1911/1950) considered the possibility that attentional difficulties might account for the schizophrenic disturbance. He later downplayed this hypothesis, however, and concluded that the basic sensory processes in schizophrenia are essentially unimpaired. Subsequent investigators thus tended to look for the primary deficit in schizophrenia at the cortical or "thought" level, until Venables (1964) and Silverman (1964), working independently of each other, reawakened interest in the possibility that the cognitive symptoms of schizophrenia may result from a more fundamental disturbance in attention. The theories of Venables and Silverman provided the basic foundation for the development of information processing approaches to schizophrenia.

Venables' Theory

Venables (1964) integrated a diversity of empirical data into a theoretical construct he called "input dysfunction." Anchoring his theory to the then prevalent arousal theories of schizophrenia, Venables (1964) related two important concepts, arousal and attention, to schizophrenia. In reviewing the two major arousal theories of the time (Mednick, 1958; Weckowicz, 1958), Venables (1964) was amazed by their conceptual similarity. He stressed that while both theories agreed on the clinical symptoms of schizophrenia, each explained them differently.

Input Dysfunction and Autonomic Imbalances

Weckowicz (1958) believed the symptoms of schizophrenia were the result of imbalances in autonomic nervous system activity. The early stages of schizophrenia, he proposed, were brought on by excessive parasympathetic activity. Compensatory parasympathetic suppression was followed by a paradoxical increase in awareness and reactivity. Accordingly, the individual becomes sensitive and may attach important meaning to insignificant events, which causes delusions. An overabundance of sympathetic activity and compensatory suppression in the chronic phase of the disorder paradoxically resulted in decreased awareness, low reactivity, and flatness of affect, causing the individual to become withdrawn, autistic, and apathetic. Central to Weckowicz's reasoning was the idea that imbalances in autonomic activity could result in the cognitive disorganization, for which he found support in experiments of perceptual constancy.

Perceptual constancy refers to the fact that objects of the same size or shape, seen at different distances, tend to be perceived as similar in size. In size constancy experiments, subjects are asked to match two objects, one presented near and one presented at a distance. In distance constancy (size estimation) experiments, subjects are asked to estimate the size of a distant object, when standard or comparison stimuli are located at the same distance from the subject. Theoretically, in both size and distance constancy, the perception of objects and cues in the peripheral field causes the reduced retinal image of an object to be corrected, thus appearing to maintain its size even when viewed from a distance.

In a perceptual constancy experiment, Callaway and Thompson (1953) found that, when normal subjects were required to make size judgments under conditions of induced sympathetic arousal, they tended to rate distant objects as being smaller than their actual size. There was a breakdown in perceptual constancy. Apparently subjects were not making full use of cues in the peripherial field, which Callaway and Thompson believed was the result of heightened sympathetic arousal. They proposed a hypothetical negative feedback mechanism in which heightened sympathetic arousal was believed to bring about a rise in the threshold of the input system in order to protect the individual. Specifically, they argued that threat induces a sympathetic discharge. This discharge then brings about a rise in the input system, which reduces the perception of threat and ultimately results in a reduction of sympathetic discharge.

Taking the matter one step further, Weckowicz (1957) reasoned that if increased sympathetic activity causes normals to be under-constant, then if chronic schizophrenics suffer from a high level of sympathetic activity, they should experience underconstancy. As hypothesized, Weckowicz (1957) found that schizophrenics tended to be underconstant when compared to nonpsychotic hospitalized patients and normal controls. In a follow-up study, Weckowicz, Somner, and Hall (1958) studied the relationship between distance constancy and level of autonomic activity in chronic schizophrenics. Again, as hypothesized, the schizophrenics were significantly more underconstant than controls. In examining intergroup differences, Weckowicz *et al.* (1958) also found that the nonparanoid patients demonstrated the greatest reduction in both size and distancy constancy. Delusional (paranoid) patients showed normal constancy and sometimes overestimation of size.

In attempting to relate normal-schizophrenic differences in perceptual constancy to the development of thought disorder, Weckowicz and Blewett (1959) provided one of the earliest statements of the information processing approach to schizophrenia. They argued that

> there is a redundancy of information in the sensory input from the environment to the organism. The cognitive processes is to a great extent concerned with the reduction of this redundancy and with selection or abstraction of some information according to certain principles and suppression of all other information. . . . [In schizophrenia] there is some change in the filtering of stimula-

tion. . . . The gates open wide, the cortex is flooded with irrelevant information. (Weckowicz & Blewett, 1959, p. 929)

This interpretation implies that in schizophrenia there is some breakdown in the early stages of information processing. The reduced size constancy exhibited by nonparanoid schizophrenics may thus have been due to an inability to process the relevant cues when making a size or distance judgment; the overconstancy exhibited by paranoid schizophrenics may have been due to an inability to filter or screen out irrelevant cues. This theme of an information processing disturbance can be found in the most modern theories of schizophrenia.

Input Dysfunction and Reciprocal Augmentation of Anxiety

The second arousal theory reviewed by Venables was that of Mednick (1958). Mednick postulated a positive feedback mechanism, reciprocal augmentation of anxiety, as the basic cause of schizophrenia. In Mednick's theory, the central construct, anxiety, was equated with the Hullian concept of drive. The primary symptoms of schizophrenia were believed to be produced by intense anxiety (high drive).

According to Hullian theory, the effect of an increase in drive is to raise the response strength of all habit tendencies aroused in a situation. Mednick (1958) argued that in the schizophrenic this process goes out of control. According to Mednick's (1958) principle of reciprocal augmentation, as drive (anxiety) builds, stimulus generalizations increase, thus increasing the number of stimuli capable of evoking anxiety. This in turn increases the overall level of drive, thereby further increasing stimulus generalization. As this process continues, the fragmented remote thoughts brought above threshold by the heightened drive are reinforced in that they reduce anxiety. Although these remote, irrelevant associations divert the individual's attention from anxiety-provoking stimuli, they eventually lead to deviant, disorganized thinking.

Venables' Basic Position

From the principle of reciprocal augmentation, Mednick deduced four testable hypotheses. Although he asserted that these four hypotheses had generally been supported, subsequent reviewers eventually uncovered conflicting, if not negative, results (Lang & Buss, 1965; Zimet & Fishman, 1970). As early as 1964, however, Venables argued that the contradictory results found in examing Mednick's as well as Weckowicz' theory could be reconciled if one assumed that there were two types of schizophrenics. As Venables (1964) stated,

Chronic schizophrenic patients—and possibly included in this category are process patients—tend to be characterized by a state of restriction of the attentional field resulting from elevated states of sympathetic and cortical activation. . . . In contrast to the chronic patient, the acute (and possibly the reactive and paranoid) patient is characterized by an inability to restrict the range of his attention so that he is flooded by sensory impressions from all quarters. (p. 41)

Venables believed that all the previous data on schizophrenia could be integrated by considering two types of schizophrenics: acute (paranoid) schizophrenics, characterized by a broading of the attentional field, and chronic schizophrenics, characterized by a restriction of the attentional field. Furthermore, in line with both Weckowicz and Mednick, this abnormal attention was believed to be caused by the physiological state of the patient. Abnormally high arousal caused a reduction in the stimulus cues utilized (span of attention); abnormally low arousal caused an increase in the span of attention.

From Callaway's work with normals and Weckowicz' work with schizophrenics, Venables reasoned as follows. Normals, under conditions of high arousal, experience underconstancy. Chronic schizophrenics exhibit underconstancy. Therefore, if the phenomenon of perceptual constancy is due to a sampling of perpheral cues in the environment, then chronic schizophrenics must suffer from a narrowing of attention. Information in the periphery is not sampled adequately. Thus, the individual fails to process critical information. Imagine what would happen, for example, if a person tried to follow a television program by attending only to the action taking place in the center of the screen. In contrast to the chronic patient, the paranoid (acute) patient, Venables believed, suffers from a widening of attention. Too many cues are sampled. Imagine trying to follow a television program while at the same time attending just as carefully to three different conversations going on in different parts of the room.

A New Look at Venables' Theory in Terms of Information Processing

Attempts to support Venables (1964) have apparently met only partial success. Spohn *et al.* (1970), for example, attempted to relate the span of apprehension, the number of items recalled for a single presentation of a multiitem stimulus, and arousal in schizophrenia. Monitoring skin conductance and heart rate during rest and performance, Spohn *et al.* (1970) controlled short-term memory factors by partialling out differences found between schizophrenic and control groups on the Wechsler Memory Scale. Consistent with a previous result (Neale, McIntyre, Fox, & Cromwell, 1969), schizophrenics showed a reduced span of apprehension when compared to normals, thus adding support to Venables' (1964) notion of a narrowing of attention in schizophrenia. No relationship was found, however, between level of arousal and the span. Others (Neale & Cromwell, 1970) have also argued that the results of investigations in which different groups of schizophrenics have been studied have not always been consistent with predictions from Venables' (1964) theory. On the other hand, relevant literature reviews (Buss, 1966; Lang & Buss, 1965; Maher, 1966; Mirsky, 1969; Yates, 1966), including a more recent treatment by Venables

(1977), not only support the hypothesis that the level of arousal in chronic schizophrenics is higher than the level of arousal in normals, but also generally support the hypothesis that chronic schizophrenics utilize a narrowed range of relevant cues. The fact that arousal did not correlate with span of attention in Spohn *et al.* (1970) may suggest that span of apprehension, which measures amount rather than speed of processing (see Saccuzzo *et al.*, 1974), may not be a valid measure of what Venables (1964) meant by narrowed attention.

More important for Venables' (1964) theory than ostensibly conflicting evidence are neuropsychological theories such as those by Kesner (1973) and Walley and Weiden (1973). Both of these theories, based on information processing models and consistent with Venables' (1964, 1977), clearly implicate arousal as one of the primary determinants of breath of attention. These theories also provide some suggestions concerning a possible neuroanatomical locus (loci) of the schizophrenic deficit, assuming that Venables' (1964) theory about the nature of schizophrenia is correct.

Kesner's Theory

Kesner (1973) presented a theoretical formulation relating advances in information processing theory to the neural basis of memory. According to Kesner's (1973) theory, memory can be divided into four components. In the first stage or component, information is received in a "cue-access system," which may be seen as analogous to Neisser's (1967) concepts of preattentive processes or filters and iconic storage. This system, characterized by a short-lasting, preperceptual information analysis operation, selects essential information for further processing. Information from the cue-access system may be transferred to either a short-term or a long-term memory system, the second and third components of memory. Retrieval of stored information, the fourth component, involves a process whereby stored information is initially processed in the cue-access system then transferred to short-term and long-term memory. Kesner (1973) defines memory as "the process of encoding information by comparing and combining sensory inputs with innate and previously acquired knowledge, storing the information, and decoding the stored information into motor components" (p. 177).

According to Kesner's (1973) definition, memory and attention are intricately linked. The most critical feature of the model, however, is the hypothesis that specific neural substrates are involved in each of the four components of memory. Specifying the most important neural substrates for each component, Kesner (1973) implicates arousal as one of the most important controlling operations of the memory process. More important in terms of Venables' (1964) theory, memory and attentional processes are linked with specific neurological substrates.

Walley and Weiden's Theory

Another neuropsychological theory (Walley & Weiden, 1973) directly relates attention and arousal through the concept of cognitive masking, a phenomenon whereby the encoding of one stimulus interferes with the encoding of another, resulting in a narrowing of attention. This theory, in which cognitive masking is directly related to arousal, supports and has direct implications for Venables' (1964) theory of schizophrenia.

In agreement with Neisser (1967), Walley and Weiden (1973) believe that pattern recognition is achieved by means of a hierarchical network of feature analyzers. On the other hand, what Neisser (1967) would call preattentive processes (filters), iconic storage (viz., sensory memory in the terminology of Walley & Weiden, 1973), and encoding all represent the function of different levels of a *single* hierarchical system. This system extends into the association area of the cortex, the highest levels of the pattern recognition network. Whereas sensory memory (iconic storage) is the result of the persistence of activity in the specific sensory projection system, encoding is due to activity in neurons in association cortex. Thus, rather than postulating scanners, filters, primary processing channels, and special storage systems, processing is simply seen as movement through a hierarchical nervous system beginning with sensory stimulation and ending in neurons in association cortex. Basing their analysis on a work by Konorski (1967), Walley and Weiden (1973) further hypothesize that conceptual learning, the formation of so-called gnostic units, involves the synapsing of the axons of neurons of one level of the hierarchy on neurons of a higher level. When new connections are made between gnostic units, the result is associative learning. In these terms, Kesner's (1973) notion of short-term memory would be viewed as activity persisting in gnostic units after encoding has taken place, while cognitive masking is caused by one set of gnostic units inhibiting the activity of another.

Walley and Weiden's theory is particularly relevant to Venables' (1964) theory because of the link between arousal and cognitive masking. Put simply, consistent with Venables' (1964) theory, the effect of cognitive masking is a decrease in the range of cue utilization (narrowing of attention). Since arousal increases cognitive masking, it produces a reduction in cue utilization. Thus, Walley and Weiden (1973), in presenting a neuropsychological theory of attention that explains how arousal produces narrowed attention, have reestablished the connection between the high arousal typically found in chronic schizophrenics and their narrowed attention.

Further analysis by Wally and Weiden (1973) provides additional insights into the possible nature of schizophrenia. According to these authors,

> the greater the complexity of the task, the greater would be the arousal induced and the narrower the range of cue utilization. Clearly, such a response to complex tasks would be self-defeating; it

obviously would be *adaptive* [italics added] for the organism to counteract this mechanism. (p. 298)

Applying these concepts to schizophrenia, in paranoid schizophrenia the adaptive mechanism must overreact, resulting in decreased arousal and hence an increase in cue utilization. In the chronic phase of the syndrome, the adaptive mechanism becomes defective through continued overuse, resulting in a loss of cue utilization. Walley and Weiden (1973) speculate that this adaptive mechanism might be accomplished through corticofugal projections, which inhibit the brainstem reticular formation. They further suggest that this adaptive mechanism is a *learned* phenomenon. Thus, according to these authors, "a failure to learn to control the reticular formation in this fashion could result in severe difficulties in coping with the demands of our complex civilization" (p. 298).

Matthysee's Pharmacological Theory

It must be remembered that Walley and Weiden (1973) are not theorizing about schizophrenia. If their theory concerning the relationship between arousal, attention, and neurological functioning is correct, however, and if Venables' (1964) theoretical formulation relating arousal, attention, and schizophrenia is correct, then corticofugal systems, or more specifically, inhibitory fibers passing out of the cortex, may play a role in certain types of schizophrenia. Indeed, the idea of a breakdown in high-level inhibitory processes is consistent with Matthysee's (1974) view of schizophrenia based on the neurotransmitter dopamine. According to Matthysee, thought disorder results from the intrusion of thoughts and fantasies that normally are not processed to the point of awareness due to the failure of normal inhibitory processes. As a result of this failure, which Matthysee believes is caused by overactivity of disinhibitory dopamine-mediated neurons, consciousness becomes flooded with irrelevant and/or anxiety-provoking thoughts.

The application of information processing concepts to Venables' (1964) theory and to the theories and empirical data that form the basis for it results in an interpretation of schizophrenia in accord with modern pharmacological viewpoints such as Matthysee's. Taken together, the data and viewpoints considered thus far point to an information processing dysfunction characterized by overutilization or underutilization of cortical input, which is caused by a disturbance in disinhibitory or inhibitory processes.

Silverman's Theory

Working independently of Venables, Silverman (1964) reached remarkably similar conclusions. He argued that acute paranoid good premorbid schizophrenics are characterized by a broadening or widening of attention, while acute poor premorbid nonparanoid schizophrenics are characterized by a restriction or narrowing of attention. The major difference between Venables' (1964) and Silverman's (1964) theories can be found in the theoretical constructs and methodology they used.

Silverman (1964) believed that individual differences in ocular fixation patterns, or eye movements, ultimately result in enduring response dispositions, or "cognitive control principles," which he conceptualized as "more or less" adjustments to the environment. Concentrating on empirically demonstrated differences found in normals, Silverman (1964) drew heavily from the research conducted by R. W. Gardner (1961), who had found two major factors in his factor analysis of measures of illusion effects. Factor I, Field Articulation, was composed of tests in which subjects must attend to certain cues and ignore others (e.g., embedded figures test). Perceptual constancy tasks, where subjects must sample or scan the sensory field, loaded high on Factor II, Scanning Control.

Silverman's formulation of schizophrenia is based on these two factors, the work of Piaget (1950), and experiments with perceptual constancy. Silverman (1964) pointed out that Piaget (1950) had shown that the young child's attention appears to anchor upon dominant objects in the stimulus field. In the course of development, the individual eventually compensates for misperceptions of size by shifting his attention to and from the center of the perceptual field. Thus, Piaget (1950) found that children tend to show underconstancy (i.e., to underestimate a far object in relation to a near object) because they center on the near object, thus failing to sample relevant cues. The child's judgments tend to be made in terms of sizes of objects as they are recorded on the retina; the adult compensates for this type of error tendency (Silverman, 1964).

Silverman (1964) related scanning and perceptual constancy by arguing that extensive scanning of a perceptual field results in overcompensation of perceptual judgments (overconstancy). On the other hand, the perceptual judgments of the minimal scanner resembles that of the child and hence results in underconstancy. Then, drawing on the findings from a group of paranoid patients who were overconstant (Raush, 1952), the work of Weckowicz who found chronic schizophrenics to be underconstant, and on numerous studies involving perceptual separation of objects from their surroundings, Silverman arrived at his formulation of schizophrenia. He hypothesized that extreme forms of scanning (minimal or excessive) characterize the attentional response disposition of most schizophrenics. In terms of individual differences, acute and paranoid schizophrenics exhibited extensive scanning and field articulation, while process, simple, catatonic, and hebephrenic schizophrenics exhibited minimal scanning and undifferentiated field articulation.

A critical aspect of Silverman's (1964) theory was his notion of "sensory input processing ideational gating." Employing a concept similar to perceptual defense, Silverman (1964) suggested that the sensory input of the paranoid patient is excessively scanned only to facilitate the rejection of input likely to be disturbing. The paranoid was seen as an individual who rapidly scanned (sampled) the environment, only to reject that information inconsistent with his beliefs.

Criticisms of Silverman's Theory

Like Venables' (1964) theory, Silverman's (1964) theory has been subjected to criticisms, most notably by Neale and Cromwell (1970) who argued, ''The literature on various deficits among schizophrenic patients does not point unequivocally towards an interpretation in terms of attention'' (p. 61). This conclusion is based mainly on the criticisms of Venables' (1964) theory already discussed, the poor correlation between eye movements and attention, and Neale and Cromwell's (1968) review of the size estimation literature.

When R. W. Gardner and Long (1962a) correlated seven measures derived from eye movement recordings with three different size-estimation tasks, only 2 of 21 correlations reached statistical significance. A subsequent study (R. W. Gardner & Long, 1962b) again failed to establish a clear relationship between eye movements and size estimation. Neale and Cromwell (1968) then peformed a critical study. Using two groups of schizophrenic subjects who had already been demonstrated to be overconstant and underconstant in a size estimation task, Neale and Cromwell (1968) presented their stimuli in a size estimation task too quickly to permit eye movements (100 msec). Since Silverman's (1964) theory predicts that the overconstancy and underconstancy are due to extreme scanning, if a stimulus is presented too fast for eye movements to occur, there should be no differences between excessive and minimal scanners; eye scanning behavior would not be involved in the judgment process. Contrary to this prediction, significant group differences were found, casting considerable doubt on the relationship between eye movements and constancy, and hence considerable doubt on the relationship between eye movements and schizophrenia. In addition to this criticism, Silverman's (1964) notion of sensory gating is subject to the same criticisms of perceptual defense in general. It can be asked, for example, how it is possible to defend (gate out) a stimulus unless it has already been perceived? If it has been perceived, then how can it be ignored?

A New Look at Silverman's Theory from an Information Processing Perspective

As was the case with Venables' (1964) theory, Silverman's (1964) theory may seem questionable unless one employs the concepts of information processing models. Although the concept of iconic storage has become a matter of controversy (Haber, 1983), the conclusion that information processing is an indirect process has not. And when processing is viewed as such, Silverman's theory can be reconciled.

As indirect, information processing has little to do with eye movements. To use a metaphor, it is the mind's eye that scans the icon and thus determines perception. It is possible to understand, then, why schizophrenics can still have a deficit in a scanning-like process in spite of Neale and Cromwell's (1968) demonstration that eye movements have little to do with differences between schizophrenics in size estimation.

In terms of either Venables' or Silverman's formulations, it can be argued that in chronic schizophrenia, processing from *iconic storage* occurs at such a sluggish rate that not enough of the relevant cues are sampled, thus resulting in underconstancy of perceptions. In paranoid schizophrenia, processing from iconic storage occurs either too rapidly or so selectively that too much of a given aspect of a perception is sampled, resulting in overconstancy. In terms of Silverman's notion of ideational gating, an individual can indeed perceive a threatening stimulus and then reject it. For example, she or he can learn not to attend to certain (threatening) elements in iconic storage, and hence, even though those elements are registered (perceived) at some level of the nervous system, they are rejected at another.

Viewing Silverman's theory from an information processing perspective helps to illustrate that traditional theories cannot simply be dismissed as wrong just because they fail to predict an empirical finding or are found to be deficient in part. These theories have much to offer the modern student. Both Venables' (1964) and Silverman's (1964) theories, for instance, take on new significance when viewed from the more comprehensive information processing perspective. The basic theme that emerges is that either not enough or too much is made available to a limited-capacity conscious control center. The conscious facility is thus deprived of critical data or overwhelmed by nonessentials.

Payne's Theory

Payne (1966) proposed a theory based on a defect in a hypothetical filter mechanism that usually serves to screen out irrelevant information. He argued that there were two basic types of schizophrenics, one type characterized by "overinclusive thinking," the other by retardation in thinking. Payne's notion of "overinclusion" stems from the earlier ideas of Cameron; his notion of retardation stems from the ideas of Babcock.

Cameron (1938) had hypothesized that schizophrenics are characterized by an inability to "preserve conceptual boundaries." This results in overly abstract thinking because ideas that may be distantly or even unrelated to a concept become a part of it. For example, the concept of evil may spill into the concept of authority. Babcock (1941), on the other hand, suggested that a main cause of schizophrenic "thought disorder" was an extreme degree of generalized motor and mental retardation, which results in concrete thinking.

Payne, Matussk, and George (1959) suggested that overinclusion was actually a deficit in attention that was caused by a breakdown of a hypothetical filter mechanism. Using various conceptual tasks (e.g., sets of proverbs) to compare matched groups of acute schizophrenics and hospitalized neurotics, Payne *et al.* (1959) found the schizophrenic groups significantly more overinclusive in spite of the fact that some of the schizophrenics were no more overinclusive than the controls. Post hoc analysis also indicated that overinclusive schizophrenics were somewhat retarded in their motor responses. Payne and Hewlett (1960) subsequently concluded that there are at least two types of schizophrenics, those characterized by overinclusion and those characterized by a general retardation in thinking. They further argued that overinclusion was the result of a fundamental disturbance in attention. Accordingly, they speculated,

> Whatever filtering mechanisms insures that only the stimuli (internal or external) that are relevant to the tasks enter consciousness and are processed, seems no longer able to exclude the irrelevant. . . . Selective perception becomes impossible so that instead of dealing with the essence of the problem, irrelevant aspects are perceived and thought about. (Payne & Hewlett, 1960, p. 69)

In subsequent work, Payne and colleagues attempted to specify more precisely the nature of their hypothesized schizophrenic defect in attention by applying information processing notions to the study of overinclusion and distractability. Payne's (1966) conclusions, entirely consistent with the Venables (1964), Silverman (1964), and information processing models, remain viable even after two decades of additional work. Payne (1966) concluded,

> Overinclusive thinking is basically not a thinking disturbance at all. It is an impairment of some central filtering process whose function it is actively to *inhibit* [italics added] external sensations, and internal thoughts which are not relevant to whatever is the focus of attention at a given time. This filter is of crucial importance, because it reduces the number of incoming data to the point at which they can be manipulated within the span of apprehension without losing crucial components. It is only this which makes rational thinking possible. (Payne, 1966, p. 95)

McGhie and Chapman's Theory

The theory of McGhie and Chapman dovetails and supports Payne (1966). Like Payne, McGhie and Chapman (1961) postulated that the basic problem in schizophrenia is due to attentional variables (viz., a breakdown in a hypothetical filter mechanism). Working essentially with acute schizophrenics, McGhie and colleagues maintained that these patients experience a widening of attention that affects their behavior.

Defining attention as the process by which an individual breaks down and effectively categorizes information, McGhie and Chapman (1961) argued that the process of attention enables one to reduce, organize, and interpret the otherwise chaotic flow of information reaching the senses. In an observational study where young schizophrenic patients were encouraged to describe their difficulties, McGhie and Chapman (1961) provided clinical data to support the position that schizophrenics are unable to screen out irrelevant incoming sensory data from conscious awareness. Examples of statements by schizophrenics surveyed by McGhie and Chapman are as follows:

> Everything seems to go through me. I just can't shut things out. I listen to sounds all the time. I let all the sounds come in that there are.
>
> Sometimes when people speak to me my head is overloaded. It's too much to hold at once.
>
> I can't move if I am distracted by too much noise. I can't help stopping to listen. (McGhie & Chapman, 1961, p. 105)

Such verbalizations by young schizophrenics led McGhie and Chapman (1961) to speculate as follows:

> Now let us suppose there is a breakdown in this selective *inhibitory* [italics added] function of attention. Consciousness would be flooded with an undifferentiated mass of incoming sensory data . . . and, if the incoming flood were to carry on unchecked, it would gradually sweep away the stable constructs of a former reality. (p. 114)

The filter mechanism that was given so much importance in Payne's and McGhie and Chapman's theory can perhaps best be viewed in terms of essential cognitive processes that precede and result in conscious thought. Because these processes are impaired in schizophrenia, normal consciousness and thinking becomes impossible. The essential idea is that an impairment at one stage of information processing adversely affects all subsequent stages. Thus, to understand the nature of thought disorder, it becomes necessary to look beyond, or rather, before the thoughts themselves, to the process that preceded them. Such was the central ingredient of Yates' (1966) theory.

Yates' Theory

Yates (1966) suggested that McGhie and Chapman's observations may be interpreted differently. Yates argued that the primary schizophrenic deficit lay not in a breakdown of the filter, but in a slowing down in the rate at which processing occurs. In line with Haber's (1969) viewpoint, he assumed that information processing occurred in stages dependent on the storage of some information while other information was being organized or transferred. Since, he argued, memory storage is limited, as shown by Broadbent (1958), Sperling (1960), and others, then slow processing would cause schizophrenics to lose more information per unit of time than in normals. Thus, only a subset of the relevant information that enters into storage will be successfully processed. In Yates' (1966) terms,

> this theory is very similar to that proposed by Chapman and McGhie, except that they stress the importance of irrelevant stimulation which is not screened out. This part of the theory seems unnecessary, however. It is here argued that the basic difficulty is an inability to process relevant information which is being presented at too fast a rate to be efficiently handled, caused by the abnormally slow rate of information processing. (p. 128)

If schizophrenics process too slowly, how is it possible to account for their reported experience of being flooded with information? One possibility is that processing takes place so slowly that the individual is unable to group information normally processed as a unit. For example, a sentence may be seen as composed of several words or a single idea. If the schizophrenic processed the words one at a time, the idea might not only get lost, but the input would seem overwhelming. In support of such an interpretation, Lawson, McGhie, and Chapman (1966) found that schizophrenics found it just as difficult to recall six words that constituted a sentence as they did six unrelated words. Normals, by contrast, showed much better recall for the sentence, apparently because they processed it as a single unit. Assuming that slow processing precludes a natural grouping of related inputs, the phenomenal experience of abnormally slow processing would be that of a flooding of information; incoming stimuli bear no relationship to one another and hence cannot be analyzed as a unit.

An Empirical Investigation of Processing Speed in Schizophrenia

The issue of processing speed in schizophrenics has been a major concern in modern empirical studies of information processing in schizophrenia. This section will focus on an ongoing attempt to attempt to evaluate speed of processing in schizophrenia using a methodological procedure known as visual masking. Visual masking and related studies illustrate how researchers have attempted to evaluate schizophrenia in terms of stages of information processing. Such studies also illustrate the thorny conceptual and methodological problems faced by researchers who have attempted, and continue to attempt, to apply information processing concepts to the study of schizophrenia.

Visual Masking Methodology

In a visual masking paradigm, an informational stimulus, known as the target, is presented in close temporal succession with a noninformational stimulus, the mask (Kahneman, 1968). Imagine, for instance, that a target consisting of a 4 × 4 matrix of letters has been briefly flashed on a screen or in a tachistoscope. In a masking experiment, a second stimulus, the mask, would be presented immediately following termination of the target or at any other predetermined interval. The mask limits the duration of the sensory signal provided by the target stimulus (Felsten & Wasserman, 1980).

Without using a mask, there is no way of knowing how long a sensory signal remains available for processing before a subject is required to respond to the target. As Felsten and Wasserman state,

> A mask permits the cognitive investigator to do something important that cannot be done by other means, namely, to deliver a pulse of information to the central nervous system with precise control on the duration of that pulse. Without using masking, visual persistence will guarantee that the duration of the information pulse experienced by the central nervous system will vary in an exceedingly complex manner. (p. 350)

To understand the importance of controlling the sensory pulse of a target, consider an early attempt to evaluate speed of processing in schizophrenics without employing a mask. Neale, McIntyre, Fox, and Cromwell (1969) compared the span of apprehension of schizophrenics and normals. Single and multi-item letter target displays were exposed for less than one-tenth of a second. Subjects were required to report as many letters as possible. Schizophrenics were as accurate as normals for single-item displays, but were unable to accurately report as many as normals from multiitem displays. The apparent inability of the schizophrenics to exact as many items, however, cannot be unequivocally interpreted in terms of slower processing. The sensory signal may be weaker or more unstable in the schizophrenics. They may process as quickly as normals but still be unable to report as many letters from the target because the initial sensory signal decayed more rapidly (i.e., remained available for less time) or contained less information to start with. Thus, the span-of-apprehension study of Neale *et al.* (1969) evaluated amount but not speed of processing, since variables other than slow processing could account for the observed performance deficit.

Early Visual Masking Studies in Schizophrenia

In an effort to deal with the limitations of Neale *et al.* (1969) and exercise control over the sensory impulse delivered to the central nervous system, Saccuzzo *et al.* (1974) employed visual masking methodology for the first time in a sample of schizophrenics. Chronic nonparanoid and paranoid schizophrenics were compared to nonschizophrenic psychiatric inpatients and normal controls. To minimize a possible confounding due to short-term memory differences, a two-choice forced discrimination task was used in which the target consisted of either a *T* or an *A*. The subject's task was simply to report which of the two targets had been presented.

A major problem faced by Saccuzzo *et al.* was that of deciding on an appropriate target duration. If the target was presented too quickly, it could be imperceptible to all subjects. If it was presented too long, however, all subjects might achieve ceiling performance. To understand the target duration problem, consider the example of the college professor who makes one exam so difficult that everyone fails and then overreacts with a second test that is so basic that all students obtain 100% scores. In neither case does the test discriminate among students of differing ability.

In the case of Saccuzzo *et al.* (1974), the problem of finding an appropriate target duration was even more complicated than finding a level that would measure performance levels between chance and ceiling. Pilot work had revealed that some schizophrenics require longer exposure durations of a stimulus than normals to achieve the same level of performance when no mask was used. To accommodate these subjects, it would have been necessary to provide a target exposure duration too long for most of the controls. But if the duration was lowered, some of the schizophrenics might have received an exposure duration that is insufficient to establish an appropriate sensory signal.

In an effort to deal with the complexities of establishing an appropriate target duration, Saccuzzo *et al.* (1974) first established the minimum exposure duration necessary to achieve 80% correct identifications of the target without a mask. Through this procedure, Saccuzzo *et al.* attempted to ensure that all subjects would have the same amount of information available before implementing the masking stimulus. In short, by determining a stimulus duration that would permit each individual subject to process as much information as all other subjects when no mask is used, Saccuzzo *et al.* hoped to rule out initial differences in the strength or quality of the sensory signal as a factor in any results that might be found when the mask was used.

Exposing the target for the previously determined duration each subject needed to achieve criterion performance, Saccuzzo *et al.* then presented a pattern noninformational masking stimulus at randomly presented intervals between offset of the target and on onset of the mask: 25, 50, 60, 200, 300, msec, and a no-mask control, which is an infinite delay of the mask. The two schizophrenics produced slower rising masking functions, indicating that they were, in fact, slower than the two control groups in processing information. In addition, however, the chronic nonparanoid group required significantly longer target exposures to achieve criterion performance without the mask. Consequently, Saccuzzo *et al.* concluded that in addition to slow processing, the nonparanoids may have the additional problem of requiring more time or a stronger stimulus to establish an adequate sensory signal. It was possible that, in Neisser's (1967) terms, iconic storage as well as processing speed was impaired in the nonparanoids.

The use of visual masking methodology provided a clear illustration of how the stages of processing that precede conscious thought might be evaluated in schizophrenic subjects and pointed to a disturbance in speed of information transfer in all schizophrenics and possibly iconic processing in certain subgroups of schizophrenics. Saccuzzo *et al.* (1974) thus provided direct empirical data in support of an information processing interpretation of schizophrenia. More work was needed, however, to establish the reliability of the findings and extend them beyond the mere demonstration of a performance deficit in schizophrenic subjects.

Saccuzzo and Miller (1977) provided confirmation of the finding that schizophrenics are impaired in their ability to evade the effects of a visual mask. Delusional paranoid schizophrenics, the type that did not show a difference in the exposure duration needed for criterion identification without a mask in Saccuzzo *et al.* (1974), were compared to normal controls. Rather than using fixed intervals as in Saccuzzo *et al.* (1974), a critical interstimulus interval (critical ISI) procedure was used in which the interval between offset of the target and onset of the mask was gradually increased for each incorrect identification of a tachistoscopically presented *T* or *A* until a predetermined criterion accuracy level was achieved.

Based on previous findings, a target duration of 6 msec was selected for all subjects. Since Saccuzzo *et al.* had not found a significant impairment for unmasked targets in the paranoids, there was little to be gained by attempting to control the sensory signal through variable target durations. On the other hand, the use of fixed target durations reduced the possibility of confounding target durations and masking performance, the major drawback of the establishing individual target durations as in Saccuzzo *et al.* (1974). Schizophrenics obtained a longer critical ISI across four separate trials, but showed no differential practice or learning effects. The finding of impaired masking functions in schizophrenics was subsequently replicated by Saccuzzo (1977), who used a fixed target duration, and by Braff and Saccuzzo (1981), who used an individually determined target duration based on the minimum duration needed for criterion recognition of unmasked targets.

A Marshalling of Evidence

Psychological studies of schizophrenia usually deal with so many unknowns that no single study, even when replicated, can hope to rule out every alternative or cover every possibility. Consequently, investigators must rely on a marshalling of evidence from a body of interrelated investigations in order to support the validity of their claims. This section examines some of the supporting evidence for the early masking studies.

The demonstration of a performance deficit in schizophrenic subjects, regardless of the task, usually tells us very little about schizophrenia. Schizophrenics perform less well than normals on just about any task, most often because of generalized deterioration that impairs performance across the board. In order to show that the masking deficit has any specific relevance to the underlying pathology of schizophrenia, it is necessary to rule against generalized deterioration. A number of solutions have been proposed to deal with the problem of generalized deficits. One approach is to include a control group known to suffer from generalized deterioration. If differences can be found between the schizophrenics and the generalized deterioration control, then generalized deterioration alone cannot account for an observed schizophrenic deficit.

Such an approach was recommended by Saccuzzo (1977). Saccuzzo observed a striking parallel between the psychological deficit literature in schizophrenia and old age. For just about every psychological deficit that had been found in schizophrenics, a similar one could be found in comparisons of young and old adult subjects, including visual masking. Since the elderly are obviously not schizophrenic, how could it be argued that a given performance deficit found in the elderly as well as in schizophrenics is directly related to the cause of schizophrenia? For example, in line with Yates, Saccuzzo and colleagues had argued that slow processing, as evaluated by the masking paradigm, was the major cause of thought disorder in schizophrenia. But how could this be if the elderly also show slow processing as evaluated by masking methodology? Saccuzzo (1977) suggested that the elderly might provide a good control group for generalized deterioration in schizophrenia studies, and moreover, if schizophrenics could not be discriminated from the elderly in a masking paradigm, then far more would be needed to rule out generalized deterioration as the cause of the masking deficit in both groups.

Brody, Saccuzzo, and Braff (1980) subsequently compared schizophrenic and elderly subjects who had been carefully screened for neurological problems, drug abuse, and problems that might impair performance on the masking task. Results showed that the elderly required a significantly higher minimum exposure to reach criterion performance for unmasked targets than both schizophrenics and normal controls. When, however, the target was exposed at a subject's individually obtained minimum duration for criterion performance, schizophrenics showed significantly poorer performance than both the elderly subjects and the normal young adult controls. Thus, the schizophrenic impairment in their masking performance was shown to be fundamentally different from a generalized deterioration control.

Further evidence against generalized deterioration has come from studies of remitted schizophrenics and from studies of schizophrenia-spectrum schizotypal personalities. S. Miller, Saccuzzo, and Braff (1979) evaluated the masking performance of individuals who had been diagnosed schizophrenic but were currently free of major symptoms and who were residing in an outpatient setting. Despite their lack of overt symptoms, these remitted schizophrenics showed a significant masking deficit compared to normal controls, which led S. Miller *et al.* (1979) to the conclusion that slow processing is an enduring trait, rather than a transitory state, of schizophrenic pathology.

In support of S. Miller *et al.* (1979), Saccuzzo and Braff (1981) compared two subtypes of schizophrenics, those with a good prognosis and those with a poor prognosis, to a group of depressed patients, a group of patients diagnosed as manic according to the criteria of Feighner *et al.* (1972), and a group of normal controls. Critical ISI was obtained eight times per subject over the course of his or her hospitalization in an acute psychiatric facility. The poor premorbid schizophrenics demonstrated a pronounced masking deficit throughout the course of their short-term hospitalization. Good premorbid schizophrenics, by contrast, showed a masking deficit only during the early stages of their disorder. To Saccuzzo and Braff (1981) these results indicated that slow processing was a trait of the genetically linked poor premorbid schizophrenic and a state for the non-genetically linked, precipitated good premorbid schizophrenic subtype.

In a second experiment, Saccuzzo and Braff (1981) compared the depressed patients, normal controls, and two subgroups of schizophrenics in a forward–backward masking paradigm. In forward masking, the mask is presented before the target. Work with normals had indicated that under conditions such as those used by Saccuzzo and Braff (1981), normals give results that do not differentiate between the two tasks (Schultz & Eriksen, 1977). Consequently, forward masking would have relevance as a control task to rule out generalized deterioration, as suggested by Chapman and Chapman (1973).

Comparison of the forward and backward masking functions of the two schizophrenic and two control groups revealed an important group by mask type by masking interval interaction. Analysis of the finding revealed that normals did not differ in their performance for the two types of mask. More importantly, the poor prognosis schizophrenics differed from the controls only in their performance on the backward masking task.

Saccuzzo and Braff's (1981) forward–backward masking comparison did not meet all of the requirements specified by Chapman and Chapman for a matched task because no data was presented demonstrating that the two types of masking procedures were equivalent with regard to reliability, discriminating power between persons, difficulty, and similarity. But results were clearly against an interpretation of generalized deterioration as in Brody *et al.* (1980) and S. Miller *et al.* (1979).

Considering all the relevant data, Saccuzzo and Braff (1981) hypothesized that slow processing, as evaluated by the backward masking task, would be found in the poor prognosis type schizophrenic even prior to the onset of schizophrenic symptoms. To test this hypothesis, Saccuzzo and Schubert (1981) and Braff (1981) independently evaluated the masking functions of individuals classified as schizotypal personalities, a nonpsychotic personality disorder believed to be genetically linked to schizophrenia. It was assumed that if slow processing was indeed a trait of individuals who fall in the poor prognostic category, then it should also be found in the schizotypal. Consistent with this prediction, both Braff (1981), who used individually determined target exposure durations, and Saccuzzo and Schubert (1981), who used a constant target exposure duration for all subjects, found an impairment in the masking functions of carefully diagnosed schizotypal personalities.

An added feature of Braff (1981) was that none of the schizotypes were medicated, indicating that their slow processing could not be attributed to medication. This finding added strength to a medication study reported by Braff and Saccuzzo (1981) in which it was found that medication did not impair the performance of schizophrenic subjects on the masking task.

More recently, Saccuzzo and Michael (1984) have supported the hypothesis that a poor masking performance in retarded schizophrenic persons is not due to a superior strategy, extending the findings of Saccuzzo, Braff, and Sprock (1982) who found that mental retardation did not worsen the schizophrenics' poor masking performance. Braff and Saccuzzo (1985) then found that the schizophrenic masking deficit is time linked, localized to intervals between 50 and 500 msec between offset of the target and onset of the mask.

Conclusion

Studies of visual masking in schizophrenia illustrate how researchers have attempted to study the information processing capabilities of schizophrenics. Such studies are supported by parallel programs of research such as those by Nuechterlein (e.g., Nuechterlein & Dawson, 1984), Knight and colleagues (e.g., Knight, 1984), and others. Taken together, these studies provide strong support for the validity of an information processing approach to schizophrenia and related spectrum disorders.

One of the more desirable outcomes of the information processing approach to schizophrenia has been the development of treatment interventions designed specifically to correct particular processing deficiencies. Magaro (chapter 14, this volume) provides an excellent overview of these new and important approaches to treatment.

III

Implications of an Information Processing Perspective for Assessment and Treatment of Psychopathology

11

Cognitive Assessment of Personality and Psychopathology

WILLIAM NASBY
Department of Psychology
Boston College
Chestnut Hill, Massachusetts 02167

JOHN F. KIHLSTROM
Department of Psychology
University of Wisconsin
Madison, Wisconsin 53705

A cognitive orientation now pervades much of clinical psychology. No longer controversial or "revolutionary," cognitive explanations of clinical disorders as well as accompanying treatment interventions have rapidly proliferated during the past decade. Although the cognitive principles and constructs which clinicians have proposed markedly differ from one explanation or intervention to the next, all share a common denominator. Cognitive explanations assume that distinct patterns of dysfunctional thoughts either cause or maintain corresponding patterns of maladaptive behavior and emotion. Similarly, cognitive interventions seek to remove dysfunctional and/or substitute functional thoughts, assuming that alleviation or even disappearance of maladaptive behavior and emotion will follow.

Despite promise, both trends ultimately risk conceptual stagnation because of limited scope: The conceptual analyses highlight the role of cognitive *products,* or what the individual consciously thinks. Rarely, though, do clinical explanations or interventions explore the cognitive *mechanisms* and *processes* that distort what the individual consciously thinks (e.g., Ingram, 1984b; Kihlstrom & Nasby, 1981).

INFORMATION PROCESSING APPROACHES TO CLINICAL PSYCHOLOGY

Refining cognitive explanations and interventions in clinical psychology requires a finer level of analysis, one that specifies how cognitive mechanisms and processes operate to produce and relieve disordered thoughts, emotions, and actions. Progress here, we believe, necessitates and presupposes an integrative model and technology of cognitive assessment. Although strategies and techniques of cognitive assessment have also proliferated recently (e.g., Kendall & Hollon, 1981; Kendall & Korgeski, 1979; Merluzzi, Glass, & Genest, 1981), few permit reasonable inferences about more than cognitive products. Arguably, many do not even assess what a person thinks but instead what a person reports thinking or, more often, reports having thought.

The cognitive perspective that currently dominates experimental psychology, the information processing paradigm (e.g., R. Lachman, Lachman, & Butterfield, 1979; Merluzzi, Rudy, & Glass, 1981), may address the limitations and oversights of cognitive assessment—somewhat. For example, experimental psychopathologists have extensively and profitably borrowed constructs and methods from the information processing paradigm to specify mechanisms and processes that may define the core deficits (or excesses) of several disorders, including schizophrenia, infantile autism, mental retardation, and organic brain syndromes. Already clinicians and psychopathologists have translated many of the experimental methods to assess organic brain syndromes. Eventually we expect that similar developments will transform and refine clinical assessment of other disorders (especially psychotic conditions) that seriously disrupt or prevent adaptive functioning.

Cognitive assessment of most disorders, however, cannot directly and indiscriminantly borrow either constructs or methods from the information processing paradigm and hope to succeed (cf. Kihlstrom & Nasby, 1981; R. J. Landau & Goldfried, 1981). For example, consider the cognitive analyses of the schizophrenic disorders which experimental psychopathologists have advanced. Although diverse, the explanations basically assume that one or more components of the information processing system have run amok: Selective mechanisms that control attention to and filtering of input break down, the processing of information occurs too slowly, sensory memory decays too quickly, and so forth. If the reader will pardon a computer metaphor, the explanations all implicate the "hardware" or the actual mechanics of the information processing system. The content of the information that the system processes, however, receives little, if any, notice. Accordingly, the experimental methods which cognitive psychopathologists have devised to examine schizophrenic disorders sample quite arbitrarily from the universe of content: Geometric shapes, strings of digits or letters, lists of words, narrative prose, and the like, do equally well.

The majority of individuals who seek and receive clinical services, however, do not suffer from an "across-the-board" breakdown of one or more control structures or processes. Instead, one can trace most of the cognitive problems of most clients to a specific domain of content—namely, social information. Most clients misconstrue particular individuals or facets of the self, distort recollections of personal experiences and social events, adopt inadequate or inappropriate strategies of interacting socially when particular encounters arise, and so forth. The mechanics of the information processing system per se operate just fine. Rather, the major problem implicates ''software'' (again, pardon the metaphor) or the social beliefs and knowledge that the system contains and the cognitive rules according to which the system operates when processing social information.

Until the late 1970s, experimental psychologists and psychopathologists who advocate the information processing paradigm have failed to address social cognition, which may explain the reluctance of most clinicians who favor a cognitive perspective to consider, let alone embrace, the approach (cf. R. J. Landau & Goldfried, 1981). The recent emergence of a *social-intelligence* viewpoint in personality (Cantor & Kihlstrom, 1983; Mischel, 1984) may provide a suitable compromise, since both the relevant domain of content and requisite level of analysis occupy center stage. Unlike the information processing paradigm, the social-intelligence viewpoint specifically emphasizes social cognition, as well as the behavioral and emotional antecedents and consequents of processing social information. But, unlike the cognitive principles and level of analysis which clinicians have preferred, the social-intelligence viewpoint also has adapted constructs and methods from the information processing paradigm to examine more finely the mechanisms and processes that control social cognition, and, therefore, retains a major asset of the information processing paradigm as well as the particular focus which clinicians who endorse a cognitive perspective will appreciate. In this chapter we examine some of the implications of this viewpoint for the clinical assessment of personality and psychopathology.

Toward an Integrative Model of Cognitive Assessment

Briefly stated, the social-intelligence viewpoint argues that social behavior is cognitively determined—or, in other words, that people behave in accordance with the meaning that they ascribe to the total situation in which social interaction takes place. This meaning is constructed by means of a set of social-cognitive processes involving perception, memory, judgment, inference, and problem solving. Thus, the interindividual differences in social behavior (i.e., differences across subjects with the objective situation held constant) are caused by individual differences in the meaning ascribed to the situation. Furthermore, intraindividual differences (i.e., differences observed across situations with the individual held constant, or across time with individuals and objective situations held constant) are caused by changes in the meaning assigned to the situation.

The Representation of Social Knowledge

Both normal and abnormal personality, from this point of view, is most appropriately construed in terms of the knowledge brought to bear by the individual on social interactions. In specifying the nature of this knowledge, the social-intelligence framework has adopted a number of constructs from current information processing models, especially ACT* (J. R. Anderson, 1983). These include the distinction between declarative and procedural knowledge (J. R. Anderson, 1976, 1983) and between episodic and semantic memory (Tulving, 1972, 1984). Each of these constructs, when applied to knowledge in the social domain, provides an important source of cognitive variation between individuals and of the cognitive basis of maladaptive behavior. As such, these forms of knowledge constitute a central target for personality and clinical assessment.

Declarative knowledge: episodic and semantic

In cognitive psychology and artificial intelligence, declarative knowledge refers to facts and beliefs about the real and imagined world of objects and events. This fund of world knowledge subsumes abstract, *semantic* knowledge about the world, as well as concrete, *episodic* knowledge about specific encounters with particular objects. Episodic memories, then, are to be distinguished from semantic ones in that the former contain, in addition to descriptions of objects, some reference to the spatial, temporal, and emotional context in which an event took place, and to the self as the agent or experiencer of that event. Episodic memories for each unique experience are encoded against a background of preexisting semantic knowledge; and context-free semantic knowledge is used in making inferences during the construction and reconstruction of some particular experience. Similarly, semantic memories develop through the accumulation and abstraction of knowledge from related episodes.

The relations among declarative memories are represented in ACT* as a graphic network of nodes representing concepts and links representing the relations among these concepts. The associative strength between nodes is represented by the length or width of the links. Thus, each fragment of the network constitutes a proposition which represents some fact in the individual's fund of semantic or episodic knowledge.

Procedural knowledge

While declarative knowledge refers to *knowing that,* procedural knowledge represents *knowing how.* It consists of the rules, skills, and strategies by which the cognitive system operates to encode, manipulate, retrieve, and utilize declarative knowledge. It includes rules of linguistic syntax, logical and mathematical operations, judgment and inference, skilled motor activities, and the like. While declarative knowledge is—at least in principle—available to conscious introspection, procedural knowledge is generally regarded as unconscious. According to ACT*, procedural knowledge begins as conscious, declarative knowledge about how to perform some overt or covert action. After extensive practice and opportunity for generalization, the procedure is rendered unconscious—though, of course, its nature can be inferred indirectly from cognitive and behavioral performance.

In ACT*, procedural knowledge is commonly represented as a production specifying some goal, an action or action sequence that can achieve that goal, and the conditions under which the action or action sequence can take place. Its format corresponds to an *if–then* statement, such that if the goal and conditions are instantiated, the action or action sequence follows automatically. Organized sets of productions define production systems which can accomplish complex cognitive and behavioral tasks.

Spreading activation

In the social-intelligence framework, the construct of spreading activation also plays a central role. According to ACT*, nodes in the declarative memory network are activated by the processing of perceptual inputs. Encoding a memory for an event, then, involves activating preexisting nodes corresponding to the features of the event, and establishing associative links corresponding to the relations among these features. Nodes that cross some threshold of activation become conscious. Once a source node has become deactivated (e.g., by processing another perceptual input), activation fades over time. Therefore, a node that has been recently activated can be reactivated more easily than one that has not; and nodes that are frequently activated retain more activation, and thus enter consciousness more readily, than those that seldom occupy the focus of attention. ACT* assumes that only a small set of nodes can be represented in consciousness simultaneously. Therefore, nodes that chronically serve as source nodes by virtue of frequent activation may prevent alternative or competing nodes from entering consciousness.

The elements of the memory store interact according to the principle of spreading activation (Collins & Loftus, 1975). Once a node in declarative memory is activated, activation spreads through the associative network along links connecting the source node to others. Source nodes that receive more attention contribute more activation. Activation spreads faster where the associative links are stronger; but, unless the source node is continually activated, activation can spread to only a limited degree before it fades. Any nodes linked to the source node that cross a threshold of activation also enter consciousness. This process is facilitated, of course, if the nodes are closely associated with the source, or if they are already near threshold by virtue of priming or chronic activation.

Implications for Personality

From the viewpoint of social-intelligence theory, declarative and procedural social memory provides the cognitive basis for the construction of social interaction. Insofar as personality is manifest in interindividual and intraindividual differences in social interaction, therefore, social memory is a major component in personality.

Declarative social knowledge: concepts and episodes

In the social domain, declarative semantic knowledge consists of the individual's repertoire of social concepts—mental representations of him- or herself (Kihlstrom & Cantor, 1985), other people (Cantor & Mischel, 1979), interpersonal behaviors (Hampson, 1982), and the situations in which social interactions take place (Cantor, Mischel, & Schwartz, 1982). This knowledge is hierarchically organized, with highly generalized, abstract social concepts subsuming more specific, concrete social entities. Much of this knowledge is summarized by the phrase "implicit personality theory," or the individual's intuitive knowledge of how individual differences are organized (Rosenberg, 1977). Another large component consists of social stereotypes, which can be considered mental representations of various outgroups (D. Hamilton, 1979). Presumably, this knowledge is astracted from direct and vicarious experience, according to the sorts of principles described by cognitive social learning theory (Bandura, 1977b; Mischel, 1973; Rotter, 1972).

Similarly, declarative episodic knowledge consists of the individual's memory for social interactions in which he or she has participated, directly or indirectly, as agent or experiencer. A central component of episodic memory is, of course, the individual's record of autobiographical memories (Kihlstrom, 1981). While memory for personal experiences has not yet been studied in any great detail (Gruneberg, Morris, & Sykes, 1978; Neisser, 1982), some principles of episodic social memory can be adduced from the study of *person memory* (Hastie *et al.*, 1980), a variant of verbal learning in which subjects are asked to remember the behaviors and characteristics displayed by specific other people. While episodic knowledge is represented propositionally in much the same manner as semantic knowledge, it does seem to have some unique organizing principles associated with self-reference, and with the spatial, temporal, and emotional context in which the remembered events take place.

Procedural social knowledge: rules and skills

In the social domain, procedural knowledge refers to the rules that people follow when engaged in social intercourse. Some of these rules guide the processing of social information such as selective attention (Cantor, 1981) and the selective encoding and retrieval of information about social entities (Hastie & Carlston, 1980); others are geared to tasks of social judgment and inference such as categorization (Cantor & Mischel, 1977), testing hypotheses about the objects of social judgment (M. Snyder, 1981c; Swann & Read, 1981a), and causal attribution (E. E. Jones, 1976; Kelley, 1972; Weiner *et al.*, 1971).

Procedural social knowledge also includes the social skills by which we negotiate social exchange (Athay & Darley, 1981). For example, there is a variety of impression-management strategies such as ingratiation (E. E. Jones, 1964) by which we can control the impressions that other people form of us (E. E. Jones & Pittman, 1982). In addition, there are scripts for various social interactions (Abelson, 1981). Scripts are similar to situation categories, in that they consist of a set of features describing the events that occur in some social interaction such as going to a restaurant; however, they differ in that these events are organized in terms of the chronological sequence in which they occur. As declarative knowledge structures, scripts enable us to categorize the situations in which we find ourselves; as procedural knowledge structures, they guide our behavior with others who are enacting the same script. As with declarative semantic knowledge, it seems likely that procedural knowledge in the social domain is acquired through precept and example, according to the principles of social learning theory.

Individual differences

The social-intelligence perspective of personality, employing the formal language of cognitive psychology, also provides a means of conceptualizing individual differences that are centrally relevant to personality and psychopathology. For example, each person necessarily possesses a different fund of episodic memories from the next. Moreover, each individual will have a somewhat different conceptual representation of the social world, and a somewhat different repertoire of rules and skills for guiding social interactions. That there will be important individual differences in the content of the social-knowledge repertoire goes almost without saying. In this chapter, however, we wish to say something about individual differences in the way in which these contents are structured, and in the cognitive *processes* that operate on them (see also Cantor & Kihlstrom, 1983).

One important dimension of individual differences is the person's expertise in a particular social domain. Expertise cuts across both declarative and procedural knowledge. By definition, of course, experts in a particular domain have acquired more "factual" knowledge, semantic and episodic, than novices. Moreover, experts may organize declarative knowledge differently than novices, establishing more associative links between the cognitive elements that define the domain, and perhaps also structuring the elements according to more complex and efficient hierarchies (e.g., Chase & Simon, 1973; Chi & Koeske, 1983). As a consequence of greater organization, areas of expertise should become more accessible, facilitating retrieval of relevant concepts and episodes to comprehend and interpret new information. Greater organization and accessibility should also free processing capacity to notice discrepancies and to assimilate exceptions. The latter characteristic may unintentionally promote conservative strategies of processing information, which may often render the expert more resistant to change than the novices (Crocker, Fiske, & Taylor, 1984). Depending on the circumstances and consequences, greater resistance to change could prove either adaptive or maladaptive.

The double-edged nature of expertise, especially in the social domain, is further revealed by its procedural aspects. Experts have developed an extensive repertoire of procedural rules to process and interpret relevant information and to plan appropriate behavior. With repeated application, procedural rules tend to become dissociated from awareness, which again frees processing capacity to pursue and accomplish other ends and goals (e.g., Shiffrin & Schneider, 1977), and which automatizes thought and action in the relevant domain. The automatic and unconscious quality of procedural knowledge, ironically enough, means that experts often run the risk of applying rules uncritically, even ''mindlessly'' (Chanowitz & Langer, 1980), and cannot easily articulate what they are doing or why (Nisbett & Wilson, 1977). If the procedural rules become inappropriate or maladaptive (e.g., because the ''rules of the game'' have changed), expertise can pose special problems. First, the inability to articulate the rules, preventing reflection and evaluation, may hinder change. In addition, even when identified, the process of replacing inappropriate, maladaptive procedures with more appropriate, adaptive ones is probably arduous and time-consuming, if only because ''old'' rules, once automatized, may not be truly lost from the repertoire, and hence may continue to dominate and intrude upon ''new'' ones.

Individual differences between chronically primed social concepts and autobiographical memories define a second, central feature of personality. Because nodes from associative networks can store activation, life contexts and experiences that often recur will produce social concepts and autobiographical memories that become and remain chronically primed (i.e., close to threshold) and easily accessed to interpret new and reinterpret old events and situations. To the extent that life contexts and experiences between individuals differ, the particular set of chronically primed social concepts and autobiographical memories will also differ (E. T. Higgins & King, 1981; E. T. Higgins, King, & Mavin, 1982). Chronically primed and easily accessible concepts and memories will generate further cognitive variation between individuals. Activation will spread repeatedly and readily to and from chronically primed concepts and memories and related nodes, and joint activation will serve both to establish and strengthen associative pathways that link easily accessible ideas and similar information.

Ideas that become chronically primed, therefore, should organize and integrate the particular networks of declarative social knowledge that an individual articulates and elaborates most (e.g., Bargh, 1982).

The selective effects of mood states identify a third dimension of individual differences. Considerable research now indicates that mood states can selectively direct attention to congruent features of the social environment, and selectively prime through spreading activation social concepts and autobiographical memories (e.g., Bower, 1981; D. M. Clark & Isen, 1982; Nasby, 1986a,b; Nasby & Yando, 1980, 1982). Moreover, the selective processing of social information constrains the particular interpretations (notably, judgments and inferences) that emerge from social events and situations. Different moods, then, may produce different interpretations of the same or a comparable situation from different individuals or from the same individual over different occasions. And, presumably, different interpretations will produce different responses to the same or a comparable event or situation.

Frequent and intense experiences of a particular mood can establish social concepts and autobiographical memories that remain chronically primed. Wittingly or unwittingly, therefore, individuals can develop cognitive expertise about some emotions but remain ignorant about others. Individuals also develop procedural rules to handle mood states. Procedural rules may control the processing of social information, which may either induce a particular mood directly (cf. Beck, 1976; Schachter & Singer, 1962) or provide "feedback" to influence the course and fate of a particular mood that already exists (cf. Mischel, Ebbesen, & Zeiss, 1973, 1976; Nasby & Yando, 1980, 1982). For example, most individuals have acquired a repertoire of strategies, cognitive and behavioral, to create and prolong the experience of pleasant moods and to curb the experience of unpleasant moods. The extent to which procedural rules successfully regulate mood states no doubt varies a great deal from one individual to the next, and earmarks an important feature of personality development (Nasby & Yando, 1980, 1982) and adaptive versus maladaptive functioning (Beck, 1976).

Toward a Technology for Cognitive Assessment

In a previous paper (Kihlstrom & Nasby, 1981), we explored a variety of techniques for assessing declarative knowledge relevant to personality and social interaction—including the kinds of maladaptive percepts, memories, judgments, and inferences that lie at the heart of psychopathology from a cognitive view. In the present chapter we undertake a similar investigation of techniques for assessing clinically relevant procedural knowledge in the social domain. Before considering specific techniques, though, we examine some of the special problems for both assessment and intervention that procedural social knowledge raises.

Procedural Social Knowledge

First, as noted earlier, procedures are by their very nature largely unconscious, inaccessible to introspective awareness. Therefore, self-report methodologies of the sort proposed for assessing the individual's fund of ostensible facts will have limited utility when it comes to his or her rules and skills. Moreover, again as noted earlier, proceduralization is largely a matter of extensive practice. While it may be possible to alter some aspect of a person's network of declarative knowledge by means of a carefully selected and cogently presented series of counterexamples, achieving the same end with a rule or skill will require much, much more time and effort.

Furthermore, as Tulving (1983) has noted, an important distinction between declarative and procedural knowledge is that the former has truth value whereas the latter does not. An individual may think that friendly people are also intelligent, that businesspeople are shrewd, that women are dependent, and so forth. Each of these "facts" is right or wrong; and if it is wrong, the erroneous knowledge can be corrected. Procedural knowledge, by contrast, does not have this property: It simply is the way which the person has of achieving certain goals under certain conditions. The procedure itself has evolved precisely because it has proved effective in achieving some specific goal, or because—in the absence of any direct, personal experience in goal-attainment—the person has been given good reason, by virtue of the precept or example of others, to think that it is so. Altering procedures would seem to require one of two principle tactics. First, the therapist may lead the client to question whether the goals are appropriate, or the conditions right, leading the person to retain the procedure in his or her repertoire but employ it under different circumstances. In the framework of ACT*, this seems more a matter of altering declarative knowledge than anything else. Second, the therapist may persuade the client that the procedure is ineffective in achieving the desired goal, or that there is a more efficient or appropriate way of doing so. In the framework of ACT*, therapy then would involve extensive retraining such that the substitute procedure replaces (or at least dominates) the original one.

Finally, it should be noted that social procedures are rules for social interactions. According to social exchange theory (Athay & Darley, 1981; Homans, 1961), each participant in a social interaction has entered the situation in order to achieve some goal. The interaction proceeds as the partners exchange love, status, money, goods, and services so that their individual goals may be met. In many cases, of course, the partners have the same goal in mind. In any event, such strategic interactions are rule governed.

Rules for Processing Social Information

Selective attention

The processing rules that selectively direct attention to some rather than other sources of personal and social information definitely warrant greater consideration from personologists and psychopathologists. After all, the mechanisms and processes that control attention define the contents of focal awareness (*what* the person consciously experiences and thinks) and provide the raw data (the activated configuration of declarative nodes) to which other processing rules apply and from which the individual interprets a particular situation or event to plan behavior. Moreover, selective attention to personal and social information may contribute significantly to strategies of regulating mood states. An experiment which Mischel *et al.* (1973) conducted illustrates the last point.

Mischel *et al.* devised a simple but effective means of assessing selective attention or exposure to personality feedback about the self among normal subjects. Before the experiment, subjects completed a series of "personality tests" and later expected to receive feedback. During the actual experiment, subjects first completed an "achievement test" of intellectual ability. To induce positive or negative moods, respectively, subjects then received bogus feedback of having either succeeded or failed; other subjects received no feedback about intellectual ability. All subjects finally received 10 minutes to examine booklets, one of which ostensibly contained personality feedback about "positive assets," the other of which ostensibly contained feedback about "negative liabilities." Mischel *et al.* surreptitiously monitored how long each subject read or studied each booklet to index selective attention. The results indicated that subjects who experienced success attended significantly longer to personality assets than subjects who either failed or received no information about intellectual ability; the latter groups did not differ. Manipulation of success–failure did not differentially affect how long subjects attended to personal liabilities. According to Mischel *et al.*, subjects who experienced success adopted a processing strategy that would maintain or even bolster the positive mood, namely, attending preferentially to personal assets. Ordinarily, however, one would not expect normal subjects who experience failure to adopt the symmetric but opposite strategy of attending more to personal liabilities, which might prolong or exacerbate the negative mood; disturbed individuals (e.g., clinical depressives and others who lack self-esteem), though, very well might.

Although no studies have yet examined selective attention to feedback about personal assets and liabilities among clinical populations, one which Swann and Read (1981a) conducted illustrates the potential of the method. Swann and Read identified two groups of participants: "self-likables" and "self-dislikables," who examined personality feedback that either confirmed or disconfirmed the self-concept. "Self-likables" attended more to positive (confirmatory) than negative (disconfirmatory) feedback. "Self-dislikables" did the opposite.

A similar procedure might contribute to the assessment of clinical disorders. For example, clients might receive an opportunity to examine booklets that ostensibly contain personality feedback about the self. Instead of just two booklets (one containing desirable, the other undesirable, feedback), the clinician might construct and present several, each containing specific and homogeneous information about a particular characteristic. Suitable characteristics would certainly include interpersonal traits (J. W. Wiggins, 1979) and emotional states (Russell, 1980). Preferential attention to feedback about some rather than other characteristics might identify areas of self-expertise and self-ignorance as well as personal concerns about interpersonal behaviors and emotional experiences. One could also extend the technique easily, allowing the client the opportunity to examine personality feedback that ostensibly refers to significant others or interaction partners.

Selective encoding

The ''depth-of-processing'' model and corresponding paradigm (Cermak & Craik, 1978; Craik & Lockhart, 1972; Craik & Tulving, 1975) have motivated and shaped much of the research that has examined the acquisition, construction, or encoding of episodic and autobiographical memories during an experimental session. Typically, the depth-of-processing paradigm tests incidental memory, via recall or recognition, of stimuli that the subject has rated or evaluated according to one or more orienting sets (e.g., semantic, structural, phonemic, orthographic). Rating semantic attributes of a stimulus presumably requires more elaborative (''deeper'') processing and produces a more distinctive and hence memorable trace than rating nonsemantic attributes.

Several experiments have extended the depth-of-processing paradigm to include self-reference orienting sets (e.g., deciding whether or not particular attributes characterize the self). Results have often indicated that self-reference enhances recall and recognition more than a variety of comparison tasks, semantic and nonsemantic alike (T. B. Rogers, 1981). Theoretically, self-reference enhances episodic memory because concepts and associations between concepts about oneself represent the most extensive and intricate network most individuals have developed, thereby permitting and producing through the application and execution of procedural rules the construction of more elaborate and distinctive traces.

Importantly, several factors qualify the general conclusion that self-reference enhances memory. Some of the factors, which should interest personologists, clinicians, and psychopathologists, include subject and stimulus characteristics as well as experimental or situational manipulations. For example, H. Davis (1979a) compared groups of depressed and nondepressed subjects who completed structural, phonemic, sematic, and self-referent ratings of nondepressed-content personal adjectives (e.g., curious, loyal, organized). Only among the nondepressives did self-reference enhance recall of nondepressed-content personal adjectives above the remaining tasks. Kuiper (e.g., Derry & Kuiper, 1981; Kuiper & Derry, 1982; Kuiper & MacDonald, 1982) has conducted a series of similar experiments, but has also sampled depressed-content personal adjectives (e.g., bleak, guilty, helpless), and extended the range of non-self-referent rating tasks. For example, Derry and Kuiper (1981) compared the recall performance of three groups (clinical depressives, nondepressed psychiatric controls, and normal nondepressives) who completed structural, semantic, and self-referent ratings of depressed- and nondepressed-content personal adjectives. Again, only the self-referent encoding task produced differences between the recall performance of the groups. Among the nondepressives (both psychiatric and normal controls) self-referent, yes ratings of nondepressed-content enhanced recall. Conversely, self-referent, yes ratings of depressed-content enhanced recall among the clinical depressives. Kuiper and Derry (1982, Experiment 1) obtained a pattern of recall from mild depressives that differed slightly: Compared to a semantic task, self-reference increased recall of *both* depressed and nondepressed content. Among nondepressives, self-reference again only facilitated recall of nondepressed content, which also occurred during a subsequent experiment (Kuiper & Derry, 1982, Experiment 2) that substituted a comparison task of other-reference (rating whether or not personal adjectives described a public figure). Mild depressives, however, recalled more self- than other-referenced depressed content.

To explain the relationships between depression and selective recall of self-referenced depressed and nondepressed material, Kuiper (e.g., Kuiper & Derry, 1981; Kuiper, MacDonald, & Derry, 1983; Kuiper, Olinger, & MacDonald, in press) has proposed a "content-specific self-schema model," which extends the previous theorizing of A. T. Beck (1967, 1976). Basically, the model assumes that depressives have developed a negative, whereas normals have developed a positive, self-schema which somehow facilitates the processing of congruent information. Ingram (1984b; Ingram *et al.*, 1983) and Nasby, 1986a,b) have offered an alternative, though perhaps complimentary, interpretation that emphasizes cognitive *processes* rather than *content*. Unlike Kuiper, who assumes that the self represents a unified, single, or monolithic structure, Ingram and Nasby have argued that individuals—normal as well as depressed—articulate and elaborate a variety of context-specific self-concepts (e.g., "self-when-elated" or "self-when-depressed"). Depressed and nondepressed individuals alike have developed and established both negative and positive concepts about the self (see Mischel *et al.*, 1973) rather than one versus the other. Presumably, then, factors and processes that selectively activate (or inhibit) negative rather than positive networks of concepts about the self and according to which individuals process (e.g., encode, store, and retrieve) self-relevant information differ between the depressed and nondepressed.

To activate positive and negative concepts about the self, Ingram *et al.* (1983) manipulated success–failure, whereas Nasby (1986a) directly induced elation–depression. Ingram *et al.* found that nondepressed subjects who had succeeded later recalled more positive self-referents than nondepressed subjects who had failed or mild depressives who had either succeeded or failed. Among the depressed subjects, however, recall of positive self-referents did not differ between the success and failure conditions. Ingram *et al.* concluded that mild depressives either do not or cannot activate positive self-concepts as readily as nondepressives to process (specifically, encode) self-relevant information following experiences of success. Nasby (1986a) found evidence that nondepressives have developed negative as well as positive self-schemata, which congruent moods can activate: Compared to "neutral" mood, depressed mood facilitated the encoding and retention of self-referenced, yes-rated (congruent), depressed content—the same effect Kuiper obtained from clinical depressives; elated mood, conversely, facilitated encoding and retention of self-referenced, yes-rated, nondepressed content. Interestingly enough, the moods did not "spill over" to affect recall of information about familiar and significant others (e.g., best friend, mother) selectively.

The results suggest, therefore, that the moods *specifically* activated or "primed" congruent networks about the self. Considered jointly, the studies which Ingram and Nasby have conducted underscore the promise of examining the processing as well as the content differences between self-concepts or self-schemata among depressed and normal individuals. Since Nasby (1986a) did not test clinically depressed subjects and since Ingram *et al.* (1983) did not sample depressed-content personal adjectives, however, we do not know yet whether depressed individuals activate negative concepts more readily than normal counterparts.

Other studies and experiments have simplified but managed to preserve the spirit of the paradigm (e.g., testing incidental memory, varying stimulus content, examining self-reference) by dropping baseline or comparison tasks, ignoring the distinction between yes and no ratings, and so forth. The revised methods should prove more tractable clinically to assess episodic memories that an individual encounters and encodes during an experimental session.

For example, Markus, Crane, Bernstein, and Siladi (1982) examined relationships between self-schemata about gender and the processing of "masculine," "feminine," and "neutral" information. Markus *et al.* first identified and then tested four groups of subjects: masculine schematics, feminine schematics, high androgynous, and low androgynous. One task, among several, required subjects to rate the self-descriptiveness of masculine, feminine, and neutral attributes. A surprise test of incidental memory followed. Feminine subjects recalled more feminine than masculine attributes and more feminine attributes than masculine subjects, who produced the converse pattern of incidental memory. Although high androgynous subjects recalled more feminine than masculine attributes, the difference did not approach that obtained from the groups of masculine and feminine subjects. Low androgynous subjects did not differentially recall feminine and masculine attributes, and recalled fewer of both than high androgynous subjects. Convergent results from other tasks suggested that masculine and feminine subjects have articulated and elaborated richly interconnected networks of attributes and concepts that organize, respectively, masculine and feminine information about the self. High androgynous subjects have developed both masculine and feminine self-schemata, whereas low androgynous subjects have established neither. Mills (1983) has reported similar results and endorsed similar conclusions.

Other experiments have addressed whether and how induced moods selectively affect the encoding and retention of autobiographical and episodic information about personality feedback. For example, Ingram (1984a) found that subjects who experienced negative mood and received negative feedback recalled more information than subjects who received the same feedback but experienced either positive or neutral mood. In addition, among subjects who experienced positive mood, those who received negative feedback about the self recalled less information than those who received positive feedback. Mischel *et al.* (1976) conducted a similar experiment, but assessed recognition memory rather than free recall. From the recognition data, Mischel *et al.* calculated d', which indexed memory strength or the ability of a subject to discriminate between targets and distractors that the personality feedback did and did not contain, repsectively. Results indicated that subjects who experienced positive mood retained less of the unfavorable feedback about the self than subjects who experienced either negative or neutral mood. Mood did not selectively affect retention of feedback about personal assets. Finally, Natale and Hantas (1982), who also tested recognition memory and calculated d' to index memory strength, obtained a pattern of results that differed somewhat: Sad mood reduced the retention of feedback about personal assets; retention of feedback about personal liabilities, however, differed insignificantly across groups that experienced a happy, neutral, or sad mood.

Clinical psychologists will find the results which Ingram (1984a), Mischel *et al.* (1976), and Natale and Hantas (1982) obtained interesting, since the experimental contexts and designs resemble the communication and processing of personality feedback that occur during treatment. More specifically, the results assume clinical significance to the extent that selective encoding of therapeutic information and personality feedback influences subsequent actions, cognitions, and emotions. And, given that mood selectively alters the impact of personality feedback—disrupting and/or facilitating "deep" or elaborate processing, respectively, of incongruent and congruent information about the self—clinicians might either assess or, perhaps better yet, manipulate the mood a client experiences when the feedback occurs to optimize the impact of the information (see Nasby & Yando, 1980, 1982). And, instead of providing global or undifferentiated feedback about personality strengths and weaknesses, clinicians might also draw finer distinctions, presenting feedback about specific attributes from either the interpersonal or emotional domain (Russell, 1980; J. W. Wiggins, 1979).

The pattern of selective encoding across specific attributes could reveal areas of interpersonal expertise and ignorance about the self or the emotional states that currently dominate the concerns and experiences of a client.

Selective retrieval

The studies of episodic and autobiographical memory we have reviewed above concern events and information which individuals encountered and processed during an experimental session, and, therefore, address most directly factors that affect encoding and acquisition. Several experiments and studies have also examined retrieval of episodic and autobiographical memories about events and personal experiences that antedate the experimental session.

For example, Markus (1977) reasoned that if a particular characteristic defines a central attribute or feature of the self (an area of self-expertise), then one should access behavioral evidence (specific examples) from autobiographical memories more readily than if the particular characteristic does not. Across a variety of behavioral domains (e.g., independence–dependence, masculinity–feminity), results have confirmed the hypothesis. Clinical applications of the same technique to assess selective accessibility and retrieval would simply require the sampling of appropriate content.

Most of the retrieval studies and experiments, though, have examined relationships between mood states, whether naturally occurring or deliberately induced, and accessibility of pleasant and unpleasant experiences. Although exceptions and deviations complicate matters, results more often than not favor a congruity hypothesis: Pleasant mood facilitates and/or disrupts accessibility and hence retrieval of positive and negative experiences, respectively; unpleasant mood often, though less consistently, does the reverse.

Two indexes, which do not always converge, have operationalized accessibility: response latency and probability of recall. Consider first studies and experiments that have measured response latency. For example, Lloyd and Lishman (1975) as well as D. M. Clark and Teasdale (1982) asked depressed patients to retrieve autobiographical memories of pleasant and unpleasant experiences and measured response latencies. Lloyd and Lishman (1975) found a negative relationship between severity of clinical depression and response latencies to retrieve unpleasant experiences. Response latencies to retrieve pleasant experiences and severity of clinical depression correlated positively but insignificantly. D. M. Clark and Teasdale (1982) examined depressed patients whose mood fluctuated diurnally. Unlike Lloyd and Lishman, however, Clark and Teasdale found no relationship between mood level and response latencies to retrieve either pleasant or unpleasant experiences, perhaps because mood level did not fluctuate enough.

Other experiments have actually manipulated happy or sad moods among normal subjects through a variety of means to examine the congruity hypothesis (e.g., Riskind, 1982; Riskind, Rholes, & Eggers, 1982; Teasdale & Fogarty, 1979; Teasdale & Taylor, 1981; Teasdale *et al.*, 1980). Consistently, results have revealed either one or both of the following effects: Individuals who experience a happy mood access pleasant events more quickly than unpleasant events and/or retrieve pleasant events more rapidly than individuals who experience a sad mood. The converse has seldom occurred. Response latencies to retrieve unpleasant experiences often do not differ between happy and sad moods. Nor does sad mood differentially affect response latencies to access and report pleasant versus unpleasant experiences.

Consider next the studies and experiments that have operationalized accessibility according to probability of recall. For example, D. M. Clark and Teasdale (1982) examined not only response latency but also probability of recall among clinical depressives whose mood fluctuated diurnally: When more depressed, subjects recalled more unpleasant than pleasant experiences; when less depressed, the opposite occurred. (Clearly, then, response latency and probability of recall do not always converge.)

A few experiments (e.g., M. Snyder & White, 1982, Experiments 1 & 2; Teasdale & Taylor, 1981) have obtained similar results from normal subjects following induction of happy or sad moods. Other experiments also have obtained significant interactions between mood states and selective retrieval of pleasant and unpleasant or happy and unhappy experiences from normal subjects, but not the "crossover" pattern that the congruity hypothesis predicts.

Autobiographical memories, then, may not only reveal domains of personal significance and insignificance, and expertise and ignorance (e.g., Markus, 1977), but also factors (specifically, moods) that bias retrieval. Because of the latter possibility, clinicians must sift and weigh the information that clients provide about previous events and experiences during interviews and therapy.

Interpretive Rules for Social Judgment and Inference

Categorization and response latency

Speeded classification or verification—the favorite method among cognitive psychologists to examine structural and processing assumptions about network models of semantic memory (e.g., R. Lachman *et al.*, 1979)—may also reveal much about categorizing social information. Although the details of specific tasks and applications differ, speeded classification or verification, quite simply, requires the subject to answer questions about category membership (e.g., "Is a canary a bird?") or attributes (e.g., "Does a canary have wings?"). Response latency or the time to answer the question provides the dependent variable of interest. Other factors equal, and given the properties of spreading activation and "priming," network models predict that directly and/or strongly linked concepts and attributes require less time than indirectly and/or weakly linked concepts and attributes to classify or verify because the application and execution of categorization rules can occur rapidly and efficiently.

Markus has used speeded classification/verification to distinguish central from peripheral attributes of the self-concept. For example, Markus (1977) first classified subjects as self-schematic or aschematic for the attribute of independence (or dependence). Later, subjects rated adjectives conceptually related to independence or dependence on a dichotomous scale of self-descriptiveness. Not surprisingly, subjects who were self-schematic for independence rated more independent adjectives as self-descriptive; and those who were self-schematic for dependence rated more dependent adjectives in this way. Independent adjectives, however, were also endorsed often by subjects classified as self-schematic for dependence, and subjects classified as self-schematic for independence often endorsed dependent items as self-descriptive, perhaps because of response sets (e.g., social desirability). The data from the response latencies proved more revealing. Self-schematics for independence responded more quickly when rating themselves on independent rather than dependent adjectives. Conversely, self-schematics for dependence responded more quickly when rating themselves on dependent rather than independent adjectives. Aschematic subjects for the dimension of independence–dependence showed no difference in response latencies for independent and dependent items. Similar findings have been obtained in the domain of gender-role orientation (Markus *et al.*, 1982; Mills, 1983). Apparently, then, subjects may say many things about themselves, for a variety of reasons. Shorter response latencies seem to indicate that the subject needs less time to find a reason—perhaps because that particular feature is already closely associated with the self-concepts and hence easily accessed or "primed."

Kuiper and MacDonald (1982) have used speeded classification/verification to assess and compare the processing of personal information about the self among depressed and normal subjects. Specifically, in response to the question "Describes you?," subjects decided whether or not personality attributes, evenly divided between depressed and nondepressed content, characterized the self. The response latencies indicated that normal subjects responded more quickly to "positive" information about the self (yes-rated nondepressed *and* no-rated depressed content) than "negative" information (no-rated nondepressed *and* yes-rated depressed content). Among depressed subjects, however, "positive" and "negative" latencies did not differ. Comparisons between the groups revealed that normal subjects classified positive information about the self more rapidly than depressed subjects; response latencies to negative information, however, did not distinguish the two groups. The results, therefore, suggest that normal subjects have established direct and strong links between a generalized concept of self and positive attributes, which depressed subjects lack. Considering negative attributes, the converse apparently does not hold. We should note, however, that Kuiper and MacDonald tested depressed subjects who experienced mild levels of the disorder. Severe depressions may very well facilitate the classification of negative attributes and features about the self.

More recently, Gotlib and McCann (1984) did obtain evidence that depressives have acquired accessible or "primed" concepts to perceive and evaluate negative information. To assess differential priming or accessibility of negative concepts among depressed and nondepressed subjects, Gotlib and McCann modified the Stroop (1935) task, which differs somewhat from speeded classification/verification. More specifically, the Stroop task includes a series of words, across which color of ink varies. The primary task requires the subject to report the color of ink rather than pronounce or otherwise classify the word per se. Because of interference effects (response competition), when words semantically match either a temporarily or chronically primed, or accessible, concept, response latencies suffer. Gotlib and McCann tachistoscopically presented to depressed and nondepressed subjects colored words of depressed, neutral, and manic content. Results supported the hypothesis: Because of accessibility and interference effects, depressed subjects responded more slowly to depressed than nondepressed content, and more slowly to depressed content than nondepressed subjects.

The results which Markus, Kuiper, and Gotlib have reported suggest that measuring response latencies, via speeded classification/verification and the Stroop task or similar procedures that pit interference against accessibility effects (e.g., Bargh, 1982) may profitably assess the content and structure of self-, person, and situation concepts, as well as the interpretive rules that individuals have acquired to categorize social information vis-à-vis declarative social knowledge.

Testing hypotheses about oneself and others

Extensive research from cognitive psychology indicates that, across tasks as diverse as concept formation, concept utilization, deductive reasoning, and problem solving, most individuals consider instances that confirm rather than disconfirm beliefs and hypotheses more compelling, diagnostic, and informative (e.g., Hovland & Weiss, 1953; Wason & Johnson-Laird, 1972). For example, given the opportunity of testing hypotheses, most individuals prefer to gather confirmatory rather than disconfirmatory evidence. The proclivity toward hypothesis confirmation also extends to the social arena. M. Snyder (1981a; M. Snyder & Swann, 1978), for example, devised a simple procedure to examine the rules or strategies that individuals formulate and implement to test hypotheses about others. More specifically, subjects chose questions from a prepared list to ask a "target" during a subsequent interview that would provide the best means of testing a hypothesis about the other—namely, assessing the extent to which the behaviors and experiences of the target match the attributes of the prototypical extravert or introvert. The list included questions that would solicit information about extraversion or introversion or neither characteristic. Across several replications and variations of the basic procedure, results consistently indicated that subjects chose to ask questions that would solicit hypothesis-confirming evidence from the target about twice as often as questions that would solicit hypothesis-disconfirming evidence.

Recently, Fong and Markus (1982) as well as Swann and Read (1981a) have extended the procedure to the realm of personality. Fong and Markus (1982) examined how self-schemata selectively influence the information people solicit to learn more about others. More specifically, Fong and Markus first identified three groups of subjects: extravert and introvert schematics, who believed, respectively, that extraversion or introversion defined a central feature of the self, and aschematics, who considered neither attribute self-relevant. All subjects then selected questions from the same list which M. Snyder and Swann (1978) had constructed to ask of and learn about a stranger (but not under conditions to test a particular hypothesis about either extraversion or introversion). Participants sought information about others that define a central feature of the self: Extraverted schematics selected more extraverted questions than did either introverted schematics or aschematics; conversely, introverted schematics selected more introverted questions than did either extraverted schematics or aschematics. Clearly, then, self-schemata may constrain the process of gathering information about others.

Swann and Read (1981a) have conducted a study that complements the one of Fong and Markus and may also contribute to clinical and cognitive assessment. Instead of examining how self-schemata influence the process of testing hypotheses about others, Swann and Read offered participants (self-perceived "assertives" or "unassertives" as well as self-perceived "emotionals" or "unemotionals") the opportunity to study the feedback of an "interaction partner" who had answered questions about participants from responses to a personality questionnaire. All four groups of participants requested more feedback (answers to questions) that would confirm rather than disconfirm the self-concept.

Efforts to obtain or solicit self-confirmatory feedback from others may stabilize the social environment, self-concepts, and interpersonal behavior. The stabilizing functions, however, may illuminate clinical problems if the confirmatory rules seek information and feedback about the self that refer to negative or undesirable attributes. Moreover, failure to demonstrate a confirmatory bias may also indicate confusion about the self or a disorganized and unstable self-concept. More positively, the same failure may signal an appropriate target or avenue of change, which the client will not resist.

Causal attributions

A final category of interpretive rules we will consider—the procedures whereby individuals attribute causes to personal and social events—has recently generated considerable interest among clinicians and psychopathologists (Metalsky & Abramson, 1981). The scope of disorders and problems to which clinicians and psychopathologists have proposed attributional perspectives now includes learned helplessness among both adults (e.g., Abramsom *et al.*, 1978) and children (e.g., Diener & Dweck, 1978), clinical depression (e.g., Beck *et al.* 1979), paranoid states, (e.g., Davison, 1966), unwarranted aggression and hostility among disturbed children (e.g., Nasby, Hayden, & DePaulo, 1980), low self-esteem (e.g., Ickes & Layden, 1978), coping reactions to accidents and victimization (e.g., Wortman & Silver, 1980), fear (e.g., Valins & Nisbett, 1971), and insomnia (e.g., G. C. Davison, Tsujimoto, & Glaros, 1973).

The techniques which clinicians, personologists, and psychopathologists have constructed to assess attributions follow either structured or unstructured formats, requiring subjects, respectively, to endorse possible causes from specified alternatives or describe "freely" the "perceived" causes of real or hypothetical events (Elig & Frieze, 1979). Whatever the format, existing techniques all measure the content of attributions, the finished products.

A cognitive approach would also examine parameters of performance other than attributional contents or products. For example, one could present each item of the questionnaire via a desktop microprocessor, tachistoscope, or slide projector and record voice onset time (VOT) to initiate a verbal description of the major cause, and response latencies to rate the event along each dimension. Over time, one could also examine recall and recognition of the questionnaire items. The latter indexes would justify stronger inferences about the interpretive rules that produce specific attributions. Suppose, for example, that a depressed client or one who risks clinical depression has developed a generalized, potent, and undifferentiated rule: "*If* I fail (regardless of the particular circumstances), *then* attribute the cause to internal, global, and stable factors" (e.g., Abramson *et al.*, 1978). To the ambiguous item, "You fail an exam," the individual should quickly initiate a verbal description of an internal, global, and stable cause—for example, "I failed the exam because of stupidity." Extreme and confident ratings of internality, globality, and stability also should occur quickly. And, over time, the individual might falsely recognize (commit "false alarms" to) lures that fit the rule but which the original questionnaire did not actually contain—for example, "You fail an exam your classmates pass" or "You fail an exam your classmates pass although they studied less than you did." From the convergent evidence that the content and pattern of ratings as well as the response latencies and memory data provide, we believe that clinicians and psychopathologists can fashion research strategies to assess attributional rules and processes more finely than the products alone.

Some comments about action rules

In large part, the study of social cognition has emphasized the structure of social information, and the processes by which it is encoded, organized, transformed, and retrieved. Correspondingly, our efforts to develop methods for the assessment of individual differences in social intelligence have emphasized these same topics. Nevertheless, the principal reason for proposing an assessment of social knowledge is the assumption that social behavior is cognitively mediated. Thus, it seems important to take some steps toward assessment strategies that directly assess the cognition–action link. Cognitively oriented social/personality psychologists have certainly not ignored the relations between social cognition and social behavior. Such concerns are manifested in the increasingly large literature on interpersonal expectancy effects (e.g., J. M. Darley & Fazio, 1980; M. Snyder & Swann, 1978), impression-management strategies (e.g., E. E. Jones & Pittman, 1982), self-verification (e.g., Swann, 1983), and scripts (e.g., Abelson, 1981).

This literature, however, is not as assiduously ''cognitive'' as some of the other material reviewed here and elsewhere (Kihlstrom & Nasby, 1981). For example, investigators of social action rules rarely commit themselves to any formal theories concerning representation or processing. Nor do their research paradigms have the kind of high-tech characteristics of some of the other work we have reviewed. Specifically, the research often relies on pencil-and-paper, self-report measures, and thus, on the person's direct introspective access to her or his procedural social knowledge. Again, the problem here is that procedural knowledge is, by its very nature, inaccessible to conscious awareness (J. R. Anderson, 1983; Nisbett & Wilson, 1977). It seems likely, moreover, that the kinds of maladaptive procedures that cause interpersonal difficulties are precisely the ones that are fully automatized, and hence inaccessible to direct awareness. We are, therefore, currently in the process of devising assessment techniques to gauge rules of social action through measures of cognitive and behavioral performance.

Conclusion

In our previous paper, we noted the essential tension in personality assessment between idiographic and nomothetic proposals. In the intervening time, we have gravitated even more toward an idiographic position. The purpose of assessment should not be to compare the individual to faceless statistical norms.

Rather, the criteria against which people should be measured ought to be set, to the greatest extent possible, by their own goals, the demands of their own peculiar life situations, and the partners with whom they must conduct social intercourse. This is congruent with the overriding perspective of the social-intelligence approach to personality, which asserts that personality does not exist in the abstract, but is constructed in the context of ongoing social interactions. It is also, of course, congruent with the cognitive–behavioral approach to clinical work, which has as its goal the remediation of specific problems, rather than the restructuring of entire personalities.

To some extent, this limited, goal-oriented perspective should mitigate the qualms which might be experienced as the clinician anticipates employing the advanced technology of the cognitive laboratory in order to map out a patient's entire fund of social knowledge. To put it bluntly, nothing of the sort is intended. Assessment should always be for some purpose, and from the cognitive–behavioral perspective those purposes should always be limited by the presenting problems of the patient or client, and other related problems that may turn up in the course of taking an anamnesis. We know from experience (Kihlstrom & Cantor, 1985) that it can take many hours and two computers only to map out a single individual's context-specific self-concepts according to procedures adopted from Rosenberg (1977) and Pervin (1976). But such a large-scale assessment will rarely be necessary. For the purpose to which personality assessment is put in traditional clinical psychology, the high-tech approach described here may seem daunting indeed. But for the limited purposes to which assessment is put by cognitive therapists, these procedures—which are specifically designed to tap the kinds of variables deemed central by practitioners—may be very much what the doctor ordered.

Acknowledgments

Preparation of this chapter was supported in part by Grant #MH-35856 from the National Institute of Mental Health and an H.I. Romnes Faculty Fellowship from the University of Wisconsin to the second author. We thank Nancy Cantor and Jeanne Sholl for their comments at various stages in the preparation of this chapter.

12

Information Processing and the Human Change Process

LA PEARL LOGAN WINFREY
MARVIN R. GOLDFRIED
Department of Psychology
State University of New York at Stony Brook
Stony Brook, New York 11794

Introduction

There has been a growing focus in the psychological literature on the role that experimental cognitive psychology and social cognition may have in understanding people's attitudes and behavior. Therapists of varying orientations are looking at how these developments can be used in assessment and intervention within the clinical setting (e.g., Goldfried & Robins, 1983; Greenberg & Safran, 1984; M. J. Horowitz, 1976; Kendall & Hollon, 1981a; Peterfreund, 1980; Turk & Speers, 1983; Wexler & Rice, 1974), and models of memory organization and schematic processing have the potential for becoming an overarching framework for understanding process and outcome in psychotherapy in general. Moreover, the language of cognitive models represents a common language that both experimentalists and practitioners can use to discuss their various approaches to human behavior. A major barrier between scientists and practitioners is therefore within sight of being eliminated, and criticisms that cognitive–behavior therapy had developed its own clinical theory of cognition, independent of existing knowledge of cognitive processes (Greenberg & Safran, 1981; Lindsay & Norman, 1977), can be redressed.

The purpose of this chapter is to (1) review some of the major work in schema theory, describing how schemata influence information processing; (2) examine

INFORMATION PROCESSING APPROACHES
TO CLINICAL PSYCHOLOGY

what this information processing perspective suggests for therapeutic strategies; and (3) note issues in need of future research.

Defining a Schema

When we ask ourselves such questions as "What is it?" or "Does the grass need cutting?" or "What do I wear to Sally's party?", we match the object or situation in question to our previous knowledge of such instances. We may find a match that indicates an appropriate response, or we may use what we know to guide the search for additional information when no match occurs. The *content* of our store of prior knowledge and the *process* of guided information search are parameters for the construct of schema.

The notion of schema is not new to experimental psychology (Bartlett, 1932; Head, 1920; Woodworth, 1938) and has recently been applied to the conceptualization of social information processing (e.g., S. E. Taylor & Crocker, 1981). Since its earliest usage, the construct has been employed with various meanings (e.g., Northway, 1940), and this practice continues in the current literature (J. R. Anderson, 1980; Kihlstrom & Nasby, 1981). Three assumptions, however, seem to be consistent across current definitions of a schema (Thorndyke & Hayes-Roth, 1979). (1) A schema is an organization of conceptually related elements, representing a prototypical abstraction of a complex concept. Specific examples are stored in a schema as are instances specifying relationships among these elements. (2) A schema is induced from the "bottom up" through repeated past experience with many examples of the complex concept it represents. (3) A schema can guide the organization of new information through the goal-directed processing of the input. Schemata, as memory structures, serve as basic units of our information processing system and, most interestingly, are defined as combined structure and process phenomena. As suggested by Neisser, schemata are "not only the plan, but also the executor of the plan" (Neisser, 1976, p. 56). Schemata are hierarchically organized such that they progress from individually specified, but related, instances of a complex concept at the "bottom" to a single, integrated representation of the concept as a whole at the "top" (Hayes-Roth, 1977). Thorndyke and Hayes-Roth (1979) further suggest that schemata of varying levels of complexity coexist in memory. This organization allows both bottom-up and top-down processing (e.g., Norman & Rumelhart, 1975). For novel experiences, bottom-up processing suggests an appropriate schema to fit the input. With more familiar instances, top-down processing can occur because a dominant model already exists to match the input (Markus & Sentis, 1980). S. E. Taylor and Crocker (1981) further suggest lateral organization and processing through a "rich web of associations," especially at the lower levels of greater specificity.

What Does a Schema Do?

J. R. Anderson (1980) has characterized schemata as enabling "quick and dirty" methods for effectively handling the information processing demands of a large and complex world. As this characterization most graphically implies, a schema offers both advantages and disadvantages to the perceiver.

To begin with the advantages, we can point to several key findings that have been reported in the experimental and social cognitive literature. Specifically, schemata have been found to (1) facilitate learning, that is, the recognition, recall, and comprehension of schematic information; (2) influence speed of information processing and problem solving; (3) allow for the chunking of information into larger, more meaningful and more readily retrieved units; (4) enable the perceiver to fill in missing data with the best guess or assumed values; and (5) provide a basis for greater confidence in prediction and decision making.

Facilitation of recognition, recall, and comprehension

Studies have repeatedly demonstrated the enhancing effect of a schema in the recognition (e.g., Cantor & Mischel, 1977) and the recall and comprehension (e.g., Bransford & Johnson, 1972) of previously presented material. These facilitative effects are believed to occur because a well-articulated knowledge structure is tapped when schema-consistent responses are required.

It should be noted, however, that some studies, such as that of Alba, Alexander, Hasher, and Caniglia (1981), have demonstrated differences in recall but *not* in recognition as a function of stored information. Based on these recognition results, Alba *et al.* argue that encoding can take place without the activation of an appropriate schema, as subjects were able to encode unrelated material well enough to recognize it later, even without prior knowledge of a familiar context. The authors conclude that the facilitative effect of a schema on recall thus represents a retrieval process, that is, greater accessibility of connecting cues in relevant inputs as part of a common activity, rather than a schema-directed encoding process.

Influence speed of information processing and problem solving

Data indicate that a schema can both facilitate (e.g., S. E. Taylor, Crocker, & D'Agostino, 1978) and slow down (e.g., Markus, Sentis, & Hamill, 1979) the processing of schema-relevant material. That a schema would affect information processing in apparently contradictory ways is one of the problems in understanding the schema construct. To be sure, the task demands may be implicated (S. E. Taylor & Crocker, 1981). For the processing of social information versus the processing of irrelevant tasks, the function of a schema may depend on unspecified attributes of the material, for example, valence or novelty. These attributes may prompt a shift from automatic to controlled processing (Schneider & Shiffrin, 1977), the latter requiring slower and more thorough memory search. Sentis and Burnstein (1979) point out, moreover, that the facilitative function of a highly integrated and unitized schema may also interfere with information processing if there is need to access subparts of a memory.

Chunking of information into meaningful and more easily retrieved units

The well-known studies of chess masters indicate that their experience gives them great facility in reproducing entire board positions even after exposures of only a few seconds (e.g., deGroot, 1965). This phenomenon has also been found in research that demonstrated an inverse relationship between reaction times to questions about schema-consistent stories and the number of relationships to be recalled (Sentis & Burnstein, 1979), as well as the finding that chunking was shown to reduce the processing time in recalling sets of facts (E. E. Smith, Adams, & Schorr, 1978).

Enabling the perceiver to fill in missing data

This characteristic of schemata is illustrated in research that has found college students, lacking information to the contrary, automatically assuming that the political attitudes of senior citizens were conservative (Fiske & Kinder, 1978). Similarly, C. E. Cohen's (1977) findings indicated that subjects intruded stereotype-consistent, but nonpresented, details in recalling the activities of a previously viewed person.

Providing greater confidence in prediction and decision making

Research in decision making has consistently demonstrated an overconfidence bias in individual's beliefs in the correctness of their responses (e.g., Koriat, Lichtenstein, & Fischoff, 1980). People have also been shown to overestimate the degree of covariation between things they believe to be associated, but be very conservative in estimating covariation when they have no clear-cut theory or expectations (D. Jennings, Amabile, & Ross, 1982). Similarly, Alba *et al.* (1981) not only found schema-enhanced recall and comprehension, but also reported that providing a schema as context greatly increased their subjects' confidence in what they recalled.

In general, the available research supports the conclusion that we remember best those things that we can relate to existing knowledge and that we make decisions with most confidence in these areas. Each positive aspect of schematic functioning may also be a liability, however, depending on the situation. For example, consider the various ramifications of defaulting incorrectly, of intruding schema-consistent information that was never presented, or of obscuring details in a well-integrated schema.

Some biases function to maintain the consistency of the schema. Two studies by L. Ross, Lepper, and colleagues illustrate this "perseverance" effect nicely. L. Ross, Lepper, Strack, and Steinmetz (1977) found that subjects imagining an event came to regard its occurrence as more likely, even when the event was subsequently *discredited.* Similarly, L. Ross, Lepper, and Hubbard (1975) found that debriefing a subject about the incorrectness of feedback they received on social sensitivity did *not* change the subjects' impressions of themselves on the social sensitivity dimension (cf. Koriat *et al.,* 1980). Furthermore, social cognition research in stereotyping suggests that disconfirming information leads *not* to the revision of a schema, but to its differentiation by the creation of subtypes. For example, a man with a stereotype of women as being quiet, passive, and not too bright, upon encountering an outgoing, assertive, and intelligent female may keep his original stereotype intact by creating a special category for this woman (e.g., "career woman"). He may eventually develop many special categories for women as his experience increases—"princess," "bitch," "showgirl"—such that nearly any female behavior can fit some category without disconfirming the overarching stereotype (S. E. Taylor, Fiske, Etcoff, & Ruderman, 1978). Other data indicate that people search for confirmatory rather than disconfirming evidence when making social decisions (M. Snyder & Swann, 1978) and decisions about objects (Wason & Johnson-Laird, 1972). Moreover, even when contradictory evidence is available in the decision-making process, individuals tend to disregard it in favor of the supporting data (Koriat *et al.,* 1980).

Another perseverance bias is the tendency to accept imperfectly matched data as schema consistent. This tendency is an extension of the default function, and it results in ambiguous or neutral data being seen as schema consistent, depending on the previous knowledge to which it is related. For example, Zadny and Gerard (1974) gave orienting instructions for viewing ambiguous actions on videotape (i.e., actors either about to steal something from a house or to remove drug-related objects). They found that subjects interpreted the behavior and recalled more information consistent with the specific set of attributed intentions. Similarly, Langer and Abelson (1974) have demonstrated how clinicians' orientations can bias the labeling of client behavior (see Turk & Salovey, this volume).

Schema-incongruent information can also be the basis for facilitated information processing. Faster rating times have been demonstrated for extremely schema-congruent items *and* extremely schema-incongruent items as compared to items that are only moderately schema related (e.g., Kuiper & Rogers, 1981; Sentis & Burnstein, 1979). This "inverted-U rating time effect" suggests a two-stage memory model in which questions involving positive and negative exemplars of a schema follow a quick and clear-cut route in arriving at a response whereas other schema-related judgments require extended memory search and, hence, more time for a response (e.g., Ebbesen & Allen, 1979).

In summary, information does not have meaning unless it fits into some cognitive context, a schema, that provides structure and processing guidelines for the interpretation of that information. Schematic processing can affect information encoding through the activation of relevant prior knowledge to assimilate input (e.g., Bransford & Johnson, 1972), as well as information retrieval, where schemata selectively guide search in memory at the time of recall (e.g., Alba *et al.*, 1981). The efficiency that results from schematic processing also results in a number of processing biases that distort our interpretation of objects and interpersonal reality. A major bias—which tends to maintain an existing schema—is the reliance on confirmatory evidence, at the expense of disconfirming evidence. Schematic biases are relevant to behavior change because they underlie the faulty thinking patterns assumed to cause dysfunctional behavior.

What Is the Role of Affect?

The literature on experimental cognitive psychology and social cognition has all but ignored emotion. Two notable exceptions are Neisser (1976) and Mandler (1975), who suggest separate and interactive systems for affective and cognitive analysis. Affective responding is qualified by cognitive interpretation (Mandler) or social experience (Neisser). Within cognitive-behavior therapy, the prevalent view is that affect is a postcognitive phenomenon, being closely linked to the cognitive system. Thus, it has been assumed that dysfunctional affective states could be changed by rational reexamination. Recently, however, several theorists have called for a reassessment of the place of affect in information processing.

Zajonc (1980) has presented a theoretical and empirical review suggesting that affective judgments are precognitive and may be independent of the perceptual and cognitive operations commonly assumed to be the basis of these affective judgments. He asserts that "preferences need no inference" as he distinguishes between "discriminada" and "preferenda" in affective processing. Discriminada function in discriminating, recognizing, and categorizing objects and events, while preferenda are defined as "interactions between some gross object features and internal states of the individual" (p. 159) that allow us to evaluate these same objects and events. Preferenda may be an insufficient basis for most higher order cognitive judgments and allow for affective processing soon after sensory input.

Other models have attempted an integrative approach to affective and cognitive processing. Bower (1981) has proposed that mood functions to activate or prime particular cognitive networks. Affect is believed to be represented in memory as "primitive emotion nodes" in a propositional network of events.

When activated, these nodes can result in the experience of the various emotions as well as the spreading of activation in the cognitive networks to which they are linked. Similarly, but in a more extensive theoretical model, Greenberg and Safran (1984) argue for the synthesis of affect and cognition, pointing out that the separation of feeling and thinking is itself a sign of dysfunction. They maintain that Zajonc's emphasis on the precognitive and independent nature of affect can lead too easily to the replacement of cognition with affect as the major antecedent variable in information processing. Moreover, Zajonc's assertion that "preferences need no inferences" refers more to automatic or unconscious processing than to the total independence of the two systems.

Greenberg and Safran's (1984) model is an expanded version of Leventhal's (1979) perceptual-motor model of emotion in which the construction of emotional experience involves three hierarchically organized mechanisms. First is the facial-motor mechanism, a largely innate expressive motor system that is responsible for the quality and distinctiveness of different feeling states. Second is schematic or emotion memory, which contains abstract representations of prior emotional experience and functions at an automatic level. It sets up expectations for future emotional events and directs attention to specific features of the perceptual field. This memory system can also generate expressive motor responses in addition to those generated in direct response to stimuli. Third is the abstract conceptual system, which is responsible for conscious, sequential volitional processing. Although it cannot directly elicit emotion, it does control the expression of emotional behavior and generates affective judgments, such as attitudes.

An important aspect of this model is the preattentive (i.e., unconscious) nature of the initial emotional processing. Only the end-product, the combination of the eliciting event, the expressive reaction, the schematic processing, and the conceptual meanings, are conscious. The component elements themselves are outside of consciousness. From this analysis Greenberg and Safran assert that

> in a sense there is no affect without cognition and no cognition without affect. Although it is certainly true that information is generated at the perceptual-motor level prior to any conscious experience, this information must still be integrated with other levels of information before arriving at the conscious experience of emotion. This process of integrating perceptual-motor information with implicit emotion schemas and with conceptual cognition results in experienced emotion. Only after this three-level integration takes place is the synthesis of emotion complete. (p. 569)

Recent empirical data yield converging support for the expressive-motor system in Greenberg and Safran's analysis. In an ingenious experiment, Laird, Wagener, Hala, and Szegda (1982) report that the emotional experience of "self-produced cue subjects" corresponds to their facial expressions. For this group, enacting facial expressions of happiness, anger, fear, and sadness made emotionally consistent material more accessible to recall. In agreement with the operation of Leventhal's facial-motor mechanism, the authors conclude that the facial expressions are attuned to basic physiological cues associated with early emotional experience. Developmental studies (e.g., Izard, Huebner, Risser, McGinnes, & Dougherty, 1980) provide further support for the largely innate nature of the facial expressive system in documenting expressive abilities in infants long before any semblance of language is acquired.

Studies of the "exposure effect," that is, increasing preference for objects following repeated exposure (e.g., Harrison, 1977), provide support for an affective schematic processing system that is similar to a cognitive schematic system. In a typical experiment, subjects are shown objects for a varying number of trials and are then asked to make liking and recognition judgments about these objects and "filler" objects not previously presented. Evidence for the unconscious nature of these affective judgments comes from the finding that, even when the recognition of "old" and "new" stimuli was reduced to a chance level, subjects could still reliably discriminate "old" and "new" stimuli on the liking dimension (Kunst-Wilson & Zajonc, 1980; Wilson, 1975). Moreover, the liking judgments were made with far greater confidence and tended to be made faster than recognition judgments (Kunst-Wilson & Zajonc, 1980).

While much work remains to be done in specifying the various ways affective and cognitive processing may interact, the work of Zajonc and his associates provides some preliminary clues. There is also substantial evidence for a mood-congruent effect, which is hinted at in the Laird *et al.* (1982) experiment discussed earlier in this section. Bower (1981) reports that subjects' hypnotically induced mood resulted in superior memory for word lists, recorded diary experiences, and childhood experiences that were affectively congruent to the induced mood. Readers made happy or sad prior to reading a story attended more to mood-congruent material, identified with the character whose mood matched their's, and recalled more about that character (Bower, Gilligan, & Monteiro, 1981). Other cognitive processes, for example, free associations, fantasies, and social perceptions, also showed this mood-dependent effect.

The work of Bower and his associates has been extended by Natale and Hantas (1982) who, in a controlled study of hypnotically induced mood, found that induced depression resulted in decreased recall of positive life events and a bias in the recall of false negative self-descriptors. The elation manipulation led to decreased recall of unpleasant memories and increased recall of pleasant events. Similar results have been reported by J. Wright and Mischel (1982) for social information memory. Researchers in this area generally conclude that mood-congruent material is made more salient in memory and is thus better recalled. The symmetrical findings for positive and negative mood suggest this is indeed a robust phenomenon.

In summary, current evidence indicates some integration between the cognitive and affective information processing systems, with schematic memory for emotional experience functioning like schematic memory for cognitive processing. The specifications of this integration remain to be empirically delineated. However, like schematic processing for cognitive memory, schematic processing for emotional experience includes enhanced memory for mood-congruent material (e.g., Natale & Hantas, 1982), greater confidence in emotionally relevant judgments (e.g., Kunst-Wilson & Zajonc, 1980), and automatic (unconscious) versus controlled processing of emotionally relevant material (e.g., Wilson, 1975). In line with this view, Turk and Speers (1983) have recently defined a schema to include both an ideational component *and* an affective component.

Self-Schemata

Self-schemata select and organize information about one's own behavior, clearly an important focus for clinicians. A schema is a useful construct for studying the self because it can represent what W. James (1910) has called the two distinct aspects of the self: the self as *knower* and the self as that which is *known*. The former, of course, represents process and the latter content or structure in the information processing model.

The function of the self as a schema in processing personal information has been most extensively studied by Markus and her colleagues (H. Markus & Sentis, 1980), and by Rogers and his associates (T. B. Rogers, 1981). This body of research has generally yielded results that parallel the findings on the function of other schemata. In his review, T. B. Rogers (1981) indicates that in comparison to tasks that are impersonal, tasks having to do with oneself are more easily encoded, the material learned is more likely to be based on direct personal experience, and the information is more likely to be recalled. In group processes, individuals best remember their own contributions as well (Brenner, 1976) and take personal credit for group products (M. Ross & Sicoly, 1979). Self-referent processing enhances general attitude behavior consistency (e.g., Cialdini, Petty, & Cacioppo, 1981; Tesser, 1978), and reviewers of cognitive dissonance theory have concluded that dissonance reduction will take place only with some cognitive involvement of the self (Greenwald & Ronis, 1978; Wicklund & Brehm, 1976). Based on this work, the self has been designated a superordinate schema (Mancuso & Ceely, 1980), while others have argued for self-schemata in several focal domains, the union of which defines the self-concept (Markus *et al.*, 1982).

Particularly relevant to our discussion are the perceptual distortions that result from self-schematic processing. Greenwald's (1980) portrait of the self as a "totalitarian ego" is a useful model for examining these. Like totalitarian societies (Orwell, 1949) and scientific paradigms (Kuhn, 1970) that control or screen out information that challenges their status quo, people also have difficulty assimilating information that is contradictory to their views of themselves.

One of the self's processing distortions, according to Greenwald, is ''ego-centricity''—seeing the self as the focus of all knowledge. This bias echoes the work of earlier self-theorists (e.g., Combs & Snygg, 1959) who asserted that ''the phenomenal self is the point of orientation for the individual's every behavior. It is the frame of reference in terms of which all other perceptions gain their meaning'' (p. 145).

As the phenomenal focus of all knowledge, the self may be viewed as the major union point of cognitive and affective processing. As Zajonc (1980) has suggested, ''Affective judgments implicate the self'' (p. 156) in the sense that affective judgments reflect the state of the self in relation to the object being evaluated. Thus, the effects of self-referent processing may not represent so much what people *know* as what people *feel* about what they know. Combining Zajonc's argument with Greenberg and Safran's (1984) model of affect, self-referent processing becomes the synthesis of cognitive and affective processing through the superordinate self-schema. Engaging in a particular behavior can now be seen as the result of a *cognitive* evaluation of what is required to achieve a specified outcome and an *affective* evaluation reflecting one's conviction about one's ability to perform the behavior successfully. This gives us an information processing analysis of Bandura's (1977a) self-efficacy theory. His ''outcome expectancies'' are the cognitive probabilities that a given behavior will lead to a desired outcome, and his ''efficacy expectancies''—which have been shown to predict an individual's behavior in a variety of domains (e.g., Bandura, 1982; DiClemente, 1981; Manning & Wright, 1983)—reflect one's affective evaluation of the self in relation to the to-be-performed behavior. This link between thinking, feeling, and behavior further underscores the need to look beyond cognition alone in planning to change dysfunctional behavior.

A second distortion noted by Greenwald (1980) is ''cognitive conservatism,'' or resistance to change. This is the perseverance bias and the tendency to favor positive or confirming evidence over negative or contradictory evidence that we have discussed above under schematic processing. It is cognitive conservatism that maintains the consistency of the self-concept. Self-consistency has certainly been underscored by a number of self-theorists (e.g., Combs & Snygg, 1959; Epstein, 1978; Lecky, 1945) as a way of maintaining coherence in what and who we are. From a clinically relevant vantage point, this tendency toward self-consistency has nowhere been better demonstrated than in the many studies indicating that depressed, socially anxious, and unassertive persons fail to assimilate positive information, but readily process negative information that they receive about themselves (e.g., Alden & Cappe, 1981; J. V. Clark & Arkowitz, 1975; Rizley, 1978). Studying a nonclinical population, Swann and Read (1981b) have shown that not only are individuals more likely to *seek* social feedback that confirms their view of themselves, but they will also *elicit* self-confirmatory social feedback when they believe others will negatively appraise them and preferentially *recall* social feedback that confirms what they believe about themselves. Likewise, communication research has found that people tend to reject messages that disagree with their prior opinions and actively construct arguments to refute the opposing-opinion message (e.g., Sherif & Hovland, 1961).

For clinicians this bias would suggest that when provided with potentially therapeutic information, clients may "get it" but not "use it" if the information is inconsistent with their self-schemata. Such roadblocks to treatment as reactance (e.g., Brehm & Brehm, 1981), resistance, and noncompliance (Wachtel, 1982) can be seen as the tendency that clients have to preserve their self-consistency, however dysfunctional their thoughts, feelings, and behavior may be. As Goldfried and Robins (1983) have pointed out, "Even when overt behavior changes do begin to emerge, clients may be slow to update the attitudes they hold about themselves on the basis of such changes" (p. 34). The cognitive part of the clinical task, then, becomes one of getting people to process the thoughts and feelings associated with the performance of new behaviors, so as to achieve a new self-consistency. Thinking about the therapeutic task in this manner requires no motivational construct such as the view that a self-defeating behavior pattern may be driven by "masochistic needs." Such a behavior pattern may be more parsimoniously explained by reference to the tendency toward self-consistency. The information processing model also easily accommodates both individuals with unrealistic self-deprecatory schemata (e.g., the socially anxious), who have difficulty processing success experiences, as well as those with unrealistic self-complimentary schemata (e.g., Type A individuals), who have difficulty processing failures.

Clinical Guidelines for Changing Self-Schemata

With a few notable exceptions, there has been little in the way of data that deal directly with how self-schemata can be changed. L. Ross *et al.* (1975) reported that individuals who initially resisted disconfirming evidence did modify their self-percpetions once they were made aware of their biasing tendency. Changes in self-perceptions were also found by Swann and Hill (1982) when recipients could not interact with the source to reject or refute self-discrepant feedback. Relatedly, social cognition research on stereotyping has found that dispersing stereotype-inconsistent evidence across many members of a group resulted in the revision of stereotypic beliefs (Weber & Crocker, 1983). These findings indicate that individuals can be responsive to information that is not representative of their currently held schemata, in spite of the strong bias to resist this information. Moreover, these data, when combined with previously reviewed findings, suggest several guidelines for assisting clients to process the thoughts and feelings associated with the performance of more adaptive behaviors. These guidelines include (1) providing a relevant context in therapy, (2) creating a new self-schema by the attention to events, (3) encouraging use of the new self-schema, and (4) sustaining the new self-schema through social interaction. We have listed these guidelines in an order that conceptually makes sense to us, noting that each of these guidelines may be pertinent at various points in the therapeutic process—which seldom proceeds in a linear fashion. In discussing these therapeutic strategies, we will be reviewing and expanding on some of the similar efforts presented by Goldfried and Robins (1983).

A Case Illustration

Before we discuss some of the clinical guidelines suggested by the information processing approach, let us present a brief case history to illustrate the use of this model.

> Ms. H., a 36-year-old divorced mother of two sons, is employed as a head teller at a local bank. She earns a limited salary but, with the help of an inheritance, is purchasing her own home. She attends a weekly weight-reduction class and has shed almost 50 pounds in the last 5 months.
>
> She initially came with her older son, who was experiencing stomach pains and fatigue for which the family physician could find no cause. Ms. H. subsequently requested help with her own difficulties, which consisted of depression, frustration at her inability to make changes in her life, and difficulty in expressing her feelings. She was working overtime at the bank doing other people's work and feeling quite angry at her well-to-do ex-husband for underpaying child support. Ms. H. saw herself as a failure and a bad mother for being divorced and wanting time away from her children. She rarely socialized and had only one close friend.

Here is a negative self-schema highlighted by schema-consistent feelings of depression and anger, and feelings of frustration about her poor occupational and social functioning. Her accomplishments were seen as schema-inconsistent and were discounted accordingly. About her weight loss she said, "That's nothing! I'm ready to give that up. . . . I haven't lost a pound in weeks!" Commenting on being a supervisor at work she stated, "I'd rather just be a regular teller. I don't make that much more, and I wouldn't have to be responsible for what everybody else does." A perseverance-default bias can be seen in her interpretation of her older son's frequent visits with his father. Relating her son's behavior to her own negative self-view, Ms. H. felt that the boy was abandoning her and that her autonomy as a parent was being threatened. Further evidence of her efforts to maintain a consistent self-schema can be seen in her pessimism about being able to effect changes in her behavior—a good example of the self-system's cognitive conservatism or resistance to change (Greenwald, 1980). We shall return to this case in the sections that follow, in conjunction with our discussion of guidelines for changing such personal biases.

Providing a Context in Therapy

Throughout the intervention process, but especially early on, preparing the client to encode new information is a necessary focus. The L. Ross *et al.* (1975) study suggests that making clients aware of their tendency to resist disconfirming information about themselves may help circumvent this bias. Thus, preparing clients to expect to process new information, even before behavior change occurs and informing them of their natural tendency to resist disconfirming evidence, is a prerequisite step in setting the stage for schema change (Goldfried & Robins, 1983).

At the very least, the therapeutic context is based on establishing rapport and providing a rationale for therapy. A good client–therapist relationship can mitigate fear of risk-taking in trying new behaviors, and a sound rationale can be a source of anxiety reduction when encoding new experiences or when confronting a setback after several successes.

In our case example, recall Ms. H's schema-consistent pessimism about being able to change her self-defeating behavior and outlook. Getting her to suspend this disbelief long enough to try new behaviors was necessary in order to initiate any change in her self-schema. Two important factors in this endeavor were providing a plausible rationale for therapy and developing a supportive therapeutic alliance with her. After completing an early assignment to follow up an invitation from a relative, she reported—with surprise—that she actually felt better after having gone out.

Another aspect of the therapeutic context is suggested by the affective, state-dependent learning data from Bower (1981) and others. Recall that this research indicated that an individual's hypnotically induced mood has the effect of making congruently toned material more accessible in memory. Thus, by affectively priming clients, we may enhance their ability to process more adaptive information. Getting clients in the "right" mood (e.g., a happy mood for depressed clients) should also aid their encoding and retrieval of the "right" information (e.g., success experiences). The data from Laird *et al.* (1982) indicate that having clients assume expressive facial poses is one way to achieve this effect.

Creating a New Self-Schema by Attention to Events

Event processing involves "bottom-up" processing, that is, focusing clients' attention on specific events that can provide them with more objective evidence on which to base their perceptions, emotions, and actions. An event can be internal physiological information or external environmental information. Self-schema theory suggests that the superordinate self-schema biases both types of information in the same manner. An internal event may be a bodily cue suggesting emotional discomfort that someone having difficulty expressing anger has come to ignore. An external event may be a failure experience that a Type A individual conveniently overlooks. Event processing is the kernal of cognitive–behavioral therapies, such as problem solving (D'Zurilla & Goldfried, 1971), rational emotive therapy (Ellis, 1962), and Beck's cognitive therapy for depression (Beck *et al.*, 1979). Indeed, altering clients' misconceptions by means of contradictory evidence is probably central to all forms of therapy (cf. Frank, 1961; Raimy, 1975).

Within the ongoing clinical interaction, calling clients' attention to small "perceptual shifts" in how they view themselves and the world can, over time, be the basis for the development of new encoding strategies. Likewise, prompting clients to perform a microanalysis of situations can lead to the use of retrieval cues not currently being used (Greenberg & Safran, 1981). This controlled type or conscious processing (Schneider & Shiffrin, 1977) deautomates the guiding schema and helps clients become aware of pertinent, previously schema-masked information for future behavioral decisions.

In the sample case described earlier, a step-by-step reenactment of Ms. H.'s angry confrontations with her son helped her to become more aware of the fact that she primarily attended to his minor infractions of house rules and his time away from her (especially that spent with her ex-husband). This focus confirmed her view of herself as a bad parent. She was neglecting other information, inconsistent with this self-view, such as her son's attempts to discuss his feelings with her and his genuine efforts to be supportive at times when she became upset. This refocusing of attention on the positive, but schema-inconsistent, events laid the foundation for more effective communication between the two, and ultimately eliminated the son's physical complaints.

We wish to emphasize the role of emotional arousal in changing self-schemata. Bandura (1977a) has argued that, in comparison to past performance, emotional arousal is not a dependable source of efficacy information. Self-schema theory, however, suggests that arousal is a natural way of indicating that an event is significant to the self-system (e.g., Epstein, 1980; Mandler, 1975). Goldfried (1982) has alluded to this phenomenon in conjunction with the therapeutic change process.

> For example, shy and unassertive individuals may rarely, if ever, have expressed their preferences or needs to others. To do so would cause them to have an experience that was "strange" or "different," which in turn would make them apprehensive . . . the therapist can utilize such concerns to demonstrate the *significance* of such change. . . . These new experiences should demonstrate to them [the clients] that they are indeed in the process of becoming different—presumably a motivation that originally brought them to therapy. (p. 108)

Therefore, when performing a new behavior, emotional arousal can be associated with a "hit," in the sense of having focused one's efforts where needed.

Another important factor in getting clients to attend to the desired information is the manner in which the information is presented. While one would expect a gradual shaping paradigm to be most effective in minimizing the biasing effects of positive (self-discrepant) information, some data suggest extreme discrepancy may be critical. In the devil's advocate procedure (Goldfried, Decenteceo, & Weinberg, 1974), for example, the therapist attempts to have clients offer their own arguments about the unreasonableness of their irrational thoughts by presenting these irrational thoughts to the clients in the most extreme form. Consistent with the Swann and Hill (1982) finding, when persons are unable to reject or refute self-discrepant information, they change their self-perceptions to accommodate it. Construing inconsistent, but objectively more functional, behavior as something one can do, as opposed to something one cannot do, enables clients to integrate the behavior as schema-consistent. In helping the client to engage in bottom-up processing, the therapist must be sensitive to the level of discrepancy a client will tolerate before rejecting the input.

To summarize, then, event processing is one way to help clients recognize their faulty schematic processing and to make available evidence they can use to reinterpret these faulty views. The goal is to accumulate sufficient schema-inconsistent evidence to induce a new schema in which to embed the new self-referent information. This analysis implies that a threshold number of events is needed to initiate a change in schematic processing, although it remains for future research to yield some parameters in this regard.

Encouraging Use of the New Self-Schema

Once clients are making desired changes in their lives, it is important to balance the bottom-up, event processing with a top-down, schema-driven perspective to ensure that a cognitive model exists to match new self-referent inputs. As a consolidation strategy, Goldfried and Robins (1983) suggest that this is particularly important during the transitional phase of change, when clients may need to surmount a "yes—but" attitude of (1) failing to appreciate how far they have come, (2) focusing on the other areas of their lives in which they have not changed, and (3) comparing their performance to that of more effectively functioning individuals.

Goldfried and Robins (1983) further offer two guidelines that are particularly relevant in facilitating top-down processing. One is adding an objective vantage point to the client's subjective outlook. The therapeutic goal here is to consolidate the client's internal attribution for success experiences, that is, to overcome the tendency of clients to reject the cause of novel success experiences as being due to their own efforts (cf. McMahon, 1973). The second guideline is retrieving past successes in order to give the new self-schema a personal history.

The objective vantage point can be provided in several ways. Therapists can provide relevant reflection, clarifications, confrontation, and other forms of feedback. They can also serve as models of objective reality and can ally themselves with the more adaptive, reality-oriented part of the client's cognitive functioning. Clients can self-monitor their success experiences in written form and use this external record to augment their transitional self-schemata, as a reminder of how they are coping. Audio- and videotape are also useful objective sources of feedback. An example from our work with Ms. H. nicely illustrates the utility of an objective vantage point. She lost a total of 75 pounds and achieved her target weight, but she continued to report difficulty accepting the positive reaction she got from others as she slimmed down. The old self continued to make external attributions for the weight loss. She credited her doctor for insisting that she reduce for health reasons and her mother for accompanying her to diet classes. She did not understand why others were "making such a fuss" as she continued to think of herself as "fat and ugly." It took the viewing of a videotaped session for Ms. H. to begin to identify, as herself, the person who had been getting the compliments. "I thought people were teasing me when they said how nice I looked! I *do* look much better than before, don't I. . . . It's really me up there!"

The second guideline is retrieving past successes. Encouraging clients to survey their successes, both current and past, serves to increase their perceived estimate that such experiences have indeed occurred (M. K. Johnson & Raye, 1981). The new self-schema can thus become stabilized by finding roots in the client's personal history. As the new self-system becomes adjusted, top-down processing will enable clients to view past behavior from the new perspective. They can more easily seek confirming evidence in past success experiences, gain confidence in what is recalled (e.g., Alba *et al.*, 1981), as well as learn from past mistakes. Consider Ms. H.'s words: "I was always blaming others for my problems. I never took charge of things for myself. Looking back, I can see that I wasn't a total failure. I haven't done so bad after all."

Maintaining the New Self-Schema through Social Interaction

Once clients are coping more effectively and processing adaptive information about themselves, the issue becomes one of whether these changes represent an enduring new self-schema or just some partial, and perhaps temporary, variation of the old self. Swann and Hill (1982) present findings suggesting that after people reach the conclusion that they have changed or are in the process of changing, the intrapersonal decision must be validated by significant others in order for perceived changes in the self to be lasting. In the case of Ms. H., as she began to view herself as a competent and likable person, her family and coworkers began to treat her in a self-confirmatory manner. Believing in one's new self-schema and behaving in a manner to verify this self-view increase the probability of self-confirmatory feedback, and a social opportunity structure

(McCall & Simmons, 1966) or environment to sustain the new self-schema is thus created.

Summary and Future Directions

Schemata extract and categorize clusters of experience, enabling us to act in a world that we can readily comprehend. Inherent in this clustering process, however, is the loss of information that results in systematic distortions. A major biasing feature of cognitive and affective processing is the reliance on confirmatory evidence at the expense of disconfirming data. This is also true of self-schemata, which exhibit a strong bias aimed at maintaining consistency in the self-system, even though this consistency may be at odds with objective reality and social feedback. Therapeutic intervention helps clients eliminate inconsistencies by focusing clients' attention on the faults in their schematic processing and helping them perform new behaviors to provide alternate sources of efficacy and outcome expectancies.

What does the schema approach offer us for understanding therapeutic change? It provides us with a model in which inferred motivational constructs are not required for conceptualizing the difficulties prompting people to seek help to change. Moreover, the model can accommodate problem behaviors based on self-deprecatory or self-complimentary schemata. What the model does *not* offer us is predictive power. Fiske and Linville (1980) point out that schema theory is not a theory but more like a metaconstruct, whose meaning is defined by its relationships with other constructs within a theoretical system (cf. Arnkoff & Glass, 1982). The process models specifying these relationships need to be made explicit. This is a particularly important issue in need of work in specifying the mechanisms of interaction between affect and cognition. The challenge is to gain operational precision in defining a schema (S. E. Taylor & Crocker, 1981). On the content issue, it is unclear how we internally represent portions of the world (see Markus & Sentis, 1980). Is stored information linked to a sensory modality (Paivio, 1971), or is it abstract (e.g., J. R. Anderson, 1980)? How is information structurally maintained, and what governs access to single or simultaneous parts in memory?

The lack of process and content specificity means that we do not know much about how a schema changes or what constitutes relevant client–therapist activities in this process. What happens to a schema that is rarely used? Is it possible to have a dormant schema? Present research has focused primarily on well-functioning adult systems. Developmental studies are needed to provide some answers to these questions. The problem of individual differences also looms large (Tellegen, Kamp, & Watson, 1982). People can cognitively represent different aspects of real-world relationships in a similar manner, or the same real world in different ways. Assessing self-schemata may provide clues for differential prescription in therapy, as well as help to define the characteristics of various clinical groups and subgroups (see Harvey, Winter, Weintraub, & Neale, 1981).

One final point is worth mentioning. Basic researchers and practicing clinicians are limited by *their own* schemata in analyzing how people process information. The exchange of hypotheses between researchers and clinicians can only help circumvent such biases and promote ''rigor and relevance'' in combining the ''sensitivity of the practicing clinician . . . with the scientific precision of the active researcher'' (A. O. Ross, 1981, p. 326). It is our contention that the use of the same information processing approach by both groups can enhance such exchange.

Acknowledgments

We are especially grateful to Rick Ingram, Jeremy Safran, and Joanne Woods for their helpful comments on an earlier draft. Work on this chapter was supported, in part, from NIMH Grants 24327 and 40196, awarded to the second author.

13

Cognitive Therapy for Depression from an Information Processing Perspective

RICK E. INGRAM
Department of Psychology
San Diego State University
San Diego, California 92182

STEVEN D. HOLLON
Department of Psychology
Vanderbilt University
Nashville, Tennessee 37240

Numerous researchers have suggested the importance of a cognitive perspective in understanding depressive disorders (Abramson *et al.*, 1978; Beck, 1967, 1976; Ingram & Reed, chapter 7, this volume; Rehm, 1977). Although this perspective is not without its problems (Coyne & Gotlib, 1983; but see also Segal & Shaw, in press), it has contributed to an understanding of depression in many ways. Perhaps the most important contribution of the cognitive approach has been in the area of therapeutic interventions for depression. In this regard, a number of therapeutic implications and strategies have been deduced from the cognitive models of depression proposed by Seligman (1974; Abramson *et al.*, 1978) and Rehm (1977). No view of depression, however, has received more therapeutic attention then Beck's (1967) model. Beck and colleagues (1979) have developed a cognitive therapy for depression that aims to teach depressed individuals to reevaluate and correct their negative cognitions. By correcting these distortions, it is argued, the factors that maintain depressive symptomatolo-

INFORMATION PROCESSING APPROACHES TO CLINICAL PSYCHOLOGY

gy will be undermined. The approach utilizes an integrated combination of behavioral and cognitive techniques in a process of hypothesis testing that seeks to alter the negative beliefs and distortions in information processing seen as underlying depression.

Beck's approach appears to have fared well in a series of carefully controlled outcome trials (Beck, Hollon, Young, Bedrosian, & Budenz, 1985; Blackburn, Bishop, Glen, Whalley, & Christie, 1981; Hollon, 1983; Hollon *et al.*, 1984; G. E. Murphy *et al.*, 1984; Rush *et al.*, 1977). Many of the trials have utilized tricyclic antidepressants, the current standard of treatment, as an active comparison intervention. In general, it would appear that cognitive therapy is at least the equal of tricyclic pharmacological therapy alone in ameliorating the acute *episode,* probably superior to drugs alone in preventing subsequent episodes, and possibly capable of enhancing overall response when combined with pharmacological interventions. Comparisons with other psychosocial approaches (Covi *et al.*, 1985; Shaw, 1977; F. G. Taylor & Marshall, 1977) have also tended to favor the cognitive–behavioral approach. In general, it would appear that cognitive therapy is an affective intervention for the treatment of depression, a point buttressed by a 1983 meta-analysis of major outcome studies (Steinbrueck, Maxwell, & Howard, 1983).[1]

The picture is thus reasonably clear regarding the effectiveness of cognitive therapy in ameliorating the symptoms of depression. What is less clear at this point, however, are the mechanisms by which cognitive therapy works. This question can actually be separated into two related components. The first concerns the precise nature of the cognitive processes in depressed individuals that are affected by cognitive therapy. As yet, these mechanisms and processes of change have not been adequately examined empirically. Perhaps one reason for this lack of research is that, to date, no one has specified these mechanisms in a complete enough manner to permit empirical investigation. Although Beck (1967, 1976) has discussed distorted thinking as underlying depression, and this concept has been elaborated in the notion of heuristics and heuristic-based biases and distortions (Evans & Hollon, in press; Hollon & Garber, in press; Kahneman *et al.*, 1982), the gamut of cognitive mechanisms that may underlie these biases has not yet been adequately conceptualized. Such a conceptualization is no doubt an evolving process, and it would seem prudent to continue our attempts to describe more precisely the variables that constitute our concepts of cognition and thinking.

The second component of the question of mechanisms of action is the specificity of particular cognitive mechanisms as they are affected by particular cog-

[1]It should be noted that although some of the cognitive approaches reviewed in this study consisted of Beck's cognitive therapy of depression, a number of other cognitive therapies were reviewed as well.

nitive therapy techniques. For example, outcome data, while generally indicating the efficacy of cognitive therapy, have not addressed the multidimensional interaction between specific therapeutic methods and the specific cognitive mechanisms involved. Although there have been some data indicating nonspecific effects of (a variation of) both cognitive as well as other therapies (Zeiss *et al.*, 1979) and specific cognitive effects of cognitive therapy (Rush, Beck, Kovacs, Wissenburger, & Hollon, 1982), this question has received inadequate attention to date. This is true not only in regard to cognitive therapy for depression (Hollon, 1981) but for other treatments and disorders as well (Arnkoff & Glass, 1982; Ingram *et al.*, 1986). We believe that continued progress in developing and refining effective treatments for depression will require adequate theoretical conceptualization that provides a framework for generating a data-based knowledge regarding the specific mechanisms of change.

The goal of the present chapter is to employ an information processing perspective in order to provide some initial steps toward such a conceptualization. Specifically, we will present an information processing framework for specifying the various relationships between the procedures of cognitive therapy for depression as developed by Beck and the cognitive components they influence. At this point, such a framework must necessarily be speculative. Our ultimate goal, of course, is to enhance the efficacy of cognitive therapy for depression. We hope eventually that such a framework will engender testable hypotheses leading to empirical research and ultimately the refinement, modification, and further development of cognitive methods.

Cognition in Depression

Before speculating on how the procedures of cognitive therapy may influence particular cognitive processes in depression, it is necessary to specify our theoretical assumptions as to what the important cognitive factors in depression are. This presents a challenge in several ways. For one, within the rapidly expanding area of cognitive–behavioral theory and research, cognitive variables have been viewed in a number of diverse ways. On the one hand, these different approaches are illustrative of the rich and vast array of theoretical constructs that presently guide the field. On the other hand, they also represent the theoretical diffusion that for the time being impedes a unified, and sometimes productive, approach to our theoretical and empirical understanding of cognitive functioning in psychopathology. Thus, given this wealth of divergent cognitive concepts, it is necessary to have some conceptual system for categorizing and distinguishing these concepts. Therefore, prior to specifying any assumptions as to the important cognitive factors in depression, we will employ a framework for delimiting the various concepts of depression. In invoking such a framework, we do not suggest that it is necessarily perfect or ideal but merely that it is a useful scheme for differentiating the major cognition components of depression while at the same time acknowledging their inextricable relations to one another.

Both Hollon and Garber (in press) and Ingram and Kendall (this volume; Ingram, 1983; Kendall & Ingram, in press) have proposed that the basic mechanisms of cognition can be viewed as falling into several conceptually distinct categories. The components within this cognitive taxonomic system are (1) cognitive structures, (2) cognitive propositions, (3) cognitive operations, and (4) cognitive products (see Ingram & Kendall, this volume, for a more detailed discussion).

Cognitive Structure

Cognitive structure can be viewed as the way or manner in which information is represented in memory. As such, it refers to the organization of memory content and encompasses concepts such as the linkages and associations among stored memories (episodic memory) and concepts and factual information (semantic memory) (Tulving, 1972).

Cognitive Propositions

Cognitive propositions, on the other hand, can be seen as the information or content that is actually represented, or stored, in various cognitive structures. Although there is no standard definition of a schema (J. R. Anderson, 1980; Kihlstrom & Nasby, 1980), most definitions to date emphasize both the structural and content components of this concept. That is, cognitive schemata, although they are frequently referred to as cognitive structures, are seldom defined without references to their particular content, for example, depressive schemata (Beck, 1967), self-schemata (Ingram *et al.*, 1983; Markus, 1977), and social schemata (Rudy & Merluzzi, 1984b; T. W. Smith *et al.*, 1983). Therefore, based on extant definitions, cognition schemata would seem to consist of both a particular cognitive structure along with the information content of the structure.

Cognitive Operations

Cognitive operations can be seen as the various processes by which the components of the cognitive processing system operate. Turk and Speers (1983) have referred to such processes as those factors that are responsible for the active manipulation of information through the system. More specifically, there are a number of constructs that appear to fall under the heading of this category. For example, rules and heuristics (Kahneman *et al.*, 1982), attentional processes (Duval & Wicklund, 1972; Ingram & Smith, 1984), encoding processes (R. Lachman *et al.*, 1979), control processes (Carver & Scheier, 1981), and spreading activation notions (Bower, 1981; Collins & Loftus, 1975; Norman, 1981) are all concepts that can be described as cognitive operations.

Cognitive Products

Finally, cognitive products can be viewed as the cognitions that result from the input of information and the interaction of cognitive structures, propositions, and operations. Variables that fall most clearly into this category include self-statements, attributions, inferences, and images.

Cognitive Variables in Depression

Within the present context, we will employ this framework for discussing our assumptions as to the cognitive factors that are implicated in the etiology and maintenance of depression. The cognitive factors will be derived from the extant cognitive models of depression. These models, are, of course, divergent in their suggestions as to what the critical cognitive factors in depression are. There do, however, appear to be some areas of general agreement concerning factors that are at least important. Given the structure, proposition, and operation distinctions, we will thus categorize these areas of agreement, while at the same time explicitly acknowledging that our own cognitive biases color our perception of these agreement points along with how they are conceptually differentiated in such a framework.

Cognitive Structures and Content (Schemata)

One factor that appears to be accepted by a number of depression researchers as an important cognitive component is referred to as a schema (Beck, 1967) or sometimes as a cognitive network (Bower, 1981; Ingram, 1984b). While there are subtle but important differences between these two concepts,[2] for purposes of the present discussion they will be viewed as essentially identical. In addition, because of its wide usage in experimental and social cognitive psychology, the term *schema* will be employed to describe this construct.

Inherent in several theories of cognitive functioning (e.g., Bower, 1981) as well as cognitive models of depression (Beck, 1967; Ingram, 1984b;) is the notion that individuals possess diverse cognitive schemata. Although the basic structures of these various schemata are similar, they are differentiated on the basis of their content.

[2]One important difference, for example, concerns processing assumptions. Whereas schema concepts typically do not include a discussion of *how* they affect cognition, network theories are somewhat better articulated in this regard (e.g., spreading activation through the network describes how information might be processed).

Among other things, schemata are viewed as the mechanisms that guide selective attention and perception (Neisser, 1967). Since there are a number of schemata, however, such cognitive functioning is guided by those that are active at any given time. Presumably, different schemata are activated by the general information processing requirements of a situation. Although this may lead to occasional cognitive bias and distortion when inappropriate schemata are activated (see, e.g., Alloy & Abramson, 1979, 1982), such distortion should generally be minimized by the switching of various schemata to guide processing. In depression, the content of the currently active schema is seen as containing predominantly negative self-referent information and is viewed as incompatible with effective and adaptive functioning.

Cognitive Operation Variables

From a process standpoint, several views converge on the notion that depression is characterized by a particular kind of automatic information processing. *Automatic* implies that processing occurs in a nonvolitional fashion, that is, the individual does not necessarily choose to think about or attend to certain information, but finds himself or herself doing so anyway. This stands in contrast to a more controlled form of processing in which the individual chooses to exert some control over the things thought about and the information attended to and the way that it is processed.

In all likelihood, most individuals engage daily in a combination of automatic and controlled processing, although there are certain experiences that are characterized more by one than the other kind of processing. Solving a difficult math problem, or writing a chapter for that matter, would seem to be an example of a primarily controlled mode of processing. Drifting off into a daydream (sometimes while trying to solve a math problem or write a chapter) is certainly more automatic in nature. Beck argues that depression is dominated by the automatic processing of negative cognitions that he has labeled automatic thoughts (Beck, 1967, 1976; Beck *et al.*, 1979). Similarly, Ingram (1984b) has argued that a central aspect of depression is an automatic recycling process that is phenomenologically experienced as a stream of negative personal memories and thoughts. In a somewhat different but related view, Seligman (1981) has also noted an automatic nature to depressogenic attributions that are seen as characteristic of at least some kinds of depression. Likewise, Rehm (1977) has suggested that a selective monitoring of negative self-relevant information occurs in an automatic fashion in depression.

A potentially different cognitive process that several models of depression address is the schema-activation process itself. On a general level, several cognitive theorists have discussed the notion that various cognitive structures can be engaged and thus become prepotent by activation that spreads through the cognitive system (Bower, 1981; Collins & Loftus, 1975; Norman, 1981). With regard to depression, several information processing oriented approaches appear to agree on the notion that a similar kind of cognitive process may serve to activate dormant cognitive structures such as the negative of depressive self-schema. The theoretical proposals of Dyck (1983), C. Hammen (1983a, 1983b), and Ingram (1983, 1984a,b), for example, all suggest that particular kinds of negative experiences may result in such an activating process. Furthermore, once this process takes place, the activation level of the depressive schema may be maintained at the expense of activating other schemata that are appropriate to situational information processing requirements (A. T. Beck, 1967; Ingram, 1983).

A final cognitive process that has been receiving recent theoretical and empirical attention in depression is the notion of self-focused attentional processes. Self-focused attention is generally referred to as attention turned inward toward aspects of the self as opposed to external-focused attention that is directed outward toward the environment and people in the environment (Carver & Scheier, 1981; Duval & Wicklund, 1972). Interestingly, a number of investigators from a variety of different theoretical backgrounds have suggested that depression may be associated with a heightened degree of self-focused attention that mediates several commonly observed features of depression. In noting parallels between social psychology research and descriptive depression research, for instance, T. W. Smith and Greenberg (1981) have suggested that the internal attributions for negative events, lowered self-esteem, and increased accuracy for some kinds of self-reports in depression may be mediated by an increased level of self-focused attention that accompanies the disorder. Employing a self-control framework, Kanfer and Hagerman (1981) and Carver and Scheier (1981) have also suggested that depressed individuals may be more self-focused than nondepressed individuals. Similarly, Beck (1967, 1976) has discussed a self-preoccupation in depression that may be analogous to self-focused attention, while Lewinsohn (1982; Lewinsohn, Hoberman, Terri, & Hautzinger, 1985), Alloy (1982), and Schmitt (1983) have also noted such an association between depression and this process. Empirically, research has begun to accumulate to document this association (Gibbons *et al.*, 1985; Ingram, Lumry, Cruet, & Siber, in press; Ingram & Smith, 1984; Pyszczynski & Greenberg, 1985; T. W. Smith, Ingram, & Roth, 1985; T. W. Smith & Greenberg, 1981). Thus, an increase in self-focused attention may well prove to be a cognitive process implicated in depression.

Cognitive Product Variables

Finally, a number of researchers have focused on the contribution of particular cognitive products (cognitions) to depression. These products appear to fall into two general classes. The first can be labeled self-statements. Beck (1967) and Hollon and Kendall (1980) have argued that depressed individuals experience a predominance of negative self-statements (or beliefs) as compared to positive self-statements (or beliefs) and that this ratio contributes to the maintenance and possible exacerbation of depression. In a similar fashion employing self-control terminology, Rehm (1977) has proposed that depressed individuals engage in substantially more self-punishment than they do self-reinforcement. Although there has been some question theoretically as to the relevance and meaning of the positive–negative self-statement construct (Arnkoff & Glass, 1982), and empirically the construct's precise relationship to psychopathology is not clear (Kendall & Hollon, 1981b), in general, research has demonstrated that depressed individuals do reliably report experiencing a relatively high number of negative self-statements (Dobson & Breiter, 1983; Harrel & Ryon, 1983; Hollon & Kendall, 1980) and engage in more self-punishment than self-reinforcement (Nelson & Craighead, 1977; Wener & Rehm, 1975).

A second general category (or perhaps, an important subcategory within the larger domain of beliefs) of cognitive products concerns the attributions that depressed individuals make. Seligman (1981) and Abramson (Abramson *et al.*, 1978) have argued that there are certain kinds of attributions that are depressogenic. For successful or positive events, these attributions are external, unstable, and specific, while for failure or negative events they are internal, stable, and global. Hence, depressed individuals are seen as making the most self-deprecating attributions possible, maximizing the effects and implications of personal failure and minimizing success. Empirically, research has generally shown that such an attribution style is associated with depression (Raps, Peterson, Reinhard, Abramson, & Seligman, 1982) although it is not clear whether it is related in a causal fashion (Seligman, Abramson, Semmel, & von Baeyer, 1979) or occurs as a corollary of the depressive state (E. W. Hamilton & Abramson, 1983). Regardless of the ultimate answer to this question, there is a good reason to believe that the depressogenic attribution pattern described by Abramson (Abramson *et al.*, 1978) and Seligman (1980) is an important cognitive factor in depression.

Cognitive Therapy for Depression

Cognitive therapy for depression (Beck *et al.*, 1979) is an active, time-limited synthesis of cognitive and behavioral change techniques designed to ameliorate the symptoms of depression largely by virtue of systematically identifying and correcting both inaccuracies in beliefs and distortions in information processing. In particular, the process of cognitive therapy can be likened to one of *collaborative empiricism,* in which the client is systematically trained to treat his or her own beliefs as if they were hypotheses to be tested (Hollon & Beck, 1979). This hypothesis testing itself can be accomplished by virtue of a review of existing information (retrospective testing): the gathering of new information (prospective hypothesis testing): or the examination of the processes used to arrive at the belief, in particular focusing attention on the operation of specific distortions (Beck, 1963, 1967).

Cognitive therapy, despite its name, is clearly an integration of cognitive and behavioral change procedures. The closest analogy is to the experimental process, in which some hypothesis is formulated (the belief), procedures are derived for testing the validity of that hypothesis (the behaviors), and the results are scrutinized to determine whether the hypothesis was confirmed or disconfirmed. In large measure, cognitive therapy involves helping the client to use his or her own behavior to test his or her beliefs, with an emphasis on uncovering any general distortions in information processing underlying systematic errors in prediction or belief.

L. Ross (1977) has suggested that beliefs can be changed in at least three fashions: (1) by empirical disconfirmation, (2) by the adoption of a new meaning system that forces a wholesale reinterpretation of existing beliefs, or (3) by systematically calling into question the processes by which a belief was derived. As discussed elsewhere by Hollon and Garber (in press), cognitive therapy appears to make use of each of these three mechanisms, with perhaps a somewhat greater reliance on, or at least preference for, the first (empirical hypothesis testing).

Cognitive therapy typically consists of at least seven overlapping stages. Not all cognitive therapies adhere to these seven stages, nor do all cognitive therapists, but, in general, the following structure will typically hold.

First is the provision of a treatment *rationale,* largely a chance to provide a major competing formulation for the client's distress than the typical "trait-like" explanations clients typically bring into treatment (e.g., "I'm a loser who can't do anything right"). This step is an initial foray into Ross' second principle: providing a competing explanation for much of the client's recent experience.

Second is some form of systematic training in *self-monitoring* or self-observation. Typically, this involves arranging a system in which mood and events, and later, cognitions, are systematically sampled and subsequently reviewed. This ongoing self-monitoring typically provides the data for subsequent hypothesis testing and appears to be somewhat freer from contamination by depressotypic distortions than is retrospective recall.

Third are a variety of *behavioral activation* strategies (e.g., pleasant activity scheduling, "chunking" complex tasks into their component parts, "success therapy," etc.), which, in and of themselves, typically have the effect of getting the client to engage in a greater frequency of purposeful behavior. In a fully integrative approach, these strategies are typically presented as behaviors which can test the differential validity of the two major explanatory constructs identified at the rationale stage, the depressed client's own trait-like negative view of the self versus some more nearly social-learning theory model in which unfortunate events are seen as the product of malleable cognitive distortions and skills deficits.

The fourth stage involves teaching the client to better *identify cognitions,* including his or her own cognitive products (typically referred to as "automatic thoughts") in a variety of situations, the larger meaning systems in which these beliefs are embedded, and the processes by which these beliefs are derived. This stage frequently makes use of the instances noted in the self-monitoring or during the behavioral activation strategies in which depressotypic cognitions were particularly apparent.

The fifth stage involves training in the *systematic evaluation of beliefs,* relying heavily on hypothesis testing (both retrospective and prospective) and the analysis of information processing strategies. The consequences of empirical hypothesis testing provide a final check on the accuracy of the client's belief ("If you were indeed totally incompetent, as you sometimes believe, how do you account for getting the job, once you were able to start getting yourself out to job interviews?"). The therapist will typically seek to teach an explicit process, involving, as a minimum, the articulation of these standard prompts: "What's the evidence for that belief?" "Is there any other alternative explanation other than the one that first occurred to you?" and "Even if you are reading the situation accurately, what are the realistic implications of that event?" Extensive use is made of these and similar prompts, with in-session discussions ideally linking to extrasession empirical (behavioral) tests of the validation of the client's specific beliefs.

The sixth stage is the articulation of the *underlying assumptions,* or world views, which seem to organize the way the client looks at himself or herself, his or her own world, or his or her future. (Ellis, 1962, refers to this level of belief as "irrational beliefs.") At this level, one is typically dealing with generic, encompassing beliefs such as "I must be successful to be worthwhile" or "Important people must approve of me at all times." Beliefs at this level are generally global, abstract, and frequently not acknowledged by the client as something he or she believes. The essence of the underlying assumptions is that they make sense out of a large number of specific instances that have already been worked through in the course of therapy.

The seventh and final stage is preparation for *termination,* with particular attention to the prevention of *relapse.* Ideally, such preparations begin early in treatment, although they do not become the primary focus of therapy until near the end of formal contacts. The whole collaborative, didactic approach is structured so as to teach principles and strategies while effecting change. It is quite conceivable that symptom reduction could be achieved even more rapidly if less emphasis were placed upon teaching in the course of therapy, but in a disorder like depression in which relapse and recurrence are probable, some attention to the imparting of stable self-management skills appears wise. Clients are trained to think of therapy not as being "curative," but rather as palliative; ideally, they have acquired skills which, if used, should help them forestall or deal with subsequent episodes of depression. An analogy is drawn between the specific components of cognitive therapy and the processes involved in taking a shower. Taking a shower is no guarantee that one will never get dirty again, but knowing how to take showers means that one has reliable control over a process that can make getting dirty a trivial event. Similarly, having learned the various self-management procedures of cognitive therapy does not provide any necessary guarantee that one will never again become depressed, but it does give one a series of procedures that can be used to deal with those depressions.

Overall, then, the process of cognitive therapy involves a series of interrelated cognitive and behavior change principles, all organized loosely around providing a deliberate, careful analysis of processes typically occurring in a more nearly automatic fashion. Whether cognitive therapy leads depressed individuals to think more like normals remains unclear. Evans and Hollon (in press), for example, have argued that cognitive therapy implicitly trains a deliberate, careful information processing strategy in the service of belief change that is far less efficient, but more conducive to accuracy, than the more typical, automatic processes utilized by both nondepressives and depressives alike.

General Categories of Cognitive Effects

Having now specified several of our assumptions concerning both cognition and the methods of cognitive therapy, it is now possible to deduce how changes in cognition may lead to the alleviation of depression. Following the classification system proposed earlier, cognitive modifications can be grouped as primarily structural/schematic (including propositions or content), at a cognitive operations level, or as affecting cognitive products.

There are at least three models with relevance to schematic change processes which appear to us to have viability. First, the existing depressotypic schemata, marked by negative views of the self, the world, and the future, may actually be altered by the processes of cognitive therapy as described above. This process of change in an existing schemata is referred to as *accommodation*. Second, an operating schemata may not be so much altered as simply *deactivated*. Few depressed individuals have ever been habitually depressed. It seems likely that even individuals currently in an episode have dormant nondepressive self-schemata. If so, then therapy may effect change not so much via accommodation as by deactivation of the depressotypic schema and activation of preexisting nondepressed schemata. Finally, it is possible that cognitive therapy accomplishes its therapeutic goal not so much by altering or deactivating existing depressotypic schema as by *developing compensatory schemata* (actually, cognitive–behavioral knowledge/action systems described by Abelson, 1981, as "scripts") which enable the individual to cope with, or compensate for, the otherwise negative impact of depressotypic information processing. In this third formulation, the operation of such a compensating schema (script), consisting largely of behavioral routines for questioning the validity of depressotypic cognitions, may intervene between the operation of depressotypic schema and eventual cognitive products to alter the nature of those products. In the sections to follow, we will evaluate the molecular impact of the various components of cognitive therapy with respect to these three competing models of change: *depressotypic schema accommodation, depressotypic schema deactivation,* and the *development of compensatory coping schemata.*

Structural Effects of Cognitive Therapy

Given that a negative or depressive self-schema is at the heart of several conceptualizations of depression, it makes good intuitive sense to assume that cognitive therapy exerts its effect by altering the content of this schema (accommodation). More specifically, decreasing the content of negative schemata and increasing the content of positive schemata logically could be expected to decrease depression and increase positive affect. As noted above, however, as logical and straightforward as this conceptualization is, there are as yet no data that directly address this issue, and, as we have suggested, competing models do exist. There are, however, some indirect observations that bear on the notion that cognitive therapy may not substantially change the content of cognitive structures. Experience with relapsed patients, for instance, suggests these individuals frequently appear to possess essentially the same (unaltered) negative self-schemata that characterized previous depressions (Hollon & Garber, in press). While this clinical anecdotal information is subject to a variety of other interpretations (e.g., this observation may only hold for the subset of clients who relapse, or may reflect the relearning of previously held beliefs), it would appear to merit systematic evaluation.

Observations of processes not directly linked to cognitive therapy may also be inconsistent with an accommodation hypothesis. The fact that depression typically has a time-limited course (Beck, 1967) and generally abates with or without treatment (Lewinsohn & Hoberman, 1982) also indirectly casts some doubt on whether recovery from depression in cognitive therapy is due to an alteration of existing cognitive structures. This assumes, of course, that natural remission from depression is not a result of cognitive structural change and that this process may work in the same way as cognitive therapy (albeit at a somewhat slower rate). Along these same lines, a comparison of other kinds of effective treatment indirectly addresses this issue. It does not seem likely, for example, that effective antidepressant medication has its therapeutic effect by directly altering the existence of negative cognitive content.

The bulk of such indirect evidence is predicated on the assumption that alleviation of depression is caused by common processes regardless of the different specific methods that affect this process. It is certainly possible, however, that natural remission, pharmacological, and cognitive therapy procedures work by affecting different processes altogether. Nevertheless, the questions raised by examining cognitive therapy relapses as well as these divergent types of recovery would seem to be a point worth considering.

While it is suggested that cognitive therapy does not necessarily exert its influence by modifying the schemata responsible for what people think about themselves (self-schemata), it may be the case that it serves to develop other cognitive schemata, in particular, *coping* schemata. Such procedural schemata (Kihlstrom & Nasby, 1980; Nasby & Kihlstrom, chapter 11, this volume) would consist of information for what to do during stressful or depressing situations and would optimally entail both cognitive and behavioral steps. Thus, with such a schema the individual may still encounter the manifestations of an activated negative self-schema, but will now have a way to cope with these manifestations and consequently hold the duration and intensity of the ensuing depression to below clinical proportions. In a sense, such a schema might be conceived of as acting like a subroutine that is accessed when a depression-inducing input is encountered. The "depression program" still runs, but the addition of a coping routine now modifies its output in a less maladaptive way. This is, of course, the third model described in the preceding section.

Process Effects

As we have previously suggested, one possibility by which cognitive therapy may alleviate depression is by deactivating the depressive self-schema. Although the other cognitive process effects are important in their own right, their ultimate effect on depression may be through their impact on the depressive self-schema. In a sense then, this schema deactivation may be seen as a higher order cognitive process that can be attacked directly through several cognitive therapy methods and also indirectly through various procedures that focus on other cognitive processes. The point we emphasize is that according to this view, once the depressive self-schema is reliably deactivated, the affect, symptoms, and characteristics associated with depression should remit.

The ability to change modes from automatic to controlled processing is undoubtedly adaptive. As noted, however, depressed individuals are more likely to be characterized by a reliance on automatic processing that may be maladaptive in two respects. First, the products of this processing are negative in nature (e.g., negative self-statements and self-deprecating attributions), and second, this processing may predominate in situations when controlled processing would be more appropriate and adaptive. Hence, fostering a switch out of the automatic mode to a more deliberate controlled mode is a critically important effect of cognitive therapy. Switching modes, though, is not sufficient in and of itself; this processing must focus on a particular kind of information. In the case of cognitive therapy for depression, this focus is on the individual's own cognition and can thus be generally referred to as metacognition. As described by Flavell (1979), metacognition entails an awareness of one's own cognition, in this case, an awareness of how cognition contributes to depression. Cognitive therapy relies heavily on helping individuals switch to a controlled mode of processing that is metacognitive in nature and focuses on depression-related cognition. This switch process, typically referred to as "distancing" (Beck *et al.*, 1979), is facilitated by having the client write down his or her beliefs for subsequent evaluation.

It should be noted that although a switch within therapy into a metacognitive mode is typically aimed at helping clients alleviate their current episode of depression, at least part of the long-term effectiveness of cognitive therapy may lie in teaching patients to initiate this process in the face of future stress. As such, clients incorporate the activation of a metacognitive sequence as part of an emerging coping schema. Thus, instead of "reacting" to life events, patients who successfully develop this cognitive coping ability switch to metacognition to vitiate their negative effects ("What things to think about did we discuss in therapy to not let this get to me? Yes, it was . . ."). Optimally, through repeated accessing, this controlled coping component becomes more automatic.

Another effect of cognitive therapy may be an effect on the quantity and quality of self-focused attention. As with automatic processing, self-focused attention is a process engaged in by many people in many situations and is generally adaptive. The excessive degree and negative content of self-focused attention in depressed individuals would appear to be more problematic. Although it was not designed to specifically influence this process, we would predict that cognitive therapy has the effect of eventually decreasing the focusing of attention on the self and increasing attention focused outwardly.

A process that is important for not only reducing depression but most likely for helping to achieve some of the aforementioned cognitive effects entails the activation of alternate schemata. The activation of any given schema, however, is not a permanent phenomena (although some, like the depressive schema, may stay activated for long periods of time). Rather, as discussed earlier, human functioning seems to be characterized by the switching of various schemata to fit the information processing parameters of particular situations. To this end, cognitive approaches seek to teach individuals how to activate various schemata that are incompatible with the depressive self-schema. These might include more positive self-schemata or the procedural schemata necessary to perform tasks that the depressed individual does not think he or she is capable of doing. Of course, since this activation takes place in the midst of a depressive episode, it is likely to be short-lived. Nevertheless, repeated activation of alternate schemata should have a number of positive effects, not the least of which is the weakening and eventual deactivation of the depressive self-schema.

Finally, from a cognitive process standpoint, the actual processing of information should be altered by cognitive therapy. Cognitive therapy contains several procedures that are explicitly designed to alter the depressed individual's characteristic negative information processing to a more positive (and presumably accurate) variety.

Effects on Cognitive Products

In this class of cognitive events, the effects of cognitive therapy appear to be relatively straightforward. Since depressed individuals are viewed as exhibiting more maladaptive self-statements and attributions (more negative and fewer positive), cognitive therapy evaluates these directly. Although it is important to note that self-statements and attributions can overlap but are not necessarily the same (Hollon & Garber, in press), cognitive therapy approaches them in a same fashion. A self-statement or attribution, for example, is the starting point for the hypothesis-testing procedure employed in cognitive therapy. While altering these products is of course important, cognitive therapy does not seek to elicit all or most negative self-statements or attributions that the individual could make and then attempt to change them. Rather, these products are addressed in order to alter the processes, structures, and content that give rise to them.

Specific Cognitive Effects

Having examined the potential ways in which cognitive therapy generally affects the various categories of cognitive variables assumed to be implicated in depression, we now turn to a discussion of the effects of the specific procedures of cognitive therapy on specific cognitive variables. Once again, the lack of empirical data in this regard must make this venture quite speculative. Nevertheless, it is possible to logically identify some of the ways in which these cognitive procedures and effects interact that may eventually lead to the generation of data in the area.

It is not likely, of course, that any one procedure affects only one cognitive factor, and conversely, that any one cognitive factor is affected by only one procedure. Acknowledging this fact, an attempt will be made to specify many of the cognitive variables influenced by a cognitive procedure. When it appears reasonable to do so, we will also attempt to specify what we think might be the *primary* cognitive effects of a procedure.

Self-Monitoring Methods

Behavioral self-monitoring

Since concretely monitoring events and specified targets can hardly be considered an effortless, overlearned task (save for some obsessive–compulsive disorders), the primary effect of behavioral self-monitoring is most likely a task that necessitates a switch to a controlled mode of processing. More specifically, such a procedure would appear to be an excellent mechanism for interrupting the automatic recycling process of negative cognitions in depression. In addition, if the behaviors being monitored are sufficiently incompatible with the predominant depressive self-schema, self-monitoring may also either precipitate a switch to another schema more appropriately able to encode the monitored events or an alteration in the depressive schema (accommodation). In line with this notion, behavioral self-monitoring may also lead to a decrease in the selective processing of personally negative information and corresponding increase in positive information.

Cognitive self-monitoring

Cognitive self-monitoring would appear to have effects similar to those of behavioral self-monitoring, with a possible difference in the strength of the effects. With regard to controlled/automatic processing, for example, it would also seem to be the case that cognitive self-monitoring requires a switch to a more controlled mode. This switch would not seem to be complete, however, since the automatic thoughts are still occurring, but now they are being monitored. Thus, while the individual has added a controlled component to this process, it is still fundamentally an automatic process. The retention of this large automatic component should also necessitate less of a switch to alternate schemata since the products being monitored are generated from the depressive schema. Finally, self-focused attention should also be at least temporarily *increased* as the individual is now both experiencing cognitions and actively monitoring them. The same is true, of course, for behavioral self-monitoring.

Behavioral Techniques

Activity scheduling

The cognitive effects of activity scheduling fall into two categories. First are the effects of the actual process of the therapist and patient collaborating to schedule activities. Foremost among these is again a switch to a more controlled processing mode that is necessary to complete this task. Additionally, because the patient must interact with the therapist, self-focused attention should be decreased. The process of carrying out the scheduled activities are a second class of cognitive effects. Controlled processing should be increased, self-focused attention should be decreased, and alternate schemata should be activated most directly by engaging in these activities.

Graded tasks

Although the variables affected by graded tasks are essentially the same as those affected by scheduling and completing activities, there are some differences, particularly in their order of importance. Perhaps the most important effect of gradual tasks is the schema necessary to accommodate the increased flow of positive information and positive cognitive products that this procedure may engender. Hence, successful completion of these tasks may serve to activate alternative schemata (although depending on the nature and complexity of the tasks, this activation may be of short duration). This is particularly true in the early stages of therapy when assigned tasks are more likely to be relatively easy and the successes generated from them "small."

The degree of controlled processing and self-focused attention affected by graded tasks will also depend on the nature of the task. More simple tasks will require less controlled and external focused attention whereas the more difficult tasks that are likely to be encountered later in therapy will require correspondingly more. Finally, since these tasks are specifically designed to ensure success, the availability of positive information will also be ensured. If the appropriate schemata are in place, then graded task assignment may also have the effect of increasing the monitoring of positive information and decreasing negative.

Scheduling specific activities

The cognitive effects of scheduling specific activities are viewed as much the same as those achieved by graded task assignment. That is, since scheduling specific activities is also to enhance favorable experiences such as success and pleasant activities, the probability of activating alternative schemata should be increased while the degree of controlled processing and external focused attention affected will depend on task complexity.

Success therapy

Again, the effects of success therapy parallel those of graded task assignment and specific activity scheduling in that alternative schemata are most likely to be activated as a result of the information engendered by these behaviors. To a somewhat lesser degree, controlled processing, self-focused attention, the monitoring of negative–positive information, and the generation of cognitive products may also be modified depending on task complexity, the amount of positive information generated from the task, and how strongly alternative schemata are activated.

The general effect of these behavioral methods may thus be to increase the availability of positive self-relevant information that will help activate alternative schemata and therefore indirectly deactivate the depression schema. Conversely, when cast in a hypothesis-testing context, such information may provide disconfirming evidence for the depressogenic schema and therefore facilitate its accommodation, or change.

Cognitive Methods

Presentation of the cognitive model

Unlike self-monitoring and behavioral methods, cognitive methods are designed to directly impact the cognitive factors that contribute to depression. The first phase in therapy always consists of presenting the cognitive model. We would argue that the primary effect of this element is to provide the initial components of what can eventually be built into a coping schema. This presentation is conceptualized explicitly as new learning and, optimally, provides depressed individuals with an alternative way of viewing depression that was not previously available to them. More specifically, it provides a framework that allows the subsequent comprehension and integration of how the individual's thoughts and behaviors contribute to depression and, more importantly, how these thoughts and behaviors can be adaptively modified. As therapy progresses, the initial elements of this framework should be reinforced and built upon until the point where the individual has developed a consolidated and functionally adaptive coping schema. The importance of developing this schema can not be overemphasized. Without the individual encoding the essential elements of the cognitive model, cognitive therapy may still reduce overt depressive symptomatology, but dependence on the therapist may be engendered and little prophylactic effect against future depression of clinical proportion will be achieved.

Identifying automatic thoughts

In many ways, this aspect of cognitive therapy probably represents an extension of cognitive self-monitoring with a somewhat more specific focus. As such its direct cognitive effects are also an extension of cognitive self-monitoring. That is, it would seem that the process of identifying automatic thoughts is useful in necessitating somewhat of a switch to a more controlled form of processing and less of a reliance on the automatic processing that generates these thoughts. Given that the cognitive techniques of cognitive therapy are predicated on the identification and subsequent modification of depression-inducing thoughts, this process is, of course, critical to cognitive therapy. With regard to direct cognitive effects other than inducing a higher degree of controlled processing, however, solely identifying automatic thoughts probably has little direct cognitive impact.

Identifying cognitive distortions

Identifying cognitive distortions is similar to the process of identifying automatic thoughts. The key difference is that, in the present context, cognitive distortions are not only identified, but attempts are made to correct them as well. This key difference is responsible for several direct cognitive effects. Perhaps the primary effect is that identifying and altering distortions serves to directly help deactivate the depressive self-schema. This effect may be accomplished in two ways. First, as cognitions are questioned, analyzed, and modified, energy should be removed from the processes that maintain the activation of the depressive schema. Second, as more accurate cognitions are engendered, different cognitive schemata should stand a greater likelihood of being activated. The relative emphasis of these two components depends on the nature of the cognition modified and how they are modified. For example, if a cognition such as "I am no good" is modified to the extent that the individual no longer expressed it (e.g., "It's not true that I'm no good") then the primary effect is to help negate the depressive schema. If, on the other hand, the cognition is replaced with another cognition (e.g., "I am a good person"), not only will some deactivation of the depressive schema take place, but an alternate schema will also receive more activation. We would argue that a combination of these two processes would provide a faster recovery from depressive symptomatology, although it may be the case that alternative activation processes do not take place until later in therapy when there has already been some deactivation of the depressive schema.

A closely related cognitive effect is the interruption of automatic processing. Since cognitions are now not only being monitored but attempts to alter them are also taking place, a much more controlled processing will account for a larger proportion of variance in the individual's way of thinking. Still, since cognitions are occurring automatically, identifying cognitive distortion does not lead to a complete controlled, metacognitive shift. Nevertheless, this cognitive method clearly involves a significant controlled component in the client's thinking.

Evaluating belief validity

Although evaluating belief validity and identifying cognitive distortion are similar, they have several nontrivial differences in the processes they affect. Whereas identifying cognitive distinctions focuses on cognitive *products* such as self-statements and/or attributions as well as information picked up and interpreted from the environment, evaluating belief validity targets the *contents* of the active schemata. Distorted information pick-up and depressive beliefs, of course, affect each other, even though they intersect the cognitive system at different points.

Despite these different intersection points, the effects of identifying cognitive distortions and evaluating belief validity are essentially the same. In evaluating belief validity, an attempt is made to modify beliefs (cognitive contents) by inferring the beliefs from cognitive products and working to test the veracity of the beliefs. The explicit goal is to modify this cognitive content. As central as this modification is to cognitive therapy, it is possible that this is not the effect achieved. It may be that what this procedure does is to facilitate the deactivation of the depressive schema. As the validity of these contents is challenged, the depressive schema could become more difficult to maintain. To the extent that alternative beliefs are articulated by the client, alternative schemata should also be activated. Similar to the effects achieved by identifying cognitive distortions, more controlled processing, a better-developed coping schema, and fewer negative self-statements and attributions should also take place as a result of this procedure.

Identifying underlying assumptions

At a later stage in therapy (a stage sometimes not progressed to), an attempt is made to identify and modify the underlying cognitive factors that appear to be linked to depression. Beck (1967; Beck *et al.*, 1979) has described these factors as underlying assumptions that, conceptualized from an information processing view, probably represent higher order constructs within schemata: constructs not directly available to the client and inferred by the therapist only after the repeated occurrence of specific cognitions and beliefs that appear linked to such higher order beliefs. It is interesting that these procedures are typically undertaken only after the client is relatively asymptomatic (Hollon & Garber, in press). Hence, rather than have direct effects on depression, this procedure seeks to alter the individual's cognitive vulnerability to future episodes of depression.

Again, it is entirely possible that in the more typical case of cognitive therapy for depression, this higher order belief modification does not occur. While cognitive therapists would doubtless favor an *accommodation* process, it is possible that one effect that does occur is an *awareness* of these attitudes rather than their change. In some sense, this parallels Freud's (1950) discussion of the difference between intellectual and emotional knowledge. The depressed individual may now know of the existence of these beliefs and be aware of their maladaptiveness, and know how they are linked to depression, but the beliefs still exist and still "feel" as though they are valid.

As L. Ross (1977) notes, of course, beliefs can change, and the present discussion is not meant to imply that such higher order assumptions cannot be altered. Nonetheless, the extent to which such actual change does occur is an open empirical question. Certainly, our anecdotal experience with relapsed patients suggests that, in some instances, less true change has occurred at this level than would have been desired. Although this latter proposal may seem to suggest that the depressed individual is doomed to continually reexperience significant depression, its implications, even if true, are not as pessimistic as they may first seem. The awareness that this procedure optimally provides may be crucial to the development of a coping schemata. With such schemata in place, when the individual experiences a future depressive-schemata activating experience, negative thoughts will again occur but with the knowledge that they are not necessarily isomorphic with "objective" reality and that a cognitive and behavioral sequence can be engaged to deal with them. Therefore, we would suggest that a possible major cognitive effect of identifying higher order assumptions may be to enhance the development of coping schemata that can be accessed during depression and that facilitates a switch into a controlled processing mode with all of the adaptive characteristics that this mode entails.

In general, cognitive techniques appear most likely to affect the activation level of the depressive schema directly by undermining the processes that maintain its activation. To the extent that more adaptive cognitions are generated to take the place of the depression schema products, alternative schema should also be activated. When these techniques are successfully applied, they should also foster a switch to a more controlled process. Finally, these should also contribute to the development of a cognitive coping schema to be actively invoked by the individual during depressing situations.

Critical Effects

In examining the effects of cognitive therapy, it becomes clear that several continually reoccur in our proposals. This is not by accident; out of the numerous effects possible, several appear to be of prime importance. Certainly, *accommodation,* or the modification of the content and/or structure of existing depressotypic schema is the process most clearly proposed by cognitive therapy. Deactivating the depressive schema, switching to a greater degree of controlled, metacognitive processing, and activating alternative schemata may be the central cognitive factors in alleviating depressive symptomatology instead of or in addition to schematic change.

In summarizing the effects of the different cognitive–behavioral procedures, it appears that both the self-monitoring techniques and behavioral methods provide the data on which the cognitive interventions are based. The behavioral methods in particular seem effective for generating data that are incompatible with the depressive schema and either force accommodation or require the activation of alternative schemata to be encoded. The data generated from these procedures in turn provide the basis for effectively implementing the cognitive procedures that serve to help directly deactivate the depressive schema. All of these procedures appear to contribute to the development of a coping schema.

Conceptual and Empirical Questions

In the preceding pages, we have outlined numerous proposals for the general and specific cognitive therapy for depression. In doing so we have been highly speculative and relied in large part on intuitive and logical reasoning rather than empirical data. No apologies are offered for this approach. There are unfortunately few data that have addressed the issues we have raised. In this light, our intention has been to lay out an initial framework for conceptualizing the information processing effects of cognitive therapy in a manner that we hope will eventually facilitate testable hypotheses concerning the various relationships between cognitive therapy and adaptive change processes. Accordingly, we now turn to a brief discussion of potential future research questions based on this analysis. It should be noted, of course, that virtually every proposal we have put forth is open to empirical confirmation or disconfirmation. We will discuss, however, several specific issues that we think are particularly interesting and meaningful.

Perhaps the most provocative proposal of those put forth in the present chapter concerns the question as to whether the content of the depressive schema is actually modified. Although it should be noted that neither of these views are seen as exclusive of other change factors, we differ in our judgments in this regard; Ingram favors primarily a deactivation process, and Hollen favors primarily an accommodation process. Most cognitive therapists would probably also favor accommodation (e.g., Beck *et al.*, 1979; Goldfried & Robbins, 1983). Similarly, well-respected cognitive and social–cognitive psychologists (e.g., Kahneman *et al.*, 1982; Nisbett & Ross, 1980) have argued that even though beliefs do not change easily, they can in fact change. This may be an effect of cognitive therapy. In describing a deactivation model, we have argued that although beliefs can and sometimes do change, highly personal beliefs may be resistant to change and may become dormant as a result of effective cognitive therapy while at the same time remaining fairly intact.

Although we believe that these competing models of change are empirically testable, there are several challenges inherent in such research. First and foremost is the need for methods to operationalize and assess depressive schema. Although considerable strides have been made in this area (e.g., H. P. Davis & Unruh, 1981; Derry & Kuiper, 1981; Ingram *et al.*, 1983; S. E. Taylor & Crocker, 1981; S. E. Taylor & Fiske, 1981), the problem has by no means been solved. Even with appropriate assessment methods, however, the difference between schema modification versus deactivation is an empirically difficult discrimination to make. Several researchers, for instance (Hammen, 1983b; Lewinsohn, Steinmetz, Larsen, & Franklin, 1981), have found evidence that the cognitive variables typically present in depressed individuals are not present when the same individuals are not depressed, that is, the variables are state dependent. Although these results are not inconsistent with the deactivation view, accepting the hypothesis that negative self-relevant beliefs were not present and active during nondepression is problematic. There always exists the possibility, for instance, that experimental methods have not tapped the relevant variables in these nondepressive states. Hence, researchers must devise careful methodologies to assess whether cognitive therapy has changed the content of cognitive structures or simply made them inaccessible. In particular, they may need to utilize stress-induction paradigms which activate ''latent'' schema, a strategy successfully employed in biological literature to detect existing, but dormant, neuroendocrine abnormalities in depression (Depue, Kleiman, Davis, Hutchinson, & Krauss, in press).

The past decade has seen a growing interest and enthusiasm for the cognitive treatment of depression. Given that there is good evidence that these methods can be effective, we would argue that the task before us now is to refine and/or modify these methods as well as perhaps develop additional methods of treatment. In this chapter we have proposed that a critical step toward accomplishing this goal is a conceptual framework that specifies how and why various procedures affect particular cognitive processes. Research generated from such a framework, even if it disconfirms the veracity of the framework, can have enormous implications for theory and research on depression. More importantly, however, we hope that such research will eventually lead to methods that will maximize the effects of cognitive therapy for the maximum number of depressed individuals.

14

Information Processing Approaches to the Treatment of Schizophrenia

PETER A. MAGARO
MARK H. JOHNSON
RALPH BORING*

Department of Psychology
Ohio State University
Columbus, Ohio 43210

Of all the psychopathologies, the schizophrenias have received the most attention. Bellack (1958) estimated that 7000 papers were published on the subject in the 20 years between 1936 and 1956. The past 20 have seen the rise in popularity of information processing models of human cognition, including efforts to identify the cognitive deficits associated with the schizophrenic disorders (Magaro, 1980, 1984). As a result of this focus on cognitive processes, a large body of literature has accumulated cataloguing the deficits associated with schizophrenia. The search for studies in the ennumeration of the perceptual and cognitive deficits associated with schizophrenia is, however, not the purpose of this chapter. Rather, we will focus upon the literature which has attempted to move beyond the identification of cognitive deficits into the means to ameliorate them, specifically, the treatment of schizophrenia through the modification of cognitive processes.

The utility of the information processing paradigm has been demonstrated by

*Present address: Department of Psychology, Arizona State University, Tempe, Arizona, 85287.

its ability to identify cognitive processes unique not only to schizophrenia but to schizophrenic subtypes as well (Magaro, 1981). This coupled with a molecular approach to cognition suggests that an information processing paradigm could provide a powerful therapeutic tool via its ability to pinpoint processes to be targeted for intervention.

Measures derived from this paradigm also could provide well-standardized methods by which to establish a diagnosis. The information processing paradigm holds promise with regard to diagnostic issues in that patterns of cognitive task markers may provide a more accurate means to diagnose pathological groups. Buchsbaum and Rieder (1979), in another content area with a similar aim, considered the possibility of diagnosing psychopathological groups on the basis of biological factors. Such an approach involved conceptualizing the dependent variable as a set of associated clinical factors. Andreasen (1983) has likewise proposed that a profitable approach to research in the affective disorders would be to identify a group of biologically homogeneous subjects, utilizing a classification system which she terms a ''biotype.'' The biotype is defined as being characterized by familial, neurochemical, neuroendocrinal, neurophysiological, neuroanatomical, and treatment response data. Some success regarding differential diagnosis of depressive subtypes has been reported using such measures as the dexamethasone suppression test, urinary MHPG levels, and sleep electroencephalograms. More relevant to our purpose is the argument of Cromwell (1978a), who states that research on the schizophrenias has been retarded for the past eight decades because of a tendency to begin each study with the selection of subjects grouped on the basis of unreliable diagnostic constructs. He contends that a more profitable approach to diagnostic classification would be to define groups by their performance on cognitive variables, with clinical factors being set as the dependent variables. The molecular approach inherent in the information processing paradigm seems well suited for identifying homogeneous diagnostic groups based upon cognitive tasks performance. That is, rather than relying upon current diagnostic practices, the information processing paradigm might prove quite useful in producing distinct pathological groupings such as depression versus schizophrenia. We mention the notion of using information process variables to provide diagnostic classification only to accent the trend to utilize the information process approach in other clinical areas besides the search for etiology. Interestingly, even though there has been a great deal of recent interest in the application of the information processing paradigm to different clinical tasks and in a number of psychopathologies (Hollon & Kriss, 1984), few therapeutic approaches have utilized the vast amount of literature which attempts to specify the exact information processing deficit associated with schizophrenia (Magaro, 1980). We will attempt to encourage such a therapeutic advance by presenting the initial review of information processing studies directed toward therapy for schizophrenics.

The format of this discussion will be as follows. First, we will briefly present an information processing framework which we have found helpful in considering the studies to be discussed in this chapter. Second, we will review and discuss the work stemming from this paradigm, which has attempted to alleviate the cognitive and perceptual deficits present in the schizophrenic disorders. Additionally, we will attempt to integrate the work currently being done with brain-injured patients which may hold promise for the treatment of schizophrenia. We will then move beyond the currently available work to provide a prescriptive approach to the treatment of schizophrenia based upon the information processing model. Finally, we will present a brief discussion of our attempt to develop a computerized treatment battery based upon current knowledge regarding the cognitive deficits associated with schizophrenia.

An Information Processing Model

The following model is presented as a framework against which to view the research discussed in this chapter. Although the popularity of multistage/multistore models has waned (R. Lachman *et al.*, 1979), we find that this model provides a useful practice framework for evaluating this literature. Figure 1 presents a schema of an information processing model.

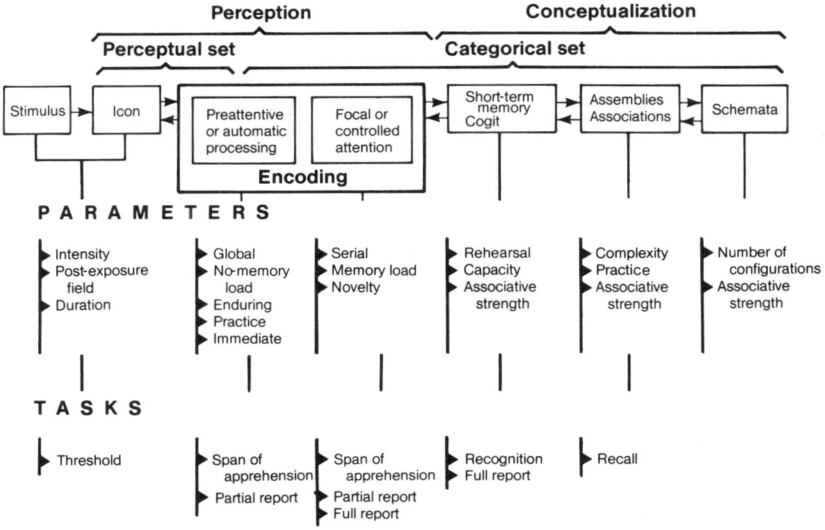

FIG. 1. ***An information processing model defining terms and processes. (From Magaro, 1980.)***

The process of deriving meaning from the environment begins with the reception of stimulus information by the organism. The initial representation of the stimulus is the icon, which is the internal representation of the external stimulus. This image is nothing more than a configuration of lines and colors which vary in length, width, or contrast. The encoding process occurs during the brief duration of the icon and is the process which operates on the stimulus representation to place it into memory. The encoding process is currently thought to occur in one of two manners: automatic or controlled (Schneider & Shiffrin, 1977). Automatic processing is thought to consist of a global, rapid processing style, while controlled processing consists of a serial, slow search process. Normal individuals shift between the two processing styles as demanded by the situation. Whereas the automatic style is most useful when processing dissimilar information, controlled processing is most useful when a careful comparison of features is necessary. For example, when searching a phone book for a common name such as Smith, a controlled processing strategy would be most useful. Conversely, if the name to be found is Xytlcemb, an automatic processing approach would probably be the most efficient.

Following encoding, the next "stage" encountered is that of the short-term or working memory, thought to comprise conscious mental processes. It is at this stage that the cogit is encountered, defined as the basic information unit which is a discrete memory representative (Hayes-Roth, 1977). Short-term memory is activated in a all-or-none fashion by recognition of the cogit in an external stimuli. A configuration of cogits which reflects all relationships between cogits simultaneously is assembled by associations to form category groups or assemblies. Assemblies in turn may be combined with other assemblies to form schemata, which in effect are more complex representations of events found in long-term memory. Finally, we see that the flow of information is bidirectional, which Neisser (1967) has termed "figural synthesis." Thus the schema "accepts information as it becomes available at sensory surface and is changed by that information; it directs movements and exploratory activities that make more information available, by which it is further modified" (Neisser, 1976, p. 54). Therefore, this information processing paradigm is based upon a constant dialectic, with the encoding processes influenced by higher order processes, namely, the schemata. (For a discussion of current research regarding the schema construct, see Alba & Hasher, 1983.) That is, not only do early processing stages determine what enters the system, but higher order processes as well exert an effect on what and how information is processed.

The preceding discussion is of necessity overly simplistic in its representation of the information processing model. A more complete discussion of this model is presented in Magaro (1980). Other chapters in this volume present complete accounts of the intricacies of this formulation, especially as applied to a variety of psychological disturbances. We have provided this presentation merely as a convenient referent for the following discussion.

Treatment Approaches

Encoding

One of the first tasks an individual must perform to receive information is to recognize and analyze the basis stimulus input. The time therefore involved in stimulus recognition and/or feature detection has become of primary importance in the search for the schizophrenia deficit. The first obvious question would be the strength and duration of the icon. Icon duration, however, has been reported to be the same in schizophrenic as nonschizophrenic subjects (Cash, Neale, & Cromwell, 1972; Magaro & Page, 1983), therefore, it may be hypothesized that any deficits observed must be due to the next information processing stage, that of encoding.

The initial encoding work was concerned with perceptual/attentional deficits. Reaction-time studies are a gross measure of encoding because they not only assess the time to encode the relevant stimulus but also the time involved in producing the correct response. However, reaction time has been a favorite experimental task for decades, and ample evidence exists demonstrating reaction-time impairments for schizophrenic subjects. Schizophrenic patients exhibit longer response latencies than normal subjects (Cancro, Sutton, & Sugarman, 1971; Rodnick & Shakow, 1940; Rosenthal, Lawler, Zahn, & Shakow, 1960) and evidence a "crossover" impairment when the preparatory interval (the time between warning stimulus and critical stimulus) is varied (Rodnick & Shakow, 1940; Tizard & Venables, 1956), which has been found to be related to the preparatory interval of the immediately preceding trial in the set (Zahn, Rosenthal, & Shakow, 1961). Further, ipsimodal and cross-modal reaction-time investigations have also noted schizophrenic performance deficits when compared to normal subjects (Nuechterlein, 1977; Sutton, Kakarem, Zubin, & Portnoy, 1961). Taken together, these studies suggest a pronounced deficit in the schizophrenic's ability to respond to the presentation of simple stimuli under certain conditions.

Steffy and his collaborators (in Cromwell, 1975) conducted a series of studies investigating the durability of the simple reaction-time and crossover deficiencies in process schizophrenics. They found that through a combination of preliminary training, positive urging, and support by the examiner the simple reaction-time scores for the process schizophrenics were lowered to normal limits: the crossover effect, however, remained unchanged. In a later effort, Kaplan (1974) was able to eliminate the crossover deficit by providing schizophrenic subjects with pretraining on temporal judgments. That is, positive transfer of temporal estimate training was found on the reaction-time attention measure in schizophrenic patients.

These reports suggest that both simple reaction-time and crossover deficits may be ameliorated using supportive and pretraining techniques, respectively. The finding that positive urging and support by the examiner lead to decrease reaction-time latencies suggests that a "noncognitive" process such as performance anxiety may play a role in this deficit. With regard to the crossover effect, direct training of temporal judgment skills may be useful in decreasing this phenomena. The demonstration that attentional/perceptual deficits may be modified via support and direct training is of great interest. Wagner (1968) addressed attentional deficits in schizophrenia by training schizophrenic subjects in attending skills.

Attentional training involved presentation of a target stimulus followed by the presentation of three stimuli, one of which was identical to the target stimulus. Subjects were to indicate which one of the three stimuli was identical to the preceding target stimulus. They received immediate feedback regarding the accuracy of their response, and correct performance was rewarded with canteen coupons. Transfer measures were taken by the Memory for Designs Test (Benton, 1946) and the Letter Circle Test. The attention training group received the training outlined above, while the control group viewed the choice display screens only and were told to pick one of the three stimuli which they "liked."

The attention training group significantly improved over their own transfer measure pretraining scores. Control subjects also demonstrated significant gains over their own transfer measure pretraining scores. Wagner interpreted this result as indicating that schizophrenic attentional deficits may be raised under conditions of contingent reinforcement; however, since all groups demonstrated an increase on the transfer measures, Wagner offered the hypothesis that this effect was due to the positive social reinforcing qualities of the experimenter. That is, Wagner invoked a motivational explanatory construct, stating that subjects would be more willing to expend effort for an experimenter who had just provided reinforcement. Thus, although Wagner's design does not allow for a precise definition of the task characteristics responsible for the gains noted, it does provide evidence concurrent with the reaction-time studies that the attentional deficits associated with schizophrenia are amenable to change if positive reinforcement is introduced into the task either by way of urging or increased contact with the tester.

In 1981, Adams, Brantley, Malatesta, and Turkat reported results of their attempt to relate the remediation of attentional deficits to clinical improvement in a 25-year-old male schizophrenic. The patient had previously been diagnosed schizophrenic and had spent 3 months in a state institution. He complained to the authors of being confused, "spaced out," being unsure in social settings, having difficulty communicating with others, and having "crazy thoughts." Additionally, the client reported considerable difficulty in following another person's conversation and was easily distracted by noises or movement of other people. Based upon this information, the authors hypothesized that the client "was not discriminating adequately between internal and external stimuli and was not attending to verbal and nonverbal cues, resulting in a deficit of social skills" (p. 461).

Treatment consisted of nine 50-minute sessions which involved practice on several tasks designed to improve the client's ability to attend to appropriate external and internal stimuli and to improve his social skills. These tasks included forward and backward digit span tasks, letter span and verbal content span tasks, a dichotic shadowed listening task, and a long-term memory retrieval task. In addition to these exercises, behavioral and cognitive–behavioral techniques including role playing, modeling, and thought stopping were also included as part of the therapy process. Following treatment, the client displayed significant improvement in his attending/focusing ability, ability to follow another's conversation under distracting conditions, and elimination of "crazy" thoughts. Follow-up consisted of monthly meetings over a 6-month period, with the client continuing to manifest the improvements noted immediately following completion of therapy.

This report suggests that the attentional deficits associated with schizophrenia may be ameliorated in young, acute, relatively intact schizophrenic patients. Obviously these results need to be replicated and extended to other schizophrenic samples before conclusions concerning the efficacy of such treatment can be made. Further, future investigations should include efforts to tease out which aspects of this approach are most effective, such as the practice provided by the cognitive tasks or the familiarity with the experimenter, which seems to increase motivation. Since a number of behavioral and experimental measurement techniques are currently available to assess aspects of a behavioral treatment (Lambert, Christensen, & DeJulio, 1984), future investigators would do well to include them in their treatment efforts.

Narrowed cue utilization has also been considered to characterize schizophrenic patients (Broen, 1968; Silverman, 1964; Venables, 1964). This inability to concurrently utilize cues from two sensory modalities has been hypothesized to be an important factor in the social maladjustment noted in chronic, nonparanoid schizophrenics. For example, social interactions often require both auditory and visual cues, such as listening to words spoken while simultaneously attending to facial expressions (Meiselman, 1973). In an attempt to broaden dual modality cue utilization, Meiselman (1973) compared chronic nonparanoid male schizophrenics who had been trained on a dual cue modality task to chronic schizophrenics who had not received such training. On a single modality task, subjects were instructed to lift their finger off a telegraph key when signaled by the onset of a light, while the dual modality task consisted of having to react to either the onset of a tone or light, with the two stimuli being presented in random order. This task has been demonstrated to produce increases in reaction-time latencies in normals and schizophrenics, although the difference between the two modality trails is significantly longer for schizophrenic than normal subjects (Kristofferson, 1967).

Results indicated that those who received training on this task showed marked gains while schizophrenics who did not receive training did not manifest this effect. Additionally, those who had received training showed marked gains over their own pretraining scores and the gain scores of the nontrained subjects. These results suggest that the narrowed cue utilization shown by chronic, nonparanoid schizophrenics is amenable to modification.

These studies demonstrate that perceptual and attentional deficits demonstrated to be present in schizophrenic patients are amenable to change. Certainly these results are encouraging and auger well for future attempts aimed at alleviating these difficulties. However, with the exception of the report by Adams *et al.*, these studies fail to tie these gains to clinical improvement.

Short-term memory

Evidence has been steadily mounting for the presence of a memory encoding deficit in schizophrenic patients who have the potential to effectively use memonic organizational properties but fail to do so at the encoding stage (Calev, Verables, & Monk, 1983). Koh and his colleagues have been successful in demonstrating that induced encoding strategies can ameliorate these deficits in young schizophrenics. Koh, Kayton, and Peterson (1976) had schizophrenic patients rate 50 words twice in succession for their pleasantness–unpleasantness characteristics. Following this rating, subjects were unexpectedly asked to recall as many of the words as possible. Results indicated that the recall performance of schizophrenics was comparable to that of normal subjects. As Koh and colleagues later noted, these results were important because "they implied that the schizophrenics' recall deficits . . . were not attributable to some permanent, structural impairment, and that these deficits can be ameliorated if schizophrenics are induced to encode the to-be-remembered words affectively and semantically" (Koh, Grinker, Marusarz, & Forman, 1981). Similar results have been reported by Koh (Koh *et al.*, 1981), utilizing a sorting task in which schizophrenic subjects were required to sort words into piles based upon their pleasantness–unpleasantness characteristics. Sorting trials continued until two consistent sorts occurred. Having met this criterion, subjects were unexpectedly asked to recall as many of the words as possible. In this condition, as with the affective rating task used in their earlier report, the performance of schizophrenic subjects was no different from that of normal controls. Thus, the encoding deficits noted to be associated with schizophrenia appear to be amenable to change by inducing affective encoding of words.

Larsen and Fromholt (1976) examined an alternative manner to lessen the encoding deficit in schizophrenia. Schizophrenics were instructed to sort cards into categories with the object of the task being to obtain two consistent sorts in a row. Following the obtainment of two sequential, consistent sorts, subjects were unexpectedly asked to recall as many of the words as possible. Under these conditions, the performance of the schizophrenics was almost identical to that of normal controls. The authors concluded that recall performance between groups was equivalent when subjects had achieved equivalence with regard to organization as evidenced by consistency in sorting.

The results of Larsen and Fromholt (1976) and Koh *et al.* (1976, 1981) suggest that the memory encoding deficits considered to characterize schizophrenic patients are reversible. Therefore, by providing schizophrenic patients with an affective encoding strategy or sufficient time to obtain stability of organization, some of the encoding deficits associated with this disorder may be alleviated. The studies reviewed up to this point suggest that a number of deficits associated with schizophrenia may be decreased or eliminated with proper training. Thus, the reaction-time, attentional, cue utilization, and memory encoding deficits which are thought to characterize schizophrenic patients are not irreversible. Rather, this small body of research indicates that quite the contrary is true: By tailoring training to fit the specific processing deficit, these deficits may be altered and eliminated.

Schemata

Building a New or Tighting an Old Schema

Schematic, or content, aspects of the information processing paradigm have received extensive attention from researchers investigating schizophrenic psychopathology, especially paranoid schizophrenia. Schemata refer to both the content of stimulus organization as well as to how stimuli are organized and structured (Hollon & Kriss, 1984). With regard to content of thought, probably the most attention has focused upon these processes in depressed groups following A. T. Beck's (1967) formulation of the depressive negative self-schema (see Ingram & Reed, this volume). Less attention has been directed to the content of assemblies and schemata of schizophrenic groups. Some attempts, however, have been made to alter or enhance the organizational processes thought to be occurring at the schematic level. Within this framework, interpersonal and problem-solving deficits are considered to be due partially from the absence or underdevelopment of schemata that contain cognitive–behavioral "scripts" for these situations.

Coche and Flick (1975) examined problem-solving behavior in schizophrenic patients because solving interpersonal problems has often been observed to be a handicap for these patients (Platt & Spivak, 1972). Three groups of psychiatric patients participated in the study, one receiving problem-solving training, one receiving no treatment, and the last receiving placebo training. Problem-solving ability was assessed before and after training using the Means–Ends Problem-Solving procedure (MEPS), in which the subject must complete unfinished stories that have interpersonal problem situations. Story responses are then scored for relevant and irrelevant means of dealing with the problem.

Training involved teaching the experimental group a series of steps which are useful in solving interpersonal issues; essentially, the series of steps provided subjects with a cognitive framework for addressing interpersonal problems. The steps included (a) identifying the problem, (b) clarifying the problem, (c) generating alternative solutions to the problem, and (d) discussing the feasibility of each solution. Results demonstrated that those subjects receiving eight problem-solving training sessions improved their problem-solving abilities as measured by the MEPS compared to control groups. The authors felt that, given the external validity of the MEPS to real-life problem solving (Platt & Spivak, 1975), these results suggested that the experimental group had made significant strides in their problem-solving ability.

In a later study, Coche and Douglas (1977) partially replicated these results in an additional sample of psychiatric patients, most of whom were schizophrenics. Problem-solving training resulted in improved impulse control, increased self-esteem, and increased feelings of competence. Thus, these studies suggest that problem-solving strategies may be taught to schizophrenics and incorporated into their schemata, resulting in improved problem-solving skills as well as gains in self-esteem, impulse control, and feelings of competence.

Interpersonal skills deficits might also be thought to be at least partially due to an inadequate repertoire of socially acceptable interpersonal responses (Wallace & Boone, 1984). An approach to ameliorate this deficit has been described by Goldsmith and McFall (1975). Schizophrenic and nonschizophrenic male inpatients were assigned to one of three treatment conditions: interpersonal skills training, pseudotherapy control, or assessment-only control. Interpersonal skills were assessed on a number of behavioral and self-report measures. Interpersonal skills training consisted of broadening the skills repertoire in a number of content domains and involved behavior rehearsal, modeling, coaching, recorded response playback, and corrective feedback. Subjects in the interpersonal skills training condition demonstrated significantly greater improvement than either control group in their ability to handle difficult interpersonal situations.

Another approach has been through the use of the structured learning therapy approach of Goldstein, Sprafkin, and Gershav (1975). A number of social ''scripts'' are taught as minute elements until the total social behavior is learned as a unit. The therapeutic goal is to establish complex social schemata that will determine social behavior. Magaro and West (1983) applied this approach with chronic psychiatric patients to teach social skills behavior. They found that by teaching the elements of interpersonal interactions, such as the sequential components involved in initiating a conversation, social skills behaviors increased. They also found that symptoms as measured by a symptom rating scale decreased as social skills increased. This is one of the few studies which found a decrease in specific types of symptomatology with the application of a therapy directed toward building social schemata.

Taken together, these studies offer support for the notion that schematic deficits may be ameliorated with proper training, that involves establishing decision-making rules, interpersonal skill, modeling behavior, and practicing interpersonal skills. We might consider this training to involve the building of an "appropriate interpersonal behavior" schema. That is, schemata containing a repertoire of appropriate behavioral skills appear to be established, which when activated direct behavioral response patterns.

Loosening the Rigid Schemata

We have been speaking of schizophrenics who have rather loose associations or weak assemblies and, hence, not very integrated schemata (see Fig. 1). However, such schemata may only characterize the nonparanoid schizophrenic. When we consider the paranoid schizophrenic, we find many rigid schemata (Magaro, 1980). Delusions may be seen as an example of a rigid schemata that is not modifiable by the usual amount of information input. The presence of delusional systems which often accompany paranoid schizophrenic disorders suggests that at least some schemata result in faulty, non-reality-based processing of information. Internal or external information may be processed in a consistently biased manner, with information consistent with the delusional system being assimilated, while incongruent information may be ignored or modified to fit the system. As those who have worked with schizophrenics, especially paranoids, can attest, modifying delusional content is a difficult, often frustrating task. We will now review efforts to produce changes in the content of delusional schematic system.

In an early report G. Davison (1966) described a combination of cognitive restructuring and relaxation therapy for 44-year-old male paranoid schizophrenic who believed that pressure points over his right eye were being caused by a spirit who helped him make decisions. Therapy consisted of redefining the cause of the pressure points as resulting solely from natural phenomena, which occurred when he became tense. Subsequent sessions over a 9-week period consisted of providing relaxation training as treatment for the pressure points, which continued to be explained as resulting from muscle tension. After 1 month the patient began to refer to the pressure points as sensations, while his conversation began to lose its "paranoid flavor." Six weeks following termination, the patient reported that the pressure points were no longer a concern and that a general improvement in his personal and professional life had occurred. Thus, the patient's delusional system was altered via subtly challenging this belief system. However, it is difficult to accurately attribute to which therapeutic agent the success was due: relaxation training, supportive psychotherapy, or the reattribution of the bodily sensations.

Watts, Powell, and Austin (1973) reported results of their attempt to modify the delusional system of paranoid schizophrenic patients. Noting that direct confrontation of the paranoid belief system might result in psychological reactance, the authors settled upon an indirect approach challenging the evidence of the belief. The belief modification program consisted of (1) challenging more weakly held beliefs, (2) asking the subject to consider alternative interpretations, and (3) examining the evidence for the subject's belief. Finally, the subject was encouraged to voice the arguments against his beliefs, as such a procedure had been demonstrated to be effective in facilitating attitude change (I. L. Janis and King, 1954). Following positive pilot data, two chronic paranoid schizophrenic patients were given this treatment. Results indicated that the belief modification program substantially reduced the strength of the paranoid belief systems. We interpret these results as having demonstrated that delusional schematic content may be altered by providing noncongruent information in a nonthreatening manner over time, allowing for their gradual integration into the schemata, resulting in a decrease of delusional symptomatology. Obviously, these results need to be cross-validated on a larger sample size. However, they are suggestive that delusional systems conceptualized as rigid schemata are amenable to alteration.

Other efforts have focused upon additional means by which to control delusional thought by altering schematic processes. Nydegger (1972) has reported his results of reattribution of delusional thoughts in a male paranoid schizophrenic. The therapist reinterpreted the delusional system as serving the purpose of keeping the patient from having to deal with certain life problems. Reattribution coupled with assertiveness training were found to produce a significant drop in number of delusional statements from 10 to 20 such statements per hour prior to therapy to a total disappearance of these statements after 6 weeks of therapy. Alford, Fleece, and Rothblum (1982) reported short-lived gains in the reduction of delusional verbalizations following cognitive restructuring and reattribution. Following discharge from the hospital, however, the delusions returned almost immediately. As troublesome schemata are ''likely to be retriggered when exposed to certain stressful events'' (Hollon & Kriss, 1984), the results of Alford *et al.* may be due to returning to a stressful environment.

As may be seen from the above discussion, schematic processes in schizophrenia are receiving attention. However, many questions remain to be answered. A number of difficulties exist with regard to issues of experimental design, including small sample sizes, inadequate outcome measures, inadequate follow-up periods, and problems arising from the concomitant use of a variety of treatment interventions. These problems make it difficult not only to ascertain what, if any, actual success has been attained, but also, to what aspect of the treatment these gains are due. However, these studies do suggest that schematic processes are amenable to change in schizophrenic patients. Future attention to specific aspects of the schematic processes pointed out by Hollon and Kriss (1984) such as theory-driven observational biases (D. Jennings *et al.*, 1982), self-fulfilling prophecy (J. M. Darley & Fazio, 1980), confirmatory biases (Rothbart, Evans, & Fulero, 1979), and conservative tendencies on the part of the individual with regard to rejection of a personally held belief (Nisbett & Ross, 1980) should produce valuable information regarding the treatment of the cognitive content of paranoid delusions.

From the above review it is obvious that a great deal of work remains to be done regarding treatment applications of the information processing paradigm to schizophrenia. Although initial efforts have attempted to attenuate and modify cognitive–perceptual deficits associated with schizophrenic disorders, this literature is far from mature. Aside from the difficulty of designing treatment interventions based upon the currently identified cognitive deficits and processes associated with schizophrenia, researchers in this area must also cope with a number of issues which plague all approaches to treatment. These include a host of confounding variables such as length of hospitalization, presence or absence of adjunct therapy (e.g., pharmacotherapy, individual psychotherapy, group psychotherapy), specificity regarding diagnosis, and severity of illness, to name a few. Further, one must contend with the pitfalls inherent in the measurement of treatment outcome, which are too numerous to enumerate here (see Lambert *et al.*, 1984). Although the list of hurdles to surmount is lengthy, the end result will hopefully justify the effort expended.

A Proposed Model for the Treatment of Paranoid and Nonparanoid Schizophrenia

In this section we will present a theoretical treatment approach for paranoid and nonparanoid schizophrenia based in part upon current literature regarding the cognitive processes thought to characterize these disorders. Following a brief exposition delineating the differences between the two schizophrenias, we will provide a basic outline for the treatment of these disorders in order to suggest the type of treatment techniques that may be developed from a theoretical interpretation of the available experimental literature on the etiology of schizophrenia. When appropriate, tasks found to be useful in the treatment of brain-injured patients will be incorporated into this discussion. Finally, we will describe an automated computer treatment battery currently being developed in our laboratory.

There is a growing body of evidence supporting the position that paranoid and nonparanoid types of schizophrenia are characterized by unique processing deficits (Magaro, 1980, 1984; Schizophrenia Bulletin, 1981). Briefly, paranoid schizophrenic patients are thought to work backward from the schemata to the icon, while the nonparanoid schizophrenic works forward. Thus, because the paranoid fails to consider the sensory context of the stimuli which provides the information that allows a fluidity of conceptualization, he or she has difficulty in situations requiring flexible schemata. The nonparanoid schizophrenic, however, shows a deficit in the organization of information in memory which prohibits the utilization of schemata.

We will now turn our attention to the treatment procedures which can be proposed from such a model of typical paranoid and schizophrenic cognitive functioning.

Paranoid Schizophrenia

Consistent with our thesis that paranoid and nonparanoid forms of schizophrenia involve different processing deficits, the following proposal for treating these disorders is tailored to the specific deficits identified as characterizing each group. The treatment that we propose involves intensive training on laboratory tasks. We argue that improved performance on these tasks would reflect a modification of the cognitive process which is responsible for the observed performance deficit on laboratory tasks. We further propose that task improvement should lead to generalized symptom reduction. A similar approach has been taken by investigators in the treatment of learning disabilities (Farnham-Diggory, 1978) and organic disorders (Gummow, Miller, & Dustman, 1983).

The treatment program for the paranoid consists of attempts to extend his perceptual input, that is, to increase recognition of a broader range of stimuli in terms of actual sitmulus properties. The first task consists of a simple cue attendance task. This involves the viewing of a scene for a specified period of time after which the subject is asked to describe a prescribed number of details within a specified time period. This training has been found not only to increase awareness about number of cues in the environment (Salamon & Suppes, 1971), but to also generalize to other dissimilar information-seeking tasks (Sieber & Lanzetta, 1966). Our program would therefore consists of having the paranoid perform this task with three task parameters (time of stimulus presentation, response interval time, and number of required responses) under the control of the therapist, beginning with simple levels and gradually increasing the difficulty by varying these parameters. Reinforcement for correct responses would also be a key aspect of training because it has been found to increase perceptual learning (Bijou & Baer, 1963). Thus, this task seeks to increase the paranoids awareness of his or her environment by gradually increasing difficulty and complexity until normal performance levels are reached.

The next stage for the treatment of the paranoid would consist of practice on a simple discrimination task to increase focal attention processes without the schematic bias. This task forces the paranoid to not only be aware of stimuli, but to also make discriminations between objects based upon their similarities and differences. With this task we seek to train the paranoid to incorporate a set of stimuli based upon the stimulus characteristics rather than being incorporated due to schema-driven processes. Training would begin with simple black–white types of discriminations, gradually becoming more complex up to and including discriminations between types of individuals, such as the difference between CIA agents and hospital staff. As with the cue attendance task, task performance would be reinforced for correct response.

The third proposed treatment task would involve training the paranoid to generate hypotheses to form new conceptual categories. We have argued that the paranoid has a conceptual bias, that is, the paranoid has strong associations which automatically activate specific schemata, preventing the recognition of discrepant stimuli. With this task we move away from primarily perceptual tasks to those requiring the integration of perceptual and schematic processes. This task, developed by Sieber and Lanzetta (1966), seeks to increase the possible number of conceptual categories or schemata into which perceptual data can be fitted. Training consists of presentation of a complex magazine picture, following which the subject is told to generate 10 hypotheses about the content of the picture as rapidly as possible. During the hypothesis generation period, a signal light remains on as long as the subject is generating different guesses about the picture content. If, however, more than 25 sec elapse between new guesses, the light goes out. The goal of training is for the subject to be able to generate 10 hypotheses in a rapid manner, precluding the extinguishing of the light for three successive pictures. Thus, this task calls upon the paranoid schizophrenic subject to form new conceptual categories using his or her new perceptual cues.

In summary, this proposed training sequence seeks to gradually increase the paranoid patient's attendance to stimuli and the production of new conceptual categories. We have not subjected this proposed treatment approach to experimental security; hence, at this time we can only demonstrate the devising of a procedure that flows from an information processing conception of the schizophrenic disorder.

Nonparanoid Schizophrenia

Unlike the paranoid, the nonparanoid schizophrenic is considered to be characterized by continually shifting concepts in the face of incoming information. That is, where the paranoid processes information from a schema-driven position, the nonparanoid appears to underutilize appropriate schematic processes. Thus, the treatment goal with the nonparanoid schizophrenic is to strengthen the conceptual framework by creating stable and enduring associations (schemata).

The first task could involve identification of gradual transpositions. This task is designed to teach the subject to rely upon conceptual rather than perceptual characteristics of the stimuli. This task consists of requiring the subject to respond to relations among stimuli, rather than responding to stimulus qualities (Reese & Lipsitt, 1970). For example, one might present the schizophrenic with two circles of different size, with the larger of the two being the correct stimulus to which to respond. Following an adequate level of performance, the individual is then presented with the circle deemed correct from the first series of trials and another larger circle. Again, the correct response would be to the new larger circle rather than the circle which was correct from the previous trial. Thus, in order to produce the correct response the subject must evaluate the stimuli using a conceptual rule (e.g., size) rather than responding to the absolute characteristics of the stimulus. Training would progress in difficulty and involve several modalities to facilitate the acquisition of conceptual abilities.

The second task designed to aid conceptual development in the nonparanoid schizophrenic involves the use of feedback in a multiple-cue learning task. As detailed by Todd and Hammond (1965), an individual is shown a series of three different-sized triangles each of which has a different number of the back. The triangles on the front of the card are related to the numbers on the back by different types of relationships. The task in this situation is to predict the numbers on the back of the card from the sizes of the triangles on the front. Providing feedback regarding the category and logical properties of the task rather than providing traditional (correct–incorrect) feedback has been found to increase performance (Todd & Hammond, 1965). Further, this increase in performance on this task has been shown to be due to an increase in cognitive consistency (Hammond & Summer, 1972). This task, therefore, would provide the conceptually deficit nonparanoid with training in several aspects of conceptual functioning: (1) dealing with predictions among relationships rather than stimulus qualities, (2) providing practice in modifying his or her conceptual categories by using feedback cues, and (3) increasing cognitive consistency through conceptually oriented feedback.

Thus, these two tasks, the transposition and multiple-cue learning task with feedback, provide a means by which the nonparanoid can develop and utilize conceptual categories. This training differs markedly from that of the paranoid schizophrenic who suffers from an overutilization of such conceptual (schematic) categories. We now turn our attention to another possible direction that could be pursued in the remediation of the cognitive deficits associated with schizophrenia.

Cognitive Rehabilitation and the Use of the Microcomputer

Although the etiology of cognitive deficits associated with brain damage may be quite different from the deficits associated with schizophrenia, approaches developed to remediate cognitive deficits associated with brain damage may be seen as a forerunner to what might be expected to be useful in the remediation of the cognitive deficits characterizing the schizophrenias.

In their review, Gummow, Miller, and Dustman (1983) divided the literature examining the management of cognitive deficits of brain-damaged adults into four basic types: (1) prosthetic environments (E. Miller, 1977), which involve the redesigning of living environments to meet the needs of the patients; (2) behavior modification techniques developed to manage problem behaviors (Goodkin, 1966); (3) cognitive stimulation, brought about by social visits, stimulating games, and reality-oriented classes (Barnes, 1974; Reinke, Holmes, & Denny, 1981); and (4) cognitive rehabilitation, which involves the designing of a program to address a specific cognitive deficit such as spatial neglect or memory deficits (Crovitz, 1979; Pattern, 1972; Weinberg *et al.*, 1979). Although we might identify treatment approaches to schizophrenia which correspond to each of the four types listed by Gummow *et al.*, it is the fourth intervention, cognitive rehabilitation, which bears most directly on the topic of this chapter.

Basically, programs designed to assist brain-damaged adults with memory, spatial, or visual deficits have utilized a forced-usage approach, consisting of repeated practice of the lost skill (Gummow *et al.*, 1983). This approach may be contrasted with the "teaching the strengths" approach seen in special education, which seeks to strengthen already dominant processes in order to overcome some deficit. The forced-usage approach has been found to increase the performance of brain-damaged adults in a number of deficient areas, including memory (Crovitz, 1979; Glasgow *et al.*, 1977), spatial deficits, and homonymous hemianopsia (Weinberg *et al.*, 1977, 1979), and left body-side neglect (Weinberg *et al.*, 1979). Gummow *et al.* (1983) concluded that diffusely organized functions such as memory and attention may be best treated in brain-damaged patients via repetitive practice and training in speeded reaction time. Further, these authors noted that short and frequent sessions are most acceptable to the patient, that the patient must be motivated to succeed, and that such training must consist of breaking down the material to be presented into simple units which gradually increase in difficulty.

As the reader may have noticed, brain-damaged and schizophrenic patients share some of the same cognitive difficulties. This is not to say that a common process underlies both. However, the success of the forced-usage approach in the treatment of brain-injured patients suggests that such treatment may also be beneficial to schizophrenic patients with similar deficits. We have seen in this chapter that the few cognitive-type interventions that have been reported present encouraging results (Adams *et al.*, 1981; Kaplan, 1974; Meiselman, 1973; Wagner, 1968). Additionally, the model for the treatment of paranoid and nonparanoid schizophrenia presented above also relies in part upon aspects of training identified by Gummow *et al.* (1983) to be important for the remediation of such deficits, such as the sequential progression from simple to more complex tasks and the use of short and frequent repetitive sessions. We would therefore expect that cognitive remediation approaches to the treatment of schizophrenia may find helpful the literature describing the rehabilitation of cognitive deficits in organic disorders.

We now turn our attention to the promising applications of the minicomputer in the treatment of cognitive deficits associated with schizophrenia. Gummow *et al.* (1983) noted that motivational concerns are crucial in ameliorating deficits with brain-damaged patients. They further noted that one promising motivational strategy involves the use of the microcomputer. Computers have a number of advantages as a trainer in areas where cognitive deficiencies exist: (1) The computer is infinitely patient; (2) it can present information in a manner that is at least acceptable and at best engaging to most adults; and (3) the computer frees the trainer or therapist to work with more than one patient at a time.

Given that many of the formulations concerning the information processing paradigm are couched in terms borrowed from the artificial intelligence field (Lachman & Lachman, this volume), it may perhaps only be fitting that we now consider the computer as a patient treatment tool for schizophrenia based upon the deficits identified from work in this area. Not only does the microcomputer possess a number of attributes which make it attractive from a practical perspective, but many of the treatment interventions we have described in this chapter seem to lend themselves quite readily to adaptation to a computer-presented format.

Over the past few years our laboratory has focused upon an assessment system that uses the model presented in Fig. 1 to identify the specific cognitive deficit. We believe that before engaging in a cognitive treatment approach, we first have to develop an assessment battery that identifies the specific cognitive deficit and provides a means to assess the effects of therapy. Our computer assessment battery employs the Commodore PET and Commodore 64 computers (Magaro & Ashbrook, 1984). To date we have written software programs for the assessment portion of the battery and then adapted commercially available games for use in the training portion of the battery. The assessment portion of the battery is based upon work from our own and other laboratories investigating the specific deficits thought to characterize paranoid and nonparanoid schizophrenics. The purpose of the battery is to diagnose the specific deficit or deficits of each individual so a prescriptive therapy could be applied. The specific cognitive tasks displayed in the battery are as follows.

Visual distraction task

The Visual Distraction Test is a variation of the Stroop (1935) procedure. Individuals are seated at a video screen and informed that their task is to name the colors of patches displayed on the screen. Twelve patches appear, three each of the colors red, blue, green, and yellow. All colors appear against a white background. The task is to name the color; the time taken to name each color and the accuracy of responses are tabulated. Next, color names printed in black against a white background are presented. The task is to read the color names as quickly as possible. Then, color names written in four discrepant colors are presented. The task is to name the color of the letters that compose the word, ignoring what the word actually says. The next condition asks for the name of the word, ignoring the color. The purpose of this task is to examine if the concept or the percept produces greater interference. The task provides a relative difference score between concept and percept interference to allow inferences about the strength of the percept relative to the concept.

Icon memory test

The features of iconic memory have been discussed above. The task that we employ to assess this stage of processing is a forced-choice span of apprehension test, a modification of the procedure used by Neale *et al.* (1969). The question which this task addresses is whether deficits can be identified in the strength of the iconic store combined with the decoding of the icon. First, visual arrays are created by allocating the letter *T* or *F* to one position of an imaginary square matrix of 16 character spaces. Each target letter, *T* or *F*, appears once on two separate arrays in each of the 16 possible matrix positions. In the next condition, a second set of arrays contain the target letter plus seven additional consonant letters. In this set of stimulus displays, a target letter is located in one of the possible 16 positions and then seven different consonant letters are randomly presented. The purpose here is to assess the ability to read simple and complex messages off the icon. The individual with such a deficit would have difficulty receiving any briefly presented information.

The encoding style test

This task is used to distinguish between automatic and controlled visual processing and is a variation of the Neisser (1963) procedure. The individual searches the array for a predesignated target letter. Two types of arrays are used. The target letter is always the letter *K*, however, distractor or context letters can be either rounded (*O, C, G, S, Q*) or straight-lined (*E, V, N, L, I*). Each trial block yields a slope statistic defined as the linear regression between reaction time and position of the target letter in the array. A second measure is the intercept, indicating the overall time to respond to the task. Following the rationale of S. Sternberg (1966), the intercept measure in a search procedure corresponds to a combination of decision making, response organization, and stimulus encoding (Neisser, 1967). The rounded distractors encourage an automatic search while the straight-lined distractors encourage a controlled search.

The purpose of the task is to ascertain which encoding strategy the individual prefers and which one is not applied when it is most appropriate to do so.

Continuous performance test

This version of the continuous performance test (CPT) is basically the same task as that employed by Erlenmeyer-Kimling and Cornblatt (1978). It is unlike the conventional CPT in that processing of two stimulus dimension (suit and number of playing card) is required, thus a relative rather than absolute target criterion is used, and successive matching-to-sample operations must be performed. Thus, there is an increased memory load requirement and a degree of complexity not characteristically found in other versions of the CPT. Of interest to us here is the separation of signal discriminability from response bias components of responding. Also of interest are the types of errors, such as errors of commission versus errors of omission, made by different groups.

Eighteen arrays are formed that partially resemble a deck of playing cards with numeral values between 1 and 9, across two suits, hearts and diamonds. In some trials, the playing card face is identical to that of the previous slide, marking a target (signal) trial. In other positions, the card face is the same as the previous one in number but not in suit, designating a nontarget (noise) trial. The remaining presentations differ in number and in suit from the previous array. The individual's task is to indicate if the card on the screen is identical in number and suit to the previous one.

Immediate memory test

This task is a variation of the S. Sternberg (1966) procedure designed to access short-term memory ability. Briefly, the task involves a set of detection trials in which a six-digit array of letters is viewed after which a box appears that is immediately filled with one numeral. The task is to indicate if the target number appeared in the original list of digits.

Semantic categorization test

This task is based on the feature comparison model of semantic memory (E. E. Smith, Shoben, & Rips, 1974). The basic idea is that a semantic categorization may require two distinct comparison stages depending on the nature of the categorization task. The representation of meaning is viewed as a collection of attributes, called semantic features. These vary continuously in the degree to which they confirm or define category membership, that is, they are weighted by their degree of "definingness." Thus, features at one extreme are essential for defining the concept, whereas features at the other extreme are only characteristic of the concept. The first comparison stage includes three processes. First, lists of features for the instance and category are retrieved, including features drawn from characteristics as well as defining dimensions. Next, these two lists are compared, with respect to all features, yielding a measure of overall similarity. This measure takes into account the proportion of the category's dimensions that are shared by the instance. The similarity measure is then compared to two criterial levels of overall similarity, a high level and a low level, that essentially serve as a response set determining the level of confidence necessary to make a decision. If similarity exceeds the high level, then the instance is judged as subsumed under the category; if it is less than the low level, it is interpreted as unrelated to the category. If similarity is in the intermediate range, a second comparison state is necessary before a decision can be determined. For both the category and the instance this second stage separates the more defining features from the characteristic ones and then compares the set of defining features of the category to those of the instance.

Recall and recognition test

These tasks follow the traditional procedure that involves the appearance of a word list followed by recall or recognition of the words. In addition to recall and recognition scores, this information is analyzed using heirarchical clustering techniques to estimate the organization patterns of information in the long-term memory store.

Summary

The individual receives training aimed at the amelioration of the specific deficit found to be present in the assessment battery. Once training is completed, the person is again tested on the assessment portion of the battery in order to evaluate performance. We are currently in the process of collecting normative data using this system. Given the marked proliferation of computer technology, we expect that other investigators will also be utilizing such an approach and other assessment, and treatment packages will hence be available to the practioner. Lynch (1984) has already presented a set of computer games to be used in a treatment of brain-injured patients. Such an approach appears to be growing in popularity, as evidence by his fifth edition of *Guide to Atari Videocomputer and Home Computer: Programs for Rehabilitation Settings*. In this rather detailed presentation of commerical software available for the Atari computer systems, Lynch presents a compilation of these programs, together with a description of which cognitive deficit each program might be most useful for. Although such programs might be extremely useful, such commercially available programs may prove to be too taxing for schizophrenic patients. A much more serious problem is the lack of a diagnostic battery to provide direction in the particular computer game that would be of most benefit to the particular patient.

Concluding Comments

As is demonstrated by the present volume, the information processing paradigm is a powerful method by which to elucidate and ameliorate cognitive deficits in a variety of disorders. Regarding the schizophrenias, the ability to identify such deficits appears to have outstripped the attempts to apply this knowledge to the treatment of these disorders. However, as the presence of certain cognitive deficits becomes more established in this area, researchers may direct their efforts more toward the treatment applications of this knowledge. Certainly the basic research identifying the deficits will remain the vital focus, yet given the information now available it appears that the time is right to apply this knowledge in a systematic manner to the treatment of cognitive processes in the schizophrenic disorders.

Acknowledgments

The authors wish to express their appreciation to the office staff here in the clinic and especially Cindy Greer for her attention to this paper.

15

Clinical Information Processing: Bias Inoculation

DENNIS C. TURK*
PETER SALOVEY
Department of Psychology
Yale University
New Haven, Connecticut 06520

Everyone makes numerous decisions daily. Frequently, these decisions are made without access to all of the potentially relevant information. Consequently, it is rare for any decision to be made without some degree of uncertainty. Many of these decisions are made in an automatic fashion, with minimal conscious processing and without serious consequences for the decision maker. This "automatic" decision making is efficient and appropriate for most everyday decisions (e.g., "What should I wear today?" "Should I order a steak and cheese grinder, a pepperoni pizza, or a gyro for lunch?") since the consequences of the decision are minor. Even when more is at stake, individuals rarely have adequate time to perform an exhaustive search and decision analysis. As Simon (1957) suggests, individuals tend to "satisfice" rather than "maximize." That is, individuals select an alternative decision that they believe to be at least adequate, if not necessarily optimal.

When using automatic modes of decision making, individuals rely upon a number of overlearned, cost-effective, inferential shortcuts or heuristics (Tversky & Kahneman, 1973). For example, they attend to salient features of a situation or individual, and they make decisions based on how representative a

*Present address: Center for Pain Evaluation and Treatment, School of Medicine, University of Pittsburgh, Pittsburgh, Pennsylvania 15260.

INFORMATION PROCESSING APPROACHES
TO CLINICAL PSYCHOLOGY

situation or person is believed to be of a general category (e.g., "He's an "Archie-Bunker" type, and thus he is likely to respond in ways that are similar to how I would expect Archie Bunker to respond in a similar situation"). Although these heuristics promote efficiency, they may contribute to less than optimal decisions.

Mental health professionals, by the nature of their work, are frequently required to make important decisions under conditions of uncertainty. Uncertainty arises from inevitable errors in observation or reporting; from variations in interpretation of the data, both between clinicians and within a single clinician over time; from the ambiguity of the language used to describe clinical findings and manifestations; from the probabalistic character of the relation between clinical information and presence of psychological distress in clients; and from changes in the clinical picture as the case unfolds, resulting from changes in the current state of knowledge and reliance on a priori theoretical orientations. Moreover, clinicians are largely dependent on the self-reports of their clients that are potentially biased, wittingly or unwittingly.

Clinical judgment has traditionally been thought to be acquired chiefly through personal experience, observation, supervision, and conversation with peers and experienced practitioners. Most training programs do not favor systematic teaching of problem solving, inferential, and decision-making skills. This neglect is not confined only to the practice of clinical psychology. Medical educators have raised similar concerns about the training of physicians (e.g., Howe, Holmes, & Elstein, 1984).

Research on decision making under uncertainty reveals that errors of judgment are often systematic rather than random, reflecting biases inherent in our cognitive apparatus rather than mere confusion (Kahneman & Tversky, 1973). These errors of judgment are shared by laypeople and by experts whose livelihoods are based on their ability to make appropriate decisions, including stockbrokers (e.g., Stael von Holstein, 1972), electrical engineers (Kidd, 1970), intelligence analysts (R. V. Brown, Kahr, & Peterson, 1974; Janis & Mann, 1977), physicians (e.g., Elstein & Bordage, 1979; Zieve, 1966), and mental health professionals (e.g., Turk & Salovey, 1985). In the next section, we will briefly describe some of the sources of bias (for more extended discussions, see Kahneman, Slovic, & Tversky, 1982; Nisbett & Ross, 1980; Turk & Speers, 1983).

Common Sources of Bias in Clinical Judgment

Confirmatory Biases

Preexisting knowledge structures, or schemata, filter incoming stimuli prior to any decision-making process. That is, through training and the development of a theoretical orientation, organized sets of expectancies become a part of (and influence) every clinician's decisional processes. These expectancies are necessary in order to sort out the plethora of information presented by clients and to make decisions reasonably quickly. They influence the types of questions that clinicians ask and the information encoded and later retrieved. However, these expectations, deriving from various theoretical orientations, can bias data-gathering processes, particularly when clinicians seek to confirm existing hypotheses (Bieri, Atkins, Briar, Leaman, & Miller, 1966; Meehl, 1954; Mischel, 1968; Sarbin, Taft, & Bailey, 1960; M. Snyder, 1981b).

As classic research on implicit personality theory has demonstrated, initial conceptualizations of clients often developed rapidly from limited information (Asch, 1946; Bruner & Tagiuri, 1954; Meehl, 1960). The particularly pernicious aspect of this tendency is that once a judgment about a client has been made, it is subsequently used as a basis for later inferences about the person, independent of the information upon which the judgment was originally based. Moreover, these judgments show great tenacity (Carlston, 1977; Srull & Wyer, 1979). That is, once such a judgment has been made, it is typically adhered to vigorously, even in the presence of new, disconfirming information (L. Ross, *et al.*, 1975; M. Rubin & Shontz, 1960). New data are often used to confirm existing hypotheses rather than to test alternatives or to generate competing formulations (see M. Snyder, 1981b). Meehl (1960) noted that clinicians form "images" of their clients within the first 4 hours of psychotherapy, and they staunchly adhere to these beliefs, expectancies, and hypotheses.

Clinicians often observe merely what they expect to observe. And since clinicians usually expect to observe pathology, they may report it even when there is little evidence on which to base such a conclusion (see Rosenhan, 1973; Turk & Salovey, in press). Such attempts to root out pathology from assessment protocols by experienced clinicians may explain the results of several studies reviewed by Mischel (1968) in which nonpsychologists and novices do as well, if not better, than experienced clinicians in their interpretation. Unfortunately, once labels are ascribed to a client they are "sticky," as Rosenhan (1973) has observed, and no matter how clients behave, they often cannot convince their therapists to change their initial assessments. The non-occurrence of deviant behavior after the initial labeling seems to be ignored.

Not only must clinicians be concerned with the influence of a priori hypotheses on the attention to and interpretation of data, but they should also be concerned about the impact of their behavior on the *creation* of confirming data, so-called self-fulfilling prophesies. That is, the behavior or questions asked by clinicians may elicit information from a client that will confirm prior expectations. For example, asking a client about his conflicts with his mother will elicit responses about such conflicts, and asking questions in an accusatory manner may elicit a hostile response from the client. In this way, the clinician may actually create the confirming evidence that he or she set out to find (see M. Snyder, 1981b; Turk & Salovey, 1985; Turk & Speers, 1983).

Anchoring and Adjustment

Anchoring, and subsequent failures in inferential adjustment, is a type of confirmatory bias whereby once a decision is made, subsequent information fails to modify expectations or appraisals to a sufficient degree (Nisbett & Ross, 1980). Initial estimates or predictions based on preliminary appraisals serve as the basis for subsequent judgments. Later appraisals and decisions are heavily influenced or "anchored" by the initial appraisal. This problem may occur even when we are aware of possible sources of bias in those initial decisions.

Some examples may serve to clarify the anchoring problem. Tversky and Kahneman (1974) provided subjects with an initial estimate of the number of African countries in the United Nations. Subjects were told that they could adjust this estimate if they thought it was inaccurate. If the initial estimate was stated as 10%, subjects adjusted it to 25%. But, if the initial estimate provided was "anchored" at 65%, subjects adjusted it to 45%. Thus, the difference in subjects' judgments, 25 versus 45%, was due entirely to the anchoring effect of the initial information with which subjects were presented. Once an initial judgment is "on the books," individuals are quite resistant to "further information, alternative modes of reasoning, or even evidential challenges" (Nisbett & Ross, 1980, p. 41).

Anchoring gives excessive weight to initial information that subsequently serves as the template against which newly acquired information is contrasted and weighed. Clinicians inferences are frequently the result of an overreliance on information revealed about a client during the intake process, despite contradictory information gleaned later during the course of psychotherapy. In fact, the psychodiagnostic system can anchor therapists' future judgments: Once clients are diagnosed psychotic, it is difficult for them to ever be seen as normal. The diagnosis of psychosis serves to "anchor" all future judgments about them. Despite evidence to the contrary, judgments will prove biased in the direction of psychosis. Perhaps these processes account for the tendency to diagnose patients as "in remission" rather than as "recovered" or "normal" when they are released from mental hospitals (see Rosenhan, 1973).

The Availability Heuristic

Information that is easily "brought to mind," perhaps because it was perceptually salient or vivid, is said to be more "available." When individuals estimate the frequency or probability of an event or outcome by the ease with which it is brought to mind, they are said to be employing the availability heuristic (Tversky & Kahneman, 1973). Unique cases of pathology, counterintuitive insights, and dramatic successes and failures are likely to be more available to the clinician than are routine examples of individuals dealing with more mundane problems, and so judgments are often unduly influenced by these memories. Freud treated a large number of patients, often as many as 10 a day during his practice. Yet he based much of his theorizing on a few rather vivid cases—a woman with a glove anesthesia, a man who dreamed of rats crawling into his anus—as opposed to the hosts of more routinely distressed (and thus less interesting and dramatic) individuals that he must have also treated.

As another example, we often overestimate the dangerousness of discharged mental patients because the occasional violent patient sticks in one's mind, with help from media coverage, while the more typical ex-patient who lives out a rather uneventful life is not as easily recalled. Since the dramatic, violent instances are more easily remembered, the clinician may judge a particular client as having a greatly inflated chance of being dangerous, ignoring base-rate data suggesting that discharged mental patients are rarely violent. This is a simple example of the lack of attention given to the non-occurrence of events which, from a probablistic, Bayesian perspective, should be given equal weight. (We are reminded of Sherlock Holmes, in "The Case of Silver Blaze," observing that when the horse was stolen, the watch dog *did not bark,* indicating that the person who stole the horse was known to the dog. The *non-occurrence* of barking was the most significant fact.)

The Representativeness Heuristic

When clinicians must judge how likely it is an individual is a member of a particular category or how likely a given outcome can be explained by a particular set of antecedents, they frequently rely on a decision-making strategy called the representativeness heuristic (Kahneman & Tversky, 1972, 1973; Tversky & Kahneman, 1974). Representativeness refers to judgments based on the degree to which a given stimulus or evidentiary base matches the essential features of some schema (or a priori hypothesis). To make accurate decisions, one must consider the probability of encountering a category member as well as a non member by chance, given that they both exhibit some diagnostic sign. However, we often under utilize some of this important base-rate information and, instead, selectively attend to information that seems to fit a certain pre-existing set of expectancies.

Contexts like the case conference often induce clinicians to make high base-rate statements about their clients or about their work, even though they think the issue is unique to their particular case. For example, at a recent case conference we attended, evidence was presented regarding an adolescent boy's concern about masturbation based solely on the results of a Draw-A-Person test, in which the boy drew a figure with hands behind the figure's back. Whether such an interpretation was based on an illusory correlation (described below) or was motivated by the clinician's desire to avoid possible errors and consequent ridicule by her peers is unclear, but it does seem to be a rather safe statement about adolescent boys—that they have some concerns regarding masturbation (see Meehl, 1973, for a detailed description of reasons why he no longer attends case conferences).

Clinicians tend to draw more confidence from a small body of consistent data than from a larger body of less consistent information. In the search for coherence, clinicians, like all individuals, often see patterns where none exist. They reinterpret data so as to increase the data's apparent consistency and ignore or discount evidence that does not fit their expectancies. In this manner, clinicians are likely to overestimate the consistency of data and consequently be overconfident in their judgments based on such data.

The Uniqueness or Preciousness Heuristic

We might postulate an extension to the representativeness heuristic that is of particular concern for clinical practitioners called the uniqueness or preciousness heuristic, perhaps captured by the frequent statement made by clinicians: "We aren't dealing with groups, we are dealing with the individual case" (Meehl, 1973). The erroneous assumption here is that probability logic does not apply to the individual case. There seems to be a tendency to neglect distributional data and to rely mainly on single case information when the context increases the uniqueness of the problem or the individual. Although each client *is* unique in many characterisitics, there is always some distributional information that should be considered. The relevance of distributional data can be masked by detailed acquaintance with the specific case or intense involvement as in psychotherapy.

In elementary courses in statistics, we all learned about normal distributions and the fact that large samples are likely to be more representative of the population studied. As a corollary, we should also have learned that small samples are more likely to deviate from the general class than large samples. Tversky and Kahneman (1971) noted that individuals seem to be unaware of this fact and believe that small samples are likely to be equally representative of the larger population. When clinicians interview clients or administer specific assessment instruments, they observe a small sample of the client's behavior and tend to assume that this sample is representative of the client's general population of behaviors.

This problem is what some have viewed as the "sign" versus the "sample" approach to the assessment of individuals (J. W. Wiggins, 1973). The client's behavior is viewed as a sign of some inherent characteristic (e.g., trait, need, conflictual area); and the observed behavior is thought to correspond directly to this underlying feature. The sample approach assumes that any observation about a client is merely a sample of his or her behavior, which does not necessarily relate to underlying personality characteristics. Clinicians must acknowledge that they only have access to a small fragment of potential information about their clients. We cannot be sure that what we have observed is a reliable sample of some general mode of responding, uninfluenced by the social context where the behavior was sampled. For example, how diagnostic would it be to learn from our client that in church he tends to be quiet and reserved or at a football game verbalizes passionately? Clinicians need to consider the reliability of any small sample of behaviors and to be cautious about making predictions based on potentially unreliable evidence.

Additionally, statistical regression is often ignored. That is, the more extreme an individual's behavior, the more likely it will ultimately be followed by behavior that is more typical or "average." Predictions based on extreme behaviors are likely to be erroneous. Regression effects may account for the observation that many clients drop out of treatment or do not come for initially scheduled interviews. It is quite possible that self-referrals are more frequent when situations and symptoms seem more severe. When examined at another point in time, the same situation might be evaluated quite differently.

Illusory Correlation

Another source of error in decision making derives from difficulties that individuals have with intuitively correlated events: They tend to perceive associations between events even when they are aware that the relation between the events is incidental (Tversky & Kahneman, 1980). For example, the Chapmans have noted in their research on this problem (Chapman, 1967; Chapman & Chapman, 1967, 1969) that certain kinds of patient responses on projective tests lead clinicians to make specific psychopathological diagnoses (e.g., distorted eyes on a Draw-A-Person test represent clinical suspiciousness and paranoia; a male patient seeing buttocks in Rorschach inkblots indicates homosexuality; or as noted earlier, creating a Draw-A-Person picture with hands behind the back is associated with masturbation) even though there is no objective evidence (i.e., validity studies) to support such relationships.

When presented with evidence to the contrary, clinicians in these studies showed remarkable consensus in believing that certain projective test percepts were clear diagnostic signs, even though no verifiable association between the response and the particular diagnosis actually exists (see L. Ross *et al.*, 1975, for a demonstration of the perserverance of beliefs even in the light of direct information to the contrary). This is not to suggest that clinicians cannot correctly observe covariation or use situational information appropriately. Rather, it suggests that when information is ambiguous, belief about covariation may influence the perception of covariation even when such associations are invalid (see Alloy & Tabachnick, 1984; R. S. Lazarus, 1966).

Debiasing the Clinician

The many potential sources of errors and biases in decision making have been detailed at length by Nisbett and Ross (1980), Meehl (1973) and in a book edited by Kahneman *et al.* (1982). After exploring the range of biases produced by the basic mechanism of information processing, you may feel that the situation is hopeless. You may be demoralized and immobilized, suffering from "learned helplessness," like M. E. P. Seligman's (1975) dogs who discover that there is little they can do to influence outcomes. You may feel like the clinician in Fig. 1.

Some of you may feel that we are about to do yet another "hatchet job" on clinical practitioners, describing in even more detail their ineptitude. You may easily call to mind the acrimonious debates that followed the publication of Meehl's treatise on clinical versus actuarial prediction (see Holt, 1970; Meehl, 1954, 1960).

We urge you to take heart and read on. It is not our intention to denigrate practitioners. The remainder of this chapter is concerned with strategies to *combat* bias and *improve* upon clinical decision making. Experience has taught us that it is insufficient to simply point out potential problems without suggesting some alternatives. The behaviorists have sensitized us to this problem with their concern about the merit of insight without corresponding behavioral change.

To change behavior, one needs to have knowledge (insight) of both problems and alternative strategies (skills), as well as some degree of confidence in one's ability to make use of these skills. We are not suggesting that all of the potential sources of bias are always detrimental. Obviously they have some survival value. Nor are we suggesting that one can ever eliminate them. Rather, we are concerned with strategies that might be utilized to circumvent some of the most troubling information processing errors. We will consider the range of alternatives (strategies) available to "inoculate" the clinician against some of the most persistent and detrimental sources of error in decision making.

The potential for biases to influence judgment is not a particularly novel idea. Philosophers, scientists, clinicians, and mystery writers alike have noted the problem. Even Freud (cited in Malcolm, 1983) was aware of the potential for biases to influence the nature of therapy (and consequently his theory). In describing his seduction theory (wish fulfillment and the nature of the Oedipal complex), he noted,

> When, I was at last obliged to recognize that the scenes of seduction had never taken place, and that they were only fantasies which my patients had made up or which *I myself had perhaps forced on them* [emphasis added], I was for some time completely at a loss. My confidence alike in my technique and its results suffered a severe blow; it could not be disputed that I had arrived at these scenes by a technical method which I considered correct. (p. 103)

Debiasing Research

What is perhaps most surprising about the clinical decision-making literature is the relative inattention that has been given to the issue of "debiasing." Most investigators are content to either identify yet another source of bias or to debate the inherent rationality of people (e.g., L. J. Cohen, 1981). Although these approaches have some merit, they are of little utility in assisting clinicians who must, in the end, rely on their judgment and come to specific conclusions about their clients.

We will base our discussion on the few papers and book chapters that have appeared and that address this issue (e.g., C. A. Anderson, 1982; Arkes, 1981; Kahneman & Tversky, 1979, 1982; Nisbett & Ross, 1980). It is important to realize that these discussions are largely speculative, and only a few attempts have been made to evaluate strategies to debias actual decisions. These have tended to focus on decisions in laboratories rather than in naturalistic settings (e.g., C. A. Anderson, 1982).

One of the major concerns in clinical practice is the potential bias provided by clinicians' theoretical orientation, idiosyncratic attitudes, beliefs, values related to their psychological needs, conflicts, prior learning history, a priori theories, and stereotypic beliefs (Turk & Salovey, 1985; Turk & Speers, 1983). Psychoanalysts have been aware of this problem for many years and have focused on the importance of countertransference or the projection of their own conflicts onto the client. The suggested strategy for dealing with this issue is the "training analysis," where analysands gain insight into their personal conflicts, needs, and so forth, and this insight is believed to be sufficient to alleviate the problems of bias in clinical judgment. Is personal analysis necessary? Although this may be a useful approach, it may be especially costly and does not directly address the many sources of bias described earlier. Moreover, personal analysis might serve to solidify the analysands' implicit theories and lead to little consideration of alternative explanations.

The available research emphasizes the efficacy of explicitly generating and evaluating competing hypotheses to prevent biased information processing. Einhorn and Hogarth (1982) and C. A. Anderson (1982) both suggest that the generation of alternative causal hypotheses to account for observed "evidence" can serve to reduce the impact of the clinician's initial theory. They suggest that an individual decision maker compare the evidence at hand with "what might have been." That is, the decision maker anchors his or her appraisal of the evidence on what hypothesis is most readily called to mind and adjusts his or her acceptance of that hypothesis based on any other alternative hypotheses possible. Failure to generate alternative hypotheses will, according to Einhorn and Hogarth (1982), result in confirmation of the initial hypothesis. However, if

FIG. 1. *The perplexed clinician contemplating what to ask his new client. He must consider the following possibilities:*

A. My *a priori* theories and stereotypes might influence what questions I ask.

B. The answers to the questions that I ask may be distorted to fit my theoretical orientation.

C. I may selectively recall information to confirm my initial hypotheses.

D. My own mood may influence what questions I ask.

E. My initial hypotheses may lead me to differentially weigh some information and discount other information.

F. Salient characteristics of the client and information provided may be more accessable.

G. I may be projecting my own conflicts and needs on to the client.

H. The questions that I ask may influence the type of information that I obtain.

I. My interpersonal style may influence her responses.

J. I may inadvertently be selectively reinforcing her provision of some information and the withholding of other material.

K. My initial predictions about the client may serve to anchor subsequent predictions making them too liberal or too conservative.

L. The client's gender may influence the questions that I ask, my interpretations of her responses, and the nature of my predictions.

M. The client's age may influence the questions that I ask, my interpretations of her responses, and the nature of my predictions.

N. The client's socioeconomic status may influence the questions that I ask, my interpretations of her responses, and the nature of my predictions.

O. The client's religion may influence the questions that I ask, my interpretations of her responses, and the nature of my predictions.

P. The client's physical appearance may influence the questions that I ask, my interpretations of her responses, and the nature of my predictions.

Q. The client reminds me of "Edith Bunker," and this fact may influence my expectancies.

R. My behavior may be influenced by what she tells me.

S. Since any question that I ask will provide some confirmatory evidence, I can never acquire disconfirming evidence for any hypothesis.

T. Once diagnosed, the client may act to confirm my initial formulation.

U. I may selectively recall salient information or characteristics.

V. I may selectively recall information to confirm my stereotype.

W. I may interpret her responses as supporting a particular hypothesis, but this may be the result of an illusory correlation.

X. My own mood may affect what I remember about the client.

Y. I may be ignoring baserates or be unaware of the appropriate baserates to employ! . . .

Z. I wonder if it is too late to become an accountant or perhaps to rejoin my old jazz band?

decision makers can generate alternatives and evaluate these, they are less likely to attend to exclusively confirmatory evidence. This view is consistent with the Kuhnian notion that theories in science are not discarded, despite evidence to the contrary, they are just *replaced* by better alternatives (Kuhn, 1962).

Asking questions that falsify one hypothesis while confirming a second is perhaps the ideal strategy. Einhorn and Hogarth (1982) describe decision making as replacement. Decision makers are more likely to give up erroneous theories if they can replace them with alternative ones. Explicit specification of alternatives should make these more "available" and consequently more capable of being tested, confirmed, and falsified. If the decision does not have an available alternative, clinicians may be biased to accept the existing hypothesis. The availability of no hypothesis may be anxiety arousing (Einhorn & Hogarth, 1983; J. C. Wright & Murphy, 1984).

It is important that decision makers generate *plausible* scenarios that are capable of explaining the observed evidence. They should consider not only "what is" but "what might have been." In addition, more attention needs to be paid to situational factors that might have influenced the observed behavior; the behavior may not be an inherent characteristic of the client. Thus, the ability of clinicians to use their imagination becomes critical to accurate decision making. Strict adherence to a theoretical perspective without ability to generate alternatives will likely lead to biased decisions. Thus, decision makers need to consider not only how the evidence fits one specific hypothesis, but how it fits or fails to fit competing hypotheses. If clinicians can generate competing, mutually exclusive hypotheses, they can ask questions that at the same time provide evidence to support one hypothesis while disconfirming a second.

Nisbett, Ross, and their colleagues (Nisbett & Ross, 1980; Nisbett, Krantz, Jepson, & Kunda, 1983) also emphasize the importance of deautomatizing decision making. They suggest that a set of maxims may be valuable in combating the biasing effects of both theories and "heuristics" (e.g., "You can always explain away the exceptions" or "What about the other three cells?").

Nisbett *et al.* (1983) also suggest that the combination of these statistical rules or maxims and formal training in the use of statistical procedures should be employed to increase the likelihood that individuals will come to less biased decisions. However, Tversky and Kahneman (1980) report that even those who are trained in decisional sciences are prone to many of the same errors as those who have not received such training. Mahoney (1976) demonstrated that even scientists trained in the scientific method and in statistics resorted to heuristics and confirmatory biases when they moved beyond their own area of expertise. The problem here may be the style rather than the content of the training that is provided. Abstract presentation of didactic information with little opportunity for direct exposure to the experience of making errors and assessment of this process would not be likely to generalize beyond the classroom.

Generating competing hypotheses and scenarios is important, but clinicians also need to consider feedback as to their own successes and failures in utilizing information to make predictions. We are reminded of Theodor Reik's 1948 book *Listening with the Third Ear,* in which he described what appears to be an amazing, intuitive insight into the hidden meaning of his client's statement that one of Reich's book was upside-down on the bookshelf, "revealing" that she had an abortion. But we are not told of the number of his incorrect interpretations. It is all too easy to recall dramatic successes and to disregard those instances in which we made an erroneous conclusion or decision.

A cautionary note: Feedback is not necessarily corrective. It can be ambiguous, misleading, and difficult to discern. Keeping a log or diary of the outcomes of specific decisions would be useful in identifying the nature of successes and failures, and these could be carefully examined to identify what factors might have contributed to the adequacy of decisions and predictions.

Clinicians should consider the utility of developing algorithms to assist in clinical decision making as analogous to those used in medical decision making (e.g., Zarin & Pauker, 1984) and described in the third edition of the *Diagnostic and Statistical Manual of Mental Disorders* (American Psychiatric Association, 1980). For example, if the options for available treatment are group versus individual, what types of questions would be employed to assist in the decision, with certain client responses leading to one type of question and other responses leading to a different set of questions?

A particular strategy that may be relevant in light of the preceding paragraph was articulated by Benjamin Franklin (quoted in Dawes & Corrigan, 1974, p. 95):

> I cannot for want of sufficient premises advise you *what* to determine, but if you please I will tell you how. My way is to divide half a sheet of paper by a line into two columns; writing over the one *Pro* and the other *Con,* then . . . I put down under the different heads short hints of the different motives, that at different times occur to me for or against the measure. When I have them all together in one view, I endeavor to estimate the respective weights, to find at length where the balance lies.

Janis and Mann (1977) describe what appears to be an analogous procedure, called the balance sheet, for assistance in decision making. What Franklin and Janis and Mann are suggesting is that the process of listing and evaluating the evidence, both for and against a hypothesis, assists the decision maker by focusing his or her attention on each side or competing hypotheses.

Bias Inoculation

Our discussion to this point has focused upon the information available regarding factors that might improve decision making—the "what" of debiasing but not the "how." Simply reading information of the type that we have been reviewing is not likely to lead to behavioral change (Bandura, 1977b). How can we "inoculate" clinical decision makers so that they make less biased decisions?

Let us first note what we mean by bias inoculation. We are using the term *inoculation* in a similar way as it is used in medicine and, more recently, in relation to stress (Meichenbaum & Cameron, 1983; Meichenbaum & Novaco, 1976; Meichenbaum & Turk, 1976). Inoculation implies that the individual is "injected" with a small quantity of a virus in order to build up an immunity. In the case of bias inoculation, we would propose subjecting individuals to small doses of information and actual experience where they have opportunities to make a range of errors with subsequent opportunities for case analyses and feedback. This procedure will assist in inoculating them against these "pathogens" in subsequent situations. Note that inoculation implies direct exposure and not simply receipt of didactic information. Here we are making a distinction between what may be viewed as a knowledge and skill deficiencies (inadequate information) from production deficencies (failures to implement appropriate skills or bring relevant knowledge to bear when appropriate for the situation at hand).

Bandura (1977b) has suggested that behavior change can be brought about in four different ways, namely, verbal persuasion, vicarious experience, emotional arousal, and performance accomplishments. Although he was specifically referring to how psychotherapies bring about changes in perceptions of self-efficacy, we believe that the sources of information that he outlined may be as relevant for assisting in short-circuiting the impact of some of the potential sources of error in decision making or what we think of as bias inoculation. We would expect that all four sources of information are important for the production of behavior change, expecially actual performance.

Borrowing from Bandura's (1977b) conception of efficacy expectations, we can distinguish between outcome efficacy, or the belief that information and training are likely to lead to desirable results, and self-efficacy, the belief held by the individual that he or she can actually perform the task at a sufficient level of proficiency. To illustrate, clinical psychologists may, after reading about Bayes' theorem (suggesting that base-rate information needs to be attended to), conclude that using this device should improve decision making (outcome efficacy). Yet, the psychologists may not believe that they have the ability to calculate all of the components of the theorem (i.e., base rates, prior odds, likelihood ratio), and, thus, they would be said to have low senses of self-efficacy. Both types of efficacy expectations seem to be necessary for confident, reliable behavior (Bandura & Cervone, 1983; Barrios & Niehaus, 1984; Condiotte & Lichtenstein, 1981).

The distinction between outcome efficacy and self-efficacy might be viewed here as a distinction between the information and skills necessary for clinicians to possess and how this information should be provided so that it is most likely to be accessed in specific situations. That is, we believe that it is necessary to provide students or clinicians with certain types of information, but this is not sufficient to guarantee its use. In addition to merely providing information, it is important to consider how it should be presented for maximal impact on behavior. Didactic presentation or verbal persuasion may be sufficient to produce high levels of outcome efficacy, but they will not lead to enhanced self-efficacy.

Most of us tend to believe that we are not prone to many of the errors described above, disregarding Fischhoff's (1975) argument that hindsight is not equal to foresight. We can look back upon another person's decision, given knowledge of its outcome, and believe that we would never have made these errors.

Metacognition

Shiffrin and Schneider (1977) have made a distinction between automatic and controlled information processing. Automatic processing is conceptualized as being routine, requiring minimal conscious attention, whereas controlled processing requires conscious awareness of cognitive activities. Novices in many areas begin with controlled processing, and as they become more expert, it becomes more automatic. The same processes may characterize clinical practice and may explain why the evidence does not support any decisional advantage of clinicians with greater number of years of experience (Crow, 1957; L. R. Goldberg, 1959). What seems important, then, is for decision makers, especially in ambiguous situations, to engage in more controlled processing and greater self-interrogation. There is a need to balance concerns about premature closure with those of problems of collecting highly redundant information that may rigidify our expectations.

An important concept that will characterize all of our suggestions for debiasing and bias inoculation is that of metacognition. According to Flavell (1979), metacognition is the awareness and monitoring of one's own cognitive processing, including memory, comprehension, knowledge, goals, and, in general, cognitive resources. Flavell has outlined three components of metacognitive inquiry that are of clinical importance. Person variables include facets of social understanding such as self-perception, self-monitoring, and, in general, what individuals know regarding themselves and others as cognitive processors. Task variables include the awareness of what cognitive resources (quantity and quality of information) can be applied to the solving of various problems. Finally, the monitoring to strategies includes the awareness of how one determines a path of action toward the accomplishment of a goal. Clinical decision makers need to attend to these components of metacognition and to become aware of their knowledge bases, attending to what they know and do not know. One way to foster this self-knowledge is to teach clinicians how to engage in appropriate self-interrogation.

It is useful to ask decision makers to identify counterarguments so that both sides of the issue can be considered. For example, we would encourage clinicians to pose to themselves such questions as "What are my hypotheses about this client and the causes of the presenting problem?" "What competing hypotheses might explain the data?" "What data would be required to falsify my initial hypotheses while providing some support for an alternative?" "What information was not present that if my hypothesis was true I would have expected?" Explicitly describing our thinking may alert us to errors and biases in our formulations and conclusions.

Self-interrogation and "thinking aloud" are important debiasing strategies as they serve to deautomatize our decisional processes and permit us to become more aware of our own thinking. In working with students, it may be helpful to provide tasks where they are asked to write up their intake cases from a theoretical perspective different from their own. This procedure will induce students to attend to alternative ways of interpreting data. Students could also role-play convincing someone else of the problems related to sources of bias and thereby generate persuasive arguments on their own.

Students and novices learn a great deal about clinical practice from their supervisors. A potentially useful strategy to employ is to have supervisors model their decision making. Bandura (1977b) has suggested that modeling is one of the ways in which people learn new behaviors. Supervisors thinking aloud about specific cases and formulations as well as predictions may serve as an important vehicle to encourage fledgling clinicians to engage in similar processes. Tapes of expert clinicians and decision makers might also be developed to illustrate the merit of self-interrogation.

Discussions and Socratic dialogues would appear to be additional strategies of some potential in clinical training. Didactic instruction and presentation are important strategies for conveying information, but verbal persuasion is less likely to lead to behavior change. Within this discussion, the applicability of the body of literature to clinical situations and cases can be raised. Examination of the biases of clients can serve to illustrate how these sources of error may inhibit optimal decisions and behavior. It seems more palatable to identify the errors in others than in ourselves.

Yet, regardless of how well didactic material is presented, decisions makers must acknowledge the *importance* of this information. Moreover, they must believe that knowledge of such information can inhibit the production of some of the major errors. Demonstrating how the awareness of biases and decision rules can prevent erroneous conclusions is especially important in enhancing outcome efficacy. Clinicians need to see that there are potential remedies for reducing errors, if not totally eliminating them. This insight is necessary, but not sufficient, to ensure that clinicians attend to biases in their clinical work.

Summary and Conclusions

We divided our chapter into two major sections. In the first, we discussed some of the limitations on human information processing and described how these can result in biases in clinical inference and judgment. In the second section, we reviewed the nascent literature on debiasing and outlined ways in which clinicians might avoid or reduce some of the judgmental pitfalls. In this manner, we attempted to inoculate the reader against some of the most common inferential traps.

Unlike other papers that have appeared on clinical judgment, we have not set out to demonstrate that clinicians are particularly poor at making decisions (see, e.g., Mischel, 1968 chap. 5). Rather we sought to convey the fact that clinicians, in common with laypeople, possess cognitive systems that foster the use of specific processing heuristics that may serve them well most of the time but may contribute to less than optimal decision making. Like bartenders, hair dressers, and cab drivers, clinicians develop and maintain cognitive representations (i.e., schemas, stereotypes, theoretical orientations) that filter the information that is observed and guide what is recalled. Moreover, these cognitive representations can influence our weighting of information and even affect our behavior so that we elicit hypothesis-consistent information. The main message of the first section of this chapter, then, is that our clinical training does *not* make us immune to biased and heuristically driven processing.

Rather, what our clinical training does lead to is *overconfidence* in our clinical judgment. Although we are well aware that computers rigidly adhering to a particular decision rule are better at common ''clinical'' judgment tasks (e.g., selecting students for graduate school, deciding whether to release a hospitalized mental patient) than are clinicians (see Meehl, 1954; Sawyer, 1966; J. S. Wiggins, 1973), we still insist that such ''mechanical'' procedures must be subject to error because they fail to consider unique characterisitics of a client or exceptional cases. The fact, however, is that they are not; but we are (L. R. Goldberg, 1968; Kahneman & Tversky, 1979). As Kahneman and Tversky (1979) note, ''A fallible predictor can retain a chance to correctly predict a few exceptional outcomes only at the cost of erroneously identifying many other cases as exceptional'' (p. 321).

Why do we tend to be poorer judges than we think? We tend to

(1) overemphasize preexisting theories and expectations in deciding what evidence is relevant and how to interpret such evidence;

(2) be unaware of biases due to limited sample size and typicality (representativeness of our sample;

(3) underutilize base-rate (distributional, prior probability) information;

(4) not recognize the predictive limitations of extreme values (regression effects);

(5) overestimate the degree of relationship between two ''intuitively'' related variables (illusory correlation);

(6) place excessive emphasis on preceptually salient information (availability heuristic);

(7) be overinfluenced by the context in which clinical work is practiced; contexts that reinforce the sanctity (or preciousness) of the individual and ignore information about distributional information and other ''group'' characteristics;

(8) be reinforced for identifying pathology and punished for reporting thoughts, feelings, and behavior that are ''within normal limits'';

(9) fail to attend to our unsuccessful predictions as well as our successful ones (how well calibrated we are).

In the second section of this chapter, we attempted to demonstrate that although most of these sources of bias derive from limitations of our information processing system, by awareness of these, attention to our own cognitive processes, careful self-interrogation, generation of competing hypotheses, and record keeping to provide feedback, we can inoculate ourselves against some of the more flagrant errors.

Thirty years ago (Meehl, 1954) correctly noted that

> psychologists should be sophisticated about errors of observing, recording, retaining, and recalling to which the human brain is subject. We, of all people, ought to be highly suspicious of ourselves. We have no right to assume that entering the clinic has resulted in some miraculous mutation and made us singularly free from ordinary errors. (pp. 27–28)

It is important to emphasize that the suggestions we made for debiasing are based largely on intuition and a only a small degree on research data. Can clinicians become less error-prone? and How? are two questions that remain open to investigation. The merit of our chapter will have to be appraised on the basis of the extent to which we have sensitized readers to the potential sources of problems and potential solutions and thereby modified the behavior of practicing clinicians, those engaged in the training of clinical students, as well as graduate students who will become leaders in the field. Moreover, if we have served to stimulate research on debiasing, then we have especially succeeded in our mission. An important caveat that we can offer in closing was noted by Barbara Tuchman (1984) in her treatise on folly: [The] tragic side of folly [is] that its perpetrators sometimes realize that they are engaged in it and cannot break the pattern'' (p. 24).

Acknowledgments

The authors wish to thank Cheryl Hader for drawing the cartoon in Fig. 1 and to Marta Moret and Lorraine Turk for their comments on an earlier draft of this chapter. We would especially like to thank the member of the first author's graduate class on clinical decision making for their cogent, perspicacious, and critical responses to many of the rudimentary ideas presented in this chapter. These students made us aware of our more extreme statements and forced us to examine our own beliefs. The class members included Carol Cornell, Connie Dobbins, Terry Eicher, Mike Ewing, Wilma Ezekowitz, Jackie Hawkins, Joan Kaufman, Bianca Martinez, and Debbie Prentice.

References

Abelson, R.P. (1981). Psychological status of the script concept. *American Psychologist,* **36,** 715–729.

Abramson, L Y., Seligman, M. E. P., & Teasdale, J. D. (1978). Learned helplessness in humans: Critique and reformulation. *Journal of Abnormal Psychology,* **87,** 49–74.

Adams, H., Brantley, P., Malatesta, V., & Turkat, I. (1981). Modification of cognitive process: A case study of schizophrenia. *Journal of Consulting and Clinical Psychology,* **49,** 460–464.

Alba, J. W., Alexander, S. G., Hasher, L., & Canigla, K. (1981). The role of context in the encoding of information. *Journal of Experimental Psychology: Human Learning and Memory,* **7,** 283–292.

Alba, J. W., & Hasher, L. (1983). Is memory schematic? *Psychological Bulletin,* **93,** 203–231.

Alden, L., & Cappe, R. (1981). Nonassertiveness: Skill deficit or selective evaluation? *Behavior Therapy,* **12,** 107–114.

Alford, G., Fleece, L., & Rothblum, E. (1982). Hallucinatory-delusional verbalizations: Modification in a chronic schizophrenic by self-control and cognitive restructuring. *Behavior Modification,* **6,** 412–435.

Allen, M. (1983). Models of hemispheric specialization. *Psychological Bulletin,* **93,** 73–104.

Alloy, L. B. (1982). Depression, nondepression, and cognitive illusions. In N. S. Jacobson (Chair), *Cognitive theories of depression: A critical reappraisal.* Symposium presented at the meeting of the Association for the Advancement of Behavior Therapy, Los Angeles, CA.

Alloy, L. B., & Abramson, L. Y. (1979). Judgment of contingency in depressed and nondepressed students: Sadder but wiser? *Journal of Experimental Psychology: General,* **108,** 441–485.

Alloy, L. B., & Abramson, L. Y. (1982). Learned helplessness, depression and the illusion of control. *Journal of Personality and Social Psychology,* **42,** 1114–1126.

Alloy, L. B., & Tabachnick, N. (1984). Assessment of covariation by humans and animals: The joint influence of prior expectations and current situational information. *Psychological Review,* **91,** 112–149.

American Psychiatric Association, (1980). *Diagnostic and statistical manual of mental disorders* (3rd ed.). Washington DC: Author.

Anderson, C. A. (1982). Innoculation and counter-explanation: Debiasing techniques in the perserverance of social theories. *Social Cognition,* **1,** 126–139.

Anderson, J. R. (1973). A theory for the recognition of items from short memorized lists. *Psychological Review,* **80,** 417–438.

Anderson, J. R. (1976). *Language, memory and thought.* Hillsdale, NJ: Erlbaum.

Anderson, J. R. (1980). *Cognitive psychology and its implications.* San Francisco, CA: Freeman.

Anderson, J. R. (1983). *The architecture of cognition.* Cambridge, MA: Harvard University Press.

Anderson, J. R., & Bower, G. H. (1973). *Human associative memory.* Washington, DC: Erlbaum.

Anderson, N. H. (1974a). Algebraic Models in perception. In Ed Carterette & M. P. Friedman (Eds.), *Handbook of Perception* (Vol. 2). New York: Academic Press.

Anderson, N. H. (1974b). Cross-task validation of functional measurement using judgements of total magnitude. *Journal of Experimental Psychology,* **102,** 226–233.

Andreason, N. C. (1982). Concepts, diagnosis, and classification. In E. S. Paykel (Ed.), *Handbook of affective disorders.* New York: Guilford Press.

Andreason, N. C. (1983). The clinical differentiation of affective and schizophrenic disorders. In M. Zales (Ed.), *Affective and schizophrenic disorders: Approaches to diagnosis and treatment.* New York: Brunner/Mazel.

Anisman, H. (1978). Neurochemical changes elicited by stress. In H. Anisman & G. Bignami (Eds.), *Psychopharmacology of aversively motivated behavior* (pp. 119–172). New York: Plenum.

Arkes, H. R. (1981). Impediments to accurate clinical judgment and possible ways to minimize their impact. *Journal of Consulting and Clinical Psychology,* **49,** 323–330.

Arkowitz, H., Hinton, R., Perl, J., & Himadi, W. (1978). Treatment strategies for dating anxiety in college men based in real-life practice. *Counseling Psychologist,* **7,** 41–45.

Arnkoff, D. (1980). Psychotherapy from the perspective of cognitive theory. In M. J. Mahoney (Ed.), *Psychotherapy process: Current issues and future directions.* New York: Plenum.

Arnkoff, D., & Glass, C. R. (1982). Clinical cognitive constructs: Examination and elaboration. In P. C. Kendall (Ed.), *Advances in cognitive-behavioral research and therapy* (Vol. 1, pp. 1–34). New York: Academic Press.

Asch, S. E. (1946). Forming impressions of personality. *Journal of Abnormal and Social Psychology,* **41,** 258–290.

Aston-Jones, G., & Bloom, F. E. (1981). Norepinephrine-containing locus of coeruleus nuerons in behaving rats exhibit pronounced responses to non-noxious environmental stimuli. *Journal of Neuroscience,* **1,** 887–900.

Athay, M., & Darley, J. M. (1981). Toward an interaction-centered theory of personality. In N. Cantor & J. F. Kihlstrom (Eds.), *Personality, cognition, and social interaction.* Hillsdale, NJ: Erlbaum.

Atkinson, R. C., & Juola, J. F. (1973). Factors influencing speed and accuracy of word recognition. In S. Kornblum (Ed.). *Attention and performance IV.* New York: Academic Press.

Atkinson, R. C., & Juola, J. F. (1974). Search and decision processes in recognition memory. In D. H. Krantz, R. C. Atkinson, R. D. Luce, & P. Suppes (Eds.), *Contemporary developments in mathematical psychology.* San Francisco, CA: Freeman.

Atkinson, R. C., & Shiffrin, R. M. (1968). Human memory: A proposed system and its control processes. In K. W. Spence & J. T. Spence (Eds.), *Advances in the psychology of learning and motivation research and theory* (Vol. 2). New York: Academic Press.

Averbach, I., & Coriell, A. S. (1961). Short-term memory in vision. *Bell System Technical Journal,* **40,** 309–328.

Averill, J. R. (1983). Studies on anger and aggression: Implications for theories of emotion. *American Psychologist,* **38,** 1145–1160.

Ayer, A. J. (1959). *Logical positivism.* New York: Free Press.

Babcock, H. (1941). *Time and the mind.* Cambridge, MA: Science-Art Publishers.

Bahrick, H. P. (1969) Measurement of memory by prompted recall. *Journal of Experimental Psychology,* **79,** 213–219.

Bahrick, H. P., & Karis, D. (1982). Long-term ecological memory. In C. R. Puff (Ed.), *Handbook of research methods in human memory and cognition.* New York: Academic Press.

Bandura, A. (1977a). Self-efficacy: Toward a unifying theory of behavioral change. *Psychological Review,* **84,** 191–215.

Bandura, A. (1977b). *Social learning theory.* Englewood Cliffs, NJ: Prentice-Hall.

Bandura, A (1982). Self-efficacy mechanism in human agency. *American Psychologist,* **37,** 122–147.

Bandura, A., & Cervone, D. (1983). Self-evaluative and self-efficacy mechanisms governing the motivational effects of goal systems. *Journal of Personality and Social Psychology,* **45,** 1017–1028.

Bargh, J. A. (1982). Attention and automaticity in the processing of self-relevant information. *Journal of Personality and Social Psychology,* **43,** 425–436.

Barnes, J. (1974). Effects of reality orientation classroom on memory loss, confusion, and disorientation in geriatric patients. *Gerontologist,* **14,** 138–142.

Barrios, F. X., & Neihaus, J. C. (1984). The influence of smoker status, smoking history, sex, and situational variables on smokers' self-efficacy. *Addictive Behaviors,* **12,** 356–364.

Bartlett, F. C. (1932). *Remembering: A study in experimental and social psychology.* London & New York: Cambridge University Press.

Baumeister, A. A., Runcie, D., & Gardepe, J. (1984). Processing of information in iconic memory: Differences between nonretarded and retarded subjects. *Journal of Abnormal Psychology,* **93,** 443–447.

Beck, A. T. (1963). Thinking in depression: I. Idiosyncratic content and cognitive distortions. *Archives of General Psychiatry,* **9,** 324–333.

Beck, A. T. (1967). *Depression: Clinical, experimental, and theoretical aspects.* New York: Harper (Hoeber).

Beck, A. T. (1976). *Cognitive therapy and the emotional disorders.* New York: International University Press.

Beck, A. T., Hollon, S. D., Young, J. E., Bedrosian, R. C., & Bundenz, D. (1985). Treatment of depression with cognitive therapy and drug therapy. *Archives of General Psychiatry,* **42,** 142–148.

Beck, A. T., Rush, A. J., Shaw, B. F., & Emery, G. (1979). *Cognitive therapy of depression.* New York: Guilford Press.

Bellack, L. (1958). *Schizophrenia: A review of the syndrome.* New York: Logos Press.

Bennett, R. M., Buss, A. H., & Carpenter, J. A. (1969). Alcohol and human physical aggression. *Quarterly Journal of Studies on Alcohol,* **30,** 807–876.

Benton, A. (1946). *A visual retention task for clinical use,* New York: Psychological Corporation.

Berlyne, D. E. (1960). *Conflict, arousal, and curiosity.* New York: McGraw-Hill.

Berlyne, D. E. (1974). Attention. In E. C. Carterette & M. P. Friedman (Eds.), *Handbook of perception* (Vol 1, pp. 123–147). New York: Academic Press.

Bever, T. G., Fodor, J. A., & Garrett, M. A. (1968). A formal limitation of associationism. In R. Dixon & D. L. Horton (Eds.). *Verbal behavior and general behavior theory.* Englewood Cliffs, NJ: Prentice-Hall.

Bickel, W. K., Stella, M. E., & Etzel, B. C. (1984). A reevaluation of stimulus overselectivity: Restricted stimulus control or stimulus control hierarchies? *Journal of Autism and Developmental Disorders,* **14,** 137–157.

Biederman, I., Glass, A. L., & Stacy, E. W. (1973). Searching for objects in real-world scenes. *Journal of Experimental Psychology,* **97,** 22–27.

Bieri, J., Atkins, A. L., Briar, S., Leaman, R. L., Miller, H., & Tripodi, T. (1966). *Clinical and social judgment.* New York: Wiley.

Bijou, S., & Baer, D. (1963). Some methodological contributions from a functional analysis of child development. In L. P. Lipsitt & C. C. Spiker (Eds.), *Advances in child development and behavior* (Vol. 1). New York: Academic Press.

Birnbaum, I. M., Johnson, M. K., Hartley, J. T., & Taylor, T. H. (1980). Alcohol and elaborative schemas for sentences. *Journal of Experimental Psychology: Learning and Memory,* **6,** 293–300.

Birnbaum, I. M., & Parker, E. S. (1977). Acute effects of alcohol on storage and retrieval. In I. M. Birnbaum, & E. S. Parker (Eds.), *Alcohol and memory,* Hillsdale, NJ: Erlbaum.

Birnbaum, I. M., Parker, E. S., Hartley, J. T., & Noble, E. P. (1978). Alcohol and memory: Retrieval processes. *Journal of Verbal Learning and Verbal Behavior,* **17,** 325–335.

Birnbaum, M. H. (1973). The devil rides again: Correlations as an index of fit. *Psychological Bulletin,* **79,** 239–242.

Blackburn, I. M., Bishop, S., Glen, A. I. M., Whalley, L. J., & Christie, J. E. (1981). The efficacy of cognitive therapy in depression: A treatment trial using cognitive therapy and pharmacotherapy, each alone and in combination. *British Journal of Psychiatry,* **139,** 181–189.

Blaney, P. H. (1986). Affect and memory: A review. *Psychological Bulletin,* **99,** 229–246.

Bleuler, E. (1950). [*The group of schizophrenia*] (English Trans.). New York: International University Press. (Original work published 1911).

Bloom, F. E., Schulman, J. A., & Koob, G. F. (in press). Catecholamines and behavior. In U. Trendelenburg & N. Weiner (Eds.), *Handbook of experimental pharmacology.* Berlin & New York: Springer-Verlag.

Boring, E. G. (1950). *A history of experimental psychology* (2nd ed). New York: Appleton-Century-Crofts, 1950.

Boucher, J. (1978). Echoic memory capacity in autistic children. *Journal of Child Psychology and Psychiatry,* **19,** 161–166.

Bousfield, W. A. (1953). The occurrence of clustering in the recall of randomly arranged associates. *Journal of General Psychology,* **49,** 229–240.

Bower, G. H. (1972). Mental imagery and associative learning. In L. Gregg (Ed.), *Cognition in learning and memory.* New York: Wiley.

Bower, G. H. (1978). Contacts of cognitive psychology with social learning theory. *Cognitive Therapy and Research,* **2** 123–146.

Bower, G. H. (1981). Mood and memory. *American Psychologist,* **36** 129–148.

Bower, G. H., Black, J. B., & Turner, T. J. (1979). Scripts in memory for text. *Cognitive Psychology,* **11,** 177–220.

Bower, G. H., Gilligan, S. G., & Monteiro, K. P. (1981). Selectivity of learning caused by affective states. *Journal of Experimental Psychology: General,* **110,** 415–473.

Boyd, R. (1979). Metaphor and theory change: What is ''Metaphor'' a metaphor for? In A. Ortony (Ed.), *Metaphor and thought.* London & New York: Cambridge University Press.

Bradshaw, J. L., & Nettleton, N. C. (1981). The nature of hemispheric specialization in man. *Behavioral and Brain Sciences,* **4,** 51–91.

Braff, D. L. (1981). Impaired speed of information processing in non-medicated schizotypal patients. *Schizophrenia Bulletin,* **7,** 449–508.

Braff, D. L., & Saccuzzo, D. P. (1981). Slowness of information processing in schizophrenia: A two factor deficit theory. *American Journal of Psychiatry,* **138,** 1051–1056.

Braff, D. L., & Saccuzzo, D. P. (in press). The time course of information processing deficits in schizophrenia. *American Journal of Psychiatry.*

Bransford, J. D., & Johnson, M. K. (1972). Contextual prerequisites for understanding: Some investigations for comprehension and recall. *Journal of Verbal Learning and Verbal Behavior,* **11,** 717–726.

Bransford, J. D., & Johnson, M. K. (1973). Consideration of some problems of comprehension. In W. G. Chase (Ed.), *Visual information processing.* New York: Academic Press.

Brehm, S. S., & Brehm, J. W. (1981). *Psychological reactance: A theory of freedom and control.* New York: Academic Press.

Brenner, M. W. (1976). *Memory and interpersonal relations.* Unpublished doctoral dissertation, University of Michigan, Ann Arbor.

Bridgeman, B., & Mayer, M. (1983). Iconic storage and saccadic eye movements. *Behavioral and Brain Sciences,* **6,** 16–17.

Broadbent, D. E. (1958). *Perception and communication.* Oxford: Pergamon.

Brody, D., Saccuzzo, D. P., & Braff, D. L. (1980). Information processing for masked and unmasked stimuli in schizophrenia and old age. *Journal of Abnormal Psychology,* **89,** 617–622.

Broen, W. E. (1968). *Schizophrenia: Research and theory.* New York: Academic Press.

Brown, G. G., Rosenbaum, G., Lewis, R., & Rouke, D. (1980). The effects of rehearsal rate in serial recall in Korsakoff amnesia. *Neuropsychologia,* **18,** 185–191.

Brown, H. I. (1979). *Perception, theory, and commitment: The new philosophy of science.* Chicago, IL: University of Chicago Press.

Brown, H. L., & Kirsner, K. (1980). A within-subjects analysis of the relationship between memory span and processing rate in short-term memory. *Cognitive Psychology,* **12,** 177–187.

Brown, J. A. (1958). Some tests of decay theory of immediate memory. *Quarterly Journal of Experimental Psychology,* **10,** 12–21.

Brown, R. V., Kahr, A. S., & Peterson, D. (1974). *Decision analysis for the manager.* New York: Holt, Rinehart, & Winston.

Bruner, J., & Tagiuri, R. (1954). The perception of people. In G. Lindzey (Ed.), *Handbook of social psychology.* Reading, MA: Addison-Wesley.

Brunson, B. I., & Matthews, K. A. (1981). The Type A coronary-prone behavior pattern and reactions to uncontrollable stress: An analysis of performance strategies, affect, and attributions during failure. *Journal of Personality and Social Psychology,* **40,** 906–918.

Buchsbaum, M., & Rieder, R. (1979). Biologic heterogenity and psychiatric research: Platelet MAO as a case study. *Archives of General Psychiatry,* **36,** 1163–1169.

Buss, A. H. (1961). *The Psychology of aggression.* New York: Wiley.

Buss, A. H. (1966). *Psychopathology.* New York: Wiley.

Butler, G., & Rabinowitz, M. (1981). An investigation of factors contributing to the apparent overselective responding of mentally retarded children. *Child Development,* **52,** 430–442.

Butters, N., & Cermak, L. S. (1974). The role of cognitive factors in the memory disorders of alcoholic patients with the Korsakoff syndrome. *Annals of the New York Academy of Sciences,* **233,** 61–75.

Butters, N., & Cermak, L. S. (1976). Neuropsychological studies of alcoholic Korsakoff patients. In G. Goldstein & C. Neuringer (Eds.), *Empirical studies of alcoholism.* Cambridge, MA: Ballinger.

Calev, A., Venables, P., & Monk, A. (1983). Evidence for distinct verbal memory pathologies in severly and mildly disturbed schizophrenics. *Schizophrenia Bulletin,* **9,** 247–264.

Callaway, E., Naghdi, S. (1982). An information processing model for schizophrenia. *Archives of General Psychiatry,* **39,** 339–347.

Callaway, E., & Thompson, S. V. (1953). Sympathetic activity and perception. *Psychosomatic Medicine,* **15,** 443–455.

Cameron, N. (1938). Reasoning, regression, and communication in schizophrenia. *Psychological Monograph,* **50** (1, Whole No. 221).

Campbell, M., Anderson, L. T., Deutsch, S. I., & Green, W. H. (1984). Psychopharmacological treatment of children with the syndrome of autism. *Pediatric Annals,* **13,** 309–316.

Campione, J. C., McGrath, M., & Rabinowitz, F. M. (1971). Component and configurational learning in children: Additional data. *Journal of Experimental Psychology,* **88,** 137–139.

Cancro, R., Sutton, S., Kerr, J., & Sugarman, A. (1971). Reaction time and prognosis in acute schizophrenia. *Journal of Nervous and Mental Disease,* **153,** 351–359.

Cantor, N. (1981). A cognitive-social approach to personality. In N. Cantor & J. F. Kihlstrom (Eds.), *Personality, cognition, and social interaction.* Hillsdale, NJ: Erlbaum.

Cantor, N., & Kihlstrom, J. F. (Eds.). (1981). *Personality, cognition, and social interaction.* Hillsdale, NJ: Erlbaum.

Cantor, N., & Kihlstrom, J. F. (1982). Cognitive and social processes in personality. In G. T. Wilson & C. M. Franks (Eds.), *Contemporary behavior therapy: Conceptual and empirical foundations* (pp. 142–201). New York: Guilford Press.

Cantor, N., & Kihlstrom, J. F. (1983). Cognitive and social processes in personality: Implications for behavior therapy. In C. M. Franks & G. T. Wilson (Eds.), *Handbook of behavior therapy.* New York: Guilford Press.

Cantor, N., & Mischel, W. (1977). Traits as prototypes: Effects on recognition memory. *Journal of Personality and Social Psychology,* **35,** 38–48.

Cantor, N., & Mischel, W. (1979). Prototypes in person perception. In L. Berkowitz (Ed.), *Advances in experimental social psychology* (Vol. 12). New York: Academic Press.

Cantor, N., Mischel, W., & Schwartz, J. (1982). A prototype analysis of psychological situations. *Cognitive Psychology,* **14,** 45–77.

Carlston, D. E. (1977). *The recall and use of observed behaviors and inferred traits in social inference processes.* Unpublished doctoral dissertation, University of Illinois, Urbana.

Carroll, J. D., & Arabie, P. (1980). Multidimensional scaling. *Annual Review of Psychology,* **31,** 607–649.

Carroll, J. D., & Chang, J. J. (1970). Analysis of individual differences in multidimensional scaling via an N-way generalization of ''Eckart-Young'' decomposition. *Psychometrika,* **35,** 283–319.

Carver, C. S. (1980). Perceived coercion, resistance to persuasion, and the Type A behavior pattern. *Journal of Research in Personality,* **14,** 467–481.

Carver, C. S., Coleman, A. E., & Glass, D. C. (1976). The coronary-prone behavior pattern and the suppression of fatigue on a treadmill test. *Journal of Personality and Social Psychology,* **33,** 460–466.

Carver, C. S., & Glass, D. C. (1978). Coronary-prone behavior pattern and interpersonal aggression. *Journal of Personality and Social Psychology,* **36,** 361–366.

Carver, C. S., & Scheier, M. F. (1978). Self-focusing effects of dispositional self-consciousness, mirror presence, and audience presence. *Journal of Personality and Social Psychology,* **36,** 324–332.

Carver, C. S., & Scheier, M. F. (1981). *Attention and self-regulation: A control theory approach to human behavior.* Berlin & New York: Springer-Verlag.

Carver, C. S., & Scheier, M. F. (1983). A control theory approach to human behavior and implications for problems in self-management. In P. C. Kendall (Ed.), *Advances in cognitive-behavioral research and therapy* (Vol. 2, pp. 127–194). New York: Academic Press.

Cash, T. F., Neale, J. M., & Cromwell, R. L. (1972). Span of apprehension in acute schizophrenics full report technique. *Journal of Abnormal Psychology,* **79,** 322–326.

Castelli, W. P. (1980). Cardiovascular statistics in the United States: Framingham and beyond. In C. Long (Ed.), *Prevention and rehabilitation in ischemic heart disease* (pp. 1–17). Baltimore, MD: Williams & Wilkins.

Cavanagh, J. P. (1972). Relation between the immediate memory span and the memory search rate. *Psychological Review,* **79,** 525–530.

Cermak, L. S., & Butters, N. (1972). The role of interference and encoding in the short-term memory deficits of Korsakoff patients. *Neuropsychologia,* **10,** 89–96.

Cermak, L. S., & Butters, N. (1973). Information processing deficits of alcoholic Korsakoff patients. *Quarterly Journal of Studies on Alcohol,* **34,** 1110–1132.

Cermak, L. S., Butters, N., & Gerrein, J. (1973). The extent of the verbal encoding ability of Korsakoff patients. *Neuropsychologia,* **11,** 85–94.

Cermak, L. S., & Craik, F. I. M. (1978). *Levels of processing in human memory.* Hillsdale, NJ: Erlbaum.

Cermak, L. S., Naus, M. I., & Reale, L. (1976). Rehearsal and organizational strategies of alcoholic Korsakoff patients. *Brain and Language,* **3,** 375–385.

Cermak, L. S., & Reale, L. (1978). Depth of processing and retention of words by alcoholic Korsakoff patients. *Journal of Experimental Psychology: Human Learning and Memory,* **4,** 165–174.

Cermak, L. S., Reale, L., & DeLuca, D. (1977). Korsakoff patients' nonverbal vs. verbal memory: Effects of interference and mediation on rate of information loss. *Neuropsychologia,* **15,** 303–310.

Cermak, L. S., & Ryback, R. S. (1976). Recovery of verbal short-term memory in alcoholics. *Journal of Studies on Alcohol,* **37,** 46–52.

Cermak, L. S., Uhly, B., & Reale, L. (1980). Encoding specificity in the alcoholic Korsakoff patient. *Brain and Language,* **11,** 119–127.

Chanowitz, B., & Langer, E. (1980). Knowing more (or less) than you can show: Understanding control through the mindlessness-mindfulness distinction. In J. Garber & M. E. P. Seligman (Eds.), *Human helplessness: Theory and applications.* New York: Academic Press.

Chapman, L. J. (1967). Illusory correlation in observation reports. *Journal of Verbal Learning and Verbal Behavior,* **6,** 151–155.

Chapman, L. J., & Chapman, J. P. (1967). Genesis of popular but erroneous psycho-diagnostic observations. *Journal of Abnormal Psychology,* **72,** 193–204.

Chapman, L. J., & Chapman, J. P. (1969). Illusory correlation as an obstacle to the use of valid psychodiagnostic signs. *Journal of Abnormal Psychology,* **74,** 271–280.

Chapman, L. J., & Chapman, J. P. (1973). *Disordered thought in schizophrenia.* New York: Appleton-Century-Crofts.

Chase, W. G., & Simon, H. A. (1973). The mind's eye in chess. In W. G. Chase (Ed.), *Visual information processing.* New York: Academic Press.

Chesney, M. A., Black, G. W., Chadwick, J. H., & Roseman, R. H. (1981). Psychological correlates of the Type A behavior pattern. *Journal of Behavioral Medicine,* **4,** 217–229.

Chevalier-Skolnikoff, S. (1973). Facial expression of emotion in nonhuman primates. In P. Ekman (Ed.), *Darwin and facial expression.* New York: Academic Press.

Chi, M. T. H., & Koeske, (1983). Network representations of a child's dinosaur knowledge. *Developmental Psychology,* **19,** 29–39.

Chiang, A., & Atkinson, R. C. (1976). Individual differences and inter-relationships among a select set of cognitive skills. *Memory and Cognition,* **4,** 661–672.

Chomsky, N. A. (1959). A review of Skinner's *Verbal behavior. Language,* **35,** 26–58.

Chomsky, N. A. (1963). Formal properties of grammers. In R. D. Luce, R. R. Bush, & E. Galanter (Eds.), *Handbook of mathematical psychology* (Vol. 2). New York: Wiley.

Chomsky, N. A. (1965). *Aspects of the theory of syntax.* Cambridge, MA: MIT Press.

Chomsky, N. A. (1980). *Rules and representations.* New York: Columbia University Press.

Church, A. (1936). An unsolvable problem of elementary number theory. *American Journal of Mathematics,* **58,** 345–363.

Cialdini, R. B., Petty, R. F., & Cacioppo, J. T. (1981). Attitude and attitude change. *Annual Review of Psychology,* **32,** 357–404.

Ciaranello, R. D., VandenBerg, S. R., & Anders, T. F. (1982). Intrinsic and extrinsic determinants of neuronal development: Relation to infantile autism. *Journal of Autism and Developmental Disorders.* **12,** 115–145.

Clark, M., & Isen, A. M. (1982). Toward understanding the relationship between feeling states and social behavior. In A. Hastorf & A. M. Isen (Eds.), *Cognitive social psychology*. New York: American Elsevier.

Clark, D. M., & Teasdale, J. D. (1982). Diurnal variation in clinical depression and accessibility of memories of positive and negative experiences. *Journal of Abnormal Psychology,* **91,** 87–95.

Clark, D. M., & Teasdale, J. D. (1985). Constraints on the effect of memory and mood. *Journal of Personality and Social Psychology,* **48,** 1595–1608.

Clark, H. H. (1984). Language use and language users. In G. Lindzey & E. Aronson (Eds.), *Handbook of social psychology* (3rd ed.). Reading, MA: Addison-Wesley.

Clark, J. V., & Arkowitz, H. (1975). Social anxiety and self-evaluation of interpersonal performance. *Psychological Reports,* **36,** 211–221.

Clark, M. S., & Fiske, S. T. (1982). *Affect and cognition.* Hillsdale, NJ: Erlbaum.

Cobb, S. (1976). Social support as a moderator of life stress. *Psychosomatic Medicine,* **38,** 300–314.

Coche, E., & Douglas, A. (1977). Therapeutic effects of problem-solving training and play-reading groups. *Journal of Clinical Psychology,* **33,** 820–827.

Coche, E., & Flick, A. (1975). Problem-solving training groups for hospitalized psychiatric patients. *Journal of Psychology,* **91,** 19–29.

Cohen, C. E. (1977). *Cognitive basis of stereotyping.* Paper presented at the meeting of the American Psychological Association, San Francisco, CA.

Cohen, D. J., & Johnson, W. T. (1977). Cardiovascular correlates of attention in autistic children: Response times to proximal and distal stimulation. *Archives of General Psychiatry,* **34,** 561–567.

Cohen, D. J., & Shaywitz, B. A. (1982). Preface to the special issue on neurobiological research in autism. *Journal of Autism and Developmental Disorders,* **12,** 103–107.

Cohen, D. J., & Young, J. G. (1977). Neurochemistry and child psychiatry. *Journal of the American Academy of Child Psychiatry,* **16,** 353–411.

Cohen, G. (1973). Hemispheric differences in serial versus parallel processing. *Journal of Experimental Psychology,* **97,** 349–356.

Cohen, J. B., Syme, S. L., Jenkins, C. D., Kagan, A., & Zyzanski, S. J. (1979). Cultural context of Type A behavior and risk for CHD: A study of Japanese-American males. *Journal of Behavioral Medicine,* **2,** 375–384.

Cohen, L. J. (1981). Can human irrationality be experimentally demonstrated? *Behavioral and Brain Sciences,* **4,** 317–370.

Colby, K. M. (1981). Modeling a paranoid mind. *Behavioral and Brain Sciences,* **4,** 515–608.

Coleman, M. (1979). Studies of the autistic syndromes. In R. Katzman (Ed.), *Congenital and acquired cognitive disorders* (pp. 265–275). New York: Raven Press.

Collins, A. M., & Loftus, E. F. (1975). A spreading activation theory of semantic processing. *Psychological Review,* **82,** 407–428.

Combs, A. W., & Snygg, D. (1959). *Individual behavior* (rev. ed.). New York: Harper.

Conant, J. B. (1947). *Understanding science: An historical approach.* New Haven, CT: Yale University Press.

Condiette, M. M., & Lichtenstein, E. (1981). Self-efficacy and relapse in smoking cessation programs. *Journal of Consulting and Clinical Psychology,* **49,** 648–658.

Conrad, C. (1974). Context effects in sentence comprehension: A study of the subjective lexicon. *Memory and Cognition,* **2,** 130–138.

Cook, R. A., Anderson, N., & Rincover, A. (1982). Stimulus over-selectivity and stimulus control: Problems and strategies. In R. F. Koegel, A. Rincover, & A. L. Egel (Eds.), *Educating and understanding autistic children* (pg. 90–105). San Diego, CA: College Hill Press.

Courchesne, E., Kilman, B. A., Galambos, R., & Lincoln, A. (1983). *Autism: Cognitive processing of novel information measured by event-related brain potentials.* Unpublished manuscript.

Covi, L., Lipman, R. S., Roth, D., Pattison, J. H., Smith, J. E., & Lasseter, V. K. (1985). *Cognitive group psychotherapy in depression.* Paper presented at the meeting of the American Psychological Association, Los Angeles, CA.

Coyne, J. C. (1982). A critique of cognitions as causal entities with particular reference to depression. *Cognitive Therapy and Research,* **6,** 3–13.

Coyne, J. C., & Gotlib, I. H. (1983). The role of cognition in depression: A critical reappraisal. *Psychological Bulletin,* **94,** 472–505.

Craighead, W. E., Hickey, K. S., & DeMonbreun, B. G. (1979). Distortion of perception and recall of neutral feedback in depression. *Cognitive Therapy and Research,* **3,** 291–298.

Craik, F. I. M. (1979a). Human memory. *Annual Review of Psychology,* **30,** 63–102.

Craik, F. I. M. (1979b). Levels of processing. In L. S. Cermak & F. I. M. Craik (Eds.), *Levels of processing in human memory* (pp. 447–461). Hillsdale, NJ: Erlbaum.

Craik, F. I. M., & Lockhart, R. S. (1972). Levels of processing: A framework for memory research. *Journal of Verbal Learning and Verbal Behavior,* **11,** 671–684.

Craik, F. I. M., & Tulving, E. (1975). Depth of processing and the retention of words in episodic memory. *Journal of Experimental Psychology,* **104,** 268–294.

Crocker, J., Fiske, S. T., & Taylor, S. E. (1984). Schematic bases of belief change. In J. R. Eiser (Ed.), *Attitudinal judgment.* Berlin & New York: Springer-Verlag.

Cromwell, R. L. (1975). Assessment of schizophrenia. *Annual Review of Psychology,* **26,** 593–619.

Cromwell, R. L. (1978a). *The use of behavioral deficits in the study of schizophrenia.* Symposium paper presented at the meeting of the American Psychological Association, Toronto, Canada.

Cromwell, R. L. (1978b). Attention and information processing: A foundation for understanding schizophrenia? In L. C. Wynne, R. L. Cromwell, & S. Matthysee (Eds.), *The nature of schizophrenia.* New York: Wiley.

Crovitz, H. (1979). Memory retraining in brain-damaged patients: The airplane list. *Cortex,* **15,** 131–134.

Crow, W. J. (1957). The effects of training upon accuracy and response set in interpersonal perception. *Journal of Abnormal and Social Psychology,* **55,** 355–359.

Crowder, R. G., & Morton, J. (1969). Precategorical acoustic storage (PAS). *Perception and Psychophysics,* **5,** 365–373.

Cutting, J. (1979). Differential impairment of memory in Korsakoff's syndrome. *Cortex,* **15,** 501–506.

Dahl, H. (1979). The appetite hypothesis of emotions: A new psychoanalytic model of motivation. In C. E. Izard (Ed.), *Emotions in personality and psychopathology.* New York: Plenum.

Daniel, A. (1980). Coronary heart disease: An overview. In M. L. Pollock & D. H. Schmidt (Eds.), *Heart disease and rehabilitation* (pp. 73–85). New York: Wiley.

Darley, C. F., Tinklenberg, J. R., Hollister, L. E., & Atkinson, R. C. (1973). Marijuana and retrieval from short-term memory. *Psychopharmacologia,* **29,** 231–238.

Darley, J. M., & Fazio, R. H. (1980). Expectancy confirmation processes arising in social interaction sequence. *American Psychologist,* **35,** 867–881.

Darwin, C. (1872). *The expression of the emotions in man and animals.* London: Murray.

Davis, D. A., & Brock, T. C. (1975). Use of first person pronouns as a function of increased objective self-awareness and performance feedback. *Journal of Experimental Social Psychology,* **11,** 381–388.

Davis, H. (1979a). Self-reference and the encoding of personal information in depression. *Cognitive Therapy and Research,* **3,** 97–110.

Davis, H. (1979b). The self-schema and subjective organization of personal information in depression. *Cognitive Therapy and Research,* **3,** 415–425.

Davis, H. P., & Unruh, W. R. (1981). The development of the self-schema in adult depression. *Journal of Abnormal Psychology,* **90,** 125–133.

Davis, M. (1965). *The undecidable: Basic papers on undecidable propositions, unsolvable problems and uncomputable functions.* Hewlitt, NY: Raven Press.

Davison, G. (1966). Differential relation and cognitive restructuring in therapy with a "paranoid schizophrenic" or "paranoid state." *Proceedings of the 74th Annual Convention of the American Psychological Association,* **1,** 177–178.

Davison, G. C., Tsujimoto, R. N., & Glaros, A. G. (1973). Attribution and the maintenance of behavior change in falling asleep. *Journal of Abnormal Psychology,* **82,** 124–133.

Davison, M. L. (1983). Introduction to multidimensional scaling and its applications. *Applied Psychological Measurement,* **1,** 373–379.

Davison, M. L., & Jones, L. E. (1976). A similarity-attraction model for predicting sociometric choice from perceived group structure. *Journal of Personality and Social Psychology,* **33,** 601–612.

Dawes, R. M., & Corrigan, B. (1974). Linear models in decision making. *Psychological Bulletin,* **81,** 95–106.

deGroot, A. D. (1965). *Thought and choice in chess.* The Hague: Mouton.

Dembroski, T. M., MacDougall, J. M., & Musante, L. (1984). Desirability of control versus locus of control: Relationship to paralinguistics in the Type A interview. *Health Psychology,* **3,** 15–26.

Dembroski, T. M., MacDougall, J. M., Shields, J. L., Petitto, J., & Lushene, R. (1978). Components of the Type A coronary-prone behavior pattern and cardiovascular responses to psychomotor challenge. *Journal of Behavioral Medicine,* **1,** 159–176.

DeMonbreun, B. G., & Craighead, W. E. (1977). Distortion of perception and recall of positive and neutral feedback in depression. *Cognitive Therapy and Research,* **1,** 311–329.

Depue, R. A., Kleiman, R. M., Davis, P., Hutchinson, M., & Krauss, S. P. (in press). The behavioral high-risk paradigm and bipolar affective disorder. VIII. Serum free cortisol in GBI-selected nonpatient cyclothymes. *American Journal of Psychiatry.*

Depue, R. A., & Monroe, S. M. (1978). Learned helplessness in the perspective of the depressive disorders. *Journal of Abnormal Psychology,* **87,** 3–21.

Derry, P. A., & Kuiper, N. A. (1981). Schematic processing and self-reference in clinical depression. *Journal of Abnormal Psychology,* **90,** 286–297.

Deutsch, J. A., & Deutsch, D. (1963). Attention: Some theoretical considerations. *Psychological Review,* **70,** 80–90.

DiClemente, C. C. (1981). Self-efficacy and smoking cessation maintenance. *Cognitive Therapy and Research,* **5,** 175–187.

Diener, C. I., & Dweck, C. S. (1978). An analysis of learned helplessness: Continuous changes in performance, strategy, and achievement cognitions following failure. *Journal of Personality and Social Psychology,* **36,** 451–462.

Dimond, S. J., & Beaumont, J. G. (1973). Differences in the vigilance performance of the right and left hemispheres. *Cortex,* **9,** 259–265.

Dobson, K. S., & Breiter, H. J. (1983). Cognitive assessment of depression: Reliability and validity of three measures. *Journal of Abnormal Psychology,* **92,** 107–109.

Dodd, D. H., & Schultz, R. F. (1973). Computational procedures for estimating magnitude of effect for some analysis of variance designs. *Psychological Bulletin,* **79,** 391–395.

Donders, F. C. (1969). Over de snelheid van psychische processen. Onderzoekingen gedaan in het Physiologisch Laboratorium der Utrechtsche Hoogeschool, 1868–1869, Tweede reeks II, 92–120. Translated by W. G. Koster in W. G. Koster (Ed.), *Attention and performance: II. Acta Psychologica,* **30,** 412–431.

Dunn, A. J., & Kramarcy, N. R. (1984). Neurochemical responses in stress: Relationships between the hypothalamic-pituitary-adrenal and catecholamine system. In L. L. Iversen, S. D. Iversen, & S. H. Snyder (Eds.), *Handbook of psychopharmacology:* **Vol. 18.** *Drugs, neurotransmitters, and behavior* (pp. 455–515). New York: Plenum.

Duval, S., & Wicklund, R. A. (1972). *A theory of objective self-awareness.* New York: Academic Press.

Dyck, D. G. (1983). Severity of depressed mood, perfectionism, and self-referenct encoding. In L. B. Alloy (Chair), *Depression and schemata.* Symposium presented at the meeting of the American Psychological Association, Anaheim, CA.

Dyer, F. H. (1973). The Stroop phenomenon and its use in the study of perceptual, cognitive, and response processes. *Memory and Cognition,* **1,** 106–120.

Dykman, B. M., & Volpicelli, J. R. (1983). Depression and negative processing of evaluative feedback. *Cognitive Therapy and Research,* **7,** 485–498.

D'Zurilla, T. J., & Goldfried, M. R. (1971). Problem solving and behavior modification. *Journal of Abnormal Psychology,* **78,** 107–126.

Ebbesen, E. B., & Allen, R. B. (1979). Cognitive processes in implicit personality trait inferences. *Journal of Personality and Social Psychology,* **37,** 471–488.

Edwards, J. L., Shigley, R. H., & Edwards, R. P. (1976). A case report of an autistic boy: Selective responding to components of bidimensional visual and auditory stimuli. *Journal of Autism and Childhood Schizophrenia,* **6,** 139–146.

Eich, J. E. (1980). The cue-dependent nature of state dependent learning. *Memory and Cognition,* **8,** 157–173.

Einhorn, H. J., & Hogarth, R. M. (1982). *A theory of diagnostic inference: I. Imagination and the psychophysics of evidence.* Unpublished manuscript, University of Chicago, Chicago, IL.

Einhorn, H. J., & Hogarth, R. M. (1983). *Diagnostic inference and causal judgment: A decision making framework.* Unpublished manuscript, University of Chicago, Chicago, IL.

Ekman, P. (1971). Universals and cultural differences in facial expressions of emotion. In J. K. Cole (Ed.), *Nebraska symposium on motivation* (Vol. 19, pp. 207–284). Lincoln: University of Nebraska Press.

Elig, T. W., & Frieze, I. H. (1979). Measuring causal attributions for success and failure. *Journal of Personality and Social Psychology,* **37,** 621–634.

Ellis, A. (1962). *Reason and emotion in psychotherapy.* New York: Lyle Stuart.

Ellis, A., & Grieger, R. (1977). *Handbook of rational-emotive therapy.* New York: Springer.

Elstein, W., & Bordage, G. (1979). Psychology of clinical reasoning. In G. Stone, F. Cohen, & N. Adler, (Eds.), *Health psychology.* (pp. 333–368). San Francisco, CA: Jossey-Bass.

Engel, G. L. (1977). The need for a new medical model: A challenge for biomedicine. *Science,* **196,** 129–136.

Epstein, S. (1978). *The unity principle versus the reality and pleasure principles, or the tale of the scorpion and the frog.* Paper presented at the National Symposium on Self-Concept, Boston, MA.

Epstein, S. (1980). The self-concept: A review and the proposal of an integrated theory of personality. In E. Staub (Ed.), *Personality: Basic issues and current research* (pp. 81–132). Englewood Cliffs, NJ: Prentice-Hall.

Erdelyi, M. H. (1974). A new look at the new look: Perceptual defense and vigilance. *Psychological Review,* **81,** 1–25.

Ericsson, K. A., & Simon, H. A. (1980). Verbal reports as data. *Psychological Review,* **82,** 215–251.

Erlenmeyer-Kimling, L., & Cornblatt, B. (1978). Attentional measures in a study of children at high-risk for schizophrenia. *Journal of Psychiatric Research,* **14,** 93–98.

Estes, W. K. (1955). Theory of elementary predictive behavior: An exercise in the behavioral interpretation of a mathematical model. In *Mathematical models of human behavior: Proceedings of a symposium.* Stamford, CT: Dunlap.

Estes, W. K. (1982). *Models of learning, memory, and choice: Selected papers.* New York: Prager.

Evans, M. D., & Hollon, S. D. (in press). Patterns of personal and causal inference: Implications for the cognitive therapy of depression. In L. B. Alloy (Ed.), *Cognitive processes in depression.* New York: Guilford Press.

Exner, J. E. (1973). The self-focus sentence completion: A study of egocentricity. *Journal of Personality Assessment,* **37,** 437–455.

Fabian, M. S., Parsons, O. A., & Silberstein, J. A. (1981). Impaired perceptual-cognitive functioning in women alcoholics: Cross-validated findings. *Journal of Studies on Alcohol,* **42,** 217–229.

Farnham-Diggory, S. (1978). *Learning disabilities.* Cambridge, MA: Harvard University Press.

Feighner, J. P., Robins, E., & Guze, S. D. (1972). Diagnostic criteria for use in psychiatric research. *Archives of General Psychiatry,* **26,** 57–63.

Fein, D., Humes, M., Kaplan, E., Lucci, D., & Waterhouse, L. (1984). The question of left hemisphere dysfunction in infantile autism. *Psychological Bulletin,* **95,** 258–281.

Fein, D., Skoff, B., & Mirsky, A. F. (1981). Clinical correlates of brainstem dysfunction in autistic children. *Journal of Autism and Developmental Disorders,* **11,** 303–315.

Felsten, G., & Wasserman, C. S. (1980). Visual masking: Mechanisms and theories. *Psychological Bulletin,* **88,** 329–353.

Fenigstein, A., Scheier, M. F., & Buss, A. H. (1975). Public and private self-consciousness: Assessment and theory. *Journal of Consulting and Clinical Psychology,* **43,** 522–527.

Festinger, L. A. (1954). A theory of social comparison processes. *Human Relations,* **7,** 117–140.

Fiedler, D., & Beach, L. R. (1978). On the decision to be assertive. *Journal of Consulting and Clinical Psychology,* **46,** 537–546.

Finkel, C. B., Glass, C. R., & Merluzzi, T. V. (1982). Differential discrimination of self-referent statements by depressives and nondepressives. *Cognitive Therapy and Research,* **6,** 173–183.

Fischoff, B. (1975). Hindsight=foresight: The effect of outcome knowledge on judgment under uncertainty. *Journal of Experimental Psychology: Human Perception and Performance,* **1,** 288–299.

Fischoff, B., & Beyth-Marom, R. (1983). Hypothesis evaluation from a Bayesian perspective. *Psychological Review,* **90,** 239–260.

Fiske, S. T. (1981). Schema-triggered affect: Application to social perception. In M. S. Clark & S. T. Fiske (Eds.), *Affect and Cognition:* The Seventeenth Annual Carnegie Symposium on Cognition. Hillsdale: Erlbaum.

Fiske, S. T., & Kinder, D. R. (1978). *Schemas and political information processing.* Paper presented at the meeting of the American Psychological Association, Toronto, Canada.

Fiske, S. T., Kinder, D. R., & Larter, W. M. (1983). The novice and the expert: Knowledge based strategies in political cognition. *Journal of Experimental Social Psychology,* **19,** 381–400.

Fiske, S. T., & Linville, P. W. (1980). What does the schema concept buy us? *Personality and Social Psychology Bulletin,* **6,** 543–557.

Flavell, J. H. (1979). Metacognition and cognitive monitoring: A new area of cognitive developmental inquiry. *American Psychologist,* **34,** 906–911.

Fleming, J. P., Miller, M. E., & Adesso, V. J. (1983). Incidental orienting tasks and the recall performance of acutely intoxicated subjects. *International Journal of the Addictions,* **18,** 143–148.

Flor-Henry, P. (1976). Lateralized temporal-limbic dysfunction and psychopathology. *Annals of the New York Academy of Sciences,* **280,** 777–797.

Fong, G. T., & Markus, H. (1982). Self-schemas and judgments about others. *Social Cognition,* **1,** 191–205.

Forgas, J. P. (1978). Social episodes and social structure in an academic setting: The social environment of an intact group. *Journal of Personality and Social Psychology,* **14,** 434–448.

Frank, J. (1961). *Persuasion and healing.* Baltimore, MD: Johns Hopkins University Press.

Frankel, F., Simmons, J. Q., III, Fichter, M., & Freeman, B. J. (1984). Stimulus overselectivity in autistic and mentally retarded children - A research note. *Journal of Child Psychology and Psychiatry,* **25,** 147–155.

Freides, D. (1974). Human information processing and sensory modality: Cross-modal functions, information complexity, memory, and deficit. *Psychological Bulletin,* **81,** 284–310.

Freud, S. (1950). *Collected papers* (J. Riviere, Ed. and Trans.). London: Hogarth Press.

Friedman, M., Byers, S. O., Diamant, J., & Rosenman, R. H. (1975). Plasma catecholamine response of coronary-prone subjects (Type A) to a specific challenge. *Metabolism, Clinical and Experimental,* **24,** 205–210.

Friedman, M., & Rosenman, R. (1959). Association of a specific overt behavior pattern with increases in blood cholesterol, blood clotting time, incidence of arcus senilis and clinical coronary artery disease. *JAMA, Journal of the American Medical Association,* **169,** 1286–1296.

Friedman, M., Thoresen, C. E., Gill, J. J., Powell, L. H., Ulmer, D., Thompon, L., Price, V. A., Rabin, D. D., Breall, W. S., Dixon, T., Levy, R. & Bourg, E. (1984). Alteration of Type A behavior and reduction in cardiac recurrences in postmyocardial infarction patients. *American Heart Journal,* **108,** 237–248.

Gardner, R. W. (1961). Cognitive control of attention deployment as determinants of visual illusions. *Journal of Abnormal and Social Psychology,* **62,** 120–127.

Gardner, R. W., & Long, R. I. (1962a). Cognitive controls of attention and inhibition: A study of individual consistencies. *British Journal of Psychology,* **53,** 381–388.

Gardner, R. W., & Long, R. I. (1962b). Control, defense, and centration effect: A study of scanning behavior. *British Journal of Psychology,* **53,** 129–140.

Garner, W. R. (1962). *Uncertainty and structure as psychological concepts.* New York: Wiley.

Garner, W. R. (1974). *The processing of information and structure.* Hillsdale, NJ: Erlbaum.

Gastorf, J. W. (1981). Physiologic reaction of Type A's to objective and subjective challenge. *Journal of Human Stress,* **7**(1), 16–20.

Gastorf, J. W., & Teevan, R. C. (1980). Type A coronary-prone behavior pattern and fear of failure. *Motivation and Emotion,* **4,** 71–76.

Gersten, R. (1983). Stimulus overselectivity in autistic, trainable mentally retarded, and non-handicapped children: Comparative research controlling chronological (rather than mental) age. *Journal of Abnormal Child Psychology,* **11,** 61–76.

Gersuni, G. V. (1965). Organization of afferent flow and the process of external signal discrimination. *Neuropsychologia,* **3,** 95–109.

Gibbons, F. X., Smith, T. W., Ingram, R. E., Pearce, K., Brehm, S. S., & Schroeder, D. J. (1985). Self-awareness and self confrontation: Effects of self-focused attention on members of a clinical population. *Journal of Personality and Social Psychology,* **48,** 662–675.

Gillberg, C., Rosenhall, U., & Johansson, E. (1983). Auditory brainstem responses in childhood psychosis. *Journal of Autism and Developmental Disorders,* **13,** 181–195.

Gillberg, C., Trygstad, O., & Foss, I. (1982). Childhood psychosis and urinary excretion of peptides and protein-associated peptide complexes. *Journal of Autism and Developmental Disorders,* **12,** 229–241.

Gjerde, P. F. (1983). Attentional capacity dysfunction and arousal in schizophrenia. *Psychological Bulletin,* **93,** 57–72.

Glanzer, M. (1982). Short-term memory. In C. R. Puff (Ed.), *Handbook of research methods in human memory and cognition.* New York: Academic Press, 1982.

Glanzer, M., & Cunitz, A. R. (1966). Two storage mechanisms in free recall. *Journal of Verbal Learning and Verbal Behavior,* **5,** 351–360.

Glasgow, R., Zeiss, R., Barrera, M., & Lewinsohn, P. (1977). Case studies on remediating memory deficits in brain-damaged individuals. *Journal of Clinical Psychology,* **33,** 1049–1054.

Glass, C. R., & Merluzzi, T. V. (1981). Cognitive assessment of social evaluative anxiety. In T. V. Merluzzi, C. R. Glass, & M. Genest (Eds.), *Cognitive assessment* (pp. 388–438). New York: Guilford Press.

Glass, D. C. (1977). *Behavior patterns, stress, and coronary disease.* Hillsdale, NJ: Erlbaum.

Glass, D. C., Krakoff, L. R., Contrada, R., Hilton, W. F., Kehoe, K., Mannucci, E. G., Collins, C., Snow, B., & Eltin, E. (1980). Effect of harassment and competition upon cardiovascular and catecholamine responses in Type A and Type B individuals. *Psychophysiology,* **17,** 453–463.

Glosser, G., Butters, N., & Samuels, I. (1976). Failures in information processing in patients with Korsakoff's syndrome. *Neuropsychologia,* **14,** 327–334.

Gödel, K. (1931). Uber formal unentscheidbare Satze der Principa Mathematica und verwandter Systeme. Translated in M. Davis (Ed.), *The undecidable: Basic papers on undecidable propositions, unsolvable problems and uncomputable functions.* Hewlitt, NY: Raven Press, 1965.

Goldberg, E., & Costa, L. D. (1981). Hemispheric differences in the acquisition and use of descriptive systems. *Brain and Language,* **14,** 144–173.

Goldberg, L. R. (1959). The effectiveness of clinicians' judgments: The diagnosis of organic brain damage from the Bender-Gestalt Test. *Journal of Consulting Psychology,* **23,** 25–33.

Goldberg, L. R. (1968). Simple models or simple process? Some research on clinical judgment. *American Psychologist,* **23,** 483–496.

Golden, C. J. (1978). *Diagnosis and rehabilitation in clinical neuropsychology.* Springfield, IL: Thomas.

Goldfried, M. R. (1982). Resistance and clinical behavior therapy. In P. L. Wachtel (Ed.), *Resistance: Psychodynamic and behavioral approaches.* New York: Plenum.

Goldfried, M. R., Decenteceo, E. T., & Weinberg, L. (1974). Systematic rational restructuring as a self-control technique. *Behavior Therapy,* **5,** 247–254.

Goldfried, M. R., & Robins, C. (1983). Self-schemas, cognitive bias, and the processing of therapeutic experiences. In P. C. Kendall (Ed.), *Advances in cognitive-behavioral research and therapy* (Vol. 2, pp. 33–80). New York: Academic Press.

Goldsmith, J., & McFall, R. (1975). Development and evaluation of an interpersonal skill-training program for psychiatric in-patients. *Journal of Abnormal Psychology,* **84,** 51–58.

Goldstein, A. P., Sprafkin, R. P., & Gershav, N. J. (1975). Structured learning therapy: Skill training for schizophrenics. *Schizophrenia Bulletin,* **14,** 83–88.

Goldstein, D., Hasher, L., & Stein, D. K. (1983). Processing of occurrence: Rote and item information by children of different ages and abilities. *American Journal of Psychology,* **96,** 229–241.

Goodkin, R. (1966). Case studies in behavioral research in rehabilitation. *Perceptual and Motor Skills,* **23,** 171–182.

Gotlib, I. H. (1981). Self-reinforcement and recall: Differential deficits in depressed and non-depressed psychiatric inpatients. *Journal of Abnormal Psychology,* **90,** 521–530.

Gotlib, I. H. (1983). Perception and recall of interpersonal feedback: Negative bias in depression. *Cognitive Therapy and Research,* **7,** 399–412.

Gotlib, I. H., & McCann, C. D. (1984). Construct accessibility and depression: An examination of cognitive and affective factors. *Journal of Personality and Social Psychology,* **47,** 427–439.

Graesser, A. C., Woll, S. B., Kowalski, D. J., & Smith, D. A. (1980). Memory for typical and atypical actions in scripted activities. *Journal of Experimental Psychology: Human Learning and Memory,* **6,** 503–515.

Greenberg, L. S., & Safran, J. D. (1981). Encoding and cognitive therapy: Changing what clients attend to. *Psychotherapy, Theory, Research, and Practice,* **18,** 163–169.

Greenberg, L. S., & Safran, J. D. (1984). Integrating affect and cognition: A perspective on the process of therapeutic change. *Cognitive Therapy and Research,* **8,** 559–578.

Greenwald, A. G. (1980). The totalitarian ego: Fabrication and revision of personal history. *American Psychologist,* **35,** 603–618.

Greenwald, A. G., & Ronis, D. L. (1978). Twenty years of cognitive dissonance. Case study of the evolution of a theory. *Psychological Review,* **85,** 53–57.

Grimm, L., & Yarnold, P. (1984). Performance standards and the Type A behavior pattern. *Cognitive Therapy and Research,* **8,** 59–66.

Grossberg, S. (1982). Processing expected and unexpected events during conditioning and attention: A psychophysiological theory. *Psychological Review,* **89,** 529–572.

Groves, P. M., & Thompson, R. F. (1970). Habituation: A dual process theory. *Psychological Review,* **77,** 419–450.

Gruneberg, M. M., Morris, P. E., & Sykes, R. N. (Eds.). (1978). *Practical aspects of memory.* New York: Academic Press.

Gummow, L., Miller, P., & Dustman, R. (1983). Attention and brain injury: A case for cognitive rehabilitation of attentional deficits. *Clinical Psychology Review,* **3,** 255–274.

Gur, R. E. (1978). Left hemisphere dysfunction and left hemisphere overactiviation in schizophrenia. *Journal of Abnormal Psychology,* **87,** 226–238.

Gur, R. C., & Sackeim, H. A. (1979). Self-deception: A concept in search of a phenomenon. *Journal of Personality and Social Psychology,* **37,** 147–169.

Haber, R. N. (1969). *Information processing approaches to visual perception.* New York: Holt, Rinehart, & Winston.

Haber, R. N. (1983). The impending demise of the icon: A critique of the concept of iconic storage in visual information processing. *Behavioral and Brain Sciences,* **6,** 1–11.

Hamilton, D. (1979). A cognitive-attributional analysis of stereotyping. In I. Berkowitz (Ed.), *Advances in experimental social psychology* (Vol. 12). New York: Academic Press.

Hamilton, E. W., & Abramson, L. Y. (1983). Cognitive patterns and major depressive disorder: A longitudinal study in a hospital setting. *Journal of Abnormal Psychology,* **92,** 173–184.

Hammen, C. L. (1983a). Cognitive and social processes in bipolar affective disorders: A neglected topic. In C. L. Hammen (Chair), *Research issues and opportunities in bipolar affective disorder.* Symposium presented at the meeting of the American Psychological Association, Anaheim, CA.

Hammen, C. L. (1983b). Self-schemas and vulnerability to depression. In L. B. Alloy (Chair), *Depression and schemata.* Symposium presented at the meeting of the American Psychological Association, Anaheim, CA.

Hammen, C. L. (1985). Predicting depression. In P. C. Kendall (Ed.), *Advances in Cognitive–Behavioral Research and Therapy* (Vol. 4). New York: Academic Press.

Hammen, C. L., Marks, Y., de Mayo, R., & Mayol, A. (1985). Self-schemas and risk for depression: A prospective study. *Journal of Personality and Social Psychology,* **49,** 1147–1159.

Hammen, C. L., Marks, T., Mayol, A., & de Mayo, R. (1985). Depression self-schemas, life stress, and vulnerability to depression. *Journal of Abnormal Psychology,* **94,** 308–319.

Hammen, C. L., Miklowitz, D. J., & Dyck, D. (in press). Stability and severity parameters of depression self schema responding. *Journal of Social and Clinical Psychology.*

Hammen, C. L., & Zupon, B. A. (1984). Self-schemas, depression, and the processing of personal information in children. *Journal of Experimental Child Psychology,* **37,** 598–608.

Hammond, K., & Summer, D. (1972). Cognitive control. *Psychological Review,* **79,** 58–67.

Hampson, S. E. (1982). *The construction of personality: An introduction.* London: Routledge & Kegan Paul.

Hannon, R., Day, C. L., Butler, C. M., Larson, A. J., & Casey, M. (1983). Alcohol consumption and cognitive functioning in college students. *Journal of Studies on Alcohol,* **44,** 283–298.

Harrell, R. H., & Ryon, N. B. (1983). Cognitive-behavioral assessment of depression: Clinical validation of the automatic thoughts questionnaire. *Journal of Consulting and Clinical Psychology,* **51,** 721–725.

Harris, G. J., & Fleer, R. E. (1974). High speed memory scanning in mental retardates: Evidence for a central processing deficit. *Journal of Experimental Child Psychology,* **17,** 452–459.

Harrison, A. A. (1977). Mere exposure. In R. G. Green and M. B. Quanty (Eds.), *Advances in experimental social psychology* (Vol. 10, pp. 39–83). New York: Academic Press.

Harvey, P., Winters, K., Weintraub, S., & Neale, J. M. (1981). Distractibility in children vulnerable to psychopathology. *Journal of Abnormal Psychology,* **90,** 298–304.

Hasher, L., Griffin, M., & Johnson, M. K. (1977). More on interpretive factors in forgetting. *Memory and Cognition,* **5,** 41–45.

Hasher, L., Rose, K. C., Zacks, R. T., Sanft, H., & Doren, B. (1985). Mood, recall, and selectivity effects in normal college students. *Journal of Experimental Psychology,* **114,** 104–118.

Hashtroudi, S., Parker, E. S., Delisi, L. E., & Wyatt, R. I. (1983). On elaboration and alcohol. *Journal of Verbal Learning and Verbal Behavior,* **22,** 164–173.

Hastie, R., & Carlston, D. (1980). Theoretical issues in person memory. In R. Hastie, T. M. Ostrom, E. B. Ebbesen, R. S. Wyer, D. L. Hamilton, & D. E. Carlston (Eds.), *Person memory: The cognitive basis of social perception.* Hillsdale, NJ: Erlbaum.

Hastie, R., Ostrom, T. M., Ebbesen, E. B., Wyer, R. S., Hamilton, D. L., & Carlston, D. E. (Eds.). (1980). *Person memory: The cognitive basis of social perception.* Hillsdale, NJ: Erlbaum.

Haugeland, J. (1981). An introduction to mind design. In J. Haugeland (Ed.), *Mind design.* Cambridge, MA: MIT Press.

Hayes-Roth, B. (1977). Evolution of cognitive structures and processes. *Psychological Review,* **84,** 260–278.

Haynes, S. G., Feinleib, M., & Kannel, W. B. (1980). The relationship of psychosocial factors to coronary heart disease in the Framingham study: III. Eight-year incidence of coronary heart disease. *American Journal of Epidemiology,* **14,** 37–58.

Hays, W. L. (1973). *Statistics for the social sciences* (2nd ed.). New York: Holt, Rinehart, & Winston.

Head, H. (1920). *Studies in neurology.* London & New York: Oxford University Press.

Heilman, K. M., Bowers, D., & Valenstein, E. (1985). In K. M. Heilman & E. Valenstein (Eds.), *Clinical Neuropsychology* (2nd ed.) (pp. 377–402). New York: Oxford University Press.

Heilman, K. M., Watson, R. J., & Valenstein, E. (1979). Neglect and related disorders. In K. M. Heilman & E. Valenstein (Eds.), *Clinical neuropsychology* (2nd ed.) London & New York: Oxford University Press.

Heilman, K. M., & Van Den Abell, T. (1979). Right hemisphere dominance for mediating cerebral activation. *Neuropsychologia,* **17,** 315–321.

Heilman, K. M., & Van Den Abell, T. (1980). Right hemisphere dominance for attention: The mechanism underlying hemispheric asymmetries of inattention (neglect). *Neurology,* **30,** 327–330.

Hester, R. K., Smith, J. W., & Jackson, T. R. (1980). Recovery of cognitive skills in alcoholics. *Journal of Studies on Alcohol,* **41,** 363–367.

Higgins, E. T., & King, G. (1981). Accessibility of social constructs: Information-processing consequences of individual and contextual variability. In N. Cantor & J. F. Kilhstrom (Eds.), *Personality, cognition, and social interaction.* Hillsdale, NJ: Erlbaum.

Higgins, E. T., King, G. A., & Mavin, G. H. (1982). Individual construct accessibility and subjective impressions and recall. *Journal of Personality and Social Psychology,* **43,** 35–47.

Higgins, R. L., & Marlatt, G. A. (1975). Fear of interpersonal evaluation as a determinant of alcohol consumption in male social drinkers. *Journal of Abnormal Psychology,* **84,** 644–651.

Hilgard, E. R. (1948) *Theories of learning.* New York: Appleton-Century-Crofts.

Hoffman, P. J. (1968). Cue-consistency and configurality in humans judgment. In B. Kleinmuntz (Ed.), *Formal representation of human judgment.* New York: Wiley.

Hollon, S. D. (1981). Comparisons and combinations with alternative approaches. In L. P. Rehm (Ed.), *Behavior therapy for depression: Present status and future directions.* New York: Academic Press.

Hollon, S. D. (1983). *Final report of the cognitive-pharmacotherapy trial: Outcome, prophylaxis, prognosis, and mechanism.* Symposium presented at the Association for the Advancement of Behavior Therapy, Washington, DC.

Hollon, S. D., & Beck, A. T. (1979). Cognitive therapy of depression. In P. C. Kendall & S. D. Hollon (Eds.), *Cognitive-behavioral interventions: Theory, research, and procedures* (pp. 153–203). New York: Academic Press.

Hollon, S. D., DeRubeis, R. J., Tuason, V. B., Evans, M. D., Weimer, M. J., & Garvey, M. J. (1984). *Combined cognitive-pharmacotherapy versus cognitive therapy alone in the treatment of depressed outpatients: Differential treatment outcome in the CPT project.* Unpublished manuscript, University of Minnesota and St. Paul-Ramsey Medical Center.

Hollon, S. D., & Garber, J. (in press). Cognitive therapy: A social-cognitive perspective. In L. Y. Abramson (Ed.), *Social-personal inferences in clinical psychology.* New York: Guilford Press.

Hollon, S. D., & Kendall, P. C. (1980). Cognitive self-statements in depression: Development of an automatic thoughts questionnaire. *Cognitive Therapy and Research,* **4,** 383–395.

Hollon, S. D., & Kriss, M. (1984). Cognitive factors in clinical research and practice. *Clinical Psychology Review,* **4,** 35–76.

Holmes, D., McGilley, B., & Houston, B. K. (1984). Task-related arousal of Type A and Type B persons: Level of challenge and response specificity. *Journal of Personality and Social Psychology,* **46,** 1322–1327.

Holmes, D., & Will, M. (in press). Expression of interpersonal aggression by angered and non-angered persons with the Type A and Type B behavior patterns. *Journal of Personality and Social Psychology,* **48,** 723–727.

Holt, R. R. (1970). Yet another look at clinical and statistical prediction: Or is clinical psychology worthwhile? *American Psychologist,* **25,** 337–349.

Holton, G. (1973). *Thematic origins of scientific thought: Kepler to Einstein.* Cambridge, MA: Harvard University Press.

Homans, G. C. (1961). *Social behavior: Its elementary forms.* New York: Harcourt, Brace, & World.

Horowitz, L. M., French, R. de S., Lapid, J. S., & Weckler, D. (1982). Symptoms and interpersonal problems The prototype as an integrating concept. In J. C. Anchin & D. J. Kiesler (Eds.), *Handbook of interpersonal psychotherapy.* Oxford: Pergamon.

Horowitz, L. M., Weckler, D. A., & Doren, R. (1983). Interpersonal problems and symptoms: A cognitive approach. In P. C. Kendall (Ed.), *Advances in cognitive-behavioral research and therapy* (Vol. 2). New York: Academic Press.

Horowitz, M. J. (1976). *Stress response syndrome.* New York: Aronson.

House, B. J. (1979). Attention to components or compounds as a factor in discrimination transfer performance. *Journal of Experimental Child Psychology,* **27,** 321–331.

Houston, B. K. (1972). Control over stress, locus of control, and response to stress. *Journal of Personality and Social Psychology,* **21,** 249–255.

Houston, B. K. (1983). Psychophysiological responsivity and the Type A behavior pattern. *Journal of Research in Personality,* **17,** 22–39.

Hovland, C., & Weiss, W. (1953). Transmission of information concerning concepts through positive and negative instances. *Journal of Experimental Psychology,* **45,** 175–182.

Howard, D. V. (1984). *Cognitive psychology.* New York: Macmillan.

Howe, K. R., Holmes, M., & Elstein, A. S. (1984). Teaching clinical decision making. *Journal of Medicine and Philosophy,* **9,** 215–228.

Howell, W. C., & Goldstein, I. L. (1971). *Engineering psychology: Current perspective in research.* New York: Appleton-Century-Crofts.

Hubel, D. H., & Wiesel, T. N. (1962). receptive fields, binocular interaction and functional architecture in the cat's visual cortex. *Journal of Physiology (London),* **160,** 106–154.

Hull, C. L. (1943). *Principles of behavior.* New York: Appleton-Century-Crofts.

Hull, J. G. (1981). A self-awareness model of the causes and effects of alcohol consumption. *Journal of Abnormal Psychology,* **90,** 586–600.

Hull, J. G., Levenson, R. W., Young, R. D., & Sher, K. J. (1983). Self-awareness reducing effects of alcohol consumption. *Journal of Personality and Social Psychology,* **44,** 461–473.

Hull, J. G., & Levy, A. S. (1979). The organizational functions of the self: An alternative to the Duval and Wicklund model of self-awareness. *Journal of Personality and Social Psychology,* **37,** 756–768.

Hull, J. G., & Young, R. D. (1983). Self-consciousness, self-esteem, and success-failure as determinants of alcohol consumption in male social drinkers. *Journal of Personality and Social Psychology,* **44,** 1097–1109.

Hull, J. G., & Young, R. D. (1985). *Alcohol and the self-conscious regulation of public behavior.* Unpublished manuscript, Dartmouth College, Hanover, NH.

Hull, J. G., Young, R. D., & Jouriles, E. (in press). Applications of the self-awareness model of alcohol consumption. *Journal of Personality and Social Psychology.*

Humphries, C., Carver, C. S., & Newman, P. G. (1983). Cognitive characteristics of the Type A coronary-prone behavior pattern. *Journal of Personality and Clinical Psychology,* **44,** 177–187.

Hunt, E. B. (1978). Mechanics of verbal ability. *Psychological Review,* **85,** 109–130.

Hunt, E. B., Lunneborg, C., & Lewis, J. (1975). What does it mean to be high verbal? *Cognitive Psychology,* **7,** 194–227.

Ickes, W., & Layden, M. A. (1978). Attributional styles. In J. Harvey, W. Ickes, & R. Kidd (Eds.). *New directions in attribution research* (Vol. 2). Hillsdale: NJ: Erlbaum.

Ingram, R. E. (1983). Content and process distinctions in depressive self-schemata. In L. B. Alloy (Chair), *Depression and schemata.* Symposium presented at the meeting of the American Psychological Association, Anaheim, CA.

Ingram, R. E. (1984a). Information processing and feedback: Effects of mood and information favorability on the cognitive processing of personally relevant information. *Cognitive Therapy and Research,* **8,** 371–385.

Ingram, R. E. (1984b). Toward an information processing analysis of depression. *Cognitive Therapy and Research,* **8,** 443–478.

Ingram, R. E., Kendall, P. C., Smith, T. W., Donnell, C., & Ronan, K. (1986). *Cognitive specificity in emotional distress.* Manuscript submitted for publication.

Ingram, R. E., Lumry, A., Cruet, D., & Sieber, W. (in press). Attentional processes in depressive disorders. *Cognitive Therapy and Research.*

Ingram, R. E., & Smith, T. W. (1984). Depression and internal versus external focus of attention. *Cognitive Therapy and Research,* **8,** 139–152.

Ingram, R. E., Smith, T. W., & Brehm, S. S. (1983). Depression and information processing: Self-schemata and the encoding of self-referent information. *Journal of Personality and Social Psychology,* **45,** 412–420.

Iversen, S. D. (1977). Brain dopamine systems and behavior. In L. L. Iversen, S. D. Iversen, & S. H. Snyder (Eds.), *Handbook of psychopharmacology: Vol. 8. Drugs, neurotransmitters, and behavior* (pp. 333–384). New York: Plenum.

Izard, C. E. (1978). On the development of emotion and emotion-cognition relationship in infancy. In M. Lewis & L. Rosenblum (Eds.), *The development of affect.* New York: Plenum.

Izard, C. E., Huebner, R. R., Risser, D., McGinnes, G., & Dougherty, L. (1980). The young infants' ability to produce discrete emotion expressions, Developmental Psychology, **16,** 132–140.

James, A. L., & Barry, R. J. (1980a). Respiratory and vascular responses to simple visual stimuli in autistics, retardates, and normals. *Psychophysiology,* **17,** 541–547.

James, A. L., & Barry, R. J. (1980b). A review of psychophysiology in early onset psychosis. *Schizophrenia Bulletin,* **6,** 506–527.

James, W. (1910). *Psychology: The briefer course.* New York: Hall.

Janis, I. L. (1972). *Victims of groupthink.* Boston, MA: Houghton Mifflin.

Janis, I. L., & Mann, L. (1977). *Decision making.* New York: Free Press.

Jefferies, R., Turner, A. A., Polson, P. G., & Atwood, M. E. (1981). The process involved in designing software. In J. R. Anderson (Ed.), *Cognitive skills and their acquisition.* Hillsdale, NJ: Erlbaum.

Jenkins, C. D. (1976). Recent evidence supporting psychologic and social risk factors for coronary disease. *New England Journal of Medicine,* **294,** 987–994, 1033–1038.

Jenkins, C. D., Rosenman, R. H., & Zyzanski, S. J. (1974). Prediction of clinical coronary heart disease by a test for the coronary-prone behavior pattern. *New England Journal of Medicine,* **290,** 1271–1275.

Jenkins, C. D., Zyzanski, S. J., & Rosenman, R. H. (1976). Risk of new myocardial infarction in middle age men with manifest coronary heart disease. *Circulation,* **53,** 342–347.

Jennings, D., Amabilem, T., & Ross, L. (1982). Informal covariation assessment. In D. Kahneman, P. Slovic, & A Tversky (Eds.), *Judgment under uncertainty: Heuristics and bias.* London & New York: Cambridge University Press.

Jennings, J. R. (1983). Attention and coronary heart disease. In D. S. Krantz, A. Baum, & J. E. Singer (Eds.), *Handbook of psychology and health* (Vol. 3, pp. 85–124.) Hillsdale, NJ: Erlbaum.

Johnson, J. E., Petzel, T. P., Hartney, L. M., & Morgan, R. A. (1983). Recall of importance ratings of completed and uncompleted tasks as a function of depression. *Cognitive Therapy and Research,* **7,** 51–56.

Johnson, M. K. (1985). The origin of memories. In P. C. Kendall (Ed.), *Advances in cognitive-behavioral research and therapy* (Vol. 4). New York: Academic Press.

Johnson, M. K., & Raye, C. L. (1981). Reality monitoring. *Psychological Review,* **88,** 67–85.

Johnson-Laird, P. N. (1977). Procedural semantics. *Cognition,* **5,** 189–214.

Jones, E. E. (1964). *Ingratiation: A social psychological analysis.* New York: Appleton-Century-Crofts.

Jones, E. E. (1976). How do people perceive the causes of behavior? *American Scientist,* **64,** 300–305.

Jones, E. E., & Pittman, T. S. (1982). Toward a general theory of strategic self-presentation. In J. Suls (Ed.), *Psychological perspectives on the self* (Vol. 1). Hillsdale, NJ: Erlbaum.

Jones, L. E. (1982). Construal of social environments: Multi-dimensional models of interpersonal perception and attraction. In N. Herschberg & L. G. Humphreys (Eds.), *Multivariate applications in the social sciences.* Hillsdale, NJ: Erlbaum.

Jones, L. E. (1983). Multidimensional models of social perception, cognition, and behavior. *Applied Psychological Measurement,* **7,** 451–472.

Jones, L. E., & Young, F. W. (1972). Structure of a social environment: Longitudinal individual differences scaling of an intact group. *Journal of Personality and Social Psychology,* **24,** 108–121.

Jones, M. K., & Jones, B. M. (1980). The relationship of age and drinking history to the effects of alcohol on memory in women. *Journal of Studies on Alcohol,* **41,** 179–186.

Juola, J. F. (1979). Pattern recognition. In R. Lachman, J. L. Lachman, & E. Butterfield (Eds.), *Cognitive psychology and information processing: An introduction.* Hillsdale, NJ: Erlbaum.

Kahneman, D. (1968). Method, findings, and theory in studies of visual masking. *Psychological Bulletin,* **70,** 404–425.

Kahneman, D. (1973). *Attention and effort.* Englewood Cliffs, NJ: Prentice-Hall.

Kahneman, D., Slovic P., & Tversky, A. (1982). *Judgment under uncertainty: Heuristics and biases*. London & New York: Cambridge University Press.

Kahneman, D., & Tversky, A. (1972). Subjective probability: A judgment of representativeness. *Cognitive Psychology*, **3**, 430–454.

Kahneman, D., & Tversky, A. (1973). On the psychology of prediction. *Psychological Review*, **80**, 237–251.

Kahneman, D., & Tversky, A. (1979). Intuitive prediction: Biases and corrective procedures. *TIMS Studies in the Management Sciences*, **12**, 313–327.

Kahneman, D., & Tversky, A. (1982). Intuitive predictions: Biases and corrective procedures. In D. Kahneman, P. Slovic, & A. Tversky (Eds.), *Judgment under uncertainty: Heuristics and biases* (pp. 414–421). London & New York: Cambridge University Press.

Kaman, V., Shikiar, R. Y., & Hautaluoma, J. (1979). *Perceived social structure, role, and communication patterns in an organization*. Unpublished paper, Coloardo State University, Fort Collins.

Kanfer, F. H. (1980). Self-management methods. In F. H. Kanfer & A. P. Goldstein (Eds.), *Helping people change: A textbook of methods* (2nd ed, pp. 334–389). Oxford: Pergamon.

Kanfer, F. H., & Hagerman, S. M. (1981). The role of self-regulation. In L. P. Rehm (Ed.), *Behavior Therapy for depression: Present status and future directions* (pp. 143–180). New York: Academic Press.

Kanfer, F. H., & Hagerman, S. M. (1985). Behavior therapy and the information processing paradigm. In S. Reiss & R. R. Bootzin (Eds.), *Theoretical issues in behavior therapy*. New York: Academic Press.

Kannel, W. B. (1979). Cardiovascular disease: A multifactorial problem (Insights from the Framingham study). In M. L. Pollock & D. H. Schmidt (Eds.), *Heart disease and rehabilitation* (pp. 15–31). New York: Wiley.

Kanner, L. (1943). Autistic disturbances of affective contact. *Nervous Child*, **2**, 217–250.

Kaplan, R. (1974). *The cross-over phenomenon: Three studies of the effect of training and information on process schizophrenic reaction time*. Unpublished doctoral dissertation, University of Waterloo, Ontario, Canada.

Kazdin, A. E. (1980). *Research design in clinical psychology*. New York: Harper & Row.

Kelley, H. H. (1972). Causal schemata and the attribution process. In E. E. Jones, D. E. Kanouse, H. H. Kelley, R. E. Nisbett, S. Valins, & B. Weiner (Eds.), *Attribution: Perceiving the causes of behavior*. Morristown, NJ: General Learning Press.

Kelly, G. H. (1955). *The psychology of personal constructs*. New York: Norton.

Kendall, P. C. (1981). Assessment and cognitive-behavioral interventions: Purposes, proposals, and problems. In P. C. Kendall & S. D. Hollon (Eds.), *Assessment strategies for cognitive-behavioral interventions*. New York: Academic Press.

Kendall, P. C. (1982). Cognitive processes and procedures in behavior therapy. In C. M. Franks, G. T. Wilson, P. C. Kendall, & K. Brownell (Eds.), *Annual review of behavior therapy* (Vol. 8). New York: Guilford Press.

Kendall, P. C., & Braswell, L. (1982). On cognitive-behavioral assessment: Models, measures, and madness. In C. D. Spielberger & J. M. Butcher (Eds.), *Advances in personality assessment*. Hillsdale, NJ: Erlbaum.

Kendall, P. C., & Butcher, J. (1982). *Research in clinical psychology*. New York: Wiley.

Kendall, P. C., & Hollon, S. D. (Eds.) (1979). *Cognitive-behavioral interventions: Theory, research, and procedures*. New York: Academic Press.

Kendall, P. C., & Hollon, S. D. (Eds.). (1981). *Assessment strategies for cognitive-behavioral interventions*. New York: Academic Press.

Kendall, P. C., & Hollon, S. D. (1981). Assessing self-referent speech: Methods in the measurement of self-statements. In P. C. Kendall & S. D. Hollon (Eds.), *Assessment strategies for cognitive-behavioral interventions:* New York: Academic Press.

Kendall, P. C., & Ingram, R. E. (in press). Future directions in the cognitive-behavioral assessment of anxiety: Let's get specific. In L. Michelson & M. Ascher (Eds.), *Cognitive-behavioral assessment and treatment of anxiety disorders.* New York: Guilford Press.

Kendall, P. C., & Korgeski, G. P. (1979). Assessment and cognitive-behavioral interventions. *Cognitive Therapy and Research,* **3,** 1–21.

Keppel, G., & Underwood, B. J. (1962). Proactive inhibition in short-term retention of single items. *Journal of Verbal Learning and Verbal Behavior,* **1,** 153–161.

Kesner, R. (1973). A neural system analysis of memory storage and retrieval. *Psychological Bulletin,* **80,** 177–203.

Kessel, F., & Bevan, W. (1985). Notes toward a history of cognitive psychology. In C. Buxton (Ed.), *Points of view in the history of psychology.* New York: Academic Press.

Kety, S. S. (1980). The syndrome of schizophrenia: Unresolved questions and opportunities for research. *British Journal of Psychiatry,* **136,** 412–436.

Kidd, J. B. (1970). The utilization of subjective probabilities in production planning. *Acta Psychologica,* **34,** 338–347.

Kietzman, M. L., Spring, B., & Zubin, J. (1980). Science of human behavior: Contributions of the psychological sciences. In H. L. Kaplan, A. M. Freedman, & B. W. Sadock (Eds.), *Comprehensive textbook of psychiatry III.* Baltimore, MD: Williams & Wilkins.

Kihlstrom, J. F. (1981). On personality and memory. In N. Cantor & J. F. Kihlstrom (Eds.), *Personality, cognition, and social interaction.* Hillsdale, NJ: Erlbaum.

Kihlstrom, J. F., & Cantor, N. (1985). Mental representations of the self. In L. Berkowitz (Ed.), *Advances in experimental social psychology* (Vol. 17). New York: Academic Press.

Kihlstrom, J. F., & Nasby, W. (1981). Cognitive tasks in clinical assessment: An exercise in applied psychology. In P. C. Kendall & S. D. Hollon (Eds.), *Assessment strategies for cognitive-behavioral interventions.* New York: Academic Press.

Kinsbourne, M. (1974). Mechanisms of hemispheric interaction in man. In M. Kinsbourne & W. L. Smith (Eds.), *Hemispheric disconnection and cerebral function* (pp. 260–285). Springfield, IL: Thomas.

Kintsch, W. (1982). Memory for text. In A. Flammer & W. Kintsch (Eds.), *Discourse processing.* Amsterdam: North-Holland Publ.

Kintsch, W., Miller, J. R., & Polson, P. G. (Eds.). (1984). *Methods and tactics in cognitive science.* Hillsdale NJ: Erlbaum.

Knight, R. A. (1984). Converging models of cognitive deficit in schizophrenia. In W. D. Spaulding & J. K. Cole (Eds.), *The Nebraska symposium on motivation: Theories of schizophrenia and psychosis* (pp 93–156). Lincoln: University of Nebraska Press.

Koegel, R. L., & Schreibman, L. (1977). Teaching autistic children to respond to simultaneous multiple cues. *Journal of Experimental Child Psychology,* **24,** 299–311.

Koh, S. D., Grinker, R. R., Sr., Marcusaz, T. Z., & Forman, P. L. (1981). Affective memory and schizophrenic anhedona. *Schizophrenia Bulletin,* **7,** 292–307.

Koh, S. D., Kayton, L., & Peterson, R. A. (1976). Affective encoding and consequent remembering in schizophrenic young adults. *Journal of Abnormal Psychology,* **85,** 156–166.

Konorski, J. (1967). *Integrative activity in the brain.* Chicago, IL: University of Chicago Press.

Kootz, J. P., & Cohen, D. J. (1981). Modulation of sensory intake in autistic children: Cardiovascular and behavioral indices. *Journal of the American Academy of Child Psychiatry,* **38,** 692–701.

Kootz, J. P., Marinelli, B., & Cohen, D. J. (1982). Modulation of response to environment stimulation in autistic children. *Journal of Autism and Developmental Disorders,* **12,** 185–193.

Koriat, A., Lichenstein, S., & Fischoff, B. (1980). Reasons for confidence. *Journal of Experimental Psychology: Human Learning and Memory,* **6,** 107–118.

Kosslyn, S. M., & Holyoak, K. J. (1982). Imagery. In C. R. Puff (Ed.), *Handbook of research methods in human memory and cognition.* New York: Academic Press.

Krames, L., & MacDonald, M. R. (1985). Distraction and depressive cognitions. *Cognitive Therapy and Research,* **9,** 561–573.

Krantz, D. H. (1969). Threshold theories of signal detection. *Psychological Review,* **76,** 308–324.

Krantz, D. H., & Tversky, A. (1971). Conjoint-measurement analysis of composition rules in psychology. *Psychological Review,* **78,** 151–169.

Krantz, D. S., Arabian, J. M., Davis, J. E., & Parker, J. S. (1982). Type A behavior and coronary artery bypass surgery: Intraoperative blood pressure and preioperative complications. *Psychosomatic Medicine,* **44,** 273–284.

Krantz, D. S., & Durel, L. A. (1983). Psychobiological substrates of the Type A behavior pattern. *Health Psychology,* **2,** 393–411.

Krantz, D. S., Durel, L. A., Davia, J. E., Shaffer, R. T., Arabian, J. M., Dembroski, T. M., & MacDougall, J. M. (1982). Propranolol medication among coronary patients: Relationship to Type A behavior and cardiovascular response. *Journal of Human Stress,* **8,** 4–12.

Krantz, D. S., Glass, D. C., Schaeffer, M. A., & Davia, J. E. (1982). Behavior patterns and coronary disease: A critical evaluation. In J. T. Cacioppo & R. E. Petty (Eds.), *Perspectives in cardiovascular psychophysiology* (pp. 315–346). New York: Guilford Press.

Krasner, L., & Houts, A. C. (1984). A study of the ''value'' systems of behavioral scientists. *American Psychologist,* **39,** 840–850.

Kristofferson, M. (1967). Shifting attention between modalities: A comparison of schizophrenics and normals. *Journal of Abnormal Psychology,* **72,** 388–394.

Kruskal, J. B. (1964). Multidimensional scaling by optimizing goodness-of-fit to a nonmetric hypothesis. *Psychometrika,* **29,** 1–28, 115–129.

Kruskal, J. B., & Wish, M. (1978). *Multidimensional scaling* (Sage University Paper Series on Quantitative Applications in the Social Sciences, No. 07-011). Beverly Hills, CA: Sage Publications.

Kuffler, S. W., & Nicholls, J. G. (1976). *From neuron to brain.* Sunderland, MA: Sinauer.

Kuhn, T. S. (1962). *The structure of scientific revolutions.* Chicago, IL: University of Chicago Press.

Kuhn, T. S. (1970). *The structure of scientific revolutions* (2nd ed.). Chicago, IL: University of Chicago Press.

Kuiper, N. A., & Derry, P. A. (1981). The self as a cognitive prototype: An application to person perception and depression. In N. Cantor & J. F. Kihlstrom (Eds.), *Personality, cognition, and social interaction.* Hillsdale, NJ: Erlbaum.

Kuipeı, N. A., & Derry, P. A. (1982). Depressed and nondepressed content self-reference in mild depressive. *Journal of Personality,* **50,** 67–79.

Kuiper, N. A., Derry, P. A., & MacDonald, M. R. (1982). Self-reference and person perception in depression. In G. Weary & H. Mirels (Eds.), *Integrations of clinical and social psychology.* London & New York: Oxford University Press.

Kuiper, N. A., & Macdonald, M. R. (1982). Self and other perception in mild depressives. *Social Cognition,* **1,** 223–239.

Kuiper, N. A., MacDonald, M. R., & Derry, P. A. (1983). Parameters of a depressive self-schema. In J. Suls & A. G. Greenwald (Eds.), *Psychological perspectives on the self* (Vol. 2). Hillsdale, NJ: Erlbaum.

Kuiper, N. A., Olinger, L. J., & MacDonald, M. R. (In press). Processing personal and social information: The role of vulnerability and episodic schemata in depression In L. B. Alloy (Ed.), *Cognitive processes in depression.* New York: Guilford Press.

Kuiper, N. A., Olinger, L. J., MacDonald, M. R., & Shaw, B. F. (1985). *Self-schema processing of depressed and nondepressed content: The effects of vulnerability to depression. Social Cognition,* **3,** 77–93.

Kuiper, N. A., & Rogers, T. B. (1979). The encoding of personal information: Self-other differences. *Journal of Personality and Social Psychology,* **37,** 499–514.

Kuiper, N. A., & Rogers, T. B. (1981). Convergent evidence for the self as a cognitive prototype: The "inverted-U RT effect" for the self and other judgments. *Personality and Social Psychology Bulletin,* **7,** 438–443.

Kunst-Wilson, W. R., & Zajonc, R. B. (1980). Affective discrimination of stimuli that cannot be recognized. *Science,* **207,** 557–558.

Kuperminc, M., & Heimberg, R. G. (1983). Consequence probability and utility as factors in the decision to behave assertively. *Behavior Therapy,* **14,** 637–646.

Laberge, D., & Samuels, S. J. (1974). Toward a theory of automatic information processing in reading. *Cognitive Psychology,* **6,** 292–323.

Lachman, J. L., & Lachman, R. (1979). Theories of memory organization and human evolution. In C. R. Puff (Ed.), *Memory organization and structure.* New York: Academic Press.

Lachman, R. (1960). The model in theory construction. *Psychological Bulletin,* **67,** 113–129.

Lachman, R., Lachman, J. L., & Butterfield, E. C. (1979). *Cognitive psychology and information processing: An introduction.* Hillsdale, NJ: Erlbaum.

Lachman, R., Lachman, J. L., & Taylor, D. W. (1982). Reallocation of mental resources over the productive lifespan: Assumptions and task analyses. In F. I. M. Craik & S. E. Trehub (Eds.), *Aging and cognitive processes.* New York: Plenum.

Ladefoged, P., & Broadbent, D. E. (1957). Information conveyed by vowels. *Journal of the Acoustical Society of America,* **29,** 98–104.

Laird, J. D., Wagener, J. J., Halal, M., & Szegda, M. (1982). Remembering what you feel: Effects of emotion on memory. *Journal of Personality and Social Psychology,* **42,** 646–657.

Lambert, M., Christensen, E., & DeJulio, S. (1984). *The assessment of psychotherapy outcome.* New York: Wiley.

Landau, R. (1980). The role of semantic schemata in phobic word interpretation. *Cognitive Therapy and Research,* **4,** 427–434.

Landau, R. J., & Goldfried, M. R. (1981). The assessment of schemata: A unifying framework for cognitive, behavioral, and traditional assessment. In P. C. Kendall & S. D. Hollon (Eds.), *Assessment strategies for cognitive-behavioral interventions.* New York: Academic Press.

Lang, P. J., & Buss, A. H. (1965). Psychological deficit in schizophrenia: II. Interference and activation. *Journal of Abnormal Psychology,* **70,** 77–106.

Langer, E. J., & Abelson, R. P. (1974). A patient by any other name.: Clinician group differences in labeling bias. *Journal of Consulting and Clinical Psychology,* **42,** 4–9.

Larsen, S., & Fromholt, P. (1976). Memonic organization and free recall in schizophrenics. *Journal of Abnormal Psychology,* **85,** 61–65.

Lawson, J. S., McGhie, A., & Chapman, J. (1966). Distractibility in schizophrenia and organic cerebral disease. *British Journal of Psychiatry,* **113,** 527.

Lazarus, A. A. (1971). *Behavior therapy and beyond.* New York: McGraw-Hill.

Lazarus, R. S. (1966). *Psychological stress and the coping process.* New York: McGraw-Hill.

Lecky, P. (1945). *Self-consistency.* New York: Island Press.

Lehnert, W. G. (1984). Paradigmatic issues in cognitive science. In W. Kintsch, J. R. Miller, & P. G. Polson (Eds.), *Methods and tactics in cognitive science.* Hillsdale, NJ: Erlbaum.

Leventhal, H. (1979). A perceptual motor processing model of emotion. In P. Pilner, K. R. Blankstein, & I. M., Spigel (Eds.), *Advances in the study of communication and affect: Vol. 5. Perception of emotions in self and others.* New York: Plenum.

Leventhal, H. (1980). Toward a comprehensive theory of emotion. In L. Berkowitz (Ed.), *Advances in experimental social psychology* (Vol. 13). New York: Academic Press.

Leventhal, H., Brown, D., Shacham, S., & Engquist, G. (1979). Effects of preparatory information about sensations, threat of pain, and attention on cold pressor distress. *Journal of Personality and Social Psychology,* **37,** 688–714.

Lewinsohn, P. M. (1982). Cognitive distortion: Consequence rather than cause of depression. In N. S. Jacobson (Chair), *Cognitive theories of depression: A critical reappraisal.* Symposium

presented at the meeting of the Association for the Advancement of Behavior Therapy, Los Angeles, CA.
Lewinsohn, P. M., & Hoberman, H. M. (1982). Depression. In A. S. Bellack, M. Hersen, & A. E. Kazdin (Eds.), *International handbook of behavior modification.* New York: Plenum.
Lewinsohn, P. M., Hoberman, H., Teri, L., & Hautzinger, M. (1985). An integrative theory of depression. In S. Reiss & R. Bootzin (Eds.), *Theoretical issues in behavior therapy.* New York Academic Press.
Lewinsohn, P. M., Mischel, W., Chaplin, W., & Barton, R. (1980). Social competence and depression: The role of illusory self-perceptions? *Journal of Abnormal Psychology,* **89,** 203–212.
Lewinsohn, P. M., Steinmetz, J. L., Larson, D. W., & Franklin, J. (1981). Depression related cognitions: Antecedent or consequence? *Journal of Abnormal Psychology,* **90,** 213–219.
Lindsay, P., & Norman, D. (1977). *Human information processing.* New York: Wiley.
Lisker, L., & Abramson, A. S. (1970). The voicing dimension: Some experiments in comparative phonetics. *Proceedings of the Sixth International Congress of Phonetic Sciences.* Prague: Academia.
Litrownik, A. J. (1984). Cognitive behavior modification with psychotic children. In A. W. Meyers & W. E. Craighead (Eds.), *Cognitive behavior therapy with children* (pp. 229–260). New York: Plenum.
Litrownik, A. J., & McInnis, E. T. (1982). Cognitive and perceptual deficits in autistic children: A model of information processing, critical review, and suggestions for the future. In P. Karoly & J. J. Steffen (Eds.), *Advances in child behavior analysis and therapy* (Vol. 1, pp. 103–155). New York: Gardner Press.
Litrownik, A. J., Mcinnis, E. T., Wetzel-Pritchard, A. M., & Filipelli, D. L. (1978). Restricted stimulus control and inferred attentional deficits in autistic and retarded children. *Journal of Abnormal Psychology,* **87,** 544–562.
Lloyd, G. G., & Lishman, W. (1975). Effect of depression on the speed of recall of pleasant and unpleasant memories. *Psychological Medicine,* **5,** 173–180.
Loberg, T. (1980). Alcohol misuse and neuropsychological deficits in men. *Journal of Studies on Alcohol,* **41,** 119–128.
Lord, C. G. (1980). Schemas and images as memory aids: Two modes of processing social information. *Journal of Personality and Social Psychology,* **38,** 257–269.
Lovaas, O. I. (1979). Contrasting illness and behavioral models for the treatment of autistic children: A historical perspective. *Journal of Autism and Developmental Disorders,* **9,** 315–323.
Lovaas, O. I., Koegel, R. L., & Schreibman, L. (1979). Stimulus overselectivity in autism: A review of research. *Psychological Bulletin,* **86,** 1236–1254.
Lovaas, O. I., Schreibman, L., Koegel, R., & Rehm, R. (1971). Selective responding by autistic children to multiple sensory input. *Journal of Abnormal Psychology,* **77,** 211–222.
Lutz, D. J., & Holmes, D. S. (1984). *Coronary-prone behavior patterns, arousal, and situation choice.* Paper presented at the meeting of the American Psychological Association, Toronto, Canada.
Lynch, W. (1984). *A guide for Atari video computers and home computer programs for rehabilitation settings* (5th ed.). Palo Alto, CA: Palo Alto Veterans Administration Medical Center.
MacAndrew, C., & Edgerton, R. (1969). *Drunken comportment: A social explanation.* Chicago, IL: Aldine.
Machlup, F., & Mansfield, U. (1983). Cultural diversity in studies of information. In F. Machlup & U. Mansfield (Eds.), *The study of information.* New York: Wiley.
MacVane, J., Butters, N., Montgomery, K., & Farber, J. (1982). Cognitive functioning in men social drinkers. *Journal of Studies on Alcohol,* **43,** 81–95.
Magaro, P. A. (1980). *Cognition in schizophrenia and paranoia: The integration of cognitive processes.* Hillsdale, NJ: Erlbaum.

Magaro, P. A. (1981). The paranoid and the schizophrenic: The case for distinct cognitive style. *Schizophrenia Bulletin,* **7,** 632–661.

Magaro, P. A. (1984). Psychosis and schizophrenia. In W. Spaulding & J. K. Cole (Eds.), *The Nebraska symposium on motivation.* Lincoln: University of Nebraska Press.

Magaro, P. A., & Ashbrook, R. (1984). The application of an information processing model to the diagnosis and treatment of functional disorders through the use of a mini-computer. *Fourth International Symposium on Models and Techniques of Cognitive Rehabilitation,* Indianapolis, Indiana.

Magaro, P. A., & Page, J. (1983). Brain disconnection, schizophrenia, and paranoia. *Journal of Nervous and Mental Disorders* **171,** 133–140.

Magaro, P. A., & West, A. N. (1983). Structured learning therapy: A study with chronic psychiatric patients and level of pathology. *Behavior Modification,* **7,** 29–40.

Maher, B. A. (1966). *Principles of psychopathology.* New York: McGraw-Hill.

Mahoney, M. J. (1974). *Cognition and behavior modification.* Cambridge, MA: Ballinger.

Mahoney, M. J. (1977). Reflections on the cognitive-learning trend in psychotherapy. *American Psychologist,* **32,** 5–13.

Malcolm, J. (1983). Annals of scholarship (Psychoanalysis, Part 1). *New Yorker,* December 3, 59–152.

Mancuso, J. C., & Ceely, S. G. (1980). The self as memory processing. *Cognitive Therapy and Research,* **4,** 1–25.

Mandler, G. (1967). Organization and memory. In K. W. Spence & J. T. Spence (Eds.), *The psychology of learning and motivation: Advances in research and theory* (Vol. 1). New York: Academic Press.

Mandler, G. (1975). *Mind and emotion.* New York: Wiley.

Manning, M. M., & Wright, T. L. (1983). Self-efficacy expectancies, outcome expectancies, and the persistence of pain control in childbirth. *Journal of Personality and Social Psychology,* **45,** 421–431.

Manuck, S. B., & Garland, F. N. (1979). Coronary-prone behavior pattern, task incentive, and cardiovascular response. *Psychophysiology,* **16,** 136–142.

Manuck, S. B., Harvey, S. H., Lechleiter, S. L., & Neal, K. S. (1978). Effects of coping on blood pressure responses to threat of aversive stimulation. *Psychophysiology,* **15,** 544–549.

Margolis, L., McLeroy, K., Runyan, C., & Kaplan, B. (1983). Type A behavior: An ecological approach. *Journal of Behavioral Medicine,* **6,** 245–258.

Markus, H. (1977). Self-schemata and processing information about the self. *Journal of Personality and Social Psychology,* **35,** 63–78.

Markus, H., Crane, M., Bernstein, S., & Siladi, M. (1982). Self-schemas and gender. *Journal of Personality and Social Psychology,* **42,** 38–50.

Markus, H., & Sentis, K. (1982). The self in social information processing. In J. Suls (Ed.), *Social psychological perspectives on the self* (Vol. 1, pp. 41–70). Hillsdale, NJ: Erlbaum.

Markus, H., Sentis, K. P., & Hamill, R. (1979). *Thinking fat: Self-schemas for body weight and the processing of weight relevant information.* Unpublished manuscript, University of Michigan, Ann Arbor.

Marlatt, G. A., & Rohsenow, D. J. (1980). Cognitive processes in alcohol use: Expectancy and the balanced placebo design. In N. K. Mello (Ed.), *Advances in substance abuse: Behavioral and Biological Research: A Research Annual* (Vol. 1, pp. 159–199). Greenwich, CT: JAI Press.

Marr, D. C. (1982). *Vision: A computational investigation into the human representation and processing of visual information.* San Francisco, CA: Freeman.

Martin, D., Abramson, L. Y., & Alloy, L. B. (1984). The illusion of control for self and others in depressed and nondepressed college students. *Journal of Personality and Social Psychology,* **46,** 125–136.

Martin, M., & Clark, D. M. (1986). On the response bias explanation of selective memory effects in depression. *Cognitive Therapy and Research,* **10,** 267–270.

Martineau, J., Garreau, B., Barthelemy, C., & Lelord, G. (1984). Evoked potentials and P300 during sensory conditioning in autistic children. *Brain and Information,* **425,** 362–369.

Martineau, J., Garreau, B., Barthelemy, C., Callaway, E., & Lelord, G. (1981). Effects of vitamin B6 on averaged evoked potentials in infantile autism. *Biological Psychiatry,* **16,** 627–644.

Martinson, W. D., & Zerface, J. P. (1970). Comparison of individual counseling and social program with nondaters. *Journal of Counseling Psychology,* **17,** 36–40.

Mason, J. W. (1975). Emotions as reflected in patterns of endocrine integration. In L. Levi (Ed.), *Emotions: Their parameters and measurement* (pp. 143–181). New York: Raven Press.

Matteson, M. T., & Ivancevich, D. B. A. (1982). Type A and B behavior patterns and self-reported health symptoms and stress: Examining individual and organizational fit. *Journal of Occupational Medicine,* **24,** 585–589.

Matthews, K. A. (1977). Caregiver-child interactions and the Type A coronary-prone behavior pattern. *Child Development,* **48,** 1752–1756.

Matthews, K. A. (1982). Psychological perspectives on the Type A behavior pattern. *Psychological Bulletin,* **91,** 293–323.

Matthews, K. A., & Brunson, B. I. (1979). Allocation of attention and the Type A coronary-prone behavior pattern. *Journal of Personality and Social Psychology,* **37,** 2081–2090.

Matthews, K. A., Glass, D. C., Rosenman, R. H., & Bortner, R. W. (1977). Competitive drive, Pattern A, and coronary heart disease: A further analysis of some data from the Western Collaborative Group Study. *Journal of Chronic Diseases,* **30,** 489–498.

Matthews, K. A., Helmreich, R. L., Beane, W. E., & Lucker, G. W. (1980). Pattern A, achievement, striving, and scientific merit: Does Pattern A help or hinder? *Journal of Personality and Social Psychology,* **39,** 962–967.

Matthews, K. A., Krantz, D. S., Dembroski, T. M., & MacDougall, J. M. (1982). Unique and common variance in structured interview and Jenkins activity survey measures of the Type A behavior pattern. *Journal of Personality and Social Psychology,* **42,** 303–313.

Matthews, K. A., & Siegel, J. M. (1982). The Type A behavior pattern in children and adolescents: Assessment, development, and associated risk. In A. Baum & J. E. Singer (Eds.), *Handbook of psychology and health* (Vol. 2, pp. 99–118). New York: Erlbaum.

Matthews, K. A., & Siegel, J. M. (1983). Type A behaviors by children, social comparison, and standards for self-evaluation. *Developmental Psychology,* **19,** 135–140.

Matthews, K. A., Siegel, J. M., Kuller, L. H., Thompson, M., & Varat, M. (1983). Determinants of decisions to seek medical treatment by patients with acute myocardial infarction symptoms. *Journal of Personality and Social Psychology,* **39,** 962–967.

Matthews, K. A., & Volkin, J. I. (1981). Efforts to excel and the Type A behavior pattern in children. *Child Development,* **52,** 1283–1289.

Matthysee, S. (1974). Dopamine and the pharmacology of schizophrenia: The state of the evidence. *Journal of Psychiatric Research,* **11,** 107.

Maurer, R. G., & Damasio, A. R. (1982). Childhood autism from the point of view of behavioral neurology. *Journal of Autism and Developmental Disorders,* **12,** 195–205.

Maynert, E. W., & Levi, R. (1964). Stress-induced release of brain norepinephrine and its inhibition by drugs. *Journal of Pharmacology and Experimental Therapeutics,* **143,** 90–95.

McCall, G. J., & Simmons, J. L. (1966). *Identities and interactions: An examination of human associations in everyday life.* New York: Free Press.

McClelland, J. L. (1979). On the time relations of mental processes: An examination of systems of processes in cascade. *Psychological Review,* **86,** 287–330.

McDowall, J. (1981). Effects of encoding instructions on recall and recognition in Korsakoff patients. *Neuropsychologia,* **19,** 43–48.

McFall, R. M., & Lillesand, D. B. (1971). Behavioral rehearsal with modeling and coaching in assertion training. *Journal of Abnormal Psychology,* **77,** 313–323.
McDowall, J. (1984). Recall of pleasant and unpleasant words in depressed subjects. *Journal of Abnormal Psychology,* **93,** 401–407.
McGeoch, J. A. (1942). *The psychology of human learning.* New York: Longmans, Green.
McGhie, A., & Chapman, J. (1961). Disorders of attention and perception in early schizophrenia. *British Journal of Medical Psychology,* **34,** 103–116.
McGuinness, D., & Pribram, K. H. (1980). The neuropsychology of attention: Emotional and motivational controls. In M. C. Wittrock (Ed.), *The brain and psychology* (pp. 95–139). New York: Academic Press.
McMahon, I. D. (1973). Relationship between causal attributions and expectancy of success. *Journal of Personality and Social Psychology,* **28,** 108–114.
Mednick, S. A. (1958). A learning theory approach to research in schizophrenia. *Psychological Bulletin,* **55,** 316–327.
Meehl, P. E. (1954). *Clinical versus statistical prediction.* Minneapolis: University of Minnesota Press.
Meehl, P. E. (1960). The cognitive activity of the clinician. *American Psychologist,* **15,** 19–27.
Meehl, P. E. (1973). Why I do not attend case conferences. In P. E. Meehl (Ed.), *Psychodiagnosis: Selected papers* (pp. 255–302). Minneapolis: University of Minnesota Press.
Meichenbaum, D. (1977). *Cognitive behavior modification: An integrative approach.* New York: Plenum.
Meichenbaum, D., & Cameron, R. (1983). Stress innoculation training: Toward a general paradigm for training coping skills: In D. Meichenbaum & M. E. Jaremko (Eds.), *Stress reduction and prevention* (pp. 115–154). New York: Plenum.
Meichenbaum, D., & Novaco, R. (1978). Stress innoculation: A preventative approach. In C. D. Spielberger & I. G. Sarason (Eds.), *Stress and anxiety* (Vol. 5, pp. 317–330). Washington, DC: Hemisphere.
Meichenbaum, D., & Turk, D. C. (1976). The cognitive-behavioral management of anxiety, anger, and pain. In P. O. Davidson (Ed.), *The behavioral management of anxiety, depression, and pain.* New York: Brunner/Mazel.
Meiselman, K. C. (1973). Broadening dual modality cue utilization in chronic nonparanoid schizophrenia. *Journal of Consulting and Clinical Psychology,* **41,** 447–453.
Meltzer, H. Y. (1979). Biochemical studies in schizophrenia. In L. Bellak (Ed.), *Disorders of the schizophrenic syndrome* (pp. 45–135). New York: Basic Books.
Merluzzi, T. V., Glass, C. R., & Genest, M. (Eds.). (1981). *Cognitive assessment.* New York: Guilford Press.
Merluzzi, T. V., Rudy, T. E., & Glass, C. R. (1981). The information processing paradigm: Implications for clinical science. In T. V. Merluzzi, C. R. Glass, & M. Genest (Eds.), *Cognitive assessment.* New York: Guilford Press.
Metalsky, G. I., & Abramson, L. Y. (1981). Attributional styles: Toward a framework for conceptualization and assessment. In P. C. Kendall & S. D. Hollon (Eds.), *Assessment strategies for cognitive-behavioral interventions.* New York: Academic Press.
Mettlin, C. (1976). Occupational careers and the prevention of coronary-prone behavior. *Social Science and Medicine,* **10,** 367–372.
Miller, E. (1977). The management of dementia: A review of some possibilities. *British Journal of Social and Clinical Psychology,* **16,** 77–83.
Miller, G. A. (1956). The magical number seven, plus or minus two: Some limits on our capacity for processing information. *Psychological Review,* **63,** 81–97.
Miller, G. A. (1974). Toward a third metaphor for psycholinguistics. In B. Weimer & D. S. Palermo (Eds.), *Cognition and the symbolic processes.* Hillsdale, NJ: Erlbaum.

Miller, G. A., Galanter, E., & Pribram, K. H. (1960). *Plans and the structure of behavior*. New York: Henry Holt.

Miller, G. A., & Gazzaniga, M. S. (1984). The cognitive sciences. In M. S. Gazzaniga (Ed.), *Handbook of cognitive neuroscience*. New York: Plenum.

Miller, S., Saccuzzo, D. P., & Braff, D. L. (1979). Information processing deficits in remitted schizophrenics. *Journal of Abnormal Psychology,* **88,** 446–449.

Mills, C. J. (1983). Sex-typing and self-schemata effects on memory and response latency. *Journal of Personality and Social Psychology,* **45,** 163–172.

Mills, C. J., & Tyrell, D. J. (1983). Sex-stereotyping encoding and release from proactive interference. *Journal of Personality and Social Psychology,* **45,** 772–781.

Milner, B. (1966). Amnesia following operation on the temporal lobes. In C. W. M. Whitty & O. L. Zangwill (Eds.), *Amnesia*. London: Butterworth.

Minsky, M. (1967). *Computation: Finite and infinite machines*. Englewood Cliffs, NJ: Prentice-Hall.

Mirsky, A. F. (1969). Neuropsychological basis of schizophrenia. *Annual Review of Psychology,* **20,** 321–348.

Mischel, W. (1968). *Personality and assessment*. New York: Wiley.

Mischel, W. (1973). Toward a cognitive social learning reconceptualization of personality. *Psychological Review,* **80,** 252–283.

Mischel, W. (1981). A cognitive-social learning approach to assessment. In T. V. Merluzzi, C. R. Glass, & M. Genest (Eds.), *Cognitive assessment*. New York: Guilford Press.

Mischel, W. (1984). Convergences and challenges in the search for consistency. *American Psychologist,* **39,** 351–364.

Mischel, W., Ebbesen, E. B., & Zeiss, A. M. (1973). Selective attention to the self: Situational and dispositional determinants. *Journal of Personality and Social Psychology,* **27,** 129–142.

Mischel, W., Ebbesen, E. B., & Zeiss, A. M. (1976). Determinants of selective memory about the self. *Journal of Consulting and Clinical Psychology,* **44,** 92–105.

Moskowitz, H. (1973). Laboratory studies of the effects of alcohol on some variables related to driving. *Journal of Safety Research,* **5,** 185–199.

Mueller, C. W., Lisman, C. A., & Spear, N. E. (1983). Alcohol enhancement of human memory: Tests of consolidation and interference hypotheses. *Psychopharmacology,* **80,** 226–230.

Mulder, G. (1983). The information processing paradigm: Concepts, methods, and limitations. *Journal of Child Psychology and Psychiatry,* **24,** 19–35.

Munsat, S. (1966). *The concept of memory*. New York: Random House.

Murdock, B. B., Jr. (1962). The serial position effect of free recall. *Journal of Experimental Psychology,* **64,** 482–488.

Murdock, B. B., Jr. (1982). Recognition memory. In C. R. Puff (Ed.), *Handbook of research methods in human learning and cognition*. New York: Academic Press.

Murphy, G. E., & Simmon, A. D., Wetzel, R. D., & Lustman, P. J. (1984). Cognitive therapy and pharmacotherapy, singly and together, in the treatment of depression. *Archives of General Psychiatry,* **41,** 33–41.

Murphy, M. D., & Puff, C. R. (1982). Free recall: Basic methodology and analyses. In C. R. Puff (Ed.), *Handbook of research methods in human memory and cognition*. New York: Academic Press.

Nagel, E. (1961). *The structure of science*. New York: Harcourt Brace.

Nasby, W. C. (1986a). *Induced moods and the selective encoding of personal information about the self*. (submitted for publication.)

Nasby, W. C. (1986b). *Egocentric versus empathic dysphoria and selective encoding of personal information about the self and others*. (in preparation.)

Nasby, W., Hayden, B., & DePaulo, B. M. (1980). Attributional bias among aggressive boys to interpret unambiguous social stimulus displays of hostility. *Journal of Abnormal Psychology,* **89,** 459–468.

Nasby, W., & Yando, R. (1980). Clinical and developmental implications of memory and affect in children. In R. Selman & R. Yando (Eds.), *New directions for child development: Clinical-developmental psychology.* San Francisco, CA: Jossey-Bass.

Nasby, W., & Yando, R. (1982). Selective encoding and retrieval of affectively-valent information: Two cognitive consequences of children's mood states. *Journal of Personality and Social Psychology,* **43,** 1244–1253.

Natale, M., & Hantas, M. (1982). Effect of temporary mood states on selective memory about the self. *Journal of Personality and Social Psychology,* **42,** 927–934.

National Society for Autistic Children. (1978). Definition of the syndrome of autism. *Journal of Autism and Childhood Schizophrenia,* **8,** 162–167.

Neale, J. M., & Cromwell, R. L. (1968). Size estimation in schizophrenics as a function of stimulus presentation time. *Journal of Abnormal Psychology,* **73,** 44–49.

Neale, J. M., & Cromwell, R. L. (1970). Attention and schizophrenia. In B. A. Maher (Ed.), *Progress in experimental personality research* (Vol. 5). New York: Academic Press.

Neale, J. M., McIntyre, C. W., Fox, R., & Cromwell, R. L. (1969). Span of apprehension in acute schizophrenics. *Journal of Abnormal Psychology,* **74,** 593–596.

Neisser, U. (1963). Decision-time without reaction time: Experiments in visual scanning. *American Journal of Psychology,* **76,** 376–385.

Neisser, U. (1967). *Cognitive psychology.* New York: Appleton-Century-Crofts.

Neisser, U. (1976). *Cognition and reality.* San Francisco, CA: Freeman.

Neisser, U. (1980a). On "social knowing." *Personality and Social Psychology Bulletin,* **6,** 601–605.

Neisser, U. (1980b). Three cognitive psychologies and their implications. In M. J. Mahoney (Ed.), *Psychotherapy process: Current issues and future directions.* New York: Plenum.

Neisser, U. (1982). *Memory observed: Remembering in natural contexts.* San Francisco, CA: Freeman.

Neisser, U. (1985). Toward an ecologically oriented cognitive science. In T. M. Shlechter & M. P. Toglia (Eds.), *New directions in cognitive science.* Norwood, NJ: Ablex.

Nelson, R. E., & Craighead, W. E. (1977). Selective recall of positive and negative feedback, self-control behaviors, and depression. *Journal of Abnormal Psychology,* **86,** 379–388.

Newcomb, T. M. (1961). *The acquaintance process.* New York: Holt, Rinehart, & Winston.

Newell, A. (1980). Physical symbol systems. *Cognitive Science,* **4,** 135–183.

Newell, A., & Simon, H. A. (1972). *Human problem solving.* Englewood Cliffs, NJ: Prentice Hall.

Newell, A., & Simon, H. A. (1976). Computer science as empirical inquiry: Symbols and search. *Communication of the ACM,* **19,** 113–126.

Nisbett, R. E., Krantz, D. H., Jepson, C., & Kunda, Z. (1983). The use of statistical heuristics in everyday inductive reasoning. *Psychological Review,* **90,** 339–363.

Nisbett, R. E., & Ross, L. (1980). *Human inference: Strategies and shortcomings of social judgment.* Englewood Cliffs, NJ: Prentice-Hall.

Nisbett, R. E., & Wilson, T. D. (1977). Telling more than we can know: Verbal reports on mental processes. *Psychological Review,* **84,** 231–259.

Niwa, S., Ohta, M., & Yamazaki, K. (1983). P300 and stimulus evaluation process in autistic subjects. *Journal of Autism and Developmental Disorders,* **13,** 33–42.

Norman, D. A. (1976). *Memory and attention* (2nd ed.). New York: Wiley.

Norman, D. A. (1981). Categorization of action slips. *Psychological Review,* **88,** 1–15.

Norman, D. A., & Bobrow, D. G. (1975). On data-limited and resource-limited processes. *Cognitive Psychology,* **7,** 44–64.

Norman, D. A., & Rumelhart, D. E. (1975). *Explorations in cognition.* San Francisco, CA: Freeman.

Northway, M. L. (1940). The concept of schema. *British Journal of Psychology,* **30,** 316–325.

Nottenburg, G., & Shoben, E. J. (1980). Scripts as linear orders. *Journal of Experimental Social Psychology,* **16,** 329–347.

Novick, B., Kurtzberg, D., & Vaughn, H. G., Jr. (1979). An electrophysiologic indication of defective information storage in childhood autism. *Psychiatry Research,* **1,** 101–108.

Novick, B., Vaughn, H. G., Jr., Kurtzberg, D., & Simon, R. (1980). An electrophysiologic indication of auditory processing defects in autism. *Psychiatry Research,* **3,** 107–114.

Nuechterlein, K. H. (1977). Reaction time and attention in schizophrenia: A critical evaluation of the data and theories. *Schizophrenia Bulletin,* **3,** 373–382.

Nuechterlein, K. H., & Dawson, M. E. (1984). Information processing and attentional functioning in the developmental course of schizophrenic disorders. *Schizophrenia Bulletin,* **10,** 106–203.

Nydegger, R. (1972). The elimination of hallucinatory and delusional behavior by verbal conditioning and assertive training: A case study. *Journal of Behavior Therapy and Experimental Psychiatry,* **3,** 225–227.

O'Leary, M. R., Radford, L. M., Chaney, E. F., & Schua, E. J. (1977). Assessment of cognitive recovery in alcoholics by use of the Trail-Making test. *Journal of Clinical Psychology,* **33,** 579–582.

Oltmanns, T. (1978). Selective attention in schizophrenia and manic psychoses: The effects of distraction on information processing. *Journal of Abnormal Psychology,* **87,** 212–225.

Ortega, D., & Pipal, J. (1984). Challenge seeking and the Type A coronary-prone behavior pattern. *Journal of Personality and Social Psychology,* **46,** 1328–1334.

Ortony, A. (1979). *Metaphor and thought.* London & New York: Cambridge University Press.

Orwell, G. (1949). *1984.* New York: Harcourt Brace.

Osgood, C. E. (1963). On understanding and creating sentences. *American Psychologist,* **18,** 735–751.

Osler, W. (1892). *Lectures on angina pectoris and allied states.* New York: Appleton.

Pachella, R. C. (1974). The interpretation of reaction time in information processing research. In B. Kantowitz (Ed.), *Human information processing: Tutorials in performance and cognition.* Hillsdale, NJ: Erlbaum.

Palkovitz, R. J., & Wiesenfeld, A. H. (1980). Differential automatic responses of autistic and normal children. *Journal of Autism and Developmental Disorders,* **10,** 347–360.

Palmer, S. E. (1975). The effects of contextual scenes on the identification of objects. *Memory & Cognition,* **3,** 519–526.

Parker, E. S., Birnbaum, I. M., Boyd, R., & Noble, E. P. (1980). Neuropsychological decrements as a function of alcohol intake in male students. *Alcoholism: Clinical and Experimental Research,* **44,** 330–3344.

Parker, E. S., Birnbaum, I. M., & Noble, E. P. (1976). Alcohol and memory: Storage and state dependency. *Journal of Verbal Learning and Verbal Behavior,* **15,** 691–702.

Parker, E. S., Morihisa, J. M., Wyatt, R. J., Scwartz, B. L., Weingartner, H., & Stillman, R. C. (1981). The alcohol facilitation effect on memory: A dose-response study. *Psychopharmacology,* **74,** 88–92.

Parker, E. S., & Noble, E. P. (1977). Alcohol consumption and cognitive functioning in social drinkers. *Journal of Studies on Alcohol,* **38,** 1224–1232.

Parker, E. S., & Noble, E. P. (1980). Alcohol and the aging process. *Journal of Studies on Alcohol,* **41,** 170–178.

Parsons, O. A. (1977). Neuropsychological deficits in alcoholics: Facts and fancies. *Alcoholism: Clinical and Experimental Research,* **1,** 51–56.

Patten, B. (1972). The ancient art of memory: Usefulness in treatment. *Archives of Neurology (Chicago),* **26,** 25–31.

Pavio, A. (1969). Mental imagery in associative learning and memory. *Psychological Review,* **76,** 241–263.

Pavio, A. (1971). *Imagery and verbal processes*. New York: Holt.

Paykel, E. S., Myers, J. K., Dienelt, M. N., Klerman, G. L., Lindental, J. J., & Pepper, M. P. (1969). Life events and depression: A controlled study. *Archives of General Psychiatry,* **21,** 753–760.

Payne, R. W. (1966). The measurement and significance of overinclusive thinking and retardation in schizophrenic patients. In P. Itoch & J. Zubin (Eds.), *Psychopathology of schizophrenia*. New York: Grune & Stratton.

Payne, R. W., & Hewlett, J. H. C. (1960). Thought disorder in psychotic patients. In H. J. Eysenck (Ed.), *Experiments in personality* (Vol. 2, pp. 3–104). London: Routledge & Kegan Paul.

Payne, R. W., Matussk, P., & George, E. I. (1959). An experimental study of schizophrenic thought disorder. *Journal of Mental Science,* **105,** 627–652.

Pernanen, K. (1976). Alcohol and crimes of violence. In B. Kissin & H. Begleiter (Eds.), *The biology of alcoholism: Social aspects of alcoholism* (Vol. 4). New York: Plenum.

Pervin, L. A. (1976). A free-response description approach to the analysis of person-situation interaction. *Journal of Personality and Social Psychology,* **34,** 465–474.

Peterfreund, F. (1980). On information and systems models for psychoanalysis. *International Review of Psychoanalysis,* **7,** 327–345.

Peterson, L. R., & Peterson, M. J. (1959). Short-term retention of individual verbal items. *Journal of Experimental Psychology,* **58,** 193–198.

Phillips, K. (1982). Investigating psychological dysfunction: Problems and prospects. In A. Burton (Ed.), *The pathology and psychology of cognition* (pp. 8–23). London: Methuen.

Piaget, J. (1950). *The psychology of intelligence*. London: Routledge & Kegan Paul.

Pittner, M. S., & Houston, B. K. (1980). Response to stress, cognitive coping strategies, and the Type A behavior pattern. *Journal of Personality and Social Psychology,* **39,** 147–157.

Pittner, M. S., Houston, B. K., & Spirdigliozzi, G. (1983). Control over stress, Type A behavior pattern, and response to stress. *Journal of Personality and Social Psychology,* **44,** 627–637.

Platt, J., & Spivak, G. (1972). Problem-solving thinking of psychiatric patients. *Journal of Consulting and Clinical Psychology,* **39,** 148–151.

Platt, J., & Spivak, G. (1975). *The MEPS procedural manual*. Philadelphia: Hahnemann Medical College and Hospital, Department of Mental Health Sciences.

Polanyi, M. (1964). *Personal knowledge*. New York: Harper & Row.

Polich, J., & Starr, A. (1984). Evoked potentials in aging. In M. S. Alpert (Ed.), *Clinical neurology of aging*. London & New York: Oxford University Press.

Popper, K. R. (1959). *The logic of scientific discovery*. New York: Basic Books.

Posner, M. I. (1978). *Chronometric explorations of mind*. Hillsdale, NJ: Erlbaum.

Posner, M. I. (1982). Cumulative development of attentional theory. *American Psychologist,* **37,** 168–179.

Posner, M. I., & Boies, S. J. (1971). Components of attention. *Psychological Review,* **78,** 391–408.

Posner, M. I., & McLeod, P. (1982). Information processing models—In search of elementary operations. In M. R. Rosenzweig & L. W. Porter (Eds.), *Annual Review of Psychology* (Vol. 33). Palo Alto, CA: Annual Reviews Inc.

Posner, M. I., & Mitchell, R. F. (1967). Chronometric analysis of classification. *Psychological Review,* **74,** 392–409.

Posner, M. I., Walker, J. A., Friedrich, F. J., & Rafal, R. D. (in press). *Effects of parietal inquiry on covert orienting of visual attention. Journal of Neuroscience.*

Post, E. L. (1936). Finite combinatory processes - Formulation I. *Journal of Symbolic Logic,* **1,** 103–105.

Poulos, C. X., Wolff, L., Zilm, D. H., Kaplan, H., & Cappell, H. (1981). Acquisition of tolerance to alcohol-induced memory deficits in humans. *Psychopharmacology,* **73,** 176–179.

Powers, W. T. (1973). Feedback: Beyond behaviorism. *Science,* **179,** 351–356.

Pribram, K. H. (1981). Emotions. In S. B. Filskov & T. J. Boll (Eds.), *Handbook of clinical neuropsychology* (pp. 102–134). New York: Wiley (Interscience).

Pribram, K. H., & McGuinness, D. (1975). Arousal, activation, and effort in the control of attention. *Psychological Review,* **82,** 116–149.

Price, V. A. (1983). *Type A behavior pattern: A model for research and practice.* New York: Academic Press.

Prior, M. (1984). Developing concepts of childhood autism: The influence of experimental cognitive research. *Journal of Consulting and Clinical Psychology,* **52,** 4–16.

Prior, M., & McGillivray, J. (1980). The performance of autistic children on three learning set tasks. *Journal of Child Psychology and Psychiatry,* **21,** 313–323.

Pryor, J. B., & Merluzzi, T. V. (1984). *Processing social interaction scripts.* Unpublished manuscript, University of Notre Dame, Notre Dame, IN.

Pylyshyn, Z. W. (1978). Computational models and empirical constraints. *Behavioral and Brain Sciences,* **1,** 93–99.

Pyszczynski, T., & Greenberg, J. (1985). Preference for self-focus in depressed and non-depressed individuals following success and failure: Counter defensive tendencies in the depressed. *Journal of Personality and Social Psychology,* **49,** 1066–1075.

Raimy, V. (1975). *Misunderstandings of the self.* San Francisco, CA: Jossey-Bass.

Raps, C. S., Peterson, C., Reinhard, K. E., Abramson, L. Y., & Seligman, M. E. P. (1982). Attributional style among depressed patients. *Journal of Abnormal Psychology,* **91,** 102–108.

Raush, H. L. (1952). Perceptual constancy in schizophrenia. *Journal of Personality,* **21,** 176–187.

Reese, A., & Lipsitt, L. (1970). *Experimental child psychology.* New York: Academic Press.

Rehm, L. P. (1977). A self-control model of depression. *Behavior Therapy,* **8,** 787–804.

Reicher, G. (1969). Perceptual recognition as a function of meaningfulness of stimulus material. *Journal of Experimental Psychology,* **81,** 275–280.

Reider, R. O., Mann, L. S., Weinberger, D. R., van Kammen, D. P., & Post, R. (1983). Computed tomographic scans in patients with schizophrenia, schizoaffective, and bipolar affective disorder. *Archives of General Psychiatry,* **40,** 735–739.

Reik, T. (1948). *Listening with the third ear.* New York: Farrar, Straus, & Giroux.

Reinke, B., Holmes, D., & Denney, D. (1981). Influence of a "Friendly Visitor" program on the cognitive functioning and morale of elderly persons. *American Journal of Community Psychology,* **9,** 491–504.

Reiss, S., & Bootzin, R. R. (1985). *Theoretical issues in behavior therapy.* New York: Academic Press.

Review Panel on Coronary-Prone Behavior and Coronary Heart Disease. (1981). Coronary-prone behavior and coronary heart disease: A critical review. *Circulation,* **63,** 1199–1215.

Rhodewalt, F. (1984). Self-involvement, self-attribution, and the Type A coronary-prone behavior pattern. *Journal of Personality and Social Psychology,* **47,** 662–670.

Rhodewalt, F., & Davison, J. (1983). Reactance and the coronary-prone behavior pattern: The role of self-attribution in responses to reduced behavioral freedom. *Journal of Personality and Social Psychology,* **44,** 220–228.

Rhodewalt, F., & Strube, M. C. (1985). A self-attribution reactance model of the process of recovery from injury in Type A individuals. *Journal of Applied Social Psychology,* **15,** 330–334.

Richardson, M. W. (1938). Multidimensional psychophysics. *Psychological Bulletin,* **35,** 654–660.

Riskind, J. H. (1982). Nonverbal expression and the accessibility of life experience memories: A congruence hypothesis. *Social Cognition,* **2,** 62–68.

Riskind, J. H., Rholes, W. S., & Eggers, J. (1982). The Velten Mood Induction Procedure: Effects on mood and memory. *Journal of Consulting and Clinical Psychology,* **50,** 146–147.

Ritvo, E. R., Freeman, B. J., Geller, E., & Yuwiler, A. (1983). Effects of fenfluramine on 14 outpatients with the syndrome of autism. *Journal of the American Academy of Child Psychiatry,* **22,** 549–558.

Rizley, R. (1978). Depression and distortion in the attribution of causality. *Journal of Abnormal Psychology,* **87,** 32–48.
Rodnick, E. H., & Shakow, D. (1940). Set in schizophrenics as measured by a composite reaction time index. *American Journal of Psychiatry,* **97,** 214–225.
Rogers, H. (1967). *Theory of recursive functions and effective computability.* New York: McGraw-Hill.
Rogers, T. B. (1981). A model of the self as an aspect of the human information processing system. In N. Cantor & J. F. Kihlstrom (Eds.), *Personality, cognition, and social interaction.* Hillsdale, NJ: Erlbaum.
Rogers, T. B., Kuiper, N. A., & Kirker, W. S. (1977). Self-reference and the encoding of personal information. *Journal of Personality and Social Psychology,* **35,** 677–688.
Rosen, L. J., & Lee, C. L. (1976). Acute and chronic effects of alcohol use on organizational processes in memory. *Journal of Abnormal Psychology,* **85,** 309–317.
Rosenberg, S. (1977). New approaches to the analysis of personal constructs in person perception. In A. W. Landfield (Ed.), *Nebraska symposium on motivation* (Vol. 19). Lincoln: University of Nebraska Press.
Rosenblum, S. M., Arick, J. R., Krug, D. A., Stubbs, E. G., Young, N. B., & Pelson, R. O. (1980). Auditory brainstem evoked responses.
Rosenhan, D. L. (1973). On being sane in insane places. *Science,* **179,** 250–258.
Rosenman, R. H., Brand, R. J., Jenkins, C. D., Friedman, M., Straus, R., & Wurm, M. (1975). Coronary heart disease in the Western Collaborative Group Study: Final follow-up experience of 8-1/2 years. *JAMA, Journal of the American Medical Association,* **233,** 872–877.
Rosenthal, D., Lawler, W. G., Zahn, T. P., & Shakow, D. (1960). The relationship of some aspects of mental set to degree of schizophrenic disorganization. *Journal of Personality,* **28,** 26–38.
Roskies, E. (1980). Considerations in developing a treatment program for the coronary prone (Type A) behavior pattern. In P. O. Davidson & S. M. Davidson (Eds.), *Behavioral medicine: Changing health life styles* (pp. 299–333). New York: Brunner/Mazel.
Ross, A. O. (1981). Of rigor and relevance. *Professional Psychology,* **12,** 318–327.
Ross, A. O., & Pelham, W. E. (1981). Child psychopathology. *Annual Review of Psychology,* **32,** 243–278.
Ross, L. (1977). The intuitive psychologist and his shortcomings: Distortion in the attribution process. In L. Berkowitz (Ed.), *Advances in experimental social psychology* (Vol. 10). New York: Academic Press.
Ross, L., Lepper, M., & Hubbard, M. (1975). Perseverance in self-perception and social perception: Biased attributional processes in the debriefing paradigm. *Journal of Personality and Social Psychology,* **32,** 880–892.
Ross, L., Lepper, M. R., Strack, F., & Steinmetz, J. (1977). Social explanations and social expectation: Effects of real and hypothetical explanations on subjective likelihood. *Journal of Personality and Social Psychology,* **35,** 817–829.
Ross, M., & Sicoly, R. (1979). Egocentric biases in availability and attribution. *Journal of Personality and Social Psychology,* **37,** 322–336.
Roth, D., & Rehm, L. P. (1980). Relationships among self-monitoring processes, memory, and depression. *Cognitive Therapy and Research,* **4,** 149–157.
Roth, D. L. & Ingram, R. E. (1985). Factors in the self-deception questionnaire: Associations with depression. *Journal of Personality and Social Psychology,* **48,** 243–251.
Rothbart, M., Evans, M., & Fulero, S. (1979). Recall for confirming events: Memory processes and the maintenance of social stereotypes. *Journal of Experimental Social Psychology,* **15,** 343–355.
Rotter, J. B. (1972). Beliefs, social attitudes, and behavior: A social learning analysis. In J. B. Rotter, J. E. Chance, & E. J. Phares (Eds.), *Applications of a social learning theory of personality.* New York: Holt, Rinehart & Winston.

Rubin, D. C., & Butters, N. (1981). Clustering by alcoholic Korsakoff patients. *Neuropsychologia,* **19,** 137–140.

Rubin, M., & Shontz, F. C. (1960). Diagnostic prototypes and diagnostic processes of clinical psychologists. *Journal of Consulting Psychology,* **24,** 234–239.

Rudy, T. E., & Merluzzi, T. V. (1984a). *Decision modeling of assertion.* Unpublished manuscript, University of Notre Dame, Notre Dame, IN.

Rudy, T. E., & Merluzzi, T. V. (1984b). Recovering social cognitive schemata: Descriptions and applications of multidimensional scaling for clinical research. In P. C. Kendall (Ed.), *Advanes in cognitive-behavioral research and therapy.* (Vol. 3, pp. 61–102). New York: Academic Press.

Rudy, T. E., & Merluzzi, T. V. (1984c). *Recovering social cognitive schemata: task effects and level of social skill.* Unpublished manuscript, University of Notre Dame, Notre Dame, IN.

Rudy, T. E., Merluzzi, T. V., & Henahan, P. T. (1982). Construal of complex assertion situations: A multidimensional analysis. *Journal of Consulting and Clinical Psychology,* **50,** 125–137.

Rumelhart, D. E., & Siple, P. (1974). Process of recognizing tachistoscopically presented words. *Psychological Review,* **81,** 99–118.

Rundell, O. H., Jr., & Williams, H. L. (1977). Effects of alcohol on organizational aspects of human memory. In F. A. Seixas (Ed.), *Currents in alcoholism, Psychiatric, psychological, social, and epidemiological studies* (Vol. 2, pp. 175–186). New York: Grune & Stratton.

Rundus, D. (1971). Analysis of rehearsal processes in free recall. *Journal of Experimental Psychology,* **89,** 63–77.

Rush, A. J., Beck, A. T., Kovacs, M., & Hollon, S. D. (1977). Comparative efficacy of cognitive therapy versus pharmacotherapy in outpatient depressives. *Cognitive Therapy and research,* **1,** 17–37.

Rush, A. J., Beck, A. T., Kovacs, M., Weissenberger, J. N., & Hollon, S. D. (1982). Comparison of the effects of cognitive therapy and pharmacotherapy on hopelessness and self-concept. *American Journal of Psychiatry,* **139,** 862–866.

Russell, J. A. (1980). A circumplex model of affect. *Journal of Personality and Social Psychology,* **39,** 1161–1178.

Rutter, M. (1978). Diagnosis and definition of childhood autism. *Journal of Autism and Childhood Schizophrenia,* **8,** 139–161.

Ryan, C. (1980). Learning and memory deficits in alcoholics. *Journal of Studies on Alcohol,* **41,** 437–447.

Ryan, C., & Butters, N. (1980). Further evidence for a continuum of impairment encompassing male alcoholic Korsakoff patients and chronic alcoholic men. *Alcoholism: Clinical and Experimental Research,* **4,** 190–198.

Ryback, R. S. (1971). The continuum and specificity of the effects of alcohol on memory: A review. *Journal of Studies on Alcohol,* **32,** 995–1016.

Sacco, W. P. (1981). Invalid use of the Beck depression inventory to identify depressed college students: A methodological comment. *Cognitive Therapy and Research,* **5,** 143–147.

Saccuzzo, D. P. (1977). Bridges between schizophrenia and gerontology: Generalized or specific deficits. *Psychological Bulletin,* **84,** 595–600.

Saccuzzo, D. P., & Braff, D. L. (1981). Early information processing deficits in schizophrenia: New findings using schizophrenic subgroups and manic controls. *Archives of General Psychiatry,* **38,** 175–179.

Saccuzzo, D. P., Braff, D. L., & Sprock, J. (1982). The effect of mental retardation and schizophrenia on information processing. *Journal of Nervous and Mental Disease,* **170,** 102–106.

Saccuzzo, D. P., Hirt, M., & Spencer, T. J. (1974). Backward masking as a measure of attention in schizophrenia. *Journal of Abnormal Psychology,* **83,** 512–522.

Saccuzzo, D. P., & Michael, B. (1984). Speed of information processing and structural limitations in retarded and dual diagnosed retarded-schizophrenic persons. *American Journal of Mental Deficiency,* **89,** 487–495.

Saccuzzo, D. P., & Miller, S. (1977). Critical interstimulus interval in delusional schizophrenics and normals. *Journal of Abnormal Psychology,* **86,** 261–266.

Saccuzzo, D. P., & Schubert, D. L. (1981). Backward masking as a measure of slow processing in schizophrenic spectrum disorders. *Journal of Abnormal Psychology,* **90,** 305–312.

Sackeim, H. R. (1983). Self-deception, self-esteem, and depression: The adaptive value of lying to oneself. In J. Maching (Ed.), *Empirical studies of psychoanalytic theory.* Hillsdale, NJ: Erlbaum.

Sackeim, H. A., & Gur, R. C. (1978). Self-deception, self-confrontation, and self-consciousness. In G. E. Schwartz & D. Shapiro (Eds.), *Consciousness and self-regulation: Advances in research.* New York: Plenum.

Safran, J. D. & Greenberg, L. S. (1985). What can cognitive psychology offer clinicians? *The Cognitive Behaviorist,* **7,** 18–21.

Salamon, G., & Suppes, J. (1971). Learning to generate subjective uncertainty: Effects of training, verbal activity and stimulus structure. *Journal of Personality and Social Psychology,* **18,** 163–175.

Sarason, I. G. (1975). Anxiety and self-preoccupation. In I. G. Sarason & C. D. Spielberger (Eds.), *Stress and Anxiety* (Vol. 2, pp. 27–44). New York: Wiley.

Sarbin, T. R., Taft, R., & Bailey, D. E. (1960). *Clinical inference and cognitive theory.* New York: Holt, Rinehart, & Winston.

Sawyer, J. (1966). Measurement and prediction, clinical and statistical. *Psychological Bulletin,* **66,** 178–200.

Schachter, S., & Singer, J. E. (1962). Cognitive, social, and physiological determinants of emotional state. *Psychological Review,* **69,** 379–399.

Schank, R. C. (1982). Inference in the conceptual dependency paradigm: A personal history. In T. W. Simon & R. J. Scholes (Eds.), *Language, mind, and brain.* Hillsdale, NJ: Erlbaum.

Schank, R. C., & Abelson, R. P. (1977). *Scripts, plans, goals, and understanding.* Hillsdale, NJ: Erlbaum.

Schau, E. J., O'Leary, M. R., Chaney, E. F. (1980). Reversibility of cognitive deficit in alcoholics. *Journal of Studies on Alcohol,* **41,** 733–739.

Scheier, M. D. (1976). Self-awareness, self-consistency, and angry aggression. *Journal of Personality,* **44,** 627–644.

Schiffman, S. S., Reynolds, M. L., & Young, F. W. (1981). *Introduction to multidimensional scaling: Theory, methods, and application.* New York: Academic Press.

Schildkraut, J. J. (1965). The catecholamine hypothesis of affective disorders. *American Journal of Psychiatry,* **122,** 509–522.

Schizophrenia Bulletin. (1981). **7,** No. 4, Special Issue: Paranoid Schizophrenia.

Schmitt, J. P. (1983). Focus of attention in the treatment of depression. *Psychotherapy: Theory, Research, and Practice,* **20,** 457–463.

Schneider, W., & Shiffrin, R. M. (1977). Controlled and automatic human information processing: I. Detection, search, and attention. *Psychological Review,* **84,** 1–66.

Schneiderman, N. (1983). Animal models of coronary heart disease. In D. S. Krantz, A. Baum, & J. E. Singer (Eds.), *Handbook of psychology and health* (Vol. 3, pp. 19–56). New York: Erlbaum.

Schopler, E. (1978). On confusion in the diagnosis of autism. *Journal of Autism and Childhood Schizophrenia,* **8,** 137–138.

Schreibman, L., Koegel, R. L., & Craig, M. S. (1977). Reducing stimulus overselectivity in autistic children. *Journal of Abnormal Child Psychology,* **5,** 425–436.

Schwartz, G. E. (1982). Testing the biopsychosocial model: The ultimate challenge facing behavioral medicine? *Journal of Consulting and Clinical Psychology,* **50,** 1040–1053.

Schwartz, R. M., & Gottman, J. M. (1976). Toward a task analysis of assertion behavior. *Journal of Consulting and Clinical Psychology,* **44,** 910–920.

Schultz, D. W., & Eriksen, C. W. (1977). Do noise masks terminate target processing? *Memory and Cognition,* **5,** 90–96.

Segal, Z. V., & Shaw, B. F. (in press). Cognition in depression: A reappraisal of Coyne and Gotlibs' critique. *Cognition Therapy and Research.*

Seidman, L. J. (1983). Schizophrenia and brain dysfunction: An integration of recent neurodiagnostic findings. *Psychological Bulletin,* **94,** 195–238.

Seligman, M. E. P. (1974). Depression and learned helplessness. In R. J. Friedman & M. M. Katz (Eds.), *The psychology of depression: Contemporary theory and research.* New York: Wiley.

Seligman, M. E. P. (1975). *Helplessness: On depression, development, and death.* San Francisco, CA: W. H. Freeman.

Seligman, M. E. P. (1981). A learned helplessness point of view. In L. P. Rehm (Ed.), *Behavior therapy for depression: Current status and future directions* (pp. 123–142). New York: Academic Press.

Seligman, M. E. P. Abramson, L., Semmel, A., & von Baeyer, C. (1979). Depressive attributional style. *Journal of Abnormal Psychology,* **88,** 242–248.

Seligman, M. E. P., & Maier, S. F. (1967). Failure to escape traumatic shock. *Journal of Experimental Psychology,* **74,** 1–9.

Semmes, J. (1968). Hemispheric specialization: A possible clue to mechanism. *Neuropsychologia,* **6,** 11–26.

Sentis, K., & Burnstein, E. (1979). Remembering schema-consistent information: Effects of a balance schema on recognition memory. *Journal of Personality and Social Psychology,* **37,** 2200–2211.

Shallice, T., & Warrington, E. K. (1970). Independent functioning of verbal memory stores: A neuropsychological study. *Quarterly Journal of Experimental Psychology,* **22,** 261–273.

Shannon, C. E. (1948). A mathematical theory of communication. *Bell System Technical Journal,* **27,** 379–423, 623–656.

Shapiro, D. (1965). *Neurotic styles.* New York: Basic Books.

Shaw, B. F. (1977). Comparison of cognitive therapy and behavior therapy in the treatment of depression. *Journal of Consulting and Clinical Psychology,* **45,** 543–551.

Shaw, B. F., & Dodson, K. S. (1981). Cognitive assessment of depression. In T. V. Merluzzi, C. R. Glass, & M. Genest (Eds.), *Cognitive assessment.* New York: Guilford Press.

Shepard, R. N. (1962). The analysis of proximities: Multidimensional scaling with an unknown distance function. *Psychometrika,* **27,** 125–140.

Shepard, R. N. (1967). Recognition memory for words, sentences, and pictures. *Journal of Verbal Learning and Verbal Behavior,* **6,** 156–163.

Shepard, R. N., & Cooper, L. A. (1982). *Mental images and their transformations.* Cambridge, MA: MIT Press/Bradford Books.

Sherif, M., & Hovland, C. I. (1961). *Social judgment.* New Haven, CT: Yale University Press.

Shiffrin, R. M. (1977). Introduction to "Human memory: A proposed system and its control processes." In G. H. Bower (Ed.), *The psychology of learning and motivation* (Vol. 11). New York: Academic Press.

Shiffrin, R. M., & Schneider, W. (1977). Controlled and automatic human information processing: II. Perceptual learning, automatic attending, and a general theory. *Psychological Review,* **84,** 127–190.

Sieber, J., & Lanzetta, J. (1966). Some determinants of individual differences in predecision information processing. *Journal of Personality and Social Psychology,* **4,** 561–571.

Silberstein, J. A., & Parsons, D. A. (1981). Neuropsychological impairment in female alcoholics: Replication and extension. *Journal of Abnormal Psychology,* **90,** 179–182.

Silver, L. B., & Segal, J. (1984). Psychology and mental health: An enduring partnership. *American Psychologist,* **39,** 804–809.

Silverman, J. (1964). The problem of attention in research and theory in schizophrenia. *Psychological Review,* **71,** 352–379.

Simon, H. A. (1957). *Models of man: Social and rational.* New York: Wiley.

Simon, H. A. (1976). Discussion: Cognition and social behavior. In J. S. Carroll & J. W. Payne (Eds.), *Cognition and social behavior.* New York: Wiley.

Simon, H. A. (1979). *Models of thought.* New Haven, CT: Yale University Press.

Simon, H. A. (1981). Studying human intelligence by creating artificial intelligence. *American Scientist,* **69,** 300–309.

Simon, H. A., & Ericsson, K. A. (1984). *Protocol analysis.* Cambridge, MA: MIT Press.

Skinner, B. F. (1957). *Verbal behavior.* New York: Appleton-Century-Crofts.

Skoff, B. F., Mirsky, A. F., & Turner, D. (1980). Prolonged brainstem transmission time in autism. *Psychiatry Research,* **2,** 157–166.

Slife, D. B., Miura, S., Thompson, L. W., Shapiro, J. L., & Gallagher, D. (1984). Differential recall as a function of mood disorder in clinically depressed patients: Between and within subject differences. *Journal of Abnormal Psychology,* **93.** 391–400.

Smith, D. (1982). Trends in counseling and psychotherapy. *American Psychologist,* **37,** 802–810.

Smith, E. E., Adames, N., & Schorr, D. (1978). Fact retrieval and the paradox of inference. *Cognitive Psychology,* **10,** 438–464.

Smith, E. E., Shoben, E., & Rips, L. (1984). Structure and process in semantic memory: A featural model for semantic decision. *Psychological Review,* **81,** 214–241.

Smith, E. E., & Spoehr, K. T. (1974). The perception of printed English: A theoretical perspective. In B. Kantowitz (Ed.), *Human information processing: Tutorials in performance and cognition.* Hillsdale, NJ: Erlbaum.

Smith, T. W., & Anderson, N. (1986). Models of personality and disease: An interactional approach to Type A behavior and cardiovascular risk. *Journal of Personality and Social Psychology,* **50,** 1166–1173.

Smith, T. W., & Brehm, S. S. (1981a). Cognitive correlates of the Type A coronary-prone behavior pattern. *Motivation and Emotion,* **5,** 215–223.

Smith, T. W., & Brehm, S. S. (1981b). Person perception and the Type A coronary-prone behavior pattern. *Journal of Personality and Social Psychology,* **40,** 1137–1149.

Smith, T. W. & Greenberg, J. (1981). Depression and self-focused attention. *Motivation and Emotion,* **5,** 323–331.

Smith, T. W., Houston, B. K., & Stucky, R. J. (1985). Effects of threat of shock and control over shock on finger pulse volume, pulse rate, and systolic blood pressure. *Biological Psychology,* **20,** 31–38.

Smith, T. W., Houston, B. K., & Zurawski, R. M. (1983). The Framingham Type A scale and anxiety, irrational beliefs, and self-control. *Journal of Human Stress* **9,** 32–37.

Smith, T. W., Ingram, R. E., & Brehm, S. S. (1983). Social anxiety, anxious preoccupation, and recall of self-relevant information. *Journal of Personality and Social Psychology,* **44,** 1276–1283.

Smith, T. W., Ingram, R. E., & Roth, D. L. (1985). Self-focused attention and depression: Self-evaluation, affect, and life stress. *Motivation and Emotion,* **9,** 381–389.

Snow, B. (1978). Level of aspiration in coronary prone and noncoronary prone adults. *Personality and Social Psychology Bulletin,* **4,** 416–419.

Snyder, C. R. (1977). "A patient by any other name" revisited: Maladjustment or attributional locus of problem? *Journal of Consulting and Clinical Psychology,* **45,** 101–103.

Snyder, C. R., Ingram, R. E., & Newburg, C. L. (1982). The role of feedback in help-seeking and helping relationships. In T. A. Wills (Ed.), *Basic processes in helping relationships*. New York: Academic Press.

Snyder, M. (1981a). On the influence of individuals on situations. In N. Cantor & J. F. Kihlstrom (Eds.), *Personality, cognition, and social interaction* (pp. 309–329). Hillsdale, NJ: Erlbaum.

Snyder, M. (1981b). On the self-perpetuating nature of social stereotypes. In D. Hamilton (Ed.), *Cognitive processes in stereotyping and intergroup behavior*. (pp. 183–212). Hillsdale, NJ: Erlbaum.

Snyder, M. (1981c). Seek and ye shall find: Testing hypotheses about other people. In E. T. Higgins, C. P. Herman, & M. P. Zanna (Eds.), *Social cognition: The Ontario symposium on persoanlity and social psychology* (Vol. 1, pp. 277–303). Hillsdale, NJ: Erlbaum.

Snyder, M., & White, P. (1982). Moods and memories: Elation, depression, and the remembering of events of one's life. *Journal of Personality,* **50,** 149–167.

Snyder, M., & Swann, W. B., Jr. (1978). Hypothesis testing processes in social interaction. *Journal of Personality and Social Psychology,* **36,** 1202–1212.

Sohmer, H., & Student, M. (1978). Auditory nerve and brainstem evoked responses in normal, autistic, minimal brain dysfunction and psychomotor retarded children. *Electroencephalography and Clinical Neurophysiology,* **44,** 380–388.

Solomon, S., Holmes, D., & McCaul, K. (1980). Behavioral control over aversive events: Does control that requires effort reduce anxiety and physiological arousal? *Journal of Personality and Social Psychology,* **39,** 729–736.

Spence, K. W. (1956). *Behavior theory and conditioning*. New Haven, CT: Yale University Press.

Sperling, G. A. (1960). The information available in brief visual presentations. *Psychological Monographs,* **74**(Whole No. 11).

Spitz, H. H. (1973). The channel capacity of educable mental retardates. In R. K. Routh (Ed.), *The experimental psychology of mental retardation*. Chicago, IL: Aldine.

Spoehr, K. T., & Lehmkuhle, S. W. (1982). *Visual information processing*. San Francisco, CA: Freeman.

Spohn, H. E., Thetford, P. E., & Woodham, F. L. (1970). Span of apprehension and arousal in schizophrenia. *Journal of Abnormal Psychology,* **75,** 113–123.

Sprouse, C. L., & Brush, D. H. (1980). Assessing a quasi-therapy group by individual differences multidimensional scaling. *Small Group Behavior,* **11,** 35–49.

Srull, T. K., & Wyer, R. S., Jr. (1979). The role of category accessibility in the interpretation of information about persons: Some determinants and implications. *Journal of Personality and Social Psychology,* **37,** 1660–1672.

Stabler, E. P. (1983). How are grammars represented? *Behavioral and Brain Sciences,* **6,** 391–421.

Stael von Holstein, C. A. S. (1972). Probabilistic forecasting: An experiment related to the stockmarket. *Organizational Behavior and Human Performance,* **8,** 139–158.

SteinBrueck, S. M., Maxwell, S. E., & Howard, G. S. (1983). A meta analysis of psychotherapy and drug therapy in the treatment of unipolar depression with adults. *Journal of Consulting and Clinical Psychology,* **51,** 856–863.

Stelmach, G. E. (1978). *Information processing in motor control and learning*. New York: Academic Press.

Stern, G. S., Harris, J., & Elverum, J. (1981). Attention to important versus trivial tasks and salience of fatigue-related symptoms for coronary-prone individuals. *Journal of Research in Personality,* **15,** 467–474.

Sternberg, R. J. (1981). Testing and cognitive psychology. *American Psychologist,* **36,** 1181–1189.

Sternberg, S. (1966). High-speed scanning in human memory. *Science,* **153,** 652–654.

Sternberg, S. (1969). Memory-scanning processes revealed by reaction-time experiments. *American Scientist,* **57,** 421–457.

Sternberg, S. (1975). Memory-scanning: New findings and current controversies. *Quarterly Journal of Experimental Psychology,* **27,** 1–32.

Stiles, W. B., Tupler, L. A., & Carpenter, J. C. (1982). Participants' perceptions of self-analytic group sessions. *Small Group Behavior,* **13,** 237–254.

Stroop, J. R. (1935). Studies of interference in serial verbal reactions. *Journal of Experimental Psychology,* **18,** 643–661.

Strube, M., Turner, C., Cerro, D., Stevens, J., & Hinchey, F. (in press). Interpersonal aggression and the type A coronary-prone behavior pattern: A theoretical distinction and practical implications. *Journal of Personality and Social Psychology,* **47,** 839–847.

Strube, M., & Werner, C. (1985). Relinquishment of control and the Type A behavior pattern. *Journal of Personality and Social Psychology,* **48,** 688–701.

Student, M., & Sohmer, H. (1978). Evidence from auditory nerve and brainstem evoked responses for an organic brain lesion in childhood with autistic traits. *Journal of Autism and Childhood Schizophrenia,* **8,** 13–20.

Suinn, R. M. (1982). Intervention with Type A behaviors. *Journal of Consulting and Clinical Psychology,* **50,** 933–949.

Sullivan, H. S. (1953). *The interpersonal theory of psychiatry.* New York: Norton.

Suls, J., Becker, M. A., & Mullen, B. (1981). Coronary-prone behavior, social insecurity and stress among college aged adults. *Journal of Human Stress,* **7,** 27–34.

Surwitt, R. S., Williams, R. B., & Shapiro, D. (1981). *Behavioral approaches to cardiovascular disease.* New York: Academic Press.

Sutton, S., Kakarem, G., Zubin, J., & Portnoy, M. (1961). The effect of shift of sensory modality on serial reaction time: A comparison of schizophrenics and normals. *American Journal of Psychology,* **74,** 224–232.

Sutton-Simon, K. (1981). Assessing belief systems: Concepts and strategies. In P. C. Kendall & S. D. Hollon (Eds.). *Assessment strategies for cognitive-behavioral interventions.* New York: Academic Press.

Swann, W. B., Jr. (1983). Self-verification: Bringing social reality into harmony with the self. In J. Suls & A. G. Greenwald (Eds.), *Psychological persepctives on the self* (Vol. 2). Hillsdale, NJ: Erlbaum.

Swann, W. B., Jr., & Hill, C. A. (1982). When our identities are mistaken: Reaffirming self-conceptions through social interaction. *Journal of Personality and Social Psychology,* **43,** 59–66.

Swann, W. B., Jr., & Read, S. J. (1981a). Acquiring self-knowledge: The search for feedback that fits. *Journal of Personality and Social Psychology,* **4,** 1119–1128.

Swann, W. B., Jr., & Read, S. J. (1981b). Self-verification processes: How we sustain our self-conceptions. *Journal of Experimental Social Psychology,* **17,** 351–372.

Swinney, D. A. (1979). Lexical access during sentence comprehension: (Re)consideration of context effects. *Journal of Verbal Learning and Verbal Behavior,* **18,** 645–660.

Takane, Y., Young, F. W., & deLeeuw (1977). Nonmetric individual differences multidimensional scaling: An alternative least square method with optimal scaling features. *Psychometrika,* **42,** 7–67.

Tanaka, M., Kohno, Y., Nakagawa, R., Ida, Y., Takeda, S., & Nagasaki, N. (1982). Time-related differences in noradrenaline turnover in rat brain regions by stress. *Pharmacology, Biochemistry, and Behavior,* **16,** 315–319.

Tanguay, P. E. (1981). Auditory brain stem study of autistic children: Whisper of the bang. In D. Park (Ed.), *The proceedings of the 1981 International Conference on Autism.* Washington, DC: NASC, The National Society for Children and Adults with Autism.

Tartar, R. E. (1975). Psychological deficit in chronic alcoholics: A review. *International Journal of the Addictions,* **10,** 327–368.

Tasi, L. Y., & Stewart, M. A. (1982). Handedness and EEG correlations in autistic children. *Biological Psychiatry,* **17,** 595–597.

Taylor, F. G., & Marshall, W. L. (1977). Experimental analysis of a cognitive-behavioral therapy for depression. *Cognitive Therapy and Research,* **1,** 59–72.

Taylor, J. (Ed.). (1958). *Selected writings of John Hughlings Jackson.* New York: Basic Books.

Taylor, S. E., & Crocker, J. (1981). Schematic bases of social information processing. In E. T. Higgins, C. P. Herman, & M. P. Zanna (Eds.), *Social cognition: The Ontario symposium on personality and social psychology* (Vol. 1, pp. 87–134). Hillsdale, NJ: Erlbaum.

Taylor, S. E., Crocker, J., & D'Agnostino, J. (1978). Schematic bases of social problem solving. *Personality and Social Psychology Bulletin,* **4,** 447–451.

Taylor, S. E., & Fiske, S. T. (1981). Getting inside the head: Methodologies for process analysis. In J. Harvey, W. Ickes, & R. Kidd (Eds.), *New directions in attribution research* (Vol. 3). Hillsdale, NJ: Erlbaum.

Taylor, S. E., Fiske, S. T., Etcoff, N., & Ruderman, A. (1978). The categorical and contextual basis of person memory and stereotyping. *Journal for Personality and Social Psychology,* **36,** 778–793.

Taylor, S. P., Gammon, C. B., & Capasso, D. R. (1976). Aggression as a function of alcohol and threat. *Journal of Personality and Social Psychology,* **34,** 938–941.

Taylor, S. P., & Leonard, K. E. (1983). Alcohol and human physical aggression. In R. G. Geen & E. Donnerstein (Eds.) *Aggression.* (pp. 77–101). New York: Academic Press.

Teasdale, J. D. (1983). Negative thinking in depression: Cause, effect, or reciprocal relationship? *Advances in Behavior Research and Therapy,* **5,** 3–25.

Teasdale, J. D. (1985). Psychological treatments for depression: How do they work? *Behavioral Research and Therapy,* **23,** 157–165.

Teasdale, J. D., & Fogarty, S. J. (1979). Differential effects of induced mood on retrieval of pleasant and unpleasant events from episodic memory. *Journal of Abnormal Psychology,* **88,** 248–257.

Teasdale, J. D. & Russell, M. L. (1983). Differential effects of induced mood on the recall of positive, negative, and neutral words. *British Journal of Clinical Psychology,* **22,** 163–171.

Teasdale, J. D., & Taylor, R. (1981). Induced mood and accessibility of memories: An effect of mood state or of induction procedure? *British Journal of Clinical Psychology,* **20,** 39–48.

Teasdale, J. D., Taylor, R., & Fogarty, S. (1980). Effects of induced elation-depression on the accessibility of happy and unhappy experiences. *Behavior Research and Therapy,* **18,** 339–346.

Teichner, W. H., & Krebs, M. J. (1974). Visual search for simple targets. *Psychological Bulletin,* **81,** 15–28.

Tellegen, A., Kamp, J., & Watson, D. (1982). Recognizing individual differences in predictive structure. *Psychological Review,* **89,** 95–105.

Temerlin, M. K. (1968). Suggestion effects in psychiatric diagnosis. *Journal of Nervous Mental Disease,* **147,** 349–353.

Tesser, A. (1978). Self-generated attitude change. In L. Berkowitz (Ed.), *Advances in experimental social psychology* (Vol. 11, pp. 289–338). New York: Academic Press.

Thomson, D. M., & Tulving, E. (1970). Associative encoding and retrieval: Weak and strong cues. *Journal of Experimental Psychology,* **86,** 255–262.

Thorndyke, P. W. (1984). Applications of schema theory in cognitive research. In J. R. Anderson & S. M. Kosslyn (Eds.), *Tutorials in learning and memory.* San Francisco, CA: Freeman.

Thorndyke, P. W., & Hayes-Roth, B. (1979). The use of schemata in the acquisition and transference of knowledge. *Cognitive Psychology,* **11,** 82–106.

Tizard, J., & Venables, P. H. (1956). Reaction time responses by schizophrenics, mental defectives, and normal adults. *American Journal of Psychiatry,* **112,** 803–807.

Todd, F., & Hammond, K. (1965). Differential feedback in two multiple-cue learning tasks. *Behavioral Science,* **10,** 429–435.

Toulmin, S. (1963). *Foresight and understanding.* New York: Harper & Row.

Townsend, J. T. (1972). Some results on the identifiability of parallel and serial processes. *British Journal of Mathematical and Statistical Psychology,* **25,** 168–199.

Townsend, J. T. (1974). Issues and models concerning the processing of a finite number of inputs. In B. H. Kantowitz (Ed.), *Human information processing: Tutorials in performance and cognition.* Hillsdale, NJ: Erlbaum.

Treismann, A. M. (1964). Monitoring and storage of irrelevant messages in selective attention. *Journal of Verbal Learning and Verbal Behavior,* **3,** 449–459.

Triandis, H. C. (1972). *The analysis of subjective culture.* New York: Wiley (Interscience).

Trousseau, A. (1882). *Clinical medicine.* Philadelphia.

Tuchman, B. (1984). *The march of folly.* New York: Alfred Knopf.

Tucker, D. M. (1981). Lateral brain function, emotion, and conceptualization. *Psychological Bullein,* **89,** 19–46.

Tucker, D. M., Antes, J. R., Stenslie, C. E., & Barnhardt, T. N. (1978). Anxiety and lateral cerebral function. *Journal of Abnormal Psychology,* **87,** 380–383.

Tucker, D. M., & Williamson, P. A. (1984). Asymmetrical neural control systems in human self-regulation. *Psychological Review,* **91,** 185–215.

Tulving, E. (1962). Subjective organization in free recall of ''unrelated'' words. *Psychological Review,* **69,** 344–354.

Tulving, E. (1972). Episodic and semantic memory. In E. Tulving & W. Donaldson (Eds.), *Organization of memory.* New York: Academic Press.

Tulving, E. (1983). *Elements of episodic memory.* London & New York: Oxford University Press.

Tulving, E. (1984). *Precis of elements of episodic memory. Behavioral and Brain Sciences,* **7,** 223–268.

Tulving, E. (1985). How many memory systems are there? *American Psychologist,* **40,** 385–398.

Tulving, E., & Thomson, D. M. (1973). Encoding specificity and retrieval processes. *Psychological Review,* **80,** 352–373.

Turing, A. M. (1936). On computable numbers, with an application to the Entscheidungs problem. *Proceedings of the London Mathematical Society (Series 2),* **42,** 230–265.

Turk, D. C., & Salovey, P. (1985). Cognitive structures, cognitive processes, and cognitive-behavioral and modification: II. Judgments and inferences of the clinician. *Cognitive Therapy and Research,* **9,** 19–34.

Turk, D. C., & Salovey, P. (in press). Toward an understanding of life with cancer. *Hospice Journal.*

Turk, D. C., & Speers, M. A. (1983). Cognitive schemata and cognitive processes in cognitive-behavioral interventions: Going beyond the information given. In P. C. Kendall (Ed.), *Advances in cognitive-behavioral research and therapy* (Vol. 2, pp. 1–32). New York: Academic Press.

Tversky, A., & Kahneman, D. (1971). The belief in the law of small numbers. *Psychological Bulletin,* **76,** 105–110.

Tversky, A., & Kahneman, D. (1973). Availability: A heuristic for judging frequency probability. *Cognitive Psychology,* **5,** 207–232.

Tversky, A., & Kahneman, D. (1974). Judgment under uncertainty: Heuristics and biases. *Science,* **185,** 1124–1131.

Tversky, A., & Kahneman, D. (1980). Causal schemas for judgments under uncertainty. In M. Fishbein (Ed.), *Progress in social psychology* (Vol. 1, pp. 49–72). Hillsdale, NJ: Erlbaum.

Tyler, S. K., & Tucker, D. M. (1982). Anxiety and perceptual structure: Individual differences in neuropsychological function. *Journal of Abnormal Psychology,* **91,** 210–220.

Ulehla, Z. J., & Adams, D. K. (1973). Detection theory and expectations of social reinforcers: An application to aggression. *Psychological Review,* **80,** 439–445.

Uttal, W. R. (1973). *The psychology of sensory coding.* New York: Harper & Row.

Valins, S., & Nisbett, R. E. (1971). Attribution processes in the development of emotional disorders. In E. E. Jones, D. Kanouse, H. H. Kelley, R. E. Nisbett, S. Valins, & B. Weiner (Eds.), *Attribution: Perceiving the causes of behavior.* Morristown, NJ: General Learning Press.

Van Egeren, L. F. (1979a). Cardiovascular changes during social competition in a mixed-motive game. *Journal of Personality and Social Psychology,* **37,** 858–864.

Van Egeren, L. F. (1979b). Social interactions, communications, and the coronary-prone behavior patterns: A psychophysiological study. *Psychosomatic Medicine,* **41,** 2–18.

Van Egeren, L. F., Abelson, J. L., & Sniderman, L. D. (1983). Interpersonal and electrocardiographic responses of Type A's and Type B's in competitive socioeconomic games. *Journal of Psychosomatic Research,* **27,** 53–59.

Velten, E. (1968). A laboratory test for induction of mood states. *Behaviour Research and Therapy,* **6,** 473–482.

Venables, P. H. (1964). Input dysfunction in schizophrenia. In B. A. Maher (Ed.), *Progress in experimental personality research* (Vol. 1). New York: Academic Press.

Venables, P. H. (1977). Input dysfunction in schizophrenia. In B. A. Maher (Ed.), *Contributions to the psychopathology of schizophrenia.* New York: Academic Press.

Voss, J. F., Tyler, S. W., & Bisanz, G. L. (1982). Prose comprehension and memory. In C. R. Puff (Ed.), *Handbook of research methods in human memory and cognition.* New York: Academic Press.

Vredenberg, K., & Krames, L. (1983). *Memory scanning in depression: The disruptive effects of cognitive schemas.* Paper presented at the meeting of the American Psychological Association, Anaheim, CA.

Wachtel, P. L. (1982). *Resistance: Psychodynamic and behavioral approaches.* New York: Plenum.

Wagner, B. R. (1968). The training of attending and abstracting responses in chronic schizophrenic. *Journal of Experimental Research in Personality,* **3,** 77–88.

Waldron, I., Hickey, A., McPerson, C., Butensky, A., Gruss, L., Overall, K., Schmader, A., & Wohlmuth, D. (1980). Type A behavior pattern: Relationship to variation in blood pressure, parental characteristics, and academic and social activities of students. *Journal of Human Stress,* **6,** 16–27.

Walker, E., & McGuire, M. (1982). Intra- and interhemispheric information processing in schizophrenia. *Psychological Bulletin,* **92,** 710–725.

Wallace, C., & Boone, S. (1984). Cognitive factors in the social skills treatment of schizophrenic patients: Implications for treatment. In W. Spaulding & J. Cole (Eds.), *The Nebraska symposium on motivation: Theories of schizophrenia and psychosis.* Lincoln: University of Nebraska Press.

Walley, R. E., & Weiden, T. D. (1973). Lateral inhibition and cognitive masking: A neuropsychological theory of attention. *Psychological Review,* **80,** 284–302.

Warren, R. E. (1974). Association, directionality, and stimulus encoding. *Journal of Experimental Psychology,* **102,** 151–158.

Warren, R. M. (1970). Perceptual restoration of missing speech sounds. *Science,* **167,** 393–395.

Wason, P. C., & Johnson-Laird, P. N. (1972). *Psychology of reasoning: Structure and content.* Cambridge, MA: Harvard University Press.

Watkins, M. J., & Gardiner, J. M. (1982). Cued recall. In C. R. Puff (Ed.), *Handbook of research methods in human memory and cognition.* New York: Academic Press.

Watts, F., Powell, G., & Austin, S. (1973). The modification of abnormal beliefs. *British Journal of Medical Psychology,* **46,** 359–363.
Weber, R., & Crocker, J. (1983). Cognitive processes in the revision of stereotypic beliefs. *Journal of Personality and Social Psychology,* **45,** 961–977.
Weckowicz, T. E. (1957). Size constancy in schizophrenic patients. *Journal of Mental Science,* **103,** 475–486.
Weckowicz, T. E. (1958). Autonomic activity as measured by the mecholyl test and size constancy in schizophrenic patients. *Psychosomatic Medicine,* **20,** 66–71.
Weckowicz, T. E. (1960). Perception of hidden pictures by schizophrenic patients. *Archives of General Psychiatry,* **2,** 521–527.
Weckowicz, T. E., & Blewett, D. B. (1959). Size constancy and abstract thinking in schizophrenic patients. *Journal of Mental Science,* **105,** 909–934.
Weckowicz, T. E., Sommer, R., & Hall, R. (1958). Distance constancy in schizophrenic patients. *Journal of Mental Science,* **104,** 1174–1182.
Weidner, G., & Matthews, K. A. (1978). Reported physical symptoms elicited by unpredictable events and the Type A coronary-prone behavior pattern. *Journal of Personality and Social Psychology,* **36,** 1213–1220.
Weinberg, J., Diller, L., Gordon, M. A., Gerstman, L. J., Lieberman, A., Lakin, P., Hodges, G., & Ezrachi, D. (1977). Visual scanning training effect on reading-related tasks in right brain damage. *Archives of Physical Medicine and Rehabilitation,* **58,** 479–486.
Weinberg, J., Diller, L., Gordon, M. A., Gerstman, L. J., Lieberman, A., Lakin, P., Hodges, G., & Ezrachi, D. (1979). Training sensory awareness and spatial organization in people with right brain damage. *Archives of Physical Medicine and Rehabilitation,* **60,** 491–496.
Weiner, B., Frieze, I., Kukla, A., Reed, L., Rest, S., & Rosenbaum, R. M. (1971). Perceiving the causes of success and failure. In E. E. Jones, D. Kanouse, H. H. Kelley, R. E. Nisbett, S. Valins, & B. Weiner (Eds.), *Attribution: Perceiving the causes of behavior.* Morristown, NJ: General Learning Press.
Weiss, J. M., Stone, E. A., & Hannell, N. (1970). Coping behavior and brain norepinephrine level in rats. *Journal of Comparative and Physiological Psychology,* **72,** 153–160.
Weisstein, N., & Harris, C. S. (1974). Visual detection of line segments: An object-superiority effect. *Science,* **186,** 752–755.
Wener, A. E., & Rehm, L. P. (1975). Depressive affect: A test of behavioral hypotheses. *Journal of Abnormal Psychology,* **84,** 221–227.
Wexler, D. A., & Rice, L. N. (1974). *Innovations in client-centered therapy.* New York: Wiley (Interscience).
Whitehead, A. N., & Russell, B. A. (1910–1913). *Principia mathematica* (Vols. 1–3). London & New York: Cambridge University Press.
Whitney, P., & Kellas, G. (1984). Processing category items in context: Instantation and the structure of semantic categories. *Journal of Experimental Psychology: Learning, Memory, and Cognition,* **10,** 95–103.
Wickens, D. D. (1970). Encoding categories of words: A empirical approach to meaning. *Psychological Review,* **77,** 1–15.
Wicklund, R. A., & Brehm, J. W. (1976). *Perspectives on cognitive dissonance.* Hillsdale, NJ: Erlbaum.
Wiggins, J. S. (1973). *Personality and prediction: Principles of personality assessment.* Reading, MA: Addison-Wesley.
Wiggins, J. W. (1979). A psychological taxonomy of trait-descriptive terms: The interpersonal domain. *Journal of Personality and Social Psychology,* **37,** 395–412.
Wilkie, W. L., & Pessemier, E. A. (1973). Issues in marketing's use of multi-attribute attitude models. *Journal of Marketing Research,* **10,** 428–441.

Wilkinson, D. A., & Carlen, P. L. (1980). Neuropsychological and neurological assessment of alcoholism: Discrimination between groups of alcoholics. *Journal of Studies on Alcohol.* **41,** 129–139.

Williams, H. L., & Rundell, O. H. (1984). Effect of alcohol on recall and recognition as functions of processing levels. *Journal of Studies on Alcohol,* **45,** 10–15.

Williams, R. B. (1975). Physiologic mechanisms underlying the association between psychosocial factors and coronary heart disease. In W. D. Gentry & R. B. Williams (Eds.), *Psychosocial aspects of myocardial infarction and coronary case* (pp. 37–50). St. Louis, MO: Mosby.

Williams, R. B. (1978). Psychological processes, the coronary-prone behavior pattern, and coronary heart disease. In T. M. Dembroski, S. M. Weiss, J. L. Shields, S. G. Haynes, & M. Feinleib (Eds.), *Coronary-prone behavior* (pp. 141–146). Berlin & New York: Springer-Verlag.

Wilson, W. R. (1975). *Unobtrusive induction of positive attitudes.* Unpublished doctoral dissertation, University of Michigan, Ann Arbor.

Wine, J. (1971). Test anxiety and direction of attention. *Psychological Bulletin,* **76,** 92–104.

Wish, M. (1976). Comparisons among multidimensional structures of interpersonal relations. *Multivariate Behavioral Research,* **11,** 297–324.

Wolpe, J., & Lazarus, A. A. (1966). *Behavior therapy techniques: A guide to the treatment of neuroses.* Oxford: Pergamon.

Woodworth, R. S. (1938). *Experimental psychology.* New York: Holt.

Wortman, C. B., & Silver, R. (1980). Coping with undesirable life events. In J. Garber & M. E. P. Seligman (Eds.), *Human helplessness: Theory and applications.* New York: Academic Press.

Wright, J., & Mischel, W. (1982). Influence of affect on cognitive social learning person variables. *Journal of Personality and Social Psychology,* **43,** 901–914.

Wright, J. C., & Murphy, G. L. (1984). The utility of theories in intuitive statistics: The robustness of theory-based judgments. *Journal of Experimental Psychology: General,* **113,** 301–322.

Yates, A. J. (1966). Psychological deficit. *Annual Review of Psychology,* **17,** 111–114.

Young, G., & Householder, A. S. (1938). Discussion of a set of points in terms of mutual distances. *Psychometrika,* **3,** 19–22.

Ytema, D. B., & Torgenson, W. S. (1961). Man-computer cooperation in decisions requiring common sense. *IRE Transactions on Human Factors in Electronics,* **1,** 20–26.

Zadny, J., & Gerard, H. B. (1974). Attributed intentions and information selectivity. *Journal of Experimental Social Psychology,* **10,** 34–52.

Zahn, T. P., Rosenthal, D., & Shakow, D. (1961). Reaction time in schizophrenic and normal subjects in relation to the sequence of series of regular preparatory intervals. *Journal of Abnormal Psychology,* **63,** 161–168.

Zajonc, R. B. (1980). Feeling and thinking: Preferences need no inferences. *American Psychologist,* **35,** 151–175.

Zarin, D. A., & Pauker, S. (1984). Decision analysis as a basis for medical decision making: The tree of Hippocrates. *Journal of Medicine and Philosophy,* **9,** 181–214.

Zeichner, A., & Pihl, R. O. (1979). Effects of alcohol and behavior contingencies on human aggression. *Journal of Abnormal Psychology,* **88,** 133–160.

Zeichner, A., & Pihl, R. O. (1980). Effects of alcohol and instigator intent on human aggression. *Journal of Studies on Alcohol,* **41,** 265–276.

Zeiss, A. M., Lewinsohn, P. M., & Munoz, R. F. (1979). Nonspecific improvement effects in depression using interpersonal skills training, pleasant activity schedules, or cognitive therapy. *Journal of Consulting and Clinical Psychology,* **47,** 427–439.

Zentall, S. S., & Zentall, T. R. (1983). Optimal stimulation: A model of disorganized activity and performance in normal and deviant children. *Psychological Bulletin,* **94,** 446–471.

Zieve, L. (1966). Misinterpretation and abuse of laboratory tests by clinicians. *Annals of the New York Academy of Sciences,* **134,** 563–572.

Zimet, C. N., & Fishman, D. B. (1970). Psychological deficit in schizophrenics and brain damage. *Annual Review of Psychology,* **21,** 113–154.

Zouzounis, J. A. (1981). *Developmental assessment of attentional processes in normals and autistics: Cardiac and behavioral responses to relevant redundant cues.* Unpublished master's thesis, San Diego State University, San Diego, CA.

Zuroff, D. C., Colussy, S. A., & Wielgus, M. S. (1983). Selective memory and depression: A cautionary note concerning response bias. *Cognitive Therapy and Research,* **7,** 223–232.

Index

B

C

D

E

F

H

T

V